Ann-Kathrin Müller

Decision Support for Biomass Value Chains for the Production of Biochemicals Considering Uncertainties

PRODUKTION UND ENERGIE

Karlsruher Institut für Technologie (KIT)
Institut für Industriebetriebslehre und Industrielle Produktion
Deutsch-Französisches Institut für Umweltforschung

Band 26

Eine Übersicht aller bisher in dieser Schriftenreihe
erschienenen Bände finden Sie am Ende des Buches.

Decision Support for Biomass Value Chains for the Production of Biochemicals Considering Uncertainties

by
Ann-Kathrin Müller

KIT Scientific Publishing

Dissertation, Karlsruher Institut für Technologie
KIT-Fakultät für Wirtschaftswissenschaften

Tag der mündlichen Prüfung: 25. Juli 2018
Referenten: Prof. Dr. Frank Schultmann, Prof. Dr. Nikolaus Dahmen

Impressum

KIT Scientific Publishing

Karlsruher Institut für Technologie (KIT)
KIT Scientific Publishing
Straße am Forum 2
D-76131 Karlsruhe

KIT Scientific Publishing is a registered trademark
of Karlsruhe Institute of Technology.
Reprint using the book cover is not allowed.

www.ksp.kit.edu

Print on Demand 2018 – Gedruckt auf FSC-zertifiziertem Papier

ISSN 2194-2404
ISBN 978-3-7315-0820-5
DOI 10.5445/KSP/1000084346

Decision Support for Biomass Value Chains for the Production of Biochemicals Considering Uncertainties

Zur Erlangung des akademischen Grades
Doktor der Ingenieurwissenschaften
der Fakultät für Wirtschaftswissenschaften
Karlsruher Institut für Technologie (KIT)

genehmigte
Dissertation
von

Dipl.-Ing. Dipl. Ing. oec. Ann-Kathrin Müller

Tag der mündlichen Prüfung: 25.07.2018
Referent: Prof. Dr. Frank Schultmann
Korreferent: Prof. Dr. Nikolaus Dahmen

Kurzfassung

Die Knappheit fossiler Ressourcen, die daraus resultierenden geopolitischen Konflikte sowie die globale Klimaerwärmung führen dazu, dass weltweit viele Stakeholder nach alternativen Rohstoffen suchen. Insbesondere die Chemieindustrie ist abhängig von fossilen Ressourcen und setzt daher aus wirtschaftlichen als auch aus gesellschaftspolitischen Gründen zunehmend biobasierte Rohstoffe für ihre Produktion ein. Die Transformation zu und Verbesserung einer Bioökonomie gewinnt daher zunehmend and Bedeutung. Um bioökonomische Konzepte in der Chemieindustrie einsetzen zu können, bedarf es geeigneter Wertschöpfungsketten für die Produktion biobasierter Chemikalien. Diese Wertschöpfungsketten unterscheiden sich sehr stark von den petro-basierten Strukturen, da sie in der Regel deutlich komplexer sind und stärker von Risiken und Unsicherheiten abhängig sind, was bei strategischen Unternehmensentscheidungen berücksichtigt werden muss. Derzeit konzentriert sich die Forschung in erster Linie auf Versorgungs- und Nachfragerisiken in Netzwerken und Lieferketten von Biokraftstoffen und Bioenergie. Eine ganzheitliche Betrachtung bioökonomischer Wertschöpfungsketten, ausgehend vom Anbau stärke- und lignozellulosehaltiger Biomassen bis hin zur Produktion von Biochemikalien und anderen Produkten für den Absatzmarkt, erfolgt bisher nicht systematisch. Vor diesem Hintergrund wird im Rahmen dieser Arbeit ein generischer Ansatz zur strategischen Entscheidungsunterstützung unter Unsicherheit für die bioökonomische Standort- und Logistikplanung entwickelt, der exemplarisch auf die Produktion Biochemikalien angewendet wird.

Der im Rahmen dieser Arbeit entwickelte Ansatz beinhaltet ein integriertes Modell und drei Untermodelle. Das Optimierungsmodell optimiert die Standorte und die Kapazitäten von Vorbehandlungsanlagen. Diese wandeln lignozellulosehaltige Biomassen in verarbeitbare Zwischenprodukte um. Mit Hilfe des Modells werden geeignete Lieferanten von vorbehandelter Biomasse ermittelt. Das Technikmodell beschreibt die Konversionsprozesse. Technische und ökonomische Bewertungen aller betrachteten Konversionsprozesse können basierend auf Fließbildsimulationen durchgeführt werden. Produktionsausbeuten, Hilfsstoffbedarf, Produktionskosten und Investitionen sind die zentralen Ergebnisse des technischen Modells. Das Risikomodell identifiziert und bewertet Risiken und Unsicherheiten, die entlang von Biomassewertschöpfungsketten auftreten. Ein Ergebnis ist das Modellieren der quantifizierbaren Risiken durch Risikokosten, welche auf Wahrscheinlichkeiten und Konsequenzen beruhen. Die Risikokosten werden in der Zielfunktion des integrierten Modells berücksichtigt. Die Wahrscheinlichkeiten werden als Monte Carlo Simulation modelliert. Die nicht-quantifizierbaren Risiken werden in Szenarien beschrieben. Zusätzlich zu den Ergebnissen der drei Untermodelle werden weitere Faktoren wie z.B. Kosten, Transportrestriktionen, existierende Infrastrukturen sowie Lieferanten etc. im integrierten Modell betrachtet. Das integrierte Modell ist als gemischt ganzzahlige, lineare Programmierung modelliert, welches verschiedene Biomassen, Transportmodi, Zwischenprodukte und Unsicherheiten darstellt. In dieser Arbeit werden drei Fallstudien betrachtet: zwei biochemische und eine thermochemische Verarbeitung in den USA. Als Ergebnis berechnet das Modell einen nahezu optimalen Standort und das entsprechende Logistiknetzwerk für die Produktion von Biochemikalien.

Die Ergebnisse sind stark abhängig vom Biomassepreis, Konversionsausbeuten und Transportmodi. Generell haben die Unsicherheiten Einfluss auf die Struktur der Wertschöpfungskette. Insbesondere die nicht-quantifizierbaren Risiken haben einen großen Einfluss und sollten daher im

Entscheidungsprozess unbedingt berücksichtigt werden. Die Wahl des Rohstoffes, das Endprodukt sowie weitere Nebenprodukte sind entscheidend für die Wirtschaftlichkeit der Wertschöpfungskette. Um die Lieferrisiken zu minimieren, sollte ein Standort im nahen Umkreis zu mehreren Lieferanten gewählt werden. Das Schiff ist der bevorzugte Transportmodus für lange Distanzen. Obwohl diese Arbeit im Wesentlichen reale Daten verwendet, sollten die Ergebnisse kritisch hinterfragt werden. Alle relevanten Daten wurden ohne weitere Validierung der Literatur entnommen. Historische Daten von Risiken können nicht generell auf die Zukunft projiziert werden. Der Ansatz nimmt fixe Kapazitäten für Produktion und Lagerhaltung an. Beide sollten basierend auf Unsicherheiten optimiert werden. Trotzdem bietet das Modell einen ersten Ansatz um verschiedene Probleme in komplexen Biomassewertschöpfungsketten darzustellen und näherungsweise optimal zu lösen.

Abstract

The scarcity of fossil resources, the resulting geopolitical conflicts and global warming are leading many stakeholders worldwide to search for alternative raw materials. In particular, the chemical industry depends on fossil resources and is due to economic and socio-political reasons increasingly using bio-based raw materials for its production. The transformation to and improvement of a bioeconomy is therefore becoming more and more important. In order to be able to use bioeconomic concepts in the chemical industry, suitable value chains are required for the production of bio-based chemicals. These value chains are very different from petro-based structures because they are usually much more complex and more dependent on risks and uncertainties. These must be taken into account in strategic corporate decisions. Research currently focuses primarily on supply and demand risks in biofuel and bioenergy networks and supply chains. A holistic approach to bioeconomic value chains, starting with the cultivation of biomass containing starch and lignocellulose up to the production of biochemicals and other products for the sales market, has not yet been systematic. Against this background, a generic approach for strategic decision support under uncertainty for bioeconomic site and logistics planning is developed within the scope of this work, which is applied to the production of biochemicals as an example.

The approach developed in this work includes an integrated model and three sub-models. The optimization model optimizes the locations and capacities of pretreatment plants. These convert lignocellulosic biomass into processable intermediates. The model is used to identify suitable suppliers of pretreated biomass. The technical model describes the conversion processes. Based on flowsheeting simulations, technical and economic evaluations of all considered conversion processes can be carried out. Production yields, utility demand, production costs and investments are the main results of the technical model. The risk model identifies and evaluates risks and uncertainties that occur along biomass value chains. One result is the modeling of quantifiable risks by risk costs, which are based on probabilities and consequences. The risk costs are taken into account in the objective function of the integrated model. The probabilities are modeled as Monte Carlo simulation. The non-quantifiable risks are described in scenarios. In addition to the results of the three sub-models, other factors such as costs, transport restrictions, existing infrastructures, and suppliers etc. are considered in the integrated model. The integrated model is modeled as mixed integer, linear programming, which represents different biomass types, transport modes, intermediates, and uncertainties. In this work three case studies are considered: two biochemical and one thermochemical processing in the USA. As a result, the model suggests a nearly optimal location and the associated logistics network for the production of biochemicals.

The results are strongly dependent on the biomass price, conversion yields and transport modes. In general, uncertainties have an impact on the structure of the value chain. Non-quantifiable risks in particular have a major impact and should therefore be taken into account in the decision-making process. The choice of raw material, the final product and other by-products is decisive for the feasibility of the value chain. In order to minimize delivery risks, a location close to several suppliers should be chosen. Barge is the preferred mode of transport for long distances. Although this work aims at using real data, the results should be critically questioned. All relevant data were taken from literature without further validation. Historical data on risks cannot generally be projected to the future. The approach assumes fixed capacities for production and storage. Both should be optimized based on uncertainties. Nevertheless, the model offers a first approach to present various problems in complex biomass value-added chains and to solve them.

Acknowlegments

This thesis has been written during my time as a research associate at the Institute for Industrial Production (IIP) at the Karlsruhe Institute of Technology (KIT). I have developed this research during a joint research project with BASF SE, which I would like to thank for their expert and monetary support.

My supervisor Prof. Dr. Frank Schultmann enabled this successful joint project. For this and his constant support and guidance I thank him sincerely. I would also like to thank Prof. Dr. Nicolaus Dahmen for the very good collaborations in biomass projects in the past years as well as his support of my thesis. Also, I would like to thank Prof. Dr. Hagen Lindstädt and Prof. Dr. Steffen Rebennack for being part of the board of examiners.

Not only the professors but also the colleagues at the institute supported me mentally and contentwise during the years. I would especially like to thank Dr. Simon Schulte Beerbühl, Andreas Rudi, Dr. Sophia Radloff, Carmen Schiel, Dr. Marcus Wiens, Tobias Zimmer and Dr. Konrad Zimmer for their discussions and motivation.

Finally, I thank my friends and family, but most of all my fiancé Sascha and my parents, for their understanding and support.

Karlsruhe, in November 2018 *Ann-Kathrin Müller*

Contents

1 Introduction **1**

1.1 Problem description 1

1.2 Objective of this work 4

1.3 Procedure 6

2 Fundamentals of biomass value chains **9**

2.1 Importance of biomass value chains 10

2.2 Definition of biomass and their cultivation 13

2.2.1 Sugary and starchy biomass 15

2.2.2 Lignocellulosic biomass 17

2.2.3 Composition of different biomass types 20

2.3 Processing of biomass 22

2.3.1 Preprocessing of biomass for biochemical conversion 23

2.3.2 Conditioning and hydrolysis 25

2.3.3 Production of biobased chemicals 29

2.3.4 Downstream processing 36

2.4 Logistics of biobased chemicals 38

2.4.1 Storage 40

2.4.2 Transport 42

2.5 Conclusion 44

3 Location planning of biomass value chains considering uncertainties . . . 45

3.1 Decision support systems . . . 46
3.2 Deterministic models for biomass location planning . . . 47
3.3 Location planning approaches considering uncertainties . . . 49
3.3.1 Definition of decision making situations . . . 49
3.3.2 Approaches for location planning under uncertainty . 51
3.4 Biomass potential and location analysis . . . 60
3.5 Approaches for assessing technical processes . . . 61
3.5.1 Material and energy flow balances . . . 62
3.5.2 Flow sheeting simulation . . . 64
3.5.3 Simulation in AspenPlus® . . . 65
3.6 Economic assessment of processes . . . 66
3.6.1 Estimation of investment . . . 66
3.6.2 Estimation of production cost . . . 69
3.6.3 Other cost . . . 71
3.7 Risk analysis and risk management . . . 72
3.7.1 Essential terms in risk management . . . 73
3.7.2 Risk assessment in biomass value chains . . . 76
3.7.3 Probability calculation . . . 82
3.7.4 Consequences of risks occurrence and their evaluation 91
3.7.5 Risk categories . . . 95
3.7.6 Risk mitigation strategies . . . 104
3.8 Approaches for location planning under uncertainties . . . 106
3.8.1 Mathematical approaches for considering risks . . . 107
3.8.2 Considered uncertainties . . . 108
3.9 Conclusion and research questions . . . 109
3.9.1 Methodological conclusion . . . 111
3.9.2 Conclusion regarding content . . . 114

4 Development of an approach for location and logistics planning for biochemicals . . . 117
4.1 General description of the approach . . . 119
4.2 Optimization sub-model . . . 122
4.2.1 Multiple-choice approach . . . 123
4.2.2 Optimization model for biorefineries . . . 125
4.3 Technical sub-model . . . 134
4.4 Risk sub-model . . . 139
4.5 Integrated model considering uncertainties . . . 144
4.5.1 Objective function . . . 151
4.5.2 Constraints . . . 154
4.6 Conclusion . . . 158

5 Determination of input parameters . . . 161
5.1 Definition of biomass potentials and locations . . . 163
5.1.1 Estimation of biomass potentials in the United States 164
5.1.2 Estimation of biomass residue cost . . . 172
5.1.3 Possible locations for the biorefinery plants . . . 176
5.1.4 Possible suppliers for the integrated model . . . 177
5.1.5 Possible locations for the integrated model . . . 181
5.2 Techno-economic analysis of biochemical processes . . . 182
5.2.1 Production of sugar syrup in biorefineries . . . 183
5.2.2 Biochemical production of biochemicals . . . 195
5.2.3 Estimation of investment and production cost . . . 202
5.3 Techno-economic analysis of thermochemical processes . . . 206
5.3.1 Production of biooil via pyrolysis . . . 207
5.3.2 Thermochemical production of biobased chemicals . 208
5.3.3 Estimation of investment and production cost . . . 212
5.4 Definition of logistical parameters . . . 213
5.4.1 Rail transport . . . 214
5.4.2 Barge transport . . . 214

5.4.3 Truck transport 215
5.4.4 Hubs 216
5.4.5 Export 217
5.4.6 Transport distances 219
5.5 Risk Analysis 220
5.5.1 Transport risks 221
5.5.2 Process risks 229
5.5.3 Environmental risks 232
5.5.4 Political risks 237
5.5.5 Supply risks 240
5.5.6 Market risks 245
5.6 Scenario construction 247
5.6.1 Basic scenario 248
5.6.2 Scenario 1: Drought 2012 248
5.6.3 Scenario 2: Customers neglect GMO feedstocks . . 249
5.6.4 Scenario 3: Incentives for lignocellulosic bioethanol 251
5.6.5 Scenario 4: Influence of transport disruption 251
5.6.6 Scenario 5: Increased conversion yields 252
5.7 Conclusion 253

6 Value chains for the production of biochemicals in the United States 255
6.1 Technical sub-model for biochemical pathways 256
6.1.1 Evaluation of biorefineries for sugar production . . . 257
6.1.2 Evaluation of butanol production 260
6.1.3 Evaluation of succinic acid production 264
6.2 Technical sub-model for thermochemical pathways 268
6.2.1 Evaluation of fast pyrolysis conversion 268
6.2.2 Evaluation of syngas production and synthesis . . . 269
6.3 Results of the optimization sub-model 270
6.3.1 Usable biomass potentials in the U.S. 271

6.3.2 Estimation of biomass residue cost 273
6.3.3 Results for biorefineries 274
6.3.4 Results for pyrolysis 275
6.4 Results of the risk sub-model 277
6.4.1 Probabilities 279
6.4.2 Consequences of the occurring risks 285
6.4.3 Risk matrix 287
6.5 Results and system configurations of the integrated model . . 291
6.5.1 Results without uncertainties 292
6.5.2 Results with uncertainties 296
6.5.3 Comparison of economic results 300
6.6 Sensitivity analysis 302
6.6.1 Transport cost and transport routes 302
6.6.2 Export shares 305
6.6.3 Biomass cost 306
6.6.4 Utility cost 309
6.6.5 Uncertainties 311
6.7 Scenario calculations 319
6.7.1 Scenario 1: Drought 2012 320
6.7.2 Scenario 2: Customers neglect GMO feedstocks . . 323
6.7.3 Scenario 3: Incentives for lignocellulosic bioethanol 326
6.7.4 Scenario 4: Influence of transport disruption 328
6.7.5 Scenario 5: Increased conversion yields 333
6.7.6 Comparison of economic results 335
6.8 Conclusion 339

7 Conclusion 341
7.1 Discussion and application 341
7.1.1 Discussion of the developed approach 341
7.1.2 Discussion of the results 346
7.1.3 Application 349

7.2 Conclusion and outlook 350
7.2.1 Conclusion 350
7.2.2 Outlook 354

8 Summary **359**

A Appendix **361**
A.1 Appendix 1 361
A.1.1 Unit processes in AspenPlus 361
A.1.2 Conversion factors of biomass processing 363
A.1.3 Cooling down of glucose syrup during transport . . . 364
A.2 Appendix 2 366
A.2.1 Sugar production of the optimization sub-model . . . 366
A.2.2 Pyrolysis production of the optimization sub-model . 368
A.2.3 Existing pretreatment plants in the U.S. 370
A.3 Appendix 3 372
A.3.1 Fault Tree of transport delays 372
A.3.2 Fault Tree of process variations 373

List of Figures

2.1 Schematic depiction of biomass value chains 9
2.2 World sugar production in 2017/2018 in million tons 16
2.3 Breakdown of lignocellulosic complex 19
2.4 Annual production of non-wood fibres 20
2.5 Production of biobased chemicals 30
2.6 Emerging routes to bio-based alcohols 35

3.1 Biomass potential types and their relation 62
3.2 Methodology for managing supply chain risks 77
3.3 Risk assessment of likelihood and consequences 81
3.4 Basic depiction of Event Tree Analysis 84
3.5 Basic depiction of Fault Tree Analysis 87
3.6 Poisson distribution with $\lambda = 4$ 90
3.7 Concepcional approach to quantify direct damage 92

4.1 Holistic two stage approach for planning biomass value chains . 120
4.2 Linear approximation of investment curves 124
4.3 Block diagram of the optimization sub-model 126
4.4 Block diagram of the technical sub-model 135
4.5 Block diagram of the risk sub-model 140
4.6 Block diagram of the integrated model 144
4.7 Subsets of the integrated model 148

5.1 Definition of considered biomass value chains 163
5.2 Production areas and yield of corn in the U.S. 166
5.3 Existing pretreatment plants in the U.S. 180
5.4 Scheme of the corn wet milling process 187
5.5 Scheme of the sugar cane processing 188
5.6 Scheme of the sorghum processing 191
5.7 Process flow sheet for the production of ABE from corn stover . 199
5.8 Process flow sheet for the production of SA from corn stover . . 202
5.9 Process flow sheet for the production of syngas from slurry . . . 209
5.10 Process flow sheet for the production of ethylene from syngas . 211
5.11 Future development of transport of corn in the U.S. 214
5.12 Top water ports by tonnage 218
5.13 Development of domestic transport of corn in the U.S. 222
5.14 Rail accidents by rail mile 223
5.15 Truck accidents by highway mile 224
5.16 History of Mississippi's level at St. Louis 225
5.17 Congestion 2002 227
5.18 Congestion 2035 227
5.19 Number of U.S. strikes and lockouts 228
5.20 Precipitation ranks of 2012 drought in the U.S. 234
5.21 Percentage of GMO corn acreage in the U.S. 239
5.22 Existing bioethanol plants in the U.S. 247

6.1 Efficiency of biomass utilization for butanol production 261
6.2 Utility demand of butanol production 262
6.3 Investment of butanol production by biomass type 263
6.4 Efficiency of biomass utilization for succinic acid production . . 265
6.5 Utility demand of succinic acid production 266
6.6 Investment of succinic acid production by biomass type 267
6.7 Biomass potentials and possible locations for pretreatment . . . 272
6.8 Biomass potentials and locations for biorefineries 276

6.9 Utilized biomass potentials and chosen locations for pyrolysis . 278
6.10 Fault Tree for varying feedstock prices 281
6.11 3D risk matrix of the identified risks of butanol 288
6.12 Risk matrix of the identified risks of butanol 289
6.13 3D risk matrix of the identified risks of SA 290
6.14 Risk matrix of the identified risks of SA 291
6.15 3D risk matrix of the identified risks of ethylene 292
6.16 Risk matrix of the identified risks of ethylene 293
6.17 Suppliers and production of butanol 294
6.18 Suppliers and production of succinic acid 296
6.19 Suppliers and production of ethylene 298
6.20 Cumulative frequency of the Monte Carlo runs for butanol . . . 315
6.21 Cumulative frequency of the Monte Carlo runs for SA 317
6.22 Cumulative frequency of the Monte Carlo runs for ethylene . . . 320

A.1 Fault Tree of transport delays 372
A.2 Fault Tree of process variations 373

List of Tables

2.1 Existing biomass conversion plants to chemicals 14
2.2 Composition of different lignocellulosic biomass 19
2.3 Pretreatment processes of lignocellulosic biomass 26
2.4 Summary of downstream processing methods 39

3.1 Percentage composition of the investment 69
3.2 Symbols used in Fault Tree Analysis 85
3.3 Approaches for considering uncertainties in BVC optimization . 108
3.4 Uncertainties in biomass value chain models 110

4.1 Sets, parameters and variables of the optimization sub-model . . 127
4.2 Sets, parameters and variables of the integrated model 149

5.1 Composition of biomass residues 168
5.2 Main cultivation areas of sugarcane, corn and sorghum 171
5.3 Harvesting and local transportation cost of corn stover 174
5.4 Nutrient prices 175
5.5 Typical yields of the wet milling process 184
5.6 Energy demand for grinding of biomass residues 192
5.7 Yield of Dilute Acid pre-treatment depending on the biomass . . 193
5.8 Yield of enzymatic hydrolysis depending on the biomass 194
5.9 Sugar syrup composition 195
5.10 Butanol fermentation yields depending on the biomass type . . . 198
5.11 Succinic acid production yields depending on the biomass type . 201

5.12 Reference cost of equipment 204
5.13 Current prices for feedstock, energy and other utilities 205
5.14 Current prices for final products 206
5.15 Biooil production yields depending on the biomass type 207
5.16 Input and output data of gasification 210
5.17 Economic input data 212
5.18 Transport cost for pretreated biomass and chemicals 216
5.19 Export shares depending on product and continent 219
5.20 Changed prices for scenario 1 249
5.21 Changed input values for scenario 2 250
5.22 Changed input values for scenario 3 251

6.1 Efficiency of sugar production depending on biomass type . . . 258
6.2 Variable production cost of biorefineries by biomass 259
6.3 Investment of sugar production from lignocelluose 259
6.4 Estimated biomass residues cost 273
6.5 Estimation of bagasse cost from natural gas cost 274
6.6 Results of the optimization sub-model for sugar production . . . 275
6.7 Results of the optimization sub-model for pyrolysis 277
6.8 Butanol: product flows without uncertainties 294
6.9 Succinic acid: product flows without uncertainties 295
6.10 Ethylene: product flows without uncertainties 297
6.11 Butanol: product flows with uncertainties 298
6.12 Succinic acid: product flows with uncertainties 299
6.13 Ethylene: product flows with uncertainties 300
6.14 Comparison of economic parameters of the three case studies . . 301
6.15 Butanol: product flows with varying transport cost 303
6.16 Succinic acid: product flows with varying transport cost 304
6.17 Ethylene: product flows with varying transport cost 305
6.18 Butanol: product flows with varying biomass prices 308
6.19 Succinic acid: product flows with varying biomass prices 309

6.20 Succinic acid: product flows with varying utility cost 311
6.21 Ethylene: product flows with varying utility cost 312
6.22 MC Simulation: Blair as alternative location (butanol) 313
6.23 MC Simulation: Bedford Park as alternative location (butanol) . 314
6.24 MC Simulation: Lafayette as alternative location (butanol) . . . 314
6.25 MC Simulation: Clinton as alternative location (SA) 316
6.26 MC Simulation: Lee as alternative location (ethylene) 318
6.27 MC Simulation: Fayette as alternative location (ethylene) 318
6.28 MC Simulation: Freeport as alternative location (ethylene) . . . 319
6.29 Butanol: product flows in scenario 1 321
6.30 Succinic acid: product flows in scenario 1 322
6.31 Ethylene: product flows in scenario 1 323
6.32 Butanol: product flows in scenario 2 324
6.33 Succinic acid: product flows in scenario 2 325
6.34 Ethylene: product flows in scenario 2 326
6.35 Butanol: product flows in scenario 3 327
6.36 Succinic acid: product flows in scenario 3 328
6.37 Ethylene: product flows in scenario 3 328
6.38 Butanol: product flows in scenario 4a 330
6.39 Succinic acid: product flows in scenario 4a 330
6.40 Ethylene: product flows in scenario 4a 331
6.41 Butanol: product flows in scenario 4b 332
6.42 Succinic acid: product flows in scenario 4b 332
6.43 Ethylene: product flows in scenario 4b 333
6.44 Butanol: product flows in scenario 5 334
6.45 Succinic acid: product flows in scenario 5 334
6.46 Ethylene: product flows in scenario 5 335
6.47 Butanol: value chain cost of the different scenarios 336
6.48 Succinic acid: value chain cost of the different scenarios 337
6.49 Ethylene: value chain cost of the different scenarios 338

A.1 List of the most common unit processes in AspePlus Simulation 361
A.2 Conversion factors of pretreatment 363
A.3 Conversion rates of hydrolysis and fermentation of ABE 364
A.4 Sugar production: results of the optimization sub-model 366
A.5 Slurry production: results of the optimization sub-model 368
A.6 Existing corn wet mills, sugar cane mills, sorghum mills 370

List of Abbreviations and Symbols

Abbreviations

C5 sugars	Sugars with five carbon atoms
C6 sugars	Sugars with six carbon atoms
ABE	Acetone-Butanol-Ethanol
AFEX	Ammonia Fiber Expansion
Aspen	Advanced Simulator for Process ENgineering
BVC	Biomass value chain
CEPCI	Chemical Engineering Plant Cost Index
DME	Dimethyl ether
DSS	Decision Support System
EP	Evolutionary Programming
ETA	Event Tree Analysis
FMEA	Failure Mode and Effect Analysis
FT	Fischer Tropsch
FTA	Fault Tree Analysis

GA	Genentic Algorithm
GAMS	General Algebraic Modeling System
GIS	Geographic information system
LHV	Lower Heating Value
LHW	Liquid Hot Water
HHV	Higher Heating Value
HMF	Hydroxymethylfurfural
HTC	Hydothermal Conversion
MC	Multiple Choice Approach
MILP	Mixed Integer Linear Programming
NPV	Net present value
NOAA	National Oceanic and Atmospheric Administration
NREL	National Renewable Energy Laboratory
NRTL	Non-Random-Two-Liquid
PML	Probable Maximum Loss
SA	Succinic acid
SOS2	Special Order Sets of type 2
USDA	US Department of Agriculture
VaR	Value at Risk

Chemical Formulas

$C_2H_4O_2$	Acetic acid
C_3H_6O	Acetone
C_4H_9OH	Butanol
$C_4H_8O_2$	Butyric acid
CO_2	Carbon dioxide
C_2H_4OH	Ethanol
CH_2O_2	Formic acid
$C_6H_{12}O_6$	Glucose, Galactose
H_2	Hydrogen
$C_3H_6O_3$	Lactic acid
H_2SO_4	Sulfuric acid
$C_4H_6O_4$	Succinic acid
$C_5H_{10}O_5$	Xylose, Arabinose
HCl	Hydrogen chloride
H_2O	Water
$C_5H_{10}O_5$	Xylose
$NaOH$	Sodium hydroxide
NH_3	Ammonia

1 Introduction

1.1 Problem description

Rising energy demand, declining fossil resources and increasing cost for energy provision lead to the necessity to search for alternative resources of sustainable energy provision. Furthermore, the global warming potential due to greenhouse gas emissions is becoming more and more crucial. The industrial use of biomass seems to be a possible alternative to conventional carbon sources (see Kaltschmitt et al. [175]).

However, not only the energy sector dependens on fossil resources. Most of the chemical processes, especially for platform chemicals (e.g. 5-hydroxy-methylfurfural, furfural, gamma-valerolactone, xylitol, 2,5-furan-dicarbo-xylic acid, levulinic acid, ethanol, etc. (see Fang et al. [111])), are based on petrol (so-called petro-chemistry). According to Chemistry World [353], the U.S. government expects the production of biobased chemicals to rise significantly. The U.S. Department of Agriculture (USDA) predicts that about 3.45 million metric tons of bio-based plastics will be produced in 2020. This relates to an increase of about 3 to 6 % per year. The total share of biobased chemicals in that market is projected to rise from 2 % to more than 22 %. Due to the above-mentioned developments, the research for producing chemicals from biomass has increased immensely (see Fiorentino et al. [117]). This includes not only the production of the chemicals itself, but also the preprocessing of biomass and downstream processes, logistics and market economics.

Biobased processes are not very efficient and demand large amounts of biomass. Although 10 % of the worldwide energy demand is covered by biomass, still large, underutilized potentials exist. Especially residues from biomass production, e.g. straw, woody residues etc. are currently being examined for large-scale applications. Contrary to sugary and starchy biomass, they do not compete with food and feed industry. Unfortunately, these feedstocks have a relatively low energy density so that often the utilization of them is currently not yet feasible (see Friedl et al. [123]). The few existing biobased chemical plants are based on the sugary and starchy biomass due to their higher performance.

Biomass value chains and the production of biobased chemicals are prone to risks such as climate change, severe weather events, availability of water, and the stability of markets (see Trager [353]). Contrary to energy conversion from biomass to heat and electricity, chemicals need to fulfill high quality demands and distribution security for their customers. Consequently, the design and robustness of the supply chain against uncertainties of all sorts are essential. Similar to conventional supply chains, biomass value chains are sensible to changes in product demand and political or regulatory decisions. However, they are particularly prone to weather effects. Additionally, as biomass processes are not state of the art yet, the technologies are not fully researched. Uncertainties and lacking knowledge are currently dominating and hindering the large-scale extension of such processes. Companies, which are pioneers in large-scale biochemical production, are trying to minimize uncertainties in their value chain to maximize their profit.

The value chain of biochemicals consists of many steps. After harvesting and collecting the biomass, it is transported to an intermediate location, the final destination or a storage. Before processing, biomass needs to be pretreated by washing, cutting, drying etc. The production of the final products can be performed by a single or multiple process steps.

The preprocessing of biomass leads to an increase of energy density and forms an intermediate product, which can then be transported more efficiently. This leads to a decoupling of processes and a multi-stage value chain network. Consequently, the process chains need to be designed carefully. The supply safety and economic feasibility depends on the chosen locations, capacities and design of process steps (centralized or decentralized) as well as on the utilized biomass (see Schwaderer [314]).

Already many studies on bioenergy and biofuel supply chains and their uncertainties exist. However, so far no research could be found, which concentrates on biochemicals and their specific uncertainties and risks within their value chain. The demand for bioenergy and biofuels influences the uncertainties of biochemicals. Hence, this work focuses on the supply chain of biobased chemicals.

An optimal location with robust logistics and feedstock supply is essential for the competitiveness of biomass value chains with petro-chemical pathways. This decision needs to be based on available biomass potentials and suppliers, transport modes, competitors and customers. These also influence the capacity of the production plant. Due to economies of scale, larger production plants are often more economic. However, biomass is a wide spread feedstock. Large demands result in high transport cost. Consequently, decision support tools need to be developed and used by stakeholders to optimize their value chains regarding feedstock choice, transport network, capacity and the respective risks.

1.2 Objective of this work

Objective of this work is to develop a decision support approach for biomass value chains under the consideration of uncertainties for the production of biobased chemicals. Many regions cultivate various biomass types. These can be used for the conversion to biochemicals. As the biomass influences multiple parameters in the model, such as suppliers, production yields, and cost, the approach should differentiate between the biomass types. Consequently, this approach includes multiple biomass.

Different sources can be used as feedstock suppliers. Already existing processing plants of the biofuel and food industry as well as possible future conversion plants from biomass residues are included in the approach. Pretreatment plants of lignocellulosic biomass do not exist yet. Hence, the location and capacity of such possible suppliers need to be optimized beforehand.

Not only various biomass types influence the value chain. The transport also has an impact on the logistics. Hence, the approach includes multiple transport modes and routes for all products within the value chain. The approach will not only propose a specific location of the biomass conversion plants, but also the logistics to and from the plants by multiple transport modes via transport hubs.

Finally, different process configurations are possible within biomass value chains. These depend on the feedstock and the transport costs. Consequently, the approach includes the optimization of conversion processes. This work aims at modeling the processes in order to assess them techno-economically. This enables the inclusion of the process parameters in the decision support tool.

The final products are often exported or can be sold at local markets. As the export cost depend on the port and the destination country, export shares of the final products are included.

Multiple uncertainties occur along the biomass value chain. These have an impact on supply, transport, harvesting yields, etc. The risks need to be identified and assessed to include them in the decision making process for location planning. This enables the choice of appropriate mitigation measures for more efficient value chains. Therefore, this work aims at including risk assessment methods in the approach.

The above presented criteria result in the development of an integrated, strategic planning approach for value chains. It should therefore include the following aspects:

- Inclusion of multiple biomass types of the first and second generation and their regional specified potentials and suppliers
- Biomass dependent process designs as well as material and energy flows
- Inclusion of regional restrictions regarding transport and cost
- Continuous modeling of capacities under consideration of investment and economies of scale for the biorefineries
- Discussion and inclusion of risks and uncertainties along the value chain from biomass production to the distribution of the final chemical product incl. export
- Demonstration of the applicability in reality based on a real data case study

1.3 Procedure

In chapter 2 the fundamentals of biomass value chains from the definition of biomass to the distribution of the final product is presented. These also include technical details of biomass characteristics as well as descriptions of processes to convert biomass to biochemicals. Additionally, the basics of logistics are described.

Many approaches exist to model uncertainties in location planning as well as biomass value chains. These consider various aspects of biomass utilization including biomass potentials, transport modes, process specifics. In order consider all aspects of biomass value chains each step needs to be assessed. Consequently, the technical and economic assessments of biomass conversion processes as well as risk assessments are presented in chapter 3. The different approaches for including risks in location planning, specifically biomass value chains is analyzed in this chapter. Based on the literature review, the considered research questions are defined.

In chapter 4 the approach for designing biomass value chains under uncertainties is developed. This includes a sub-model for the determination of future biorefinery locations for the conversion of lignocellulosic biomass. As the biomass influences the chosen processes as well as the efficiency of process, the simulation of conversion technologies is shown in the technical sub-model. Uncertainties of biomass value chains are estimated by the risk sub-model. The results of these three sub-models are utilized as input for the integrated location model.

An example case refers to the United States of America where large amounts of well known biomass sources as well as a well developed infrastructure exist. The input data for the integrated model and the three sub-models is presented in chapter 5. These include biomass potentials, economic parameters such as investment and production cost, logistics and infrastructure as well as technical parameters of the processes. The identified risks are described. The approach is applied in different scenarios to analyze the influence of extreme events.

The results are discussed in chapter 6. These include supplier locations of pretreated biomass and their capacities, material and energy flow balances of the processes as well as probabilities and consequences of risks. The output of the sub-models as well as of the integrated model are presented. The integrated model defines possible future setups of value chains for the production of biobased chemicals.

Chapter 7 reflects on the approach, which has been developed in this work. The applicability as well as the model restrictions will be discussed and reviewed critically.

This work closes with a short summary in chapter 8.

2 Fundamentals of biomass value chains

In this chapter, the fundamentals of biomass value chains are presented. Biomass value chains are complex setups. In order to enable a feasible concept, both, technical and logistic factors need to be considered. Currently, biomass of the first and second generation (see section 2.2 for a definition) are the most promising feedstocks. These are provided by multiple suppliers and are transported in a distribution network of multiple transport modes. According to Adams et al. [5], value chains do not only include production sites and logistics but also operators, stakeholders, and policy makers as well as final customers. The five main steps in the biomass supply chain are cultivation and harvesting, pre-treatment, storage, transport, and biomass conversion facilities. In figure 2.1, the basic setup of a biomass value chain is depicted. It includes the different steps of the product chain from biomass sources to the final utilization of the biochemical and the process variations in each step.

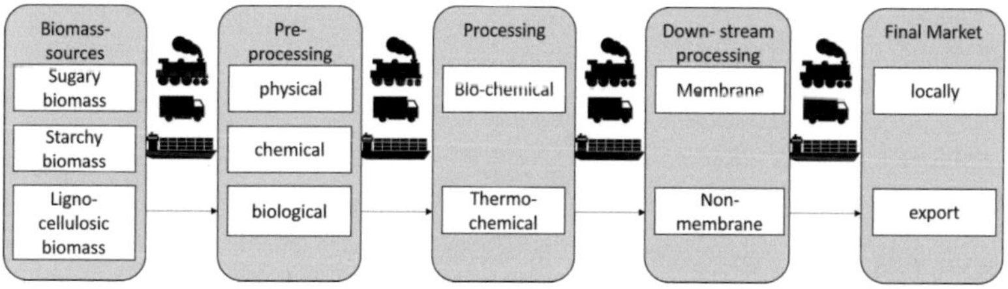

Figure 2.1: Schematic depiction of biomass value chains

The objective of biomass value chain optimization is to minimize cost as well as to improve the ecological footprint whilst ensuring a continuous feedstock supply. In section 2.1, the state of the art of biochemical production is presented. The basics on the definition of biomass and description of sugary, starchy and lignocellulosic biomass are described in section 2.2. Biomass can be converted by many different technologies to biochemicals. The technical basics are described in section 2.3. These include preprocessing steps, biochemical and thermal-chemical conversion as well as downstream processing steps. Biomass cultivation, conversion and demand satisfaction need to be secured by an efficient supply chain. Therefore, an optimized supply chain management is essential. The logistics of biomass value chains are presented in section 2.4. The overall section 2 is concluded in section 2.5.

2.1 Importance of biomass value chains the production of biochemicals

In the past, the importance of biomass-based products has increased significantly. Due to limited fossil reserves, the economy is forced to develop new value chains and transform it to renewable resources. The aim of many political directives is, hence, the development of an "environmentally, economically and socially sustainable global economy" (see de Jong et al. [169]). Biomass value chains can be categorized by the feedstock that is utilized, the products and the process (see de Jong et al. [169]). Philp et al. [285] define biochemicals as all "chemicals that can be produced through biomass origin and/or a bioprocessing route." The variety of biobased chemicals is extensive: propane- and butane diols, amino acids, ethanol, butanol, carboxylic acids etc.

The U.S. Department of Energy has issued a report on biobased chemicals which are predicted to be most likely essential building blocks for the future (see Werpy et al. [383]). This list was issued in 2004 and has been updated in 2010. Since the beginning of the 2000s, the production of biobased chemicals has increased frequently and is predicted to rise by more than 22 % compared to those years until 2025 (see USDA [366]). According to Philp et al. [285], biobased chemicals not only need to fulfill economic benefits but also need to comply with ecological and social standards to be competitive with petrochemicals. Just like fossil-based chemicals, biobased products need to fulfill national standards such as the Toxic Substances Control Act (TSCA) of the U.S. Environmental Protection Agency (EPA) or the European REACH (Registration, Evaluation, Authorization, and Restriction of Chemicals) regulations.

Although extensive research (see Brethauer et al. [60]) has been done in the past years to produce biochemicals from lignocellulosic biomass, the few existing production plants are based on sugary or starchy biomass (for definitions see section 2.2). Agricultural residues and wood biomass are not as easy convertible to biochemicals. As lignocellulosic biomass is not only built up of glucose (see section 2.2.2), the produced amount of biochemicals is lower on mass basis than when utilizing sugar as feedstock (see Hatti-Kaul et al. [150]). Biochemical conversion (e.g. via fermentation) is economically feasible if the production yield is high. Thermochemical conversion is currently not yet available in large-scale productions due to economic reasons (see Trippe [356]).

The production yields and economic benefits might lead to the assumption that biochemicals should be produced from first generation biomass, but sugar, grains and other resources are also used as food and feed. The conversion to chemicals is extensively discussed in the "food or fuel" debate (see Kaltschmitt et al. [175]). Many people worldwide suffer from hunger, so that food should not be used for the production of energy, fuels or chemicals (see Thompson [347]).

The utilization of biomass for the provision of energy has been state of the art for centuries. The most common use of biomass is the combustion of wood for the conversion to heat. Biogas production for the integration in natural gas systems has increased in the past years, especially due to rising subsidies from politics to enhance the development of a bioeconomy (see Dieckmann et al. [95]). Nevertheless, especially in Germany, the biogas plants are strongly dependent on the subsidies and might not be economically feasible without them.

Contrary to bioethanol production for biofuels, the production of biochemicals is not as advanced. Worldwide almost 100 million cubic meters of bioethanol were produced in 2016. Additionally, the production capacity of biodiesel reached almost 40 million cubic meters. According to the U.S. Department of Energy [103], the U.S. are the worldwide leader in bioethanol production with more than 57 % of the worldwide production in 2015. Brazil is the second largest producer of bioethanol. Whilst the bioethanol in the U.S. is processed from corn, the main feedstock in Brazil is sugar cane (see U.S. Department of Energy [103]). Only few production plants exist which convert biomass to chemicals. In the following table 2.1, large-scale production sites in operation are summarized. Especially large chemical companies such as BASF, DuPont, Bayer etc. are leaders in transforming the chemical production towards a more sustainable bioeconomy. They have mostly agreed to cooperations with companies, who are either their supplier or the developer of a certain bacteria string. In the past 10 years, the development has increased rapidly (see table 2.1).

Especially the production of building blocks is of importance as they can be processed to other high quality chemicals, polymers, bioplastics etc. A study of the nova-Institute [7] has identified a production capacity of about

2 million tons in 2013. The major building blocks are succinic acid and 1,4-butanediol, even though they are "brand new drop-ins" to the market.

Contrary to the production of biochemicals from biomass, value chains for the food industry by using first generation biomass are well established. For example, the existing system for the utilization of corn in the United States to produce animal feeds, starch and glucose syrup for soft drinks and bakery ingredients is very advanced. Also the utilization of sugar cane in Brazil or palm oil in Malaysia and Indonesia only have minimal optimization potentials, which mostly accrue in the residue utilization. Biomass value chains for the food and feed industry are often identical to biochemical or biofuel setups. Nevertheless, the capacities of conversion facilities for food applications are mostly lower than for biochemical plants. This reduces the complexity of supplier and transport networks.

2.2 Definition of biomass and their cultivation

The National Renewable Energy Laboratory (NREL) defines biomass as "any plant-derived organic matter. Biomass available for energy on a sustainable basis includes herbaceous and woody energy crops, agricultural food and feed crops, agricultural crop wastes and residues, wood wastes and residues, aquatic plants, and other waste materials including some municipal wastes."

Biomass resources can be clustered into the following groups: in general biomass and its biofuels can be defined as first or second generation and more recently also as third generation biomass. Biomass of the first generation is mostly sugary and starchy as well as oilseed biomass (see Sheldon [322]). In section 2.2.1, the characteristics of first generation biomass are described.

Table 2.1: Existing biomass conversion plants to chemicals

Product	Company	Capacity [kt/a]	Location	Year of operation	Source
Succinic acid	Myriant	13.6	Lake Providence, USA	2014	[131]
	Reverdia (JV DSM&Roquette)	10	Cassano Spinola, Italy	2012	[302]
	BioAmber&Mitsui	20	Rayong, Thailand	2015	[48]
	BioAmber&Mitsui	30	Sarnia, Canada	2015	[47]
	BASF SE & Purac	10	Montmelo, Spain	2014	[1]
Propanediol	DuPont & Tate&Lyle	60	Loudon, TN, USA	2006	[99]
Furandicarboxylic acid	Avantium&BASF	50	Antwerp, Belgium	tbd	[304]
L-Aspartic acid	Flexible Solutions International	5	Taber, Canada	2011	[51]
Itaconic acid	Pfizer Food Science	5 - 7	New York, USA	1989	[267]
	Pfizer Food Science	5 - 7	Sandwich, UK	1989	[267]
	Cargill/Cultor Food Science	30	Eddyville, USA	1996	[267]
	Iwata Chemicals	3.5	Kogyo, Japan	1970	[267]
	Rhodia	1 - 5	Melle, France	1995	[267]
	Tianli Biolog. Fermentation	2	Yunnan, China	1993	[267]
	Leizhou Yueli Itaconic Acid	1	Guangdong, China	1999	[267]
	Jiangshan Guoguang Biochem.	2 - 4	Zhejiang, China	1996	[267]
Levulinic acid	GFBiochemicals	10	Caserta, Italy	2017	[135]

Lignocellulosic biomass, such as woody biomass or crop residues, are defined as second generation. The peculiarities of lignocellulosic biomass are explained in section 2.2.2. In the present past, biomass such as algae or energy crops are defined as third generation. The latter is currently only available in laboratory scale. Therefore, third generation biomass is excluded from the scope of this work.

Biomass of the first generation mostly compete with food and feed production (see Sheldon [322]). Hence, the utilization for the production of biochemicals is heavily criticized in the public debate. The development of biobased chemicals is currently still in progress. Biochemicals are prone to high quality issues so that no state of the art process based on lignocellulosic biomass exists.

In the following the specifics of sugary, starchy and lignocellulosic biomass are explained.

2.2.1 Sugary and starchy biomass

Sugary and starchy biomass belong to the category of first generation biomass. They are easier to utilize than lignocelluloses, as they do not have to be processed by complex conversion technologies. Contrary to lignocellulosic biomass, they do not contain lignin, which inhibits fermentation.

Sugary biomass

Sugary biomass is mostly built up of aldohexoses, C6-sugars, such as glucose, fructose, mannose and galactose as well as their derivatives. Sugar beets and sugar cane are examples for sugary biomass. The main content is sucrose, a disaccharide made up of α-D-glucose and β-D-fructose. They are combined by an α-β-1,2-glycosidic bound.

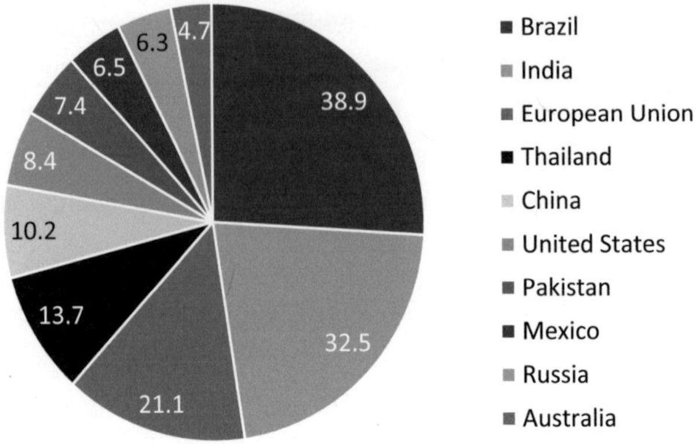

Figure 2.2: World sugar production in 2017/2018 in million tons (USDA [119])

Sugary biomass contains more than 70 % water. The sugar content is about 70 to 80 % of the dry mass, which is about 17 % of the wet biomass (see Lewandowski [204]). Microorganisms can especially metabolize glucose. Hence, it is utilized as feedstock for ethanol, acetic acid, isopropanol or n-butanol production.

In 2013/2014, almost 180 million tons of sugar were produced. With more than 39 million tons, the majority of sugar was processed in Brazil. Eastern countries such as India, China and Thailand produced together about 52 million tons of sugar. The distribution of the different countries is shown in figure 2.2. The larger share of sugar with 80 % is produced from sugar cane, which grows in tropical regions. The remaining 20 % are based on sugar beet (see USDA [119]).

Starchy biomass

According to Lewandowski [204], starch consists of many hundreds and thousands of α-1,4-glucosidic linked, unbranched D-glucose units (amylose) and/or of α-1,6- glucosidic, branched glucose chains (amylopectin). Starch is the most common compound for energy storage of plants. Cereals consist of 80 % endosperm, which contains starch and gluten. Other compounds are bran and hull (about 15 %) and germ (2-5 %). Contrary to sugar, starch is a macro molecule, which can hardly be digested by bacteria. Hence, the polysaccharides need to be hydrolyzed by enzymes and water.

Examples for starchy biomass are corn, wheat and barley as well as vegetables such as potatoes. Corn is one of the main feedstocks for bioenergy and biofuel production. The supply chains are well established and the product quality of corn syrup has a high standard. Almost 40 % of the total produced starch is based on corn, whilst the United States are the largest producer and exporter of corn. Other major crops for starch production are potatoes, wheat as well as cassava (see Lewandowski [204]).

2.2.2 Lignocellulosic biomass

Examples for lignocellulosic biomass are wood and agricultural residues, such as corn stover, bagasse, wheat straw as well as energy crops. For detailed information see Thakur [342]. These feedstocks have been studied intensively in the past years as they do not compete for utilization with the food and feed industry such as biomass of the first generation. Lignocellulosic biomass are composed of cellulose, hemicellulose and lignin, which form a complex compound. Further components are proteins, fatty acids and ash. The composition varies depending on the type of biomass. The following paragraphs are based on detailed information of Thakur [342]. Consequently, the utilization is currently less feasible but is assumed to be more sustainable as lignocellulosic biomass often occurs as waste.

Cellulose

Cellulose is built up of long chains of glucose monomers which are linked by β-1,4-glycosidic bonds. It can make up for 40 to 60 % of the cell wall of lignocellulosic biomass. A single cellulose molecule may consist of up to 10,000 glucose units. Hence, cellulose is a polysaccharide. They are interconnected by hydrogen bonds and form strong micro fibrils. Before glucose from cellulose can be fermented the crystalline structure needs to be cracked.

Hemicellulose

Hemicellulose consists also of polysaccharides, but not only of glucose but also of xylose, arabinose, galactose, mannose, thamnose and facose (pentoses and hexoses). Xylose, a C5-sugar, is the main component of hemicellulose. It is linked by β-1,4-glycosidic bonds.

Lignin

Lignin is a highly polymer substance made up of phenyl-propane derivatives. These strong bonds result in the non-fermentability of lignin. It forms the strong outer wall of the cell and covers the hemicellulose and cellulose. High lignin contents lead to low fermentation yields. As shown in figure 2.3 the lignin complex as the outer barrier needs to be split up by pretreatment to access hemicellulose and cellulose. Depending on the type of biomass, the composition of lignin, cellulose and hemicellulose as well as other compounds can vary (see table 2.2). The influence of biomass specific characteristics are presented in section 2.2.3.

Tye et al. [361] have summarized the potentials of different non-wood lignocellulosic biomass. The most agricultural residues are produced from the major biomass types, such as sugar cane, barley, corn, sorghum, wheat, etc.

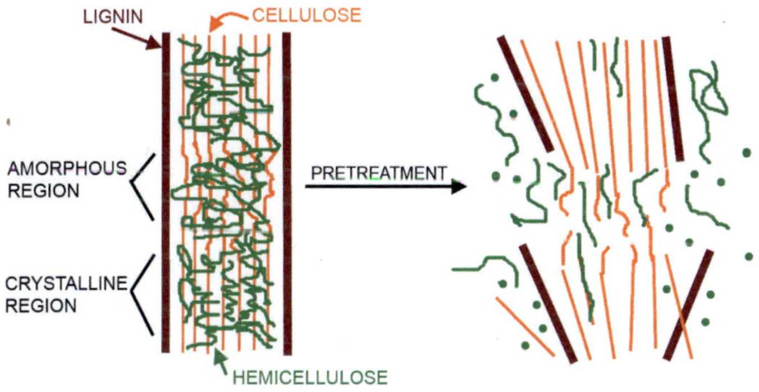

Figure 2.3: Breakdown of lignocellulosic complex (Mosier [239])

Table 2.2: Composition of different lignocellulosic biomass (Lee et al. [200])

in % of dry mass		Wheat straw	Corn stover	Barley straw
Cellulose		37.6	37.5	40.1
Hemicellulose				
	Xylan	19.5	21.7	18.98
	Arabinan	2.8	2.8	1.93
	Galactan	1.1	1.6	0.98
Lignin		13.5	18.9	19.37
Protein		3.8	3.1	-
Ash		6.4	6.4	4.45
Extractives		13	7	5.99
Acetate		4.6	1	4.45

This leads to an annual cellulose availability of 131.9 to 160.5 million tons of corn stover, 210.4 to 309.0 million tons of rice straw and 474.3 million tons of sugarcane bagasse, just to name the most important potentials (see Tye et al. [361]). In figure 2.4, the worldwide annual production of non-wood fibers, mostly residues from agricultural production is shown.

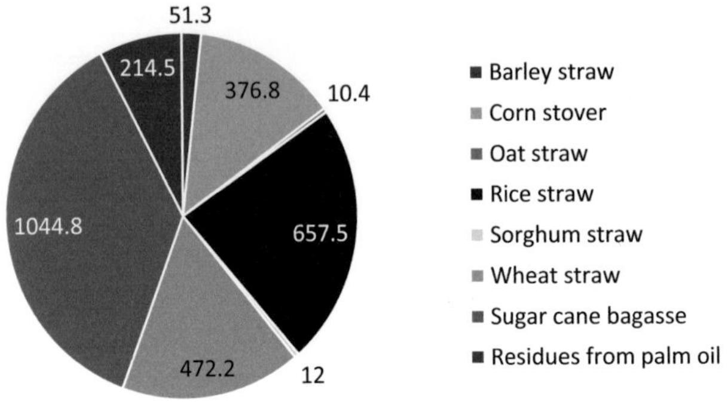

Figure 2.4: Annual production of non-wood fibres (Tye et al. [361])

2.2.3 Composition and characteristics of different biomass types

Depending on the type of biomass, the composition varies greatly. In the following, the major components and their influence on the processability of biomass will be discussed. These are the lignin content, the sugar composition, the ash content, the lower heating value and the water content.

Lignin content

The lignin content of biomass is the most crucial parameter regarding the processability by fermentation (see Tippkötter [349]). Depending on the chosen technology it can influence the efficiency immensely. High lignin contents result in lower cellulose and hemicellulose concentrations. In case of fermentations this leads to lower yields, as lignin is not fermentable. On the other hand, efficient preprocessing steps that lead to high sugar contents in the fermentation broth also result in high concentrations of inhibitors. Thermochemical processes can convert lignin more easily and break down the overall complex but only with a high energy input.

Sugar composition

The most important factor regarding biochemical processes is the sugar composition (see Tippkötter [349]). Depending on the bacteria, hexoses (especially glucose) are better fermentable than C5 sugars such as xylose. Glucose can be found mainly in starch (e.g. wheat or corn) whilst sugary biomass contains the same amount of glucose as fructose (C5-sugar) in the so-called sucrose. Lignocellulosic biomass is built up of multiple sugars such as glucose, xylose, arabinose, galactose and mannose. Contrary to biochemical processes, thermochemical production is independent on the sugar composition but is mainly focused on the carbon content of biomass.

Ash content

Biomass contains not only organic but also inorganic components. Experiments (e.g. by combustion) can determine the ash content and has normally a value of 3 to 10 % per dry ton. Ash is composed of minerals of silicon, aluminum, calcium and magnesium. Biomass with a high ash content is often handled as feedstock with low quality (see Trippe [356]). According to McKendry [220], ash can influence handling as processing of biomass. Bacteria cannot utilize ash in fermentations. This results in lower yields. In thermochemical production it can even lead to process related problems, especially in combustion processes ash can react to slag.

LHV and HHV

The lower heating value (LHV) is defined as the released energy whilst combustion with air (see McKendry [220]). The LHV is mostly mass or volume based. One can differentiate between the lower heating value and the higher heating value (HHV). The HHV is the complete energy, which is released whilst the fuel is burned including the latent heat of steam. Hence, it gives the maximum available energy of a biomass. The actually utilizable energy depends on the conversion technology and the type of energy. As the LHV cannot be measured experimentally, the vaporization heat of the water is subtracted from the HHV (see Kaltschmitt et al. [175]).

Water content

McKendry [220] distinguishes between two different water contents: the intrinsic and extrinsic water content. Contrary to the latter, intrinsic water content is not influenced by the weather. The extrinsic water content depends on the harvesting conditions. The moisture of biomass influences the conversion to alcohols or gases/oils. Thermochemical processes require a low water content, whilst biochemical processes can also utilize high moistures as in grasses or manure.

2.3 Processing of biomass

In the following section, the different preprocessing and conversion steps for producing biochemicals from biomass are presented. Depending on the type of biomass, different conversion steps are needed. Generally, physical-chemical, biochemical, and thermochemical processes exist to convert first and second generation biomass to biobased chemicals. These can either be used as solely pre-processing of biomass or for the total processing route.

2.3.1 Preprocessing of biomass for biochemical conversion

Biomass often needs to be preprocessed for further conversion to biochemicals. Objective of the preprocessing is the easier access and further processability of the feedstock. Additionally, pretreatment leads often to energetic densification of the feedstock. This results in more economic transports. Depending on the biomass and the conversion technology, different preprocessing steps are needed. Mostly mechanical processes are used for preprocessing of starchy, oily as well as sugary biomass. The large-scale processes include corn wet milling, sugar mills or rapeseed extraction. The majority of the preprocessing of first generation biomass is milling or extraction.

All biomass types are milled before further processing. The milling process can facilitate the extraction processes. It also increases the surface area, which accelerates chemical and biological reaction processes.

2.3.1.1 Pretreatment of sugary and starchy biomass

Glucose is necessary for the production of biochemicals by fermentation. Glucose can be produced from sugary and starchy biomass. The pretreatment of these is comparatively easy. These include mainly cleaning and crushing steps. The process of milling sugary biomass such as sugar cane or sugar beet is mostly combined with extraction. At first, the biomass is milled in multiple mills. After milling in hammer mills or in mills with revolving knifes, the sugar syrup is extracted from the broth by washing with counter flowing water. Afterwards, the sugar water needs to be cleaned for example with lime to remove impurities. The residues from sugar extraction can be used for animal feed, biogas production or energy provision by combustion (see Friedl et al. [123]).

Friedl et al. [123] distinguish two different processes for pretreating starchy biomass: dry and wet milling. To achieve higher purities, starchy biomass is often milled with water in the so-called wet milling process. Multiple products can be gained in this process. The main product is starch, which can be converted to glucose syrup by hydrolysis. Other products are proteins, germs and fibers. These can be separated from the other products before fermentation. The crops are cut by revolving knives. The germ is separated by a series of hydro cyclones. Afterwards, the fibers are parted from the remaining products (proteins and starch) by screens.

In dry milling processes the direct utilization of the complete crop for fermentation is envisaged. Dry milling processes are mostly more economic and are often used for biofuel processes. Nevertheless, the quality of the products from dry milling and, hence, the feedstock for bioethanol fermentations, is low. Consequently, the yield from fermentation is less than from wet milling. The grain is separated in four physical components: germ, flour, fine grits and coarse grits. The residues from dry milling and fermentation can be dried and sold as Distillers Dried Grain with Solubles (DDGS) (see Friedl et al. [123]).

2.3.1.2 Pretreatment of lignocellulosic biomass for biochemical conversion

The pretreatment of lignocellulosic biomass for the production of biochemicals does not differ from the preprocessing for biofuel production. Bajpai [35] provides a summary on pretreatment technologies of lignocellulosic biomass. He describes five main types of techniques: physical, physicochemical, chemical, cellulose solvent-based lignocellulose and biological pretreatment. **Physical pretreatments** focus on the solely mechanical comminution of lignocellulose by grinding, milling etc. or high-energy radiation. **Physico-chemical pretreatments** are based on physical and chemical principles. The lignocellulosic complex is split up by physical forces such as heat or pressure. Additionally, they are catalyzed by chemical reactions. The most common processes are steam explosion, liquid hot water pretreatment (LHW), ammonia fiber explosion (AFEX) or carbon dioxide explosion. Contrary to the physical pretreatment **chemical preprocessing** only uses chemical reactions to break up the lignocellulose. Lignin can be split by oxidatives such as ozone, sulfur trioxide or hydrogen peroxide, by acids and alkali or by sulfites. A common pretreatment is also the Organosolv process. **Cellulose solvent-based lignocellulose pretreatment** This pretreatment has gained more and more interest in research as it increases the cellulose accessibility. This leads to higher hydrolysis rates and fermentability compared to conventional lignocellulosic pretreatment technologies. Solvents used for these processes are ionic liquids, aqueous n-Methylmorpholine-n-oxide, urea or sodium hydroxide and N,N-Dimethylacetamide. As in all biochemical processes, microorganisms can be used in **biological pretreatment** to degrade lignocellulose. These are for example white-rot fungi or brown-rot fungi. A short summary of the advantages and disadvantages of the major pretreatment processes is presented in table 2.3.

2.3.2 Conditioning and hydrolysis for biochemical conversion

Especially lignocellulosic biomass cannot be fully pretreated by the above mentioned processed. Hence, the remaining poly- and oligomers need to be broken down for fermentation as bacteria and yeasts can only metabolize sugars. During pretreatment processes, inhibitors can be produced, which harm the fermentation and reduce the yield. The pretreated biomass first needs to be conditioned to remove the inhibitors. Afterwards, the broth is hydrolyzed to produce sugar monomers for fermentation.

Table 2.3: Pretreatment processes of lignocellulosic biomass (Kumar [192])

Process	Principle	Advantage	Disadvantage
physicochemical			
Steam Explosion	explosive decompression at 160-260°C (high-pressure steam)	only water, low disposal cost	incomplete decomposition of the lignin-carbohydrate matrix, by-products
AFEX	90°C, high pressure, explosive decompression, ammonia addition	ammonia may improve fermentation rate	only for low lignin contents
LHW	160-190°C, distilled water, pH of 4-7	only few toxic by-products, small particle sizes	low glucose yield
chemical			
Ozonolysis	treatment with ozone decomposes lignin (C=C bonds)	no toxic by-products, at ambient conditions	high cost
Dilute Acid	concentrated acids (H_2SO_4, HCl)	decomposes the majority of hemicellulose to dissolved sugars	high cost, generation of furfural and HMF
Organosolv	Mixture of organic solvents and anorganic acid catalysis, 180-195°C	easy recovery of organic solvents, lignin isolated as valuable product	expensive solvents, tight process control
biological			
rot funghi	decompose lignin and cellulose	low energy demand	long reaction times
physical			
pulsed electric field	short burst of high voltage	ambient conditions, easy construction	high investments

Contrary to biochemical processes, thermochemical processes are not as sensible to varying biomass qualities and do not need to be broken down to sugars. Pretreated biomass does not need to be conditioned for further thermochemical processing. Hence, the in the following explained conditioning and hydrolysis steps are only necessary in biochemical production processes. Consequently, they are neglected in the following sections.

2.3.2.1 Conditioning

Depending on the type of pretreatment process (see section 2.3.1), different toxic by-products, so called inhibitors, are produced, which can influence further processing. Especially biochemical processes for the production of biochemicals are sensible to inhibitors. According to Pienkos and Zhang [286], mainly five groups exist, which influence the fermentation.

In the following, these materials will be explained:

- **Furfural** and **Hydroxymethylfurfural (HMF)** interfere with the activity of dehydrogenases and cause the inhibition of glycolysis. This results in reduced growth rates and cell yields.
- **Phenols** inhibit cell growth and sugar transport once they partition into membranes.
- **Acids** cause the collapse of pH gradients and, hence, cellular energy generation. The hydrophobicity interferes the ability of the compound to pass through the cell membranes.
- **Aldehydes** are hydrophobic, but contrary to acids and alcohols do not cause a collapse of pH or the membrane structure
- **Alcohols** are less toxic than acids and aldehydes, but their toxicity also results from hydrophobicity. This can cause a breakdown of the membrane structure.

Different processing possibilities exist to reduce the inhibitors in the fermentation broth. According to Pienkos and Zhang [286], these can either be biological, chemical or physical. For biological reduction of inhibitors, enzymes (e.g. laccase and lignin-peroxidase) or fungi (e.g. *Coniochaeta ligniaria*) can be added to the hydrolysate. The acids in the fermentation broth are neutralized by bases, such as sodium hydroxide ($NaOH$), calcium hydroxide ($Ca(OH)_2$), potassium hydroxide (KOH), or ammonia hydroxide (NH_4OH). Using physical conditioning the inhibitors are not treated and neutralized but are removed from the hydrolysate, for example by liquid-liquid extraction.

2.3.2.2 Hydrolysis

Before the fermentation of lignocellulosic biomass, especially the cellulose and hemicellulose components are further broken down by enzymes to monomer sugars. This process is called hydrolysis. It is often the most time consuming processing step within the overall production. Enzymes cannot decompose lignin anaerobically. The characteristics of the biomass define the type of process as well as the process conditions. During hydrolysis, starch, cellulose, hemicellulose, and other oligomers are split up to sugars and monomers. For the processing of starch, two different process types are distinguished by Friedl et al. [123]. Enzymatic and acid treated hydrolysis are explained in the following sections.

Enzymatic hydrolysis

In enzymatic hydrolysis, enzymes are used to convert cellulose to glucose. Mostly biomass is pretreated by steam explosion, acids, organic solvents, hydrogen peroxide etc. to make it accessible for enzymes. The endoglucanases split the connections within the long chains of cellulose molecules.

At the new free ends exoglucanases split the cellubiose molecules from the non-reducible ends of the cellulose.

Acid treated hydrolysis

In the past, hydrolysis plants used acids for hydrolysis. Either concentrated acids at normal temperature or dilute acids at 200 degrees Celsius can be used for acid treated hydrolysis. Different processes exist to break down the oligomers by acid treatment. These are, for example, Bergius-process with diluted hydrochloric acid, Tennessee Valley Authority (TVA) process with concentrated sulfuric acid and the arkenol process. Details of these processes can be found by Friedl et al. [123]. Processes with a high acid concentration lead to high yields, high sugar concentrations and low reaction times. Nevertheless, acids can inhibit the fermentation.

2.3.3 Production of biobased chemicals

For the production of biobased chemicals many different process routes exist, which can be combined in various manners. In this section, the basics of thermal-chemical processes are described. These are, for example, combustion, gasification or pyrolysis. The fundamentals of biochemical processes such as fermentation and hydrolysis, are presented in the following. The large variety of possible products from biomass is shown in figure 2.5.

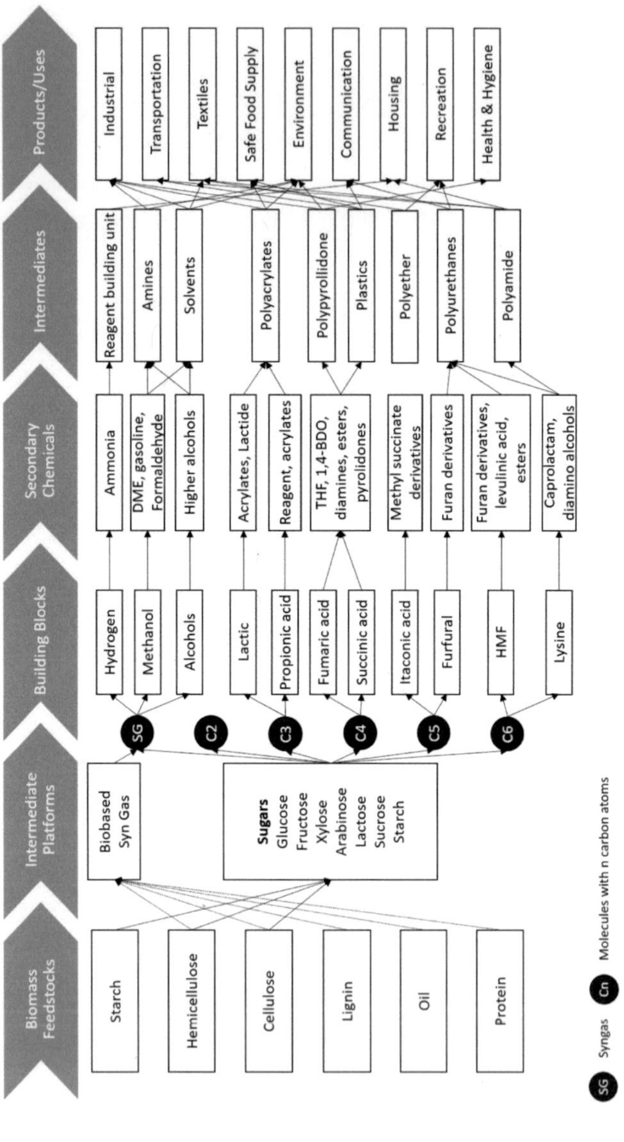

Figure 2.5: Production of biobased chemicals (NREL [383])

2.3.3.1 Thermochemical processes

According to Bridgwater [61], especially pyrolysis and gasification are suitable for the production of chemicals. These have been studied by, e.g. Trippe [356], Meyer [227] and Schwaderer [314]. Thermochemical processes, especially synthesis of gasified biomass, have the advantage that they can produce a large variety of different products. A negative aspect of thermochemical processes is the high energy demand, which is necessary to convert biomass (see Kaltschmitt et al. [175]). The combustion of biomass produces heat and can, consequently, be used for the conversion to energy in combined heat and power plants (CHP). Due to the focus of this work, the production of heat and energy is excluded from the scope.

Gasification

According to Hofbauer et al. [155], fuel gases are produced during gasification by two methods. Biomass can be either partially or fully oxidized. This produces a mixture of carbon monoxide (CO), carbon dioxide (CO_2), hydrogen (H_2) and methane (CH_4). The second route is the treatment with steam or pyrolytic gasification (see Bridgwater [61]). The solid fuel is heated up, reacts with oxidizers, such as air or steam, and is converted to a flammable gas. This gas can then be oxidized to CO_2 and water (H_2O). The process of gasification has three phases: heating, pyrolytic decomposition, and the gasification itself. The produced syngas can be utilized for further chemical conversion processes, such as Fischer Tropsch Synthesis. Gasification is an endothermic process. Equation 2.1 presents the reaction.

$$\begin{aligned} &CH_xO_y(Biomass) + O_2(fromair) + H_2O(steam) + CO_2 \\ &\rightarrow \\ &CH_4 + CO + CO_2 + H_2 + H_2O(unusedsteam) + C(coke) + tar \end{aligned} \tag{2.1}$$

Pyrolysis

Contrary to gasification, pyrolysis is performed without an oxidizing material (see Hofbauer et al. [154]). Hence, it is heated by exclusion of oxygen. Liquid (e.g. pyrolysis oils) as well as solid (e.g. char) materials are produced during pyrolysis. Depending on the duration of the process, one can distinguish between three different types of pyrolysis: slow, intermediate and fast.

Aim of the slow pyrolysis is the production of primary solid products (char). The first two faces of gasification (heating and pyrolytic decomposition) is given enough time for full reactions. As a full oxygen-free environment is almost impossible, some gasification processes occur nevertheless. The so produced gases can be utilized for energy provision for the process. Liquid products (e.g. bio-oil) are mostly produced during fast pyrolysis. The second phase will not be fulfilled completely, so that liquids are the main product. Pyrolysis gas is also used for energy provision. Up to date the pyrolysis reactions are not fully understood, so that the formulations of reaction equations is not possible (see Hofbauer et al. [155]).

Fischer Tropsch Synthesis

Trippe et al. [356] describe the Fischer Tropsch (FT) Synthesis for the production of gasoline and diesel. For the production of biofuels via FT Synthesis various reactions take place. The basic principle of the FT Synthesis is formation of $-CH_2-$ monomers, which then polymerize to longer products, such as paraffins, olefins, and oxygenated hydrocarbons. The reactions can be generally formulated as follows.

$$nCO + (2n+1)\,H_2 \rightleftharpoons C_nH_{2n+2} + nH_2O \tag{2.2}$$

$$nCO + 2nH_2 \rightleftharpoons C_nH_2 + nH_2O \tag{2.3}$$

These two equations describe the exothermic reactions of syngas to paraffins (see equation 2.2) and olefins (see equation 2.3).

In parallel, the undesired water-gas shift reaction and methane formation occur. By adapting FT synthesis conditions, these pathways can be reduced. High operating pressures result in longer carbon chains and a decrease of methane production. In order to achieve maximum product yields the reaction should take place at low temperatures, high operating pressures, and $H_2 : CO$ ratios of about 2 (see Trippe [356]).

Hydrothermal Conversion (HTC)

The term "hydrothermal" has its origin in geochemistry and mineralogy. It defines hot, liquid water reserves under high pressure, the so-called hot compressed water. It mostly has a temperature above 373 K and a pressure of more than 0.1 MPa. Other influencing factors are the dry matter content of the feed, the particle size, the process duration, the pH-value of the feed and additives. For further details see Vogel [375].

In HTC, the thermochemical processes of heating and pyrolytic decomposition are run through. The presence of liquid water benefits the hydrolysis reactions. In the end, the main product is a lignite similar solid fuel.

Other related processes are the hydrothermal liquefaction (HTL) and the hydrothermal gasification (HTG) (see Vogel [375]).

2.3.3.2 Biochemical processes

Biomass is a heterogeneous good and can vary greatly in its composition (see section 2.2). Enzymes and microorganisms on the other hand are very sensible to variations. Different pretreatment techniques, as shown in section 2.3.1, convert biomass to more homogeneous and fermentable sugars.

Biochemical processes have the advantage that they are carried out at low temperatures around 303 to 313 K. This results in low energy cost. The downside is the long reaction times, which lie often between twenty and seventy hours, depending on the batch size. Fermentation are historically performed in batch reactors. Currently, low reaction times and the maximum yields (e.g. due to sugar concentration and inhibitory products) limit the performance of fermentations. Therefore, batch systems are being optimized in current research (see Formenti et al. [120]). Research mainly focuses on simultaneous saccarification and fermentation (SSF). According to Kaltschmitt et al. [175], especially fed-batch reactors seem to increase the production yield. Continuous production only makes sense in large scale applications, as it is less flexible, it is sensible to substrate qualities and results in low fermentation rates (see Kaltschmitt et al. [175]). Once the polymers are broken down to C5 and C6 sugars, microorganisms, such as bacteria or yeasts, can metabolize the feedstock to produce biochemicals.

As seen in figure 2.6, the routes for producing alcohols, which have a large share in biochemical production, are mostly based on fermentation. Alcohols can be used as platform chemicals and be converted to a large variety of other chemicals.

In general, two different fermentation types are differentiated: anaerobe and aerobe, which are explained in the following based on Friedl et al. [123].

Anaerobe fermentation

This process produces biochemicals by fermenting sugars with bacteria or yeast at anaerobic conditions, meaning without oxygen being present. During fermentation, an incomplete oxidation of the substrates to carbon dioxide and other by products occurs. During glycolysis, glucose transfers to the intermediate product pyruvate.

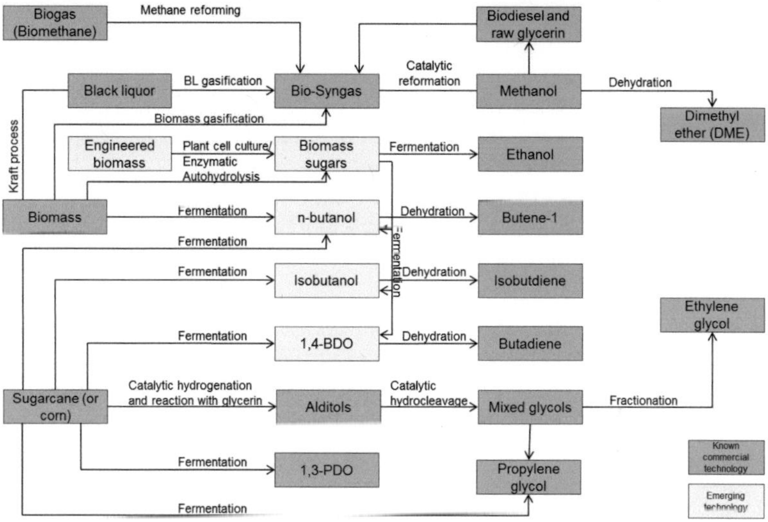

Figure 2.6: Emerging routes to bio-based alcohols (Nexant [260])

Aerobe fermentation

Contrary to anaerobe fermentation, this type occurs with oxygen being present. Pyruvate is decomposed to intermediate products for the biosynthesis of the cell, respectively for the production of adenosine triphosphate (ATP) as energy supply for the cell. This metabolism is also called cell breathing. The main reaction is the consumption of oxygen by producing carbon dioxide (see equation 2.4).

$$aC_6H_{12}O_6 + bO_2 + cNH_3 \rightarrow CH_XO_yN_z + dCO_2 + eH_2O \tag{2.4}$$

2.3.4 Downstream processing

Before the final products, derived from thermochemical and biochemical production, can be used as chemicals, they often need to be cleaned and processed. In the following, the different downstream processing techniques based on thermochemical and biochemical production are shortly presented.

2.3.4.1 Downstream processing of thermochemical products

After gasification or pyrolysis, the products can be processed to facilitate downstream processes or to upgrade the product.

Upgrading of pyrolysis products

According to Samolada et al. [311], biomass pyrolysis liquids can be upgraded to bio-gasoline via hydrogen processing and catalytic cracking. Catalytic hydrotreatment is very cost intensive in terms of processing cost and investment. Fluid catalytic cracking seems to be cheaper. It converts oxygenated feedstocks to fractions of lighter hydrocarbons. Pyrolysis char can be upgraded to active char. Instead of being converted to energy, it can be used for emission reduction and soil upgrading (see Funke et al. [126]).

Raw syngas cleaning

The synthesis gas, which is produced from biomass gasification, still contains impurities. These may inhibit downstream processes, such as Fischer-Tropsch synthesis, by harming the catalyst. These impurities are mainly nitrogen, chlorine, sulfur, and ash. According to Woolcock and Brown [386], different technologies exist to clean syngas from biomass. In general, they distinguish between hot and cold gas cleaning depending on the operating temperature of the process. While cold gas cleaning has a high energy demand as the gas needs to be cooled down and be reheated afterwards, the processing conditions of hot gas cleaning are still too extreme. Hence, cold gas cleaning technologies are still state of the art. For details on the different processes see Woolcock and Brown [386].

2.3.4.2 Downstream processing of biochemical products

The final products need to be separated from the fermentation broth. Many different technologies exist to isolate the different products from each other. Some processes, such as gas stripping, adsorption, liquid-liquid extraction etc., can be used for *in-situ* separation of the final products. As the fermentation products often inhibit the fermentation process itself, the separation of them during the process is endeavored. Distillation and rectification have been the most known and utilized downstream processing technologies, but for large-scale applications they are mostly too energy intensive. In general, the processes can be distinguished in non-membrane and membrane separation. These are briefly described in the following. The most common technologies as well as their advantages and disadvantages are summarized in table 2.4.

Non-membrane separation

The main non-membrane separation techniques are thermal processes. Most of these processes convert the product to a gaseous phase. As a large share of the fermentation broth consists of water, thermal processes are highly energy intensive. On the other hand the purity of the products are high. Non-membrane technologies include distillation, rectification, liquid-liquid extraction, and gas stripping (see Duerre [98]).

Membrane separation

Due to the high energy demand of non-membrane technologies, research has increased immensely in the past years to enhance the separation from fermentation broth via membranes. Membranes have the advantage that they built up a physical barrier between the final products and the fermentation broth. This decreases the inhibitory effect that many products have on the microorganisms. As a disadvantage, the pores of membranes clog often. Pertraction, pervaporation, and adsorption are examples for membrane separation techniques (see Duerre [98]).

2.4 Logistics of biobased chemicals

The main logistical operations in the material flow include multiple steps from feedstock origin to the final market. The supply chain of biobased chemicals is made up of harvesting, handling storage, loading and unloading of transportation vehicles, and transport of the different products.

The transported bulk materials include all aggregate phases: solid, fluid and gaseous. Contrary to the transport mode and the materials, the available infrastructure depends on the region. Capacities and usable transport modes might be restricted. Transport cost and legal constraints, such as speed or transport volume, are given by the considered region (see Meyer [227]).

Depending on the size of the biomass suppliers, they might also own their private transport system. Nevertheless, private and public transport networks as well as their respective cost are treated equally in this study (see Meyer [227]).

Table 2.4: Summary of downstream processing methods (Duerre [98])

Process	Principle	Advantages	Disadvantages
Distillation	Separation of the products due to different boiling points	high purities possible	high energy demand
Gas-stripping	Cleaning with gas, condensation of solvent and steam	easy process, minor risk of plugging or fouling	low selectivity, incomplete removal of solvents, higher energy demand as membrane processes
Liq.-liq. extraction	contact of the water insoluble solvent with the fermentation broth	high capacity and selectivity, minor risk of plugging and fouling	expensive process
Pertraction	similar to liq.-liq. extraction with membrane which separates extract from fermentation broth	high selectivity, easy processing	large membrane area necessary, possible plugging and fouling
Pervaporation	selective diffusion of solvents through non porous mem brane, recollection of vaporized products by vacuum	easy processing	possible plugging and fouling
Adsorption	adherence of solvent on e.g. silicates	low energy demand	high material cost, low capacity, low flexibility, possible fouling

2.4.1 Storage

Biomass is mostly a seasonal good, especially in case of agricultural crops, but the majority of processing facilities operates continuously throughout the year. Consequently, at some point, biomass needs to be stored to overcome the temporal gap of supply and demand.

Campaign production of the final product in the same season as the harvest would require larger production capacities which will be then left unused throughout the rest of the year.

Depending on the biomass type, different storage options and restrictions need to be respected. Due to hygroscopic properties of some biomass, the moisture content of stored biomass can increase under wet weather conditions. This can be avoided by closed storage facilities. A trade-off between more expensive storage systems and biomass quality exists (see Meyer [227]).

During storage, two different effects occur according to Dieckman et al. [96]. On the one hand, the water content in biomass may decrease depending on the ambient conditions. This leads to an increase of heating value and a decline of transport mass. On the other hand, in case the ambient conditions are wet, biomass deteriorates during storage. The deterioration rate λ depends on the moisture content of the biomass and the biomass itself.

The deterioration of biomass reduces the quality and, hence, the value of the good. Eksioglu et al. [105] define the deterioration as in equation 2.5. The actual usable biomass amount $u_{b,l,k}$ is by $(1-\lambda_b)$ lower than the stored amount $v_{b,l}$

$$\sum_{k=1}^{K} u_{b,l,k} \leq v_{b,l} \cdot (1-\lambda_b) \qquad \forall b,l \qquad (2.5)$$

Dieckmann et al. [96] describe different risks, which go along with storage. These are:

- Loss of substances due to biological processes (loss risk)
- Self-incineration (hazard potential)
- Fungi growth (health risks)
- Odor pollution (environment risk)
- Reallocation of water content (quality risk)
- Agglomeration due to frost effects (technical risk)
- Abrasion of fine particles (quality risk)
- Trickle away of water (environmental risk)

Not only biomass needs to be stored in biomass value chains, but all occurring products. As delays might occur, the storage at each fixed location within in the biomass value chain is needed. Just-in-time transports are hardly feasible. Hence, at most transportation hubs and facilities, storage for each product should be implemented. The size of the storage needs to be optimized depending on the uncertainties, which may occur in the supply chain (see Dieckmann [96]).

Different storage types and restrictions exist. The storage type influences the cost and the deterioration rate. Low cost often lead to high storage losses (e.g. on field storage without protection). Especially biomass can depreciate during storage, causing less processable quantity and quality. This can be overcome by installing silos or warehouses. On the other hand, these cause investments, which increase the storage cost (see Dieckmann [96]).

2.4.2 Transport

Even more than conventional supply chains, biomass based supply chains are restricted by specific constraints. Biomass has a low energy density and, hence, the transport is, depending on the type of biomass, sometimes bound by volume less than mass capacity. Due to the low energy content, the transport over long distances is often infeasible as the cost are too high (see Schwaderer [314]). Many works exist, which estimate the supply cost curves of biomass. The transport of biomass is similar to other goods, which are transported as bulk. This leads to similar modeling structures for different feedstocks, regions and conversion technologies (see Meyer [227]). The transport of biomass is restricted either by the mass or volume of the transported good. The higher the density of the (pretreated) biomass is, the more the transport is bound by mass restrictions. Therefore, biomass is often pretreated to enable economic transport for long distances. Volume bound transport often occurs in case of second generation biomass such as straw or woody residues. These biomass are often only transported by short distances if they are not pretreated. The maximum economic feasible transport distance depends on the type of biomass. High feedstock qualities, and therefore energy densities, result in longer distances. Transport cost are related to the choice of transport mode and the transport distance (see Trippe [356]). Much research is performed to optimize the logistics of biomass transport (see Zimmer et al. [404], Hamelinck et al. [146], Mafakheri et al. [211], a.o.). Especially the pretreatment of biomass to liquids or compressed solids by pelletization, pyrolysis, or torrefaction may reduce long distance transport cost. Even though some of these processes are very cost intensive, in terms of energy cost and investments, the additional pretreatment is feasible in the long run. Among others, Schwaderer [314], Kerdoncuff [180], and Uslu et al. [369] have studied the influence of energy densification processes to increase the efficiency of biomass transport.

Bulk materials are mainly transported by rail, barge or truck. Pipeline transport can be possible for biofuels, but in the case of biochemicals the needed network has not yet been established. Nevertheless, Kumar et al. [190] have studied the transport of corn stover via pipeline. Due to the low feasibility, it is neglected from this study. Depending on the type of product, different transport modes can be applied (see Meyer [227]).

The majority of biomass is transported by truck. Especially for short distance transport, this transport mode is the most feasible. Depending on the region, where biomass is harvested, transported and processed, different trucks and sizes are available. Even in Europe the restrictions can reach from 28 tons in Switzerland to 40 tons in Germany and about 60 tons in Sweden. Trucks in the United States may transport up to 80 tons (see Dieckmann et al. [96]).

If the conversion facilities are close to the railway system, then the products may also be transported by rail. Rail transport is mostly carried out in standard wagons. Railways can transport 40 to 60 tons per wagon depending on the rail system (see Dieckmann et al. [96]).

In general, biomass can be transported by barge, but mostly the transport cost for short distances are too expensive and the cultivation fields too distant from waterways, that barge transport is not feasible. Furtermore, for the transport via ship, different production characteristics need to be considered. Barge transport is mostly preferred for long distance transportation. According to Dieckmann et al. [96], transport ships can reach lengths of 39 to 110 meters and a width of 5 to 11.4 meters. Consequently, the transportable biomass volume is between 220 and 3000 tons per ship.

2.5 Conclusion

Biomass value chains are complex networks built up of different types of usable biomass, preprocessing and processing technologies and respective products. In this chapter, the various biomass types have been defined. The influence of the biomass composition on quality and processes was presented. Depending on the processing technology, biomass needs to be pretreated accordingly. For biochemical processes, especially starchy and lignocellulosic, biomass needs to be broken down to fermentable sugars, which is mostly glucose and xylose. Thermochemical processes on the other hand require a certain particle size for efficient conversion. After processing, the different products are cleaned and separated from by-products in downstream processes. The choice of biomass and product mostly define the possible conversion processes.

Due to the seasonality and the wide spread production of biomass, the supply chain is prone to specific challenges. Biomass needs to be stored throughout the year as it accrues only in harvesting season, but most processes work continuously. The low energy density of biomass influences the efficiency of transport. Sometimes densification technologies, such as pelletization or torrefaction, are used to increase the feasibility of long-range transportation. Depending on the product type, different transportation methods can be used. These are mainly barge, rail and truck transport, whilst truck is the most common transportation mode.

3 Location planning of biomass value chains considering uncertainties

In the following sections, the basics of location planning under uncertainties are presented. After an introduction to decision support systems in section 3.1, a selection of discrete location planning approaches, which exist in literature is presented in section 3.2. In section 3.3, the different approaches for integrating uncertainties in location modeling are shown. A crucial aspect when developing location planning models for biomass value chains is the available biomass for conversion. The basics for estimating biomass potentials is presented in section 3.4. Knowledge on the technical processes are necessary to convert biomass to biochemicals. Hence, approaches for simulating the processes of biomass conversion as described in section 3.5. The estimation of investment and production cost is an essential part of the assessment of biomass value chains (see section 3.6). Location planning approaches are strongly dependent on the efficiency and economic feasibility of the production process. Therefore, the optimization and simulation of material and energy flow balances is essential for an optimal configuration of a biomass value chain. The uncertainties need to be included in location planning models. The existing methods for risk analysis are presented in section 3.7. A literature review of approaches dealing with location planning and risk assessment in biomass value chains is presented in section 3.8. Finally, the research questions and the configuration of the developed approach in this work are presented in section 3.9.

3.1 Decision support systems

Production systems, logistical networks and information infrastructure have become more and more complex and interconnected in the past years and decades. Within these systems a large variety of decisions need to be made. The decision situations are dominated by uncertainties and complexity (see Vahidov and Kersten [371]).

Due to the rising complexity of the systems, the need for models to support the decision process has increased immensely. Hence, computable approaches to provide decision support systems (DSS) have been developed in the past years (see Burstein and Holsapple [64]). DSS are often computer-based systems that support decision-makers by making the process more productive, agile, innovative and reputable due to standardized algorithms (see Burstein and Holsapple [64]). According to Blanning [50], a DSS needs to at least provide results for one of the following tasks: simulation or optimization of decisions, data selection or aggregation, parameter estimation or equalization of decisions. The correlations between the different tasks need to be defined clearly to enable an efficient work.

According to Shim et al. [323], a DSS consists of three main components: data management, model management and dialogue management. A well established and effective DSS is characterized by short development times, a high pre-customization and a high customization possibility (see Gachet [127]). For more details on DSS see Schaetter [312]. DSS are needed for different problems. Peidro et al. [278] summarize these to strategic, tactical and operational planning problems, which correlates to long-, mid- or short-term decisions. Whilst strategic problems influence the supply chain designs for 5 to 10 years in the long run, tactical decisions are based on a year or two time frame and try to optimize the use of resources such as warehouses, suppliers, transports, etc. Operational decisions are mostly addressed by scheduling problems and have only short planning periods of only a few weeks.

DSS can be classified in five types as defined by Power [292]. Model-driven DSSs support the decision making process by quantitative models, which optimize or simulate the situation but are restricted by the available data. Data-driven models try to cope with large amounts of data as in e.g. data warehouses or file systems. Collaboration and communication systems are supported by communication-driven DSSs and are mostly applied in network and communication technology. Document-driven DSSs provide document retrieval and analysis within computer storage systems that include files such as documents, images, or videos. The most subjective DSS is knowledge-driven DSS as it includes person-computer systems with a high expertise in the field of the decision problem and the necessary skills.

Operations research models are an approach for a model-driven decision support for the location planning in value chains. Location planning systems are mostly used for strategic decisions. The location of a production plant is fix for more than ten years. In the following section deterministic operations research models for the location planning of biochemical production plants are presented.

3.2 Deterministic operations research models for biomass location planning

Many approaches exist to optimize the location of future biomass conversion plants. These models include various aspects of biomass value chains and focus on different regions. Depending on the stage of development and focus of research, the approach deals with high complexity. Existing approaches consider for example multiple biomass, multiple technologies, multi-stage production, multiple transport modes, storage, etc. These models are built up as location or network planning, transport optimization or production planning tools (see De Meyer et al. [226]).

A deterministic model is built up of an objective function and constraints (see Rausch [300]):

$$Min\, F(x) = c^T \cdot x \tag{3.1}$$

$$subject\, to$$

$$A \cdot x \geq b \tag{3.2}$$

$$x \geq 0 \tag{3.3}$$

Objective is often to minimize cost or maximize the net present value or profit over time. The produced amount x is multiplied with the various cost c^T of the value chain. The model is subject to different constraints. In general, the produced amount x needs to be positive and the utilized amount needs to be larger as the available capacity b. The coefficient matrix is represented by A.

For each step of the value chain, models exist, which for example optimize harvesting schedules or biomass collection, biomass production steps or storage duration and locations (see Foulds and Wilson [122], Rentizelas et al. [301], Frombo et al. [125], a.o.). Weintraub and Romero [382] have performed a literature review on operations research models for the management of agriculture and forestry. Storage capacities and storage effects have been analyzed by Rentizelas et al. [301]. Schwaderer [314] developed an approach, which considers multiple biomass and technologies. It optimizes the location(s) of future biomass conversion plants for energetic and material use under consideration of lignocellulosic biomass by thermal conversion technologies. The capacity of these plants are optimized by the model by including economies of scale regarding the investment. As a large variety of models exist, a full literature review cannot be presented in this work and is therefore neglected. In section 3.8, the relevant literature regarding biomass value chains and uncertainties is presented.

3.3 Location planning approaches considering uncertainties and risks

In Operations Research, many different approaches exist to handle uncertainties and risks. These include scenario-based analysis, (conditional) value at risk, fuzzy programming and stochastic programming. Depending on the level of detail, the uncertainties are included more or less precise. Highly detailed modeling approaches require detailed data to assess the influence of uncertainty. For the description of risk analysis see section 3.7.

First, decision making situations are defined in the following section 3.3.1. Different approaches in location planning for dealing with uncertainties are presented in section 3.3.2.

3.3.1 Definition of decision making situations

Decisions can be distinguished in five groups based on their consideration of risks, respectively uncertainty. In the following, these decisions are explained as published by Rausch [300].

- **Decision under certainty**
  This is the most common and generally least complicated decision making problem. All information of the environment is available or

assumed to be fix. All decisions can be made based on deterministic models (see section 3.2).

- **Decision under risk**
  Contrary to the decision under certainty, not all information is available in the case of decision making under risks. The only information available, is the likelihood of a possible event. Hence, one or many factors can have multiple characteristics, which may have different probability distributions. These decision making problems can be included in stochastic optimization models (see section 3.3.2).

- **Decision under fuzzyness**
  This class relies on the methods of Fuzzy-Set-Theory. Here model parameters can be defined vaguely. To solve such problems, fuzzy modeling can be applied.

- **Decision under uncertainty**
  As in the class described above, also different characteristics are possible, but in this case likelihoods for each event are not available. For solving a decision under uncertainty different processes of the normative decision theory need to be applied such as the Maximin-, Laplace- or Regret Rule. Alternatively approaches of the robust optimization may lead to good solutions.

- **Decision under conflict**
  Contrary to a decision under uncertainty, the environment is replaced by a rational opponent in case of a conflict. These problems are mostly solved with the help of game theoretical approaches.

Depending on the type of decision and situation, which is considered in the case study, different approaches can be applied. The existing approaches are presented in the following section.

3.3.2 Approaches for decision making in location planning under uncertainty

Many different mathematical approaches exist to model location planning decisions under uncertainty. Basically, all deterministic models can be tested for their robustness by sensitivity analysis. In this case deterministic parameters are varied and their effect on objective values and the setup of value chains can be tested. Hence, sensitivity analysis shows the vulnerability of the objective values regarding changing input data. This approach can be combined with any decision making model. Its advantage is the easy application and the low methodological effort, but the results are less robust.

Peidro et al. [278] have analyzed different quantitative models for supply chain planning under uncertainty. They have categorized the different models by problem type, source of uncertainty and modeling approach. For the differentiation of uncertainties see section 3.7. Peidro et al. [278] identified four different modeling approaches. These are analytic models, models based on artificial intelligence, simulation models as well as hybrid models. Many different approaches can be assigned to these categories. These clusters are briefly presented in the following.

- **Analytical models**
  robust optimization, stochastic optimization, games theory, linear programming, parametric programming
- **Models based on artificial intelligence**
  multi-agent system, fuzzy linear programming, fuzzy multi-objective programming, fuzzy goal programming, fuzzy numbers, reinforcement learning, evolutionary programming, genetic algorithms
- **Simulation models**
  discrete event simulation, system dynamics

- **Hybrid models**
  linear programming and simulation, model protective control (MPC), stochastic dynamic programming, mixed integer linear programming (MILP) and discrete event simulation, genetic algorithm and simulation, MILP and system dynamics

3.3.2.1 Analytical models

Analytical models are defined as decision support approaches by theoretical modelling and mathematical equations in applied sciences (see Mula et al. [240]). The above presented approaches are explained in more detail in the following.

Scenario analysis

In scenario analysis three different types can be distinguished: non- stochastic and stochastic scenario analysis as well as optimization under uncertainty. With the help of scenario analysis different input data is varied according to defined scenarios. The model is solved for each defined scenario and is assessed in a second step. The definition of a best alternative is the main default of the scenario analysis. Scenario analysis is especially suitable in case of non-quantifiable data, but can also be applied in case of risks with given distribution functions (see Schaetter [312]). Schaetter [312] summarizes three different types of scenarios: predictive, explorative and normative scenarios.

Games theory

Cachon and Netessine [65] have described the application of games theory in supply chain analysis. Games theory in general analyzes the interactive decisions of multiple agents in a supply chain. In case multiple agents aim to find a new location of a biochemicals plant, games theory searches for the optimal solution for all participants with or without them knowing of the decision of another participant in the game. However, all participants know of other actors taking part in the "game".

(Conditional) Value at Risk

Conditional Value at Risk is also called Mean Excess Loss or Mean Shortall (see Uryasev [363]). Value at Risks (VaR) models can be assigned to stochastic optimization models. This approach is often used to measure risks and include them in a stochastic context. Unfortunately, VaR models are hard to solve numerically as it influences the convexity of the model. Conditional Value at Risk models have recently been in the focus of research to address this problem (see Goh and Meng [138]). Conditional Value at Risk models can, in general, be described as defined by Uryasev [363].

$$Min\,F\left(\alpha,z\right)=\alpha+v\sum_{j=1}^{J}z_j \tag{3.4}$$

$$subject\,to$$

$$z_j\geq f\left(x,y_j\right)-\alpha \tag{3.5}$$

$$z_j\geq 0;x\in X;j=1,\ldots,J \tag{3.6}$$

The objective function 3.4 is described by the auxiliary variables z_j and the VaR function $\alpha(x,\beta)$. The VaR function is the "smallest percentile of the loss distribution with confidence level β" (see Uryasev [363]).

Robust optimization

Robust optimization is a subsection of stochastic optimization. Ben-Tal and Nemirovski [43] define robust optimization as "modeling methodology, combined with computational tools, to process optimization problems in which the data is uncertain and is only known to belong to some uncertainty set". Objective of robust optimization is to calculate nearly optimal solutions, which hardly react sensitively to different scenarios. According to Rausch [300], robust optimization has the advantage compared to stochastic models, that it includes an expected value and is more adaptable.

$$Min\,F(x,y) = c^T \cdot x + d^T \cdot y \tag{3.7}$$

$$subject\,to$$

$$A \cdot x \geq b \tag{3.8}$$

$$B \cdot x + C \cdot y \geq e \tag{3.9}$$

$$x \geq 0; y \geq 0 \tag{3.10}$$

The first term of the objective function 3.7 and the first restriction (see equation 3.8) defines the design component x of the model and includes only deterministic cost c^T and coefficient matrix A and no uncertain coefficients. The optimized value of the decision variable cannot be changed. The control component y is defined by the second term of the objective function 3.7 and its respective cost d_T. The second restriction 3.9 includes scenario dependent control components (coefficient matrix C and control variable y), which are restricted by the scenario boundary e. It provides a solution for the control variable y and describes uncertain parameters. Many authors define concepts to formulate a robust model from the general structure as described above. For further information on these models see Rausch [300].

Stochastic programming

The deterministic model according to section 3.2 can be adapted to stochastic modeling as follows:

$$Min\, F(x) - c_u^T \cdot x \tag{3.11}$$

$$subject\, to$$

$$A_u \cdot x \geq b_u \tag{3.12}$$

$$A_d \cdot x \geq b_d \tag{3.13}$$

$$x \geq 0 \tag{3.14}$$

Uncertain cost are represented by c_u^T. The deterministic constraints are defined as in equation 3.13 by the deterministic coefficient matrix A_d and deterministic boundaries b_d. The uncertain constraints as in equation 3.12 are formulated similarly by an uncertain coefficient matrix A_u and uncertain boundaries b_u (see Rausch [300]). In general, the same variable types as in deterministic modeling can be applied only that the constraints are not defined by fix boundaries. These are linear, integer-linear, and non-linear functions. Additionally, the model fulfills the following characteristics.

- The model includes only linear objective functions and constraints in which the variable are non-negative and real.
- All functions are linear and utilize variables, which are restricted to non-negative integer. Special cases include mixed-integer with real and integer variables as well as mixed-binary optimization models in which variables only take the binary value 0 or 1.
- In non-linear models all functions are non-linear

Deterministic models can be solved by efficient solution procedures, as the calculation times depend on the complexity and size of the problem. In contrast, the calculation time of stochastic models increases exponentially with rising problem size. Those are so called NP-hard optimization models. NP-hard solutions are not related to a polynomial of the problem size and, hence, are not bound in their calculation times.

Two different types of stochastic models exist: one-stage and two stage approaches. The first defines a single strategy for which the model is optimal in a certain period. Two stage approaches only give a fixed solution for the first stage. The strategy of the following stages depend on the actually chosen design of the uncertain input parameters.

3.3.2.2 Models based on artificial intelligence

Copeland [84] defines artificial intelligence as "the ability of a digital computer or computer-controlled robot to perform tasks commonly associated with intelligent beings." Hence, these systems can learn from previous experiences and adapt future decisions. Nevertheless, up to date the computational programs cannot simulate the same flexibility as of human beings.

Multi-agent system

According to Giannakis and Louis [136], multi-agent systems model the collaboration of multiple decision makers in supply chains. Each agent is responsible for a certain role. The agents can interact with each other, within or across organizations. Multi-agent systems are particularly useful for the analysis of collective cooperation problems where joint coordination of supply chain actors leads to a higher performance of the overall system.

Fuzzy linear programming

In fuzzy-based approaches, the uncertainties in data are quantitatively modeled fuzzy sets, which approximate probabilities of vague information. This approach tries to quantify expressions such as "highly effects" or "much larger than" (see Comes [82]). Due to its complexity this approach is rarely used in logistical optimization. The data processing is very time consuming and demands a high expertise.

$$\widetilde{Min}\, F(x) = c^T \cdot x \tag{3.15}$$

$$subject\, to$$

$$A \cdot x \tilde{\geq} b \tag{3.16}$$

$$x \geq 0 \tag{3.17}$$

The fuzzy objective function is influenced by the decision variable x. The cost c^T and the boundaries b are a column vector of fuzzy numbers. The coefficient A is a matrix of fuzzy numbers (see Delgado et al. [92]). Other applications of the fuzzy theory are Fuzzy multi-objective programming, Fuzzy goal programming and Fuzzy numbers.

Reinforcement learning

According to van Otterlo and Wiering [273], reinforcement learning, also called approximate dynamic programming, analyzes how agents act in an environment. Their objective is to maximize their cumulative reward. RI is often formulated as a Markov decision process with the following steps: (1) fix set of environment and fix set of actions, (2) analysis of probabilities for the transition from state s to s' under action a and (3) the immediate reward after transition as well as (4) the assessment of stochastic rules that describe the observation of each agent. The observations and decisions of each agent are compared at each time step.

Evolutionary programming

Falcone et al. [110] describe the application of evolutionary programming (EP) in supply chain optimization. EP simulates the phenotypical relationship between populations. For modeling the mutation it uses Gaussian distribution. Seven steps are necessary to optimize a supply chain by EP: (1) creation of an initial population, (2) computation of the fitness of each individual, (3) generation of a single descendant, (4) evaluation of each descendant, (5) comparing all solutions to select the ancestors of the next generation, (6) apply mutation to produce new descendants, and (7) repeat (2)-(6) until the stopping criterion is met.

Genetic algorithm

Genetic algorithms are similar to EP. Individuals evolve throughout generations and generate new populations. Falcone et al. [110] summarize GA to five steps: (1) creation of initial population, (2) evaluation of each solution by fitness function, (3) selection of most fitted individuals by selection strategy, (4) application of mutation to generate a new population from the selected individuals, and (5) repeat steps (2)-(4) until the stopping criterion is met.

3.3.2.3 Simulation models

Contrary to algebraic models, simulation models do not use algebraic equations, but try to model real behavior as precise as possible with the help of a software program and mathematical expressions (see Harling [148]).

System Dynamics

Forrester [121] has described the system dynamics approach. System dynamics represents real world problems nonetheless the complexity and non-linearity it brings and can include loops. The biggest challenge of system dynamics is to model a large number of mostly non-linear inter-temporal relationships between the variables. According to Ranganath [298], system dynamic models are based on problem statements, variable identifications and looping of causal behaviors of these variables.

Monte Carlo Simulation

According to Mahedevan [212], Monte Carlo simulation is a numerical experimentation technique. At first a random number of a distribution function is used as input for a computational model. A large number of experiments is carried out in such manner. The outputs of the computational models are compared and statistics are computed to analyze the influence of the distribution functions. Monte Carlo simulations are often applied due to their easy application. Meyer [227], Trinks[355] and Luo [210] are examples for such applications, which include the following steps:

1. Generate input values from random variables of a probability distribution function
2. Calculate deterministic computational model and check system for failures
3. Repeat steps (1) and (2) for a large number of times N
4. Analyze, compare and interpret the results of all model runs

3.3.2.4 Hybrid models

Hybrid models combine the advantages of simulation and analytic models. They are often a combination of the above-mentioned approaches such as linear programming and simulation or mixed integer linear programming with system dynamics.

According to Peidro et al. [279], the majority of models coping with uncertainties were analytic models up to 2009. Almost half of the considered models were analytic approaches. Most of the models included only a single source of uncertainty.

3.4 Biomass potential and location analysis

Biomass is a widely spread product. The available biomass type and amount depends on the considered region. Often geographic information systems (GIS) are used to estimate the available potentials. These are software systems, which are based on geographical data to gather, process and visualize data. The respective data can be organized by multiple layers. These layers can include data on politics, streets, climate, weather, cultivated area etc. and can be combined and interlinked to provide new data (see Schwaderer [314]). In general, different types of potentials are defined. According to Kaltschmitt et al. [175], these include theoretical, technical, economic, harvestable and sustainable potential. In figure 3.1, the different potential types and their relation are depicted. The different potential types are explained in the following.

- **Theoretical potential**
  The theoretical potential describes the total physically available biomass potential within a certain region and time frame based on the energy content of the biomass. It defines the upper limit of the theoretically usable energy.

- **Technical potential**
  Due to technical restrictions such as harvesting rate, storage or conversion losses, etc., the theoretical potential cannot be fully used. The biomass, which can be used based on the given restrictions and also include legal or ecological constraints, is called technical potential.

- **Economic potential**
  The economic potential describes the part of the technical potential, which can be utilized despite economic restrictions. Influencing parameters of political or business economics may vary and, hence, the calculated economic potential.

- **Usable potential**
  The usable potential is restricted by already existing facilities. Theoretically, the usable potential converges to the economic potential on the long run.

- **Sustainable potential**
  In case of defined sustainability criteria, the sustainably usable potential is the amount of the technical potential, which can be harvested due to climate, nature protection or soil quality restrictions.

The potential estimation is performed by multiplying the theoretical values with factors such as utilization in slope classes or the remaining amount on the field. Finally, the already utilized amount is subtracted to receive the usable potential.

3.5 Approaches for assessing technical processes

The process for converting biomass to biochemicals is an essential part of the biomass value chain. Especially biochemical processes such as fermentation are prone to high uncertainties as they utilize sensible microorganisms. According to Froehling [124], three main approaches exist to estimate the efficiency of processes: material and energy balancing, regression analysis and flow sheeting simulation.

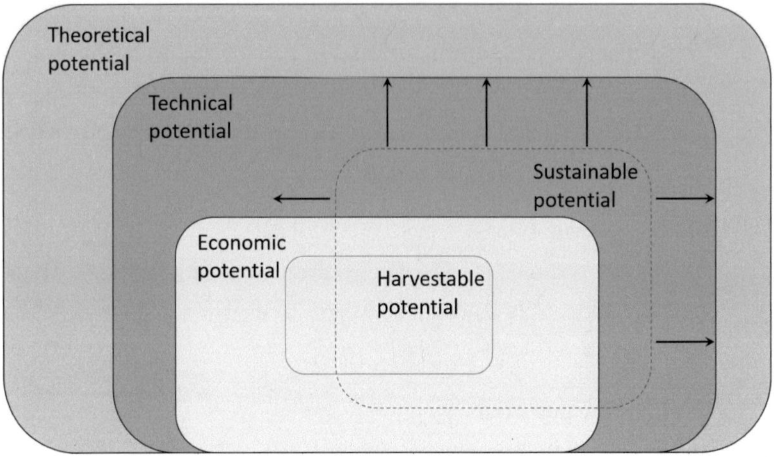

Figure 3.1: Biomass potential types and their relation (Kaltschmitt et al. [175])

As many biomass processes are not yet realized in industrial scale, these approaches can support the design of conversion facilities. The results of the simulations, material and energy flow balances, provide a basis for technical and economic assessments. These can influence the decision, whether the investment is feasible or not, depending on technical efficiency and production cost.

In the following the approaches are described similar to e.g. Trippe [356], Schwaderer [314], and Schulte Beerbühl [42]).

3.5.1 Material and energy flow balances

The efficiency of biomass conversion processes influence the supply chain immensely. More or less feedstock is needed depending on the product yield from biomass for a fix demand. The lower the product to biomass yield is, the more biomass needs to be transported to the facility.

Not only the efficiency influences the robustness of a biomass value chain, but also the energy and utility demand of the process. Both depend on the process and the utilized biomass resource. Material and energy flow balances are the basis for process efficiency estimation. Different approaches exist to perform the analysis. As Schwaderer [314] points out, the approaches for material and energy balancing are limited. Approaches from engineering are necessary to accurately describe technical processes. These include non-linearity of relations between substances and the thermodynamic and chemical dependencies of substances.

Depending on the biomass type, different process configurations are necessary to convert biomass to biochemicals. Coherent system boundaries need to be defined to be able to compare different processes. Within these boundaries, the material and energy balances are calculated. The processes can be assessed based on efficiency parameters such as yield, selectivity and conversion rate, which are all based on the law of mass conversion as defined in equation 3.18. The sum of all input mass streams m_{in} must be equal to all output mass streams m_{out} plus potential mass losses m_{loss} (see Trippe [356]).

$$\sum m_{in} = \sum m_{out} + \sum m_{loss} \tag{3.18}$$

The most common measure to assess processes for biomass conversion is the yield of a production. It is defined among others by Vauck and Mueller [373] as the ratio of actually produced substance to the maximum possible produced amount based on stoichiometric calculations (see equation 3.19).

$$Percent\ yield\ Y_i = \frac{actual\ yield}{theoretical\ yield} = \frac{n_i - n_{i0}}{n_{ji}} \tag{3.19}$$

Not only the mass of a system needs to be in balance, but also energy cannot be created or destroyed. According to the first law of thermodynamics the total energy of a system remains constant (see equation 3.20). All input energy e_{in} is converted to output energy e_{out} and energy losses e_{loss}.

$$\sum e_{in} = \sum e_{out} + \sum e_{loss} \tag{3.20}$$

3.5.2 Flow sheeting simulation

Flow sheeting simulations can be used to estimate material and energy flows of possible large-scale installations. The approaches can vary from *black box* models of a production up to very detailed simulations of computational fluid dynamics (CFD) on a molecular basis. Depending on the level of detail, the interactions between the molecules are simulated more or less precisely. The more detailed the simulation model is, the more data and knowledge of the process is needed. Hence, the implementation and calculation of the model itself is more challenging. In regard to the addressed question an adequate approach for the simulation needs to be chosen. For the conceptual design of facilities in the process industry mostly flow sheeting simulation is used. These are based on thermodynamic and chemical equilibrium and therefore define a medium level of detail. The simulations can be used in multiple stages of the plant lifetime: from process development to the optimization of an already existing plant (see Schulte Beerbühl [42]).

Flow sheeting simulation tools have the advantage that they include a large variety of databanks. These provide thermodynamic, chemical and physical base data and models. In general two different types of flow sheeting simulations can be differentiated: sequential-modular and simultaneous systems. The first calculate each unit operation for itself in the sequence of the production. In case of re-circulations, the partial streams are calculated in iterations. Simultaneous models utilize a matrix. All balances of the unit operations are used as input in those matrixes and are solved all at once (see Kerdoncuff [180]).

3.5.3 Simulation in AspenPlus®

Many commercially flow sheeting simulation software exist. The most popular tools are SuperPro Designer, ChemCad, AspenPlus® and IPSEpro. As described by Trippe [356], Peters, Timmershaus & West [282] provide a summary of other flow sheeting software.

The application of AspenPlus® by the company Aspen Technology, Inc., for the assessment of processes for the conversion of biomass has been proven by many authors (Schwaderer [314], Trippe [356], Kerdoncuff [180], Kumar et al. [189]). It is generally used for the assessment and optimization of processes in chemical engineering by calculating energy and mass flows of systems. AspenPlus® can be combined with other software such as Excel or Matlab. Unit processes are defined for the simulation of a system. For further details on the unit processes see appendix A.1.1. The mass and energy balances are calculated utilizing input data as well as physical, chemical, and thermodynamic databases. Design specifications enable the manual definition of temperatures, pressures, etc. of unit processes. Additionally, with FORTRAN codes, MATLAB links and other user defined calculation operations, the simulations can be designed to the individual needs of the user. Sensitivity analysis can be conducted to analyze the influence of single parameter settings.

3.6 Economic assessment of processes for the production of biochemicals

The economic assessment of different biochemical processes is essential when comparing different production routes from various biomass. Depending on the biomass, the process can vary and accordingly can the investment and processing cost of the production site. As only few biorefineries are in operation to this day, only literature values are available for an economic assessment. The literature values are based on many assumptions and cannot always be applied to all production plants due to their individuality. Consequently, a detailed individual estimation of the production plant is not feasible and is also bound to a large effort.

3.6.1 Estimation of investment

Investments are defined as the total capital demand of a facility to procure the necessary equipment and take them into operation. An investment consists of multiple parts (see Meyer [227]). Properties, infrastructure for water and electricity, repair and maintenance as well as controlling equipment are a few examples of additional investments to the already existing facility. The total investment is the sum of all these components. In general, the applied method of investment estimation leads to different degrees of accuracy in the calculation. Detailed investment estimations require detailed data input but result in more precise calculations. According to Meyer [227], these can be between -30 to + 50 % for estimating the order of magnitude by turnover ratios and can reach up to -5 to +10 % in case of detailed analysis by code of accounts. Different approaches exist to estimate the investments. Trippe [356] discusses various methods such as summarized calculation, factor methods and detailed individual calculation. He proposes that for the estimation of investment of different biomass conversion technologies, the sub-processes should be depicted by block flow diagram. The total investment is estimated with the help of differentiated surcharge rates. Therefore, the main components need to be defined.

All equipment is considered as main components, which are shown in the block flow diagram. The needed data for the investment estimation are based on different sources. Peters, Timmerhaus, & West [282] and Chauvel [75] provide a large data base on basic components. Humbird [162] has calculated investment of a bioethanol biorefinery and published many investments of single units.

At first, the capacity of a base investment is defined. In chemical industry, this is mostly an annual or hourly quantity of either the final product or the feedstock to the plant.

Economies of scale are taken into account for the estimation of the investments. The capacity of a production plant increases triple, whilst the surface of single equipment only rises twofold. This results from the relation between volume and surface area. Investment is mostly dependent on the material, which is used for the equipment and, hence, on the surface area. The specific investment decreases with rising capacity. Equation 3.21 shows the correlation between the investment I_{ref} of a reference investment and its capacity C_{ref} and the actual capacity $C_{current}$ and investment $I_{current}$ of a current facility. The factor R defines the size degression. Normally this factor can have a value between 0.6 and 0.8 (see Trippe [356]).

$$I_{current} = I_{ref} \cdot \left(\frac{C_{current}}{C_{ref}} \right)^R \tag{3.21}$$

Additionally, investments depend not only on the capacity but are also related to the year of their estimation. Reference investments are mostly provided for a certain capacity and a specific year. For more realistic estimations, both, capacity and year need to be consdiered. Investments can be approximated according to equation 3.22 to adapt them to the current year. The ratio between the investment in the current $I_{current}$ to a reference year I_{ref} is equivalent to the proportion of the price index of the current $P_{current}$ to the reference year P_{ref}.

$$I_{current} = I_{ref} \cdot \frac{P_{current}}{P_{ref}} \tag{3.22}$$

Different price indexes exist, which adapt the price of the reference investment to the current price. The price indexes include rising cost for material, personnel, or inflation. The most known price indexes are the Chemical Engineering Plant Cost Index (CEPCI), the German Kölbe Schulze Index and the Nelson-Farrar Cost Index. They are being published by American and German journals. The CEPCI is an aggregated index of eleven single indexes and is based on data from 1947 on. The Kölbe Schulze index relies on data from 2005 and aggregates seven single indexes (see Meyer [227]).

Additionally to the investments, other cost such as for engineering, construction and administration of the facility need to be included. These are independent on the consumption and the operation of the plant and are calculated by a fix percentage of the investment. Possible values for the percentages are presented in table 3.1.

These can be distinguished in direct and indirect cost. Direct cost can directly be accounted to a specific facility. Indirect cost are general cost, which do not depend to a cost object.

Table 3.1: Percentage composition of the investment (Aden et al. [6])

Costs	share of investment in %
Direct cost	
Building	1.5
Infrastructure	9
Sales	10
Construction	10
Indirect cost	
Engineering	25

3.6.2 Estimation of production cost

The specific production cost are defined by the total cost of the facility per year and the revenues of byproducts based on the produced amount of the biochemical. The production cost are based on the results of the material and energy flow balances as well as on the investment. The total yearly cost C^{total} of a facility is calculated as investment related cost $C^{investmentdependent}$ plus operational cost $C^{operation}$ plus personnel $C^{personnel}$ and other cost C^{other} as defined in equation 3.23. These cost are presented in the following (see Meyer [227]).

$$C^{total} = C^{investmentdependent} + C^{operation} + C^{personnel} + C^{other} \tag{3.23}$$

Investment dependent cost

Investment dependent cost are based on the total investment. Investment dependent cost include depreciation, repair and maintenance (R&M) cost, taxes and insurance (see equation 3.24). The larger a production plant, the harder it is to repair and maintain and, hence, the R&M cost rise. Taxes, insurance and depreciation increase with the total investment. These cost occur nevertheless if a product is produced or not.

$$C^{investmentdependent} = I \cdot \frac{1}{n} + I \cdot \left(1 + f^{capital}\right) \cdot \frac{i}{2} + I \cdot \left(f^{maintenance} + f^{taxes}\right) \tag{3.24}$$

Operational cost

Operational cost are based on the consumption and include cost for feedstock, energy and utilities as well as for disposal of by-products and waste. These cost depend on the operating hours of the process or the produced amount respectively. Biochemical products are mostly dependent on feedstock cost. These can make up for up to 60 % of the consumption related cost (see Trippe [356]).

Consumption related cost are calculated by the mass flow m_j of input material j and the price p_j for the input material j.

$$C^{consumption} = \sum_j m_j \cdot p_j \tag{3.25}$$

The total consumption related cost are built up as the sum of the input material streams of the feedstock or utilities, which are processed during a certain time period and their respective cost. The consumption of the products can be estimated by material and energy flow balances from the flowsheeting simulations (see section 3.5).

Process cost

Process cost are cost, that occur independently on the facility load factor and the energy consumption of the process. Personnel cost are the most common type of process cost. They can also be estimated based on the capacity of the production plant. The larger a plant is the more personnel is needed for the operation. Holland and Wilkinson [156] provide an equation 3.26, which estimates the personnel cost c_{pers} based on relation of the reference capacity C_{ref} to the current capacity $C_{current}$ multiplied with the number of people required N_{ref} for the reference plant and the average annual salary p_{pers} per person.

$$c_{pers} = p_{pers} \cdot N_{ref} \cdot \left(\frac{C_{current}}{C_{ref}} \right)^{0.25} \tag{3.26}$$

3.6.3 Other cost

Additionally to the production cost, many other cost affect biomass value chains. These influence the economic feasibility of the supply chain. Hence, they are presented in the following. These cost include transport, storage, export, and transshipment cost. The cost for biomass are already included in the production cost.

Transport cost

The specific cost of transportation c^T can be defined by specific fix and variable cost terms (see equation 3.27). The fix cost present the share, which does not depend on the transport distance. Fix transport cost c^T_{fix} include for example personnel cost as well as the investment related cost of the transport mode. Variable transport cost $c^T_{variable}$ depend on the distance d, which is traveled. The largest share of variable transport cost is made up of fuel cost. Transport cost are mostly defined per amount of transported product. The transport mode influences the fix and variable transport cost. For example, due to large investments in the ship, barge transport has high fix cost. These are compensated by low specific variable transport cost (see Meyer [227]).

$$c^T = c^T_{fix} + c^T_{variable} \cdot d \tag{3.27}$$

Storage

Storage cost can be defined by the investment, which is necessary for the storage capacity. If the company does not want to invest in additional storage facilities, it can also rent storage capacity. The storage rent and investment depend on the type of storage and the capacity of the storage facility (see Rentizelas et al. [301]).

Transshipment cost

Multimodal transport has many advantages. It is often time efficient and less cost intensive for long distance transport. However, due to transshipment from one transport mode to another, additional handling cost need to be considered. The transported good needs to be transferred. Depending on the transport type and product, this can lead to high transshipment cost.

Export cost

The final products of a conversion plant can also be exported to other cities, states, countries or continents. Depending on the export port, different cost occur. These are influenced by the product, which is exported, the export terminal and the receiving terminal.

3.7 Risk analysis and risk management

In this section the existing approaches for risk analysis and risk management are described in general and specifically for biomass value chains. Risks can often lead to disruptions in supply chains, which in turn, reduces the profitability of the value chain. Due to recent trends, supply chains are more and more sensible to disruptions. Hendricks and Singhal [152] see increased complexity, outsourcing and partnerships, single sourcing, limited buffers, focus on efficiency, over-concentration of operations and poor planning and execution as the main drivers for disruptions in supply chains. According to them, these can be mitigated by improving the accuracy of demand forecasts, integrating, and synchronizing planning and execution, reducing the mean and variance of lead times, by collaborating with supply chain partners, investing in visibility, increasing flexibility of supply chains, postponement strategies, and investing in technologies. Often risk assessment and risk management need to be performed to conquer these disruptions and to find the suitable mitigation strategy. The objective of this section is to provide an introduction to risk analysis.

At first, different definitions of risk and uncertainties are presented in section 3.7.1. In section 3.7.2, approaches for assessing risks in biomass value chains are described. Probabilities and consequences are essential for assessing risks. Hence, an introduction into probability calculations is presented in section 3.7.3. The estimation of risk consequences is presented in section 3.7.4. Risks can be clustered into different risk categories. These are shown in section 3.7.5. Finally, different risk mitigation strategies are discussed in section 3.7.6.

3.7.1 Essential terms in risk management

Ayyub [28] defines risk as "the potential of losses and rewards resulting from an exposure to a hazard or as a result of a risk event." According to Waters [380] risk and uncertainty need to be differentiated and can be defined as follows. **Uncertainty** cannot be quantified, meaning that events might occur in the future, but no information can be provided on the likelihood of their occurrence, hence concrete information on certain parameters is absent.

Risk on the other hand can be defined by probability of an incident (see Knight [183]). According to Wu et al.[168], risks are comprised of three main components:

- **likelihood of occurrence** also often called probability, can be measured either objectively based on historic data of such events or subjectively based on intuition.
- **the consequences of this occurrence** are a multiple of simultaneous events, which may also interact with each other.
- **exposure to such an event** is the most crucial part, which needs to be well understood when handling risks as it influences the effectiveness of risk management.

Ayyub [28] defines **event consequences** as "the degree of damage or loss from some failure". Among many, Ziegenbein [402] defines risk as the product of probability and the effect of the event.

$$Risk = probability\ of\ an\ event \cdot loss\ of\ the\ event\ happening \tag{3.28}$$

The product is also called the **expected loss** of the event, meaning the probability weighted average (see Hubbard [160]). Risk has to include some probability of a loss, but does not include gains.

Many different terms exist in risk research. Not only risks and uncertainties are differentiated. Risk cannot only be defined as likelihood multiplied with consequences (see equation 3.28). Ayyub [28] defines the main terms in risk analysis. **Hazard** is an event, which poses potential harm to another person or thing. According to Villagrán de Léon [91], hazard is the likelihood or possibility of an extreme event with a certain intensity in a certain region to a certain time. **Reliability** can be defined as the complementary value of failure probability. A system is reliable if it can operate at its design function even though the boundary conditions have varied. Crichton [85] formulates a risk function as dependency on hazard and vulnerability (see equation 3.29).

$$R = f(hazard, vulnerability) \tag{3.29}$$

The reaction of a system against risks and uncertainties can be described by different terms. **Vulnerability** is defined as the sensitivity of a system to harm (see Bohle [54]). Vulnerability depends on the susceptibility, resilience and exposition of a system (see Bohle [54]). **Resilience** is defined as the ability of a system to cope with external stress factors and disruptions, to minimize possible losses and to recover to the initial state (see Holling [157], Rose [307]).

Waters [380] differentiates between internal and external risks. **Internal risks** occur within the respective supply chain. These include risks such as "late deliveries, excess stock, poor forecasts, financial risks, minor accidents, human error, faults in information technology systems". These risks are not as critical to stakeholders as they can be managed directly by the company. Management strategies are for example additional stock, multiple suppliers, etc. **External risks** include all risks, which have their origin and take place outside the supply chain and are harder to control. These are risks such as "earthquakes, hurricanes, industrial action, wars, terrorist attacks, outbreaks of disease, price rises, problems with trading partners, shortage of raw materials, crime, financial irregularities, etc."

Kajüter [173] defines three types of approaches for including risk management in the supply chain. **Risk management with supply chain orientation** is considered in case a company identifies, assesses and steers risks systematically. Generally, this occurs mostly in areas, which focus on materials, good, or information flows. The risk assessment is then in the hand of the regarded company. The next step is **risk analysis within the supply chain**. This comprises the identification, assessment and steering of risks of multiple companies within various value chains. The collaboration focuses on an informal basis. The systematic inclusion of risk management in planning and reporting to the supply chain does not take place. **Supply chain risk management** is a structured approach to cooperatively analyze, steer and control as well as communicate risks in the supply chain. Companies strongly work together and have incorporated an approach to jointly establish a risk management process.

A cross-functional team of risk experts should be assembled. These should characterize the major sources of risk as well as assess and prioritize these risks. Finally, the identified risks should be monitored and actions need to be defined to improve the risk management process (see Hendricks and Singhal [152]).

In general, there are three core actions in risk management, which need to be performed by the expert team (see Waters [380]):

1. identification of risks
2. assessment of their consequences
3. design of appropriate measures

3.7.2 Methodology for assessing risks in biomass value chains

Risks can be assessed according to the ISO 31.000/2009 [262] process. In figure 3.2 the methodology for analyzing and assessing risks according to Ziegenbein [402] is presented.

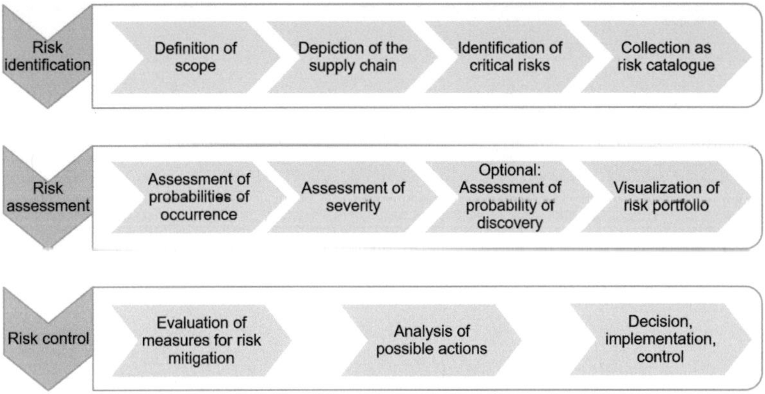

Figure 3.2: Methodology for managing supply chain risks (Ziegenbein[402])

3.7.2.1 Identification of risks

According to the ISO 31.000/2009 [262], risk identification is defined as follows "the aim of this step is to generate a comprehensive list of risks based on those events that might create, enhance, prevent, degrade, accelerate, or delay the achievement of objectives. It is important to identify the risks associated with not pursuing an opportunity. Comprehensive identification is critical, because a risk that is not identified at this stage will not be included in further analysis." The steps as seen in figure 3.2, scope definition, depiction of the supply chain, risk identification and risk catalog, need to be performed in this part.

For the identification of risks, they firstly need to be systematized and clustered. The identification is a critical process because only risks, which have been identified can be avoided or reduced (see Aven [26]). As the risks are very specific for each case, they need to be analyzed in a structured and systematic manner. Copying the risks of a similar case is not sufficient as some risks might remain unidentified.

Mullai [241] describes the risk identification steps in more detail. At first the background of the assessment should be known. After performing a preliminary risk analysis, the responsible person to conduct the risk analysis should be identified. Also, other interested parties need to be identified and included in the project. Risk generating activities as well as the occurring problems need to be identified. A set of objectives for risk analysis should be defined as well as the boundaries of the study. Appropriate methods and techniques for risk assessment need to be selected. Finally, all relevant risk-related data need to be collected. One approach is to differentiate risks according to the origin of their source. Vahrencamp and Siepermann [18] differentiate between endogenous and exogenous risks. Endogenous uncertainties mostly occur within a company, exogenous risks are affected by the environment.

The categorization of risks is adapted to the list presented by Waters [380] and include

- environmental risks (natural and political)
- physical risks
- transport risks
- supply risks
- market risks
- technical risks
- economic risks

Melnyk [223] differentiates into natural risks, demand shifts, supplier problems, human behavior, information and technology, financial and legal risks. Tang and Tomlin [338] share a similar classification of risks: supply, process, demand, intellectual property, behavioral, political and social risks.

Different approaches exist to identify risks. The most known methods are Failure Mode and Effect Analysis (FMEA), Event Tree Analysis (ETA) and Fault Tree Analysis (FTA), which are discussed in detail in section 3.7.3. Nevertheless, the greatest problem is, that it is impossible to identify every possible risk (see Waters [380]). The four main reasons, why not all conceivable risks can be identified are that inherently unknowable risks exist, risks depend on time and progress and might change with a different scope, and secondary risks (risks that result from risk treatment) exist.

After the identification of risks, they need to be assessed. The process of risk assessment is described in the following section.

3.7.2.2 Assessment of risks

The ISO 31.000/2009 [262] defines Risk Assessment as follows:

> "Risk analysis involves developing an understanding of risk and impacts both positive and negative. Risk analysis provides input for risk evaluation and decisions on the most appropriate risk treatment strategies and methods. Risk analysis can also provide input for making decisions where the options involve different types and levels of risk assumption, mitigation, reduction, and avoidance."

Many different methods for the assessment of risks exist. Hubbard [160] provides an overview of possible approaches. The appropriate method may be chosen depending on the application. The most common method is expert intuition, which is not based on any quantified data. A more systematic approach is an expert audit, in which experts develop comprehensive checklists. In simple stratification methods rating scales, such as traffic light symbols are used. Weighted scores are used as risk indicators where each risk is multiplied with a weighting factor. In traditional financial analysis, conventional financial analysis tools such as a discount rate are used. Multi-criteria decision making (MCDM) and analytic hierarchy process (AHP) also used weighted scores but in a more structured manner. The most detailed analyses are provided by probabilistic models where the odds and magnitudes of losses are computed. This approach is mostly chosen in insurance or financial industry (see Zimmer [403]).

In more detail, the analysis process can be described by the following steps: (1) system definition, (2) hazard identification, (3) exposure and consequences analysis, (4) likelihood estimation and quantification, (5) risk estimation and presentation, and, finally, (6) sensitivity analysis. Mullai [241] has described each step in more detail. Step (4) will be presented in more detail in section 3.7.3 and 3.7.4.

Ayyub [28] describes different approaches to perform reliability assessments of systems. The **Advanced Second-moment Method** is based on performance functions, which depend on a resistance (e.g. supply) and load (e.g. demand) of a system. In case of a positive performance, the system is in survival state. Negative performance functions occur in case of failure states. **Monte Carlo** simulation techniques use samples of a system to estimate the failure probability. These samples are randomly generated. If the majority of samples leads to a failure, then the overall system is most likely to fail. **Time-dependent Reliability Analysis** is similar to the general reliability functions, but they are dynamic as they depend on time and are not constant.

The main steps in risk assessment are, according to Ziegenbein [402], the assessment of probabilities and occurrence, assessment of the severity of the risk and the visualization of a risk portfolio. The result of risk assessment visualized as a risk matrix is depicted in figure 3.3. This work uses this risk definition for the risk assessment. Aim of this study is to cluster the identified risks in risk matrices as presented below.

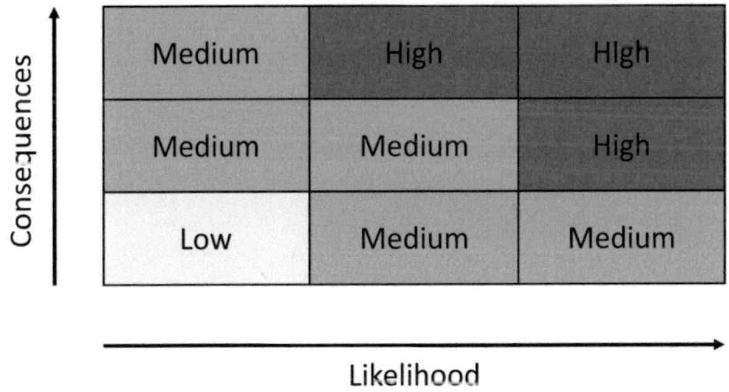

Figure 3.3: Risk assessment of likelihood and consequences

In the matrix, the risks are clustered and displayed by likelihood and consequences. The most critical risks can be identified at once and risk mitigation can be enforced. Nevertheless, the clustering is subjective and the difference is often not as fix. Necessary risk mitigation strategies can be defined based on the risk assessment. In the next section, the necessary steps are presented.

3.7.2.3 Design of appropriate measures

Risk mitigation strategies aim at minimizing the effects of risks, either by minimizing probabilities or by reducing the consequences (see Hubbard et al. [160]). In general, four alternatives exist for managing risks: avoidance, reduction, transfer and acceptance (see Hubbard [160], Mullai [241], USCG [144]).

After comparing and ranking the risks, strategies and measures need to be defined. Mullai [241] and Ziegenbein [402] present the main steps of risk management as in figure 3.2: identification of options, decision making, planning and implementations of the actions. For more detail on risk management steps, please see Mullai [241].

3.7.3 Probability calculation

In this section, the estimation of probabilities for the calculation of risks is presented. Three approaches can be chosen for the estimation of probabilities (see Waters [380]). The likelihood of an event can be calculated if the situation is known. In case of uncertain prediction, one can consider historical data of an event and provide empirical probabilities with this information. The third possibility is the personal opinion of experts, which are often qualitative and subjective.

Different approaches exist, which support the user in assessing the probability of risk occurrences. According to Vesely et al. [374] two different approaches can be distinguished: inductive and deductive. Even though this handbook was published by the U.S. Nuclear Regulatory Commission, the described methodologies can be applied to multiple topics.

Inductive approaches try to formulate a general conclusion from individual cases. Many methods have been developed to describe the context between single and general events. Examples are the Fault Hazard Analysis (FHA), Failure Mode and Effect Analysis (FMEA), or the Preliminary Hazards Analysis (PHA) (see Vesely et al. [374]).

Contrary to the inductive approaches, the **deductive methods** reason from the general to the specific problem. These approaches are more investigations of a situation and occur more accidentally than intentionally. An example for such an approach is the Fault Tree Analysis (FTA). According to Vesely et al. [374], "inductive methods are applied to determine **what** system states (...) are possible; deductive methods are applied to determine **how** a given system state (...) can occur."

After estimation of probabilities, these can be categorized by their likelihood of occurrence. Waters [380] defines the five following categories of probabilities.

- **very unlikely** events might happen but hardly noticeable for people
- **rare**: people only meet this event once or twice in their working life
- **occasional** events occur sometimes
- **frequent** and regularly to people
- **very likely**: this event occurs often

In the following, different approaches for probability estimations are explained. These include Failure Mode and Effect Analysis, Event Tree Analysis, and Fault Tree Analysis.

3.7.3.1 Failure Mode and Effect Analysis

The Failure Mode and Effect Analysis (FMEA) is a popular approach. Ayyub [28] distinguishes between design and process FMEA. According to him a failure mechanism causes a failure mode within a system. A failure mode is how a specific process may possibly fail in up- or downstream processes. FMEA is mostly based on data, which is available based on past experiences. As defined by Dani [89], the FMEA is performed by the following steps: (1) recognition and evaluation of potential failures and the effects of that failure, (2) assessment of severity of the risk, (3) detection of the failure, (4) estimation of a risk priority number ($severity \cdot occurence \cdot detection$), (5) identification of actions, which can reduce the risk and (6) documentation of the entire process.

3.7.3.2 Event Tree Analysis

Event Tree Analysis (ETA) is based on the assumption that the system is successful if a single route of events is fulfilled. As described by Ayyub [28] the event tree is initiated by an event followed by a reaction. This can either lead to a success or a failure of the branch. In case the branch succeeds the movement is commonly upwards (see figure 3.4). On the contrary, a failure is marked by a downward branch. The basic outcome is the identification of successful scenarios. All other paths mark a failure with varying levels of likelihood and consequence. A strength of this methodology is the effective depiction of interdependence within the system.

The basic scheme of the ETA is presented in figure 3.4.

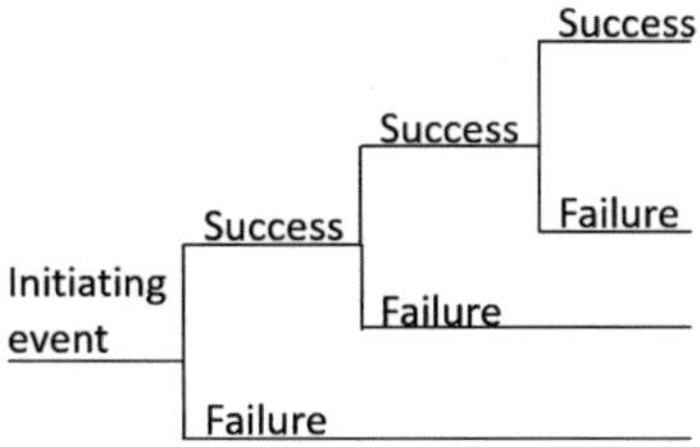

Figure 3.4: Basic depiction of Event Tree Analysis (Ayyub [28])

3.7.3.3 Fault Tree Analysis

Fault Tree Analysis (FTA) is often used to visualize failures within a complex system. As defined by Ayyub [28] the fault tree is a graphical model which combines single events by deductive reasoning to top event failures. At first, the top event needs to be determined. Then other events need to be set, which lead to the top event. Based on logical connectivity by gates the lower level events are clustered.

Fault trees are often linked to event trees as they can quantify parts of event trees. The most common events that are defined as top events in supply chains are losses of production or failures in safety systems (see Borghesi [56]). Basic events are often given by statistical data and are represented by components or human fault. The main definitions of lower level events are presented in the table 3.2 below.

Table 3.2: Symbols used in Fault Tree Analysis (Ayyub [28])

Symbol	Name	Description
	OR Gate	causality never passes through an OR gate, inputs are identical to output
	AND Gate	specifies a causal relationship between the inputs and the output
	Decomposable event	can and should be decomposed further to basic events
	Basic event	cannot be decomposed further into lower level events, probabilities need to be calculated for these events
	undeveloped event	can be decomposed further but as they are mostly negligible they are not considered further
	transfer nodes	inclusion of the top event in another Fault Tree

The logic gates AND and OR can be calculated as presented in the two following equations (see equations 3.30 and 3.31). As a result of the FTA, the likelihood of the top event of a tree can be estimated. The main limiting factor is the complexity and size of the tree.

Hence, all probabilities can be combined by AND and OR gates and the likelihood of the next top event can be calculated. These combinations are performed until the identified main top event can be calculated from the basic events.

AND-gates are defined as such that both events need to occur in order to lead to the top event. Hence, the probabilities of two single events $P(A)$ and $P(B)$ are multiplied as defined in equation 3.30 to the joint probability $P(AandB)$ of the top event.

$$P(AandB) = P(A \cap B) = P(A) \cdot P(B) \tag{3.30}$$

OR-gates let single events through, meaning that the next top event occur in case only one of the basic events take place. The possibility that both can occur is neglected in the OR-gate. As defined in equation 3.31 the single probabilities $P(A)$ and $P(B)$ are summarized and the AND-gate $P(AandB)$ is subtracted.

$$P(AorB) = P(A \cup B) = P(A) + P(B) - P(A) \cdot P(B) \tag{3.31}$$

The basic depiction of how fault trees are composed is shown in figure 3.5. The basic events are 1, 2 and 3. Events 2 and 3 are combined by an AND-gate to the top event 4. The event 1 is connected by an OR-gate with event 4 to the main top event 5. Hence, for this example, the probability of event 5 would be as presented in the following equation 3.32.

$$\begin{aligned} P(5) &= P(1) + P(4) - P(1) \cdot P(4) \\ &= P(1) + P(2) \cdot P(3) - P(1) \cdot P(2) \cdot P(3) \end{aligned} \tag{3.32}$$

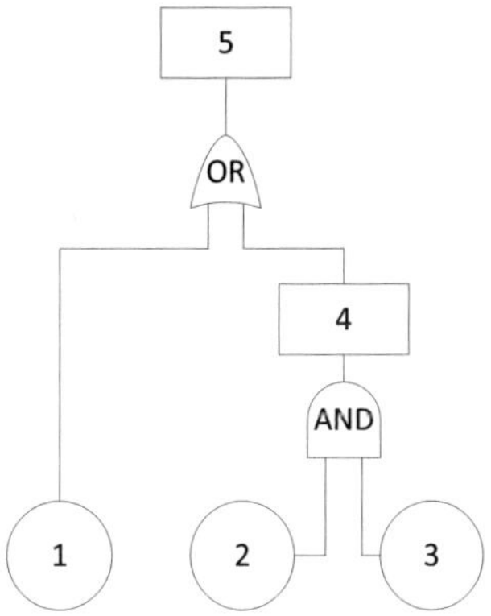

Figure 3.5: Basic depiction of Fault Tree Analysis

3.7.3.4 Estimation of probabilities

The probability of an event is essential to assess risks. It shows the proportion of times that it occurs (see Waters [380]). In a frequentist interpretation of probabilities a low (high) probability corresponds to a low (high) occurrence frequency of an event. In case of a probability of zero the event never occurs. In contrast, a value of one means that the event always take place. A value between these represents the likelihood. According to Waters [380], three types for estimation of probabilities exist: calculation, observation and subjective estimates.

- **Calculation**

  If knowledge of a situation is available then the theoretical probabilities can be calculated as follows:

$$Probability\ of\ an\ event = \frac{number\ of\ ways\ that\ the\ event\ can\ occur}{number\ of\ possible\ outcomes} \tag{3.33}$$

- **Observation**

  In this case historical data of actually happened events in the past is used to calculate the likelihood of an event:

$$Probability\ of\ an\ event = \frac{number\ of\ times\ that\ the\ event\ can\ occur}{number\ of\ observations} \tag{3.34}$$

- **Subjective estimates**

  Contrary to the previous approaches the subjective estimation is not recommended. The estimation relies on the experience and opinions of people and not on real data.

The estimation of probabilities and, hence, the setup of likelihood functions are a key factor in assessing risks. In general, two different types of probability functions can be distinguished. They can either be discrete or continuous (see Borghesi and Gaudenzi [56]).

Discrete probability functions can be given as follows in equation 3.35, where X is a random variable and where p depends on the value of θ.

$$L(\theta \mid x) = p_\theta(x) = P_\theta(X = x) \tag{3.35}$$

This function is the likelihood function of θ with the given value of the outcome x of X. Continuous probability functions are defined by the following equation 3.36:

$$L(\theta \mid x) = f_\theta(x) \tag{3.36}$$

whilst X is a random variable of a continuous probability distribution. The distribution is defined by the function f which depends on the value θ.

In biomass value chains, risks are often independent from previous risks. Consequently, Poisson distributions are the most common function type. Depending on the type of failure, different probability functions can be applied. According to Ayyub [28] also exponential distribution, Weibull functions, lognormal distribution etc. can be used to approximate the probability of a failure. The basics of Poisson distributions are described in the following excursus.

Excursus: Poisson distribution

The **Poisson distribution** is a discrete probability distribution. It expresses the probability of a given number of events occurring in a fixed interval of time and/or space. These events should occur what known average rate and independently of the last event. According to Ayyub [28] the number of natural hazards such as hurricanes, earthquakes can be considered as a variable number with a Poisson distribution. The random variable is defined as a number of success in case of many ($n \rightarrow \infty$) BERNOULLI-experiments with a very low success rate ($p \rightarrow 0$) (see Schira [313]).

$$P_\lambda(k) = \frac{\lambda^k}{k!} e^{-\lambda} \qquad (3.37)$$

With λ being the average number of events per interval, e is Euler's number, k takes values 0,1,2,... and k! is the factorial of k.

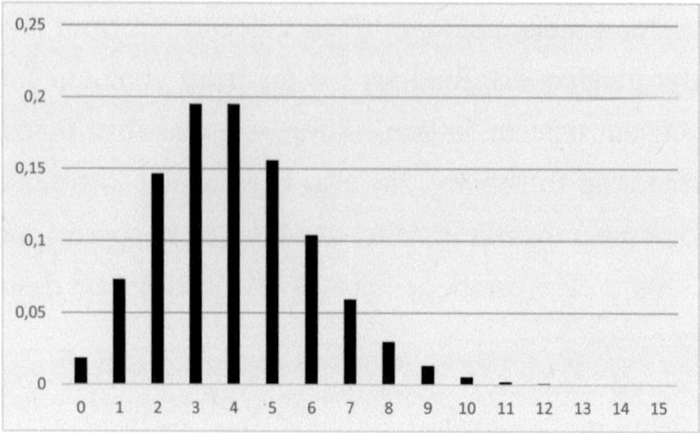

Figure 3.6: Poisson distribution with $\lambda = 4$

3.7.3.5 Correlation between risks

Risks can influence other risks and lead to correlations. These can result in varying probabilities. According to Merz [224], the dependencies and correlations between risks can lead to an over- or underestimation of vulnerabilities and can, hence, influence the results of the vulnerability analysis.

Different methods can be applied to assess the correlation between risks. Multivariate stochastic methods, such as factor analysis, can be used for structure analysis. Expert based approaches, such as Decision Making Trial and Evaluation Method (DEMATEL), can also be applied. Whilst the first assesses stochastic correlations, the second enables the analysis of causal structures. The stochastic correlations can be estimated by various approaches. These are for example the correlation analysis by Pearson, the main component resp. factor analysis as well as the definition of the Cronbach α. These approaches lead to linear correlations between the indicators. Statistic methods only give an indication of direct dependencies and not of indirect influences (see Merz [224]).

This work neglects the correlation of risks. Many risks result in a complex identification and quantification of correlations. This is beyond the scope of this scientific analysis. The identification of uncertainties along the overall value chain is already quite challenging.

3.7.4 Consequences of risks occurrence and their evaluation

The second step in evaluating risks is to assign a value to the consequence of a risk. In many cases, a direct measure can be defined. For example, the effect of an event is the cost that can occur if the hazard occurs. Depending on the risk, the quantification of the consequence is more or less obvious. In case of transport, there are different methods to estimate the cost of delay. For instance, penalty cost for a delay can be estimated or cost for the speeding up process to ensure an on-time transport can be considered (see Waters [380]). Some risks cannot be defined by cost but rather by time. A project, which will not terminate on time, is a risk, which is not easily transferable to cost. In general, risk consequences can be clustered and defined as negligible, minor, moderate, serious, critical or catastrophic (see Waters [380]).

Two different approaches exist to estimate the consequences of a risk. Borghesi and Gaudenzi [56] present the Probable Maximum Loss (PML) and the Maximum Foreseeable Loss (MFL). The maximum monetary loss, which can affect a business by the probable risk, can be measured by the PML. Direct and indirect consequences of risk occurrence can be estimated by different approaches, which are presented in literature. The chosen method depends on the scope of research. It can reach from macroeconomic total losses via the effect on a single loss category on regional level to the monetary loss of single objects (see Merz [224]).

The approaches to estimate direct and indirect consequences are presented in the following sections.[1]

3.7.4.1 Quantification approaches of direct risks

According to Messner and Meyer [225], no standard evaluation methodologies for quantifying direct damages exist. Often the methods depend on the aim of the study, the level of detail or data availability. Nevertheless, the process of quantifying risks is mostly similar. It is depicted in figure 3.7.

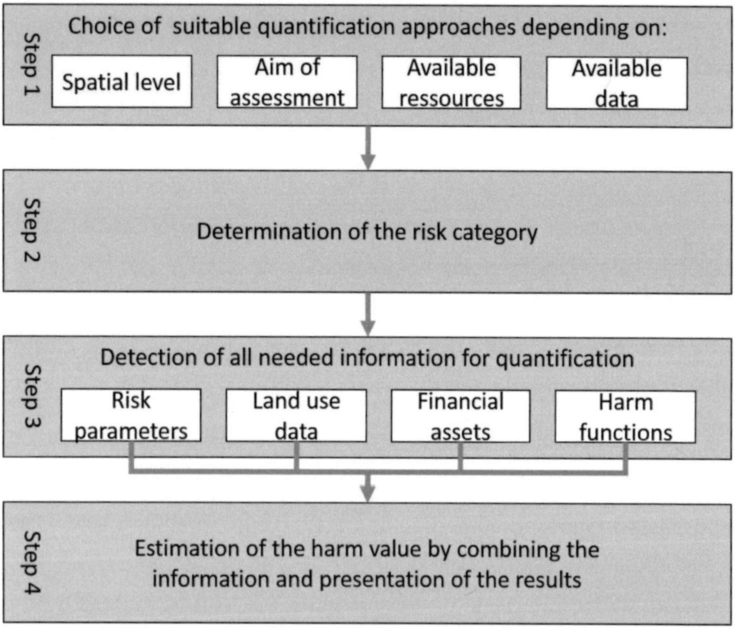

Figure 3.7: Concepcional approach to quantify direct damage (Messner and Meyer [225])

The following steps need to be performed.

[1] The following sections summarize the descriptions provided by Merz [224].

1. **Identification of suitable quantification approach**
   In the first step, the system boundaries are defined. The loss potential of single industry locations can be assessed as well as macro-scale approaches for assessing losses for the whole economy.

2. **Definition of considered loss categories**
   The processing of loss assessment depend on the defined categories. On regional level for example the losses of buildings will be considered, but inventory will be defined out of scope.

3. **Collection of all needed data and information for loss assessment**
   The regional impact of a risk and its consequences are assessed in this step. Hence, the necessary data needs to be collected on the respective defined level. Therefore, either bottom-up or top-down approaches can be chosen. Bottom-up approaches are more complex as a single production plant will be used as basis for the industrial exposition to risks on regional level.

4. **Combination of all collected data**
   To overlay the defined losses on regional level the data can be assessed in GIS systems. All methods for loss quantification are bound to various uncertainties. These need to be considered in the final assessment of the results.

3.7.4.2 Quantification approaches of indirect risks

According to Green and van der Veen [142], the size of the affected area or infrastructure and the duration of the disruption have the largest influence on the risk consequences. The spatial scale define, which type of quantification method can be used (see Green and van der Veen [142]).

Cochrane [81] clustered the approaches for quantifying indirect damages into the following:

- interview of companies and assessment of historic events
- Input-Output models
- Computational General Equilibrium
- Econometric models
- Hybrid models

Of these, only the first is applicable for very detailed damage analysis. Historic data or the expertise of companies are used to quantify the consequences of infrastructure disruptions (see Balducci et al. [40]). This method needs large amounts of data, hence the effort is high. Nevertheless, the results are very detailed and realistic. The output of such damage analysis is for example the economic damage of not produced value (see Green and van der Veen [142]).

The other approaches are based on a lower level of detail and are, therefore, more applicable for macro-economic analysis. **Input-Output models** are the most common method for economic damage analysis (see Okuyama [268]). They are static linear models, which correlate all input and output streams between economic sectors based on production relations. Input-Output models do not need large amounts of detailed data sets. Unfortunately, the identified correlations are only linear, the damage is independent from varying economic parameters and limited products and capacities are not considered.

Computable General Equilibrium (CGE) models are market simulation models which optimize the behavior of single consumers (see Shoven and Whalley [325]). In contrast to Input-Output models, CGE arc non-linear and include also price variability as well as variable products and capacities. For this method a larger amount of data is necessary.

Econometric models are based on time series. Due to their large data demand, they are only seldom used for the quantification of macroeconomic indirect damage (see West and Lenze [384]).

The combination of the above described approaches are performed in **hybrid models**. Consequently, they are mostly dependent on the applicant. The most known hybrid model is the Multi-Hazard Loss Estimation Methodology of the US Federal Management Agency. It is based on input-output parameters which, are extended by GIS data (see Cochrane [81]).

3.7.5 Risk categories

In biomass value chains many different risks occur. In this section, the predominant risk categories will be described. These risks are applicable to different types of biomass value chains and are not restricted to a certain biomass type. Specific definitions of biomass related risks will be described in section 5.5.

Many different clusters and descriptions of risks and uncertainties exist in literature. Sodhi et al. [329] groups risks into supply, process and demand as well as corporate-level risks. Waters [380] clusters risks based on Mason-Jones and Towill [218] in internal, supply chain and external risks. Other classifications differentiate between physical, financial, information and organizational risks. The categories of Mason-Jones and Towill [218] also include environmental, demand and supply, process and control risks. Minahan [232] distinguishes between supply market, supplier, regulatory and supply strategy risks.

Waters [380] provides a list, which is by no means exhaustive, of common risks in supply chains:

- natural, *environment*
- economic, financial, *supply*, *market*, *transport*
- physical, operations, *products/process*, technical
- information, safety
- strategic, management, organization, planning
- human, criminal, local permits, *political*

The risks, which are indicated in italic letters, are the most adequate for describing biomass value chains. These value chains are not very critical to human mankind so that terrorism or other criminal and safety risks do not apply. Many risks are a matter of definition so that for example product, physical and technical risks can be defined similarly. Therefore, the risks, which are indicated in italic letters, will be considered in this work and are, hence, described in more detail in the following sections.

3.7.5.1 Supply risks

Sodhi et al. [329] define supply risks as all risk events that can be associated with the suppler side. Examples for this include supply cost, delivery and quality of the product as well as the reliability of the supplier. Supply risks have increased in the past years as more and more production is being outsourced by the company so that they rely on an external supplier. In addition, the supply chain has changed to a reduction of the number of suppliers and increased the global sourcing of products (see Sodhi et al. [329]).

Tang and Tomlin [338] define different supply risks. **Supply cost risk** describe the variation of the effective per-unit price, which leads to an increase of raw material prices of the own production. In case a business partner gives up the contract between himself (the supplier) and his customer, this can be seen as a **supply commitment risk**. The customer needs to search for a new supplier, risking additional cost or reduced quality. Short-term supply disruptions are defined as **supply continuity risk**.

3.7.5.2 Transport and storage risks

Kummer and Sudy [193] define **transport risks** based on existing literature as all individual risks, which occur in the context of the physical transport of goods. This includes the risk of destruction of the good during transport or the risk of a transport delay. The effect of transport risk to a participant of the supply chain depends on the type of contract that was chosen. These can either be on the side of the customer, supplier or infrastructure provider.

Storage risks regard to all individual risks in context with the storage of goods and affect either the good or the storage site itself (see Kummer and Sudy [193]).

Transport risks can be caused by other risks such as environmental risks (e.g. floods, hurricanes etc.). In general, transport and storage damages can be affected by different factors but always regard to spatial and temporal bypassing. The likelihood of transport risks depend on the probability of other risks (e.g. environmental risks), but can be easily estimated based on historical data. The estimation of the consequences of transport risks is mostly straightforward.

Kummer and Sudy [193] define the following transport and storage risks, which apply to all types of supply chains and are, consequently, also applicable to biomass value chains:

- **Transport volume risk**
  This includes all risks, which harm the transported volume, e.g. theft, terror or accidents. Transport volume risks lead to delays in the supply. To secure the supply additional cost occur in different scenarios

and stages of the supply chain: express goods (logistics), additional production and set-up cost (production), revenue reduction through discounts (marketing) etc.

- **Transport quality risk**
  In the case of transport quality risks, the quality of the good can depreciate during the transport. Especially wet biomass can deteriorate during long transport periods. Reduced revenues can result from this.

- **Storage volume and quality risk**
  The risks, which affect the transport of goods, are also valid for the storage of products. The quantity and quality of biomass can be reduced by weather conditions or suboptimal storage during storage.

- **Transport and storage cost risk**
  Higher transport or storage cost than planned result in risks for the company, which needs to bear the cost.

- **Transport and storage value risk**
  If the value of the transported or stored product decreases during transport or storage, the procurement and marketing unit of the company bear the risks depending on the product. Transport and storage value risks do not necessarily need to be affected by depreciated goods, but can also have other causes such as the sudden lack of demand for a product.

- **Transport time risk**
  In case of a delay of the transport, production stops might be necessary as the feedstock might not be available. This may lead to the provision of the needed good of the expected quality but to a later date. Transport delays can be caused by accidents, congestion, extreme weather events, strike etc. The delay can be so long that sometimes the transport is canceled completely.

- **Storage time risk**
  Storage time risks are relevant for products, which can only be stored for a certain time. This is especially relevant for easily perishable goods. Depending on the type of biomass, the feedstock might also be perishable. As some biomass are seasonal goods, they need to be stored for a year. Consequently, biomass needs to be pretreated accordingly to reduce storage risks.

- **Transport and storage location risk**
  This risk occurs, when the good cannot be transported to the defined destination or cannot be stored at the defined location. Transport to a false location can lead to additional cost by rerouting the product.

Kummer and Sudy [193] define strategies to reduce transport and storage risks. These include a close location to the supplier or strong cooperation with a supplier, identification of safe routes, choice of transport mode, design of the storage.

3.7.5.3 Process risks

Process risks in biomass supply chains can include many different risks, which can depend on the process itself, but also depend on environmental influences. These risks are presented in the following.

According to Gunukula et al. [145], technological and market risks exist. Risks occur mostly in the development and scale-up of emerging technologies for the production of chemicals based on renewable resources technology. In addition, the lack of economies of scale may inhibit the market entry for low profit margin biochemicals. In case of platform technologies, which can produce not only single products, but multiple chemicals, this may reduce the risk as the output is more flexible to market requirements.

Sodhi et al. [329] also list the default of the manufacturing design, the yield of the production, inventory imbalances and an inadequate capacity of the production plant. In general, all risks that lead to variances in the production are crucial for the profit of the company.

Process risks can affect both: quantity and quality. Especially in case of biomass, it is almost impossible to produce a constant composition and yield. As all natural goods, the harvest depends on soil, weather, and other natural impacts (see Gunukula et al. [145]).

3.7.5.4 Market and demand risks

Demand risks are faced by all companies worldwide and include both, product volume and mix. These risks include the forecasting of the demand for the final product and a change in technology or in consumer preference (see Sodhi et al. [329]).

Forecasting reflects the discrepancy between the company's forecast and the actual demand of the customer(s). Either the company has produced a too high volume of the product and needs to find additional customers or too less product can be provided, which results in reduced revenues. Sodhi et al. [329] describe reasons for forecasting errors: "long lead times for production, seasonality of demand, high product variety, and short product life cycles". Especially in case of commodity products, holding inventory might be an appropriate measure to reduce demand risks based on forecasting errors.

Changes in technology or in consumer preferences is closely related to long-term forecasting errors. This does not only affect the demand of the customer, but also capacity investment decisions in the company and, hence, the return of the investment (see Sodhi et al. [329]). Technology risks can be reduced by Joint-Ventures with competitors, constant research and development of new technologies, products and consumer preferences.

Other market related risks include, for example, the variability of exchange rates. The changes in global markets and currencies are relevant in case of imports and exports. This might either change the benefit of the company but revenues might also be decreased if a product price was fixed in a foreign currency (see Sodhi et al. [329]).

3.7.5.5 Environmental risks

Whyte and Burton as part of The Scientific Committee on Problems of the Environment (SCOPE) [385] have defined environmental risks as risks, which "arise in, or are transmitted through, the air, water, soil or biological food chains, to man". These risks can have different causes, either by mankind or by nature. As they have in common, that they harm impartial citizens, measures need to be implemented, which manage these risks.

Environmental risks are always connected to other risks. For example, traffic accidents can relate to extreme snow fall or hurricanes and tornadoes can cause blackouts. Soil degradation, floods and pesticides/fertilizers are among the major environmental risks of 63 developing countries, which also affect biomass cultivation (see Whyte and Burton [385]).

3.7.5.6 Weather risks

According to Langholtz et al. [197], the effect of extreme weather events, climate variability and change have been assessed only to a comparatively small extent. Agricultural production is highly dependent on the weather circumstances and are sensitive to climate changes. Eaves and Eaves [100] found that the price of grain ethanol is more volatile to weather impacts than the import of gasoline. The Intergovernmental Panel of Climate Change (IPCC) [116] gave the prediction that extreme weather events increase in frequency, spatial extension, duration and/or intensity, which will most likely affect the agricultural production immensely. Extreme weather events are hail, wind, tornadoes, extreme temperatures, drought, and precipitation, which might result in floods. Especially the drought of 2012 in the U.S. showed the vulnerability of crops to weather extremes. These have already become more severe in the past decades and may continue to do so in the future. Potential vulnerabilities caused by climate variability and change on the biochemical supply chain (see Langholtz et al. [197]).

Increasing average temperatures, local changes in rainfall amount and intensity, changes in climatic variability and the incidence of extreme events, in the incidence of pests and disease can affect crop yields (see Marshall et al. [215]). Multiple stakeholders are affected by biomass related weather risks (see Morrow et al. [238]):

1. producers
    - short-term (days to months) direct impacts on yield due to unfavorable weather conditions and increased exposure
    - long-term (years to decades) yield impacts due to declining suitability of feedstocks to new climate conditions
2. feedstock logistics
    - biomass shortages due to yield impacts and/or disruption of transportation networks
    - increased competition for biomass among brokers
    - longer transportation distances to obtain needed biomass quantities
3. biorefinery
    - price volatility, potentially reducing profitability
    - reduced reliability of water for refining options
    - direct damage to facilities

4. consumers
    - fuel/energy price volatility
    - reduced reliability of fuel supply

3.7.5.7 Political risks

Political risks include all risks, which are influenced by decisions of policy makers. These risks are hardly quantifiable. Political decisions are made by individuals based on the public opinion. Corporations, investors and governments face changing decisions, events, or conditions. This can lead to an unexpected loss of value of an economic action. Political risks are defined as "the risk of a strategic, financial, or personnel loss for a firm because of such nonmarket factors as macroeconomic and social policies (fiscal, monetary, trade, investment, industrial, income, labor, and developmental), or events related to political instability (terrorism, riots, coups, civil war, and insurrection)" (see Kennedy, Jr. [74]).

Macro- and micro-level political risks exist. **Macro-level risks** affect not only a certain corporation, but all protagonists. Such risks include government currency adaptions, regulatory changes or corruption. Some research parties model macro-level risks. A political risk index has been developed by the Eurasia Group. Another Global Political Risk Index is published by The Economist, Economist Intelligence Unit or The PRS Group, Inc. (see Kobrin [185], Clark [80]).

In contrast, **micro-level risks** only have an impact on a single firm or sector. Regional or local political climates may affect a business endeavor in a certain region. Policies are designed to foster commercialization of biobased products (e.g. biofuels/ethanol) from corn to non-food crops (see Energy Policy Act of 2005 [367]).

3.7.6 Risk mitigation strategies

As defined by Ayyub [28], risk mitigation is an action to reduce the probability or the consequences of an event. Therefore, efficient management processes are necessary. Ayyub [28] describes four possible strategies to mitigate risks:

- **Risk reduction or elimination** is the most effective approach. Hence, the amendment of the system structure might lead to an elimination or reduction of the probabilities or consequences of risks.
- **Risk transfer** shifts the risk to a party within the project or process chain, which is best able to manage them or to an insurance company.
- **Risk avoidance** aims at neglecting projects which could cause the risks.
- In case the risks cannot be avoided **risk absorbance** is the only possible method by covering the risks by enough finances.

Smith and Petley [327] define three main strategies to reduce the impact of hazards. Firstly, this is the mitigation of risks to reduce the loss burden. Secondly, the events can be modified by protection from hazards. And finally, the adaption and, hence, the modification of human vulnerability to hazards is a risk mitigation strategy.

According to Waters [380], two approaches exist on how to react to risks. Firstly, the risk can be ignored. This leads mostly to reactive approaches and managers think about risk mitigation once the problem has occurred. The second option is to proactively develop measures, which is mostly the more expensive, but prepare for the best response.

Sodhi et al. [329] describe different strategies to reduce the impact that a risk has on the supply chain. The main three risk mitigation strategies include, firstly, the alignment of partnerships with suppliers and customers by contracts to increase the purchasing security. Secondly, the supply chain needs to be designed flexible. Thirdly, buffers or redundancies reduce especially supply and process risks.

According to Hopp et al. [158], different risk mitigation strategies exist. In general, risks can be prevented, responded to or the company can be protected against risks. **Risk prevention strategies** are forecasting of uncertainties and risk reduction techniques. Both approaches aim at not even being affected by risks. In case the stakeholder is aware of a risk, he/she can take necessary measures to avoid effects. **Response strategies** detect risks and respond with high speed to them. Fast reactions minimize the consequences of risks. The faster a supply chain is up and running, the earlier business is back to usual. If severe risks are identified, often **protection strategies** are necessary. These include additional protection of and by inventory, capacity and information. The lack and susceptibility of these assets induce a higher vulnerability to risks of the stakeholder.

Tang and Tomlin [338] have defined two risk mitigation strategies in case supply risks occur. **Flexible supply strategies via multiple suppliers** can reduce the dependency on a single supplier. In case one supplier drops out, another supplier can be contacted. Especially supply commitment risks can be reduced by **flexible supply strategies via flexible supply contracts.**

Sodhi and Tang [329] have defined nine robust supply chain strategies. Some of these improve the supply management of a company and some the demand management. In the following, these strategies are summarized. See Sodhi and Tang [329] for more details. Postponement delays the product specialization and increases the product flexibility. Strategic stock leads to an increase of product availability. A flexible supply base enables the shift of production among suppliers. The production can also be shifted from between in-house production and a supplier as so called make-and-buy strategy. Economic supply incentives increase the product availability as it enables the adjustment of order quantities. Flexible transportation leads to varying transport routes in case of transport disruptions. Product demand can be controlled by revenue management to influence the customer's selection. Dynamic assortment planning also influences the control of product demand. As product changes might shock customers, a silent rollout can result in a better the product control to customers. Flexible supply contracts allow the shift of order quantities across time and suppliers. A flexible manufacturing process leads to a high flexibility in producing different products and meeting customer demands.

Risk mitigation strategies may have a positive effect, but can also lead to an increase of risks in other sections. For example, adding capacity to decrease the risks of delays, procurement security and inventory. This will result in an increase of capacity risks. Likewise, the increase of inventory will decrease e.g. delays, but will lead to a rise of inventory risks. For further examples and descriptions see Sodhi et al. [329]. Assessed risks can be included into location planning models under uncertainties. Existing approaches will be described in the following.

3.8 Approaches for location planning in biomass value chains under uncertainties

Technical feasibility studies and the development of technical production processes have increased in the past years (see section 2.1). The research on location planning models has exploded in the past years to improve biomass value chains. Not only deterministic location and network planning models are in the focus of international research, but also the consideration of uncertainties within the biomass value chain has become of more and more interest. Whilst until 2010, only a few papers have been published, the number of journal publications has increased since then (see Bairamzadeh [34]). In the following, the developed approaches to deal with uncertainties as well as the considered risks will be presented.

3.8.1 Mathematical approaches for considering risks

The majority of the approaches, which were applied for location planning are analytic methodologies (see section 3.3.2.1). Especially sensitivity analysis and Monte Carlo methods were studied extensively. Although they are in many cases not mentioned explicitly, they are often combined with other methods. Other approaches are robust optimization, two-stage stochastic modeling, multi-stage stochastic modelling, fuzzy programming, value at risk optimization, scenario analysis and simulation. Analyzed approaches are summarized and clustered in table 3.3. Many of the approaches in literature are stochastic programming approaches. A few have used Value at Risk models or robust optimization.

Table 3.3: Approaches in biomass value chain optimization under uncertainty

Approach	Source
Monte Carlo analysis	[27], [159], [181],[206], [227], [233], [166], [165], [316], [394]
Stochastic programming	[27], [29], [31], [32], [72], [76], [130], [133], [216], [217], [228], [271], [270], [306], [318], [351], [395]
Two-Stage stochastic programming	[207], [272], [291], [390], [393], [394]
Value at Risk	[88], [137], [177], [186]
Fuzzy programming	[36], [38],[39], [350]
Scenario analysis	[20], [37], [182], [234], [299], [319], [320], [392], [397], [398]
Robust optimization	[34], [209], [317], [340], [352], [396]
Simulation	[102], [101]

3.8.2 Considered uncertainties

After a literature review of the existing models to cope with risks in biomass value chains, the identified uncertainties were clustered in five groups. Within these clusters, subgroups were defined as follows:

- **Biomass supply uncertainties**: purchase price, yield/availability, seasonality
- **Transportation and logistics uncertainties**: transport cost, storage cost, disruptions
- **Production and operations uncertainties**: conversion rate, investments and production cost

- **Demand and price uncertainties**: sales price, demand
- **Other uncertainties**

The most common risks, which have been considered in existing approaches, are varying biomass yields as well as sales price and demand uncertainties. Other risks, which were studied to a larger extent are cost in general, but transport, storage, biomass and production cost in specific. The variation of cost in general is often performed in the sensitivity analysis and is rather easy to include in location planning models. In literature, also more technical variations, such as seasonality of biomass, conversion rates of processes and disruptions in transport, have been considered. These do not only have an effect on the overall cost of the value chain, but also on the performance of the system. In case of varying conversion rates, different amounts of feedstock are needed. Seasonality of biomass leads to insecure supply or maybe even the lack of feedstock. Logistic disruptions have the same effect. The results of the literature review is presented in table 3.4.

3.9 Conclusion and research questions

This work considers value chains of first and second generation biomass. These value chains include the cultivation of biomass and the transport from the harvesting field to a storage facility. After storage the biomass is converted by different pretreatment processes to pretreated biomass. Then, the pretreated biomass is converted by thermochemical or biochemical processes to chemicals. The performance of the conversion processes depends on the biomass type and needs to be assessed carefully. The final products are either sold to the local market or transferred to a port, from which they can be exported worldwide.

Table 3.4: Uncertainties in biomass value chain models

Uncertainty	Uncertainty	Source
Biomass supply	Purchase price	[27], [29], [31], [39], [137], [159], [181], [233], [271], [270], [166], [165], [352], [393], [398]
	Yield	[27], [29], [31], [34], [39], [72] [76], [88], [130], [133], [159], [177], [207], [206], [181], [272],[270], [299], [306], [318], [317], [319], [320], [340], [350], [352], [351], [390], [394], [395], [397], [398]
	Seasonality/Quality	[209], [318], [317], [392]
	Demand	[76]
Transport	Transport cost	[39], [159], [177], [317], [319], [398]
	Storage	[317],[319], [320], [394]
	Disruptions	[32], [182], [217], [291]
Process	Conversion rate	[34], [159], [350], [394], [397]
	Production cost	[39], [101], [206], [350], [352], [398]
Demand	Sales price	[20], [27], [29], [31], [39], [88], [101], [271], [270], [398]
	Demand	[27], [29], [20], [31], [34], [72], [102], [130], [133], [159], [177], [186], [206], [234], [272], [270], [306], [340], [350], [352], [351], [394], [395], [397]
Others		[36], [207], [206], [181], [233], [320], [352], [393]

Along this value chain, different risks and uncertainties occur, which influence the decision of a location for such facilities. These risks need to be identified and considered in the DSS. Accordingly, the following research questions can be formulated.

A How can multiple aspects of biomass value chains, namely techno-economic assessments, uncertainties, and location and logistic planning be combined in one model?

B To which extent do biomass types influence the location of biochemical conversion plants?

C Despite risks occurring in biomass value chains, can a robust location be defined?

D Which technology is more suitable for large-scale production? How can different technologies be compared?

E Which risks have an influence on the biomass value chain for the production of biochemicals and how can these be measured?

F Which location and value chain setup is suited best considering various risks in the biomass value chain?

An approach to address the above presented research questions is developed in section 4.

3.9.1 Methodological conclusion

Contrary to other approaches, analytic models have the advantage that they optimize the defined conditions and propose the best possible solution of the system. Simulation models on the other hand may show results for defined scenarios, but in case of large systems, the evaluation of all possible connections is very challenging. Biomass value chains are very complex as they include many different aspects. Consequently, simulations models are neglected in this work. As presented in section 3.3.2, many different approaches exist to perform location planning under uncertainty. Objective of this work is not to consider uncertain capacities or uncertain demands, but to design the biomass value chain as such that fix demands of customers can be fulfilled. Consequently, the production capacity is considered as fix value. This work assumes that the price for biobased chemicals is equal to petrochemicals. Hence, the overall demand for biochemicals is identical as for conventional chemicals as the chemical properties of the product are alike. Consequently, the demand is secure and does not need to be considered as an uncertainty. Fuzzy and stochastic programming models are often applied for uncertain mass balances or uncertain information. In this work, these values are assumed to be fix and certain. Consequently, the chosen approach is an analytic operations research model. Nevertheless, to include the variability of risks in the model, a hybrid model as defined in section 3.3.2.4 by combining the analytic location model with the simulation method of Monte Carlo is applied.

Uncertainties, which influence the design of the biomass value chain and the economic feasibility of the production of biochemicals, are the focus of this work. To assess the economic feasibility of the value chain, the cost, which are inflicted by the risks, need to be included in the objective function. Many consequences of risks in biomass value chains can be quantified and monetized. This work utilizes Fault Tree Analysis for the identification and quantification of the single results. This approach summarizes single risk events to quantifiable main risks, which are easier to quantify. Each uncertainty causes cost, which occur once it takes place. Therefore, the cost for each edge of the network need to be estimated. Uncertainties, which cannot be quantified, can be analyzed by scenario calculations to assess their influence on the value chain. The main uncertainty categories, which are considered in this work are supply, market, process, environmental, transport, and political risks.

In order to include realistic data on conversion technologies these need to be simulated thermodynamically. Biomass influence the technology itself, but also the efficiency and needed feedstock as well as utility demands. As these restrictions influence the feasibility of the biomass value chain, they need to be considered thoroughly. The processes are modeled by flowsheeting simulation in AspenPlus. This software is well known and has already been applied by many others. The material and energy flow balances from the simulations can be used as basis for the investment and production cost estimations. Both, technical and economic parameters are used as input parameters in the analytic model.

Finally, both first and second generation biomass should be considered in the analytic model due to the following reasons: demand for sustainability, restricted first generation biomass supply and the rising food and tank discussions. First generation biomass is already fully used in existing pretreatment plants. Second generation biomass biorefineries are very scarce. Hence, large potentials exist to be used for biochemical plants.

The biorefinery locations can be used as suppliers for the biochemical plants. Consequently, the locations need to be optimized based on conversion rates and biomass potentials in an upstream model.

Merz [224] differentiates between uncertainty and sensitivity analysis. Uncertainty analysis is the analysis of the relative contribution of different input variables to the uncertainty of the model results. Sensitivity analysis analyzes the effect of variations of the input factors on the variability of the model. In this work, sensitivity calculations are performed to analyze the influence of varying cost (e.g. regarding export, biomass, utility prices).

3.9.2 Conclusion regarding content

The most central content in all publications is the limitation to the production of biofuels or bioenergy. Contrary to those two products, the demand for biochemicals is not as large and certain, the market is smaller and the availability of biomass is more restricted as the demand for the biofuel production also needs to be fulfilled. In existing publications the focus on biochemicals could not be found (see section 3.8). Hence, the consideration of specifically this market in contrast to the biofuel value chains is new to the scientific world. The influence of biofuels on the production of biochemicals as risk will be described in more detail in section 5.5.6. Consequently, this work focuses on biochemicals.

In a few publications the conversion rate of the process is considered as a risk, but the values are assumed and not calculated. As the conversion yield depends on the chosen biomass, the calculation of the efficiency of different processes is essential. Not only the yield of the processes vary, depending on the biomass, but also the configuration of the processes itself. The type of the chosen process as well the size of the production plant influence the investments and production cost.

Until now, the existing models only focus on a few single uncertainties, which occur in the biomass value chain. The advantage of this approach is that the influence of only a few risks can be clearly identified. Contrary to these approaches, multiple risks occur in reality. Although the influence of a single uncertainty cannot be quantified if many risks are included, the focus on only a few aspects restrict the possibilities. It might also lead to neglecting significant risks. Hence, the inclusion of all identified risks within the biomass value chain is crucial.

Additionally, biomass value chains not only depend on the biomass and the technology but also on the logistics. Therefore, multiple transport modes as well as intermodal transport via hubs are included in this work. The products are finally brought to local, national, and international customers.

This work and the developed model, as described in chapter 4, include the following assets.

- multiple biomass of the first and second generation
- inclusion of already existing pretreatment plants
- multiple transport modes and hubs
- process variation depending on the biomass
- estimation of investment and production cost by biomass and process
- risk assessment
- intermediate products
- export of final products

4 Development of an approach for location and logistics planning for biochemicals considering uncertainties

The previous sections introduced biomass value chains (see chapter 2), approaches to model location planning under uncertainty (see section 3), and techno-economic assessment of processes (see section 3.5). Also general risks (see section 3.7), which can occur within biomass value chains were defined. Based on the presented methodologies and concepts, research questions were defined in section 3.9. The following approach has been developed to answer these research questions. Aim of the model-based assessment is to provide decision support for the configuration of biomass value chains considering uncertainties and risks related to the net present value (NPV). Objective of the approach is to maximize the NPV of the overall value chain. Hence, the nearly optimal setup of the value chain under uncertain circumstances is proposed. The configuration of the value chain includes the location, the logistics, the process setup, the types of used biomass, and the suppliers. Existing and future locations of suppliers are considered. As various factors influence the profitability and efficiency of biomass value chains, multiple aspects are included in the model, which are explained below. Outcome of the model is the proposition of a location and a logistical concept to produce chemicals from biomass either thermochemically or biochemically.

The approach is based on an integrated model (see section 4.5), which proposes a location for the production of biochemicals under uncertain conditions. This model needs multiple input parameters. Some of them are calculated in previous models, which are defined as sub-models. The detailed setup of the approach is explained in section 4.1.

The approach provides a decision support tool that covers the use of multiple biomass types (first and second generation biomass) as well as the pretreatment of these biomass to convertible feedstocks by thermochemical or biochemical processes. Since currently only few pretreatment facilities of second generation biomass exist, the locations of such production sites are modeled in the optimization sub-model (see section 4.2). This results in possible supplier locations of pretreated biomass of which the feedstock for the final conversion to biochemicals can be sourced. The processes itself can be implemented at the same location but can also be split up if it is technically and economically feasible. For the estimation of yields and cost the technical sub-model (see section 4.3) is implemented.

The transport of different products in the value chain is enabled by various transport modes and can be transshipped at hubs. The final product can be exported to international sales markets or fulfill local demands. As the location of export terminals influences the location of the biochemical production plant, the ports are included in the integrated model.

Not only deterministic values influence the feasibility and design of a biomass value chain, but also risks and uncertainties like accidents, weather etc. have an impact on the decision and the value chain setup. Therefore, the risk assessment of the value chains is essential and needs to be included in the decision support tool (see section 4.4).

4.1 General description of the approach

The overall location and logistics planning problem is composed of an integrated model and three sub-models. The integrated model provides decision support for the production of biochemicals from pretreated biomass considering uncertainties. The sub-models provide the needed input data for the integrated model by a data exchange format to interchange the parameters and results. These sub-models are:

4.2 **optimization sub-model**: optimization of the location of pretreatment plants of second generation biomass as feedstock supplier for biochemicals

4.3 **technical sub-model**: techno-economic analysis of biomass conversion technologies of pretreatment and biochemical production for the calculation of yields, investment and production cost

4.4 **risk sub-model**: risk assessment of the considered uncertainties (likelihood and consequences) in biomass value chains for risk cost

The dependencies of the integrated model and the sub-models are depicted in figure 4.1. These optimize biorefinery locations (on the left), perform techno-economic assessments of available technologies (middle) and evaluate risks and uncertainties (on the right).

For the approach and its implementation, substantial amount of data is needed. This includes technical process data such as yields, energy, and utility demand. Economic cost data of production and investment as well as of supply, transport, utilities etc. are essential to estimate the economic feasibility of the value chain. Additionally, data on biomass potentials, predefined locations and other details of logistics are needed. The assessment of risks along the biomass value chain is a core part of this approach.

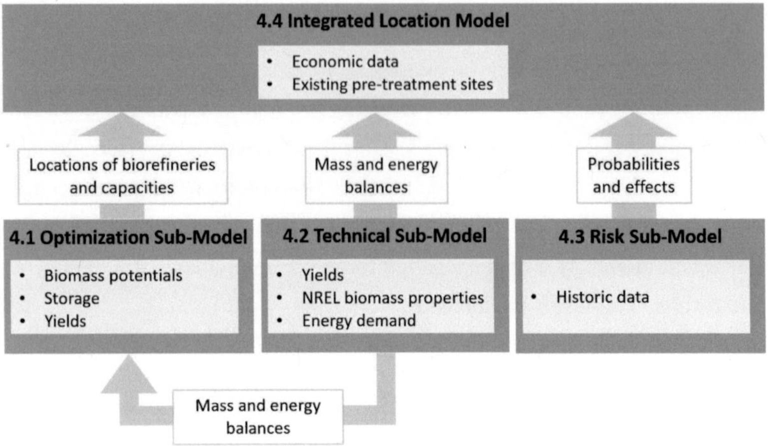

Figure 4.1: Holistic approach for planning biomass value chains

Therefore, the relevant risk data, such as effects and probabilities of these risks need to be analyzed. This needed data is modeled before the location planning of the biochemical production takes place.

Biomass is mostly preprocessed before it is converted to biochemicals. The type of biomass and the respective available conversion technologies influence the further processing. Pretreatment of biomass increases the efficiency of the downstream production processes and transport. Especially in case of lignocellulosic biomass, the pretreatment facilitates processing and reduces transport cost due to its energy densification. The preprocessing can either be done via mechanical, thermochemical or biochemical technologies. The main pretreatment products are pellets, biooil or sugar syrup. In general, facilities, which include the preprocessing technologies can be defined as biorefineries. The development of biorefineries for processing second generation biomass has increased immensely in the past years (see Stichnothe et al. [334]). Contrary to corn wet mills or sugar mills, biorefineries are not yet state of the art. As production sites of first generation biomass to sugars already exist and fully utilize the available biomass potential, the locations of these plants are assumed to be fix and will not be optimized by the following approach. The locations of potential lignocellulosic biorefinery production sites need to be optimized based on a mathematical model as so far only few such facilities exist in large scale. In order to include them as possible suppliers in an integrated model, that provides decision support for the value chain of biochemical production, they are estimated by an **optimization sub-model**. Biomass potentials, storage restrictions and harvesting yields are the main input data for the optimization sub-model. As a result, the chosen locations of biorefineries as well as their product capacities are calculated.

Different conversion technologies exist to produce biochemicals. These define the final product, the energy demand and the demand of different utilities. Not only technical aspects of the conversion technologies are essential but also their investment and other related cost. The production cost and yield of the conversion to biochemicals decide if the value chain is feasible. Hence, for the economic profitability, the conversion technologies are assessed techno-economically in a **technical sub-model**. The results, the mass and energy balances, of the sub-model are used as input data for the integrated model. The technical sub-model is based on the conversion rates of the reactions, chemical properties of biomass and other products and the energy and utility demand for the processing steps.

The third sub-model is the basis for risk assessment. Mostly historic data is used to estimate the consequences and probabilities of different risks and uncertainties. Based on these data the cost of each risk can be estimated and included in the integrated model. These risks are assessed for transport modes, products in the value chain and the conversion technologies. Uncertainties, which are not evaluated in the **risk sub-model**, are analyzed by scenario analysis.

In the following, first the optimization sub-model for location planning of biorefineries will be introduced in section 4.2. The technical sub-model for simulating the technologies as well as estimating the investment and production cost is presented in section 4.3. In section 4.4 the risk assessment sub-model is explained. Afterwards, the integrated model as decision support for location and logistic planning of the production of biochemicals from pretreated biomass will be shown in section 4.5.

4.2 Optimization sub-model

This section introduces the optimization sub-model to estimate the location of biorefineries to pretreat lignocellulosic biomass. Contrary to given capacities of existing first generation biomass processing plants, the size of the biorefineries is not fixed.

Due to the low energy content of lignocellulosic biomass, the transport distance and, hence, the transport cost are crucial for the feasibility of the production plant and overall value chain. Biomass is widely spread and not concentrated in an area. Higher biomass demand leads to larger transport distances to collect the biomass. Therefore, the capacity of biorefineries is restricted by two contrary variables. On the one hand, large production plants can benefit from economies of scale. High capacities result in lower specific investments. On the other hand, transport cost rise immensely with increasing distances from the production facility. Schwaderer [314] has developed an approach, which optimizes the location and capacity of a production plant based on the available biomass potential and non-linear investment curves. His model includes the multiple choice approach, which will be shown in the following in section 4.2.1. Objective of the optimization sub-model is to optimize the capacity and location of a biorefinery. Contrary to the approach by Schwaderer [314], the optimization sub-model does not include the optimization of technology choices. This work assumes that the best available technology is known by the operator. The model of Schwaderer [314] includes multiple biomass, a single transport mode, multiple processes and variable capacities modeled by investment functions. These features were adapted in the optimization sub-model.

4.2.1 Multiple-choice approach

Investments I^{new} of production plants can benefit from economies of scale. These are non-linearly dependent on the ratio of capacity of a reference system C^{basis} to the capacity of a new production plant C^{new}. The factor which influences the non-linearity is the size degression factor R. The non-linear size degression is multiplied with the investments I^{basis} of the reference system. This results in the investments of a potential new asset. This approach can be applied to single units and also to overall production plants. Nevertheless, the size degression factors might need to be adapted.

$$I^{current} = I^{ref} \cdot \left(\frac{C^{current}}{C^{ref}} \right)^{R} \tag{4.1}$$

In general, values of R = 0.6 to 0.8 can be assumed for biorefineries (see Trippe [356]) for the size degression factor. In the following, a mean value of 0.7 will be assumed. Based on the given reference values for a biorefinery of a certain capacity and the economies of scale, the investment for an optimized capacity can be calculated by equation 4.1.

The non-linear cost curves can be estimated by linearization of the curve as shown in figure 4.2.

As the formulation of the optimization sub-model is a Mixed Integer Linear Programming problem, the non-linear cost curves need to be linearized.

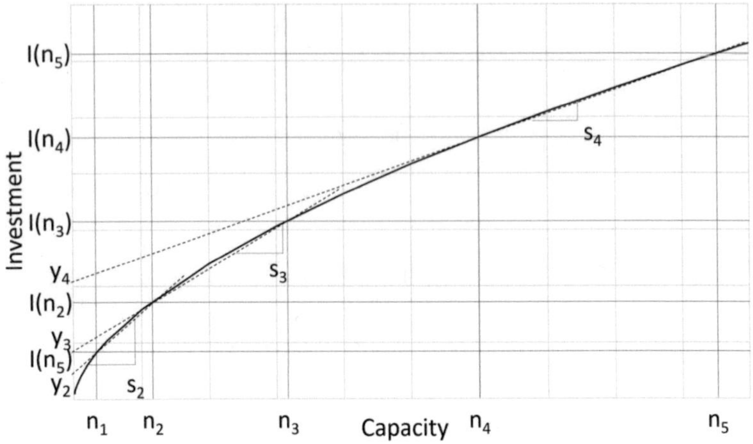

Figure 4.2: Linear approximation of investment curves(Schwaderer [314])

For the linear approximation of the cost curves the multiple-choice (MC) approach is chosen. This approach defines linear curves in certain segments. Depending on the capacity, a segment is chosen and, based on the linear curve, an investment is calculated. Many predefined segments lead to more detailed results. Schwaderer [314] has tested the special ordered set of type 2 (SOS2) and the MC approach and has concluded that the MC is more adequate. For more detail on the approaches, please see Schwaderer [314]. The approach is formulated as shown in equations 4.2 to 4.5.

The decision variable ω_g represents the optimal capacity in the interval $[n_{g-1};n_g]$. Due to the binary variable μ_g for all $g \in 2,...,G$, it can only have a positive value for a single section $[n_{g-1};n_g]$.

$$Min \sum_{g=2}^{G} (s_g \cdot \omega_g + y_g \cdot \mu_g) \tag{4.2}$$

subject to

$$n_{g-1} \cdot \mu_g \leq \omega_g \leq n_g \cdot \mu_g \qquad \forall g \subset 2,...,G \tag{4.3}$$

$$\sum_{g-2}^{G} \mu_g \leq 1 \tag{4.4}$$

$$\mu_g \in 0;1 \qquad \forall g \in 2,...,G \tag{4.5}$$

Investment estimation is performed with the help of three linear equations in the sections $[n_1;n_2]$, $[n_2;n_3]$ and $[n_3;n_4]$ whereas n_g with $g \in \{1,...,G\}$ are the support points. Investment occurring for the support points n_g are given as $I(n_g)$. The minimum capacity is represented by n_1 and the maximum by n_4. The slope of the equations is given by s_g and y_g gives the y-axis intercept in the section $[n_{g-1};n_g]$ with $g \in \{2,...,G\}$ respective line.

4.2.2 Optimization model for biorefineries

In this section, the optimization sub-model is presented. The general setup of it is depicted in figure 4.3. Many different input parameter are needed to perform the optimization. The results of the optimization sub-model are used as input parameters for the integrated model.

The following model determines a NPV-optimal location and capacity of biorefineries, which produces pretreated biomass from second generation (lignocellulosic) biomass These pretreated biomass can be sugars, oils, pellets etc. The biomass is harvested from the field and is stored locally before it is transported to the conversion facilities. During storage, deterioration and drying of the biomass occurs, based on its water content. After the transport of deteriorated biomass, it is processed in biorefineries with variable capacities.

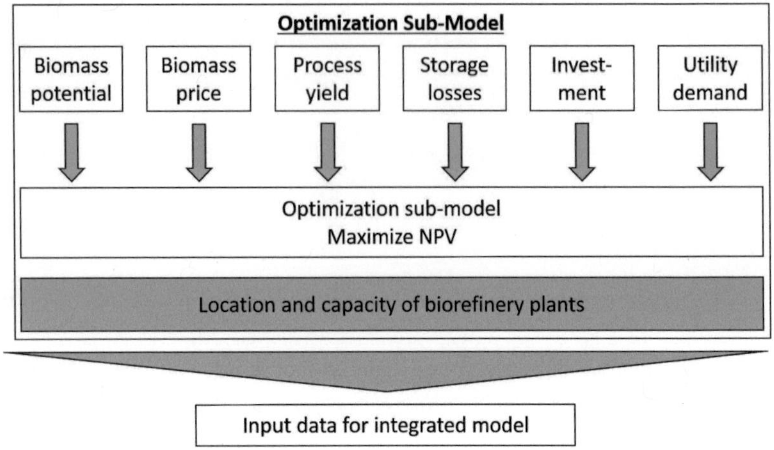

Figure 4.3: Block diagram of the optimization sub-model

This work assumes that the operator choses the best available technique for the pretreatment of the biomass, based on the given boundary conditions. Therefore, a technology optimization such as in Schwaderer [314] is not considered. In addition, the transport is restricted to truck only. As the transport distances for biomass utilization are quite short (about 30 to 50 miles), this work assumes that rail transport is too expensive and barge transport is not feasible. Hence, multi-modal transport is not implemented in the model.

In the following, the developed model will be explained. The used sets, parameters and variables are summarized in table 4.1.

Table 4.1: Sets, parameters and variables of the optimization sub-model

Parameter	Description	Unit
Sets		
$b \in \{1,...,B\}$	biomass type	
$i,j \in \{1,...,I\}$	locations of suppliers and possible production plants	
$u \in \{1,...,U\}$	utilities	
$g \in \{1,...,G\}$	capacity intervals for investment approximation	
Parameters		
General parameters		
$d_{i,j}$	distances between location i and j	$[miles]$
M	Big M	$[-]$
Biomass and Products		
$A_{b,i}$	maximum harvest of biomass b at location i	$[t/a]$
H_j	demand for final product	$[t/a]$
λ_b	biomass deterioration	[%]]
Economic Parameters		
$c_b^{T,fix}$	distance independent transport cost of feedstock f with transport t	$[\$/t]$
$c_b^{T,var}$	distance dependent transport cost of feedstock f with transport t	$[\$/(t \cdot mi)]$
c_b^{ut}	variable production cost by biomass b	$[\$/t]$
c_b^{B}	cost of biomass b	$[\$/t]$
p^{PB}	price of pretreated biomass	$[\$/t]$
c_{inv}	specific investment	$[\$/t]$
n_g	upper fulcrum of the capacity interval g	$[t/a]$

Table 4.1: Sets, parameters and variables of the optimization sub-model

Parameter	Description	Unit
s_g	slope of the respective investment curve in the capacity interval g	$[t/a]$
σ	annuity factor	$[-]$
r	interest rate	$[-]$
T	time of operation	$[years]$
Z_t	yearly payments	$[\$/a]$
Process		
α_b	conversion yield depending on biomass b	$[\%]$
$m^{ut}_{b,u,p}$	amount of utility	$[t_{ut}/t_{PB}]$
Variables		
Continuous variables		
R^P	revenues of pretreated biomass	$[\$/a]$
C^B	biomass cost	$[\$/a]$
C^T	transport cost	$[\$/a]$
C^I	investment	$[\$/a]$
C^U	utility cost	$[\$/a]$
$m^{SB}_{b,i}$	mass flow of stored biomass	$[t/a]$
m^{PB}_{j}	mass flow of pretreated biomass	$[t/a]$
$m^{B}_{b,i,j}$	mass flow of harvested biomass	$[t/a]$
$\omega_{j,g}$	continuous capacity variable of the capacity interval g at production location i	$[t/a]$
Binary variables		
$\mu_{j,g}$	binary variable depending on capacity interval g at location i	$[0,1]$

4.2.2.1 Objective function

The objective of the optimization sub-model is to maximize the net present value (NPV) of the overall value chain from biomass production and harvesting to the pretreated biomass. The optimal capacity shall be constrained by an economically meaningful amount of given harvest used. The maximization of the NPV ensures that in case of positive profits the maximum amount is produced.

In general, the NPV can be defined as in equation 4.6:

$$NPV = \sum_{t=0}^{T} \frac{C_t}{(1+r)^t} - C^I \tag{4.6}$$

All net cash flows C_t are divided by the discount rates r over the time span t from now to the end of the considered time horizon T. The NPV is calculated by subtracting the investment from the discounted cash flows. This work assumes that the investment at the time $t = 0$ is fully paid by equities. The yearly payments are considered to be constant during the operational time as the revenues for biochemicals are directly dependent on the main cost contributor, the biomass price. Hence, the difference of both will remain more or less constant. Normally, the operational time of a production plant is longer than the considered depreciation time. Consequently, the residual value of the investment is assumed to be zero.

Based on the above presented assumptions, the NPV can be simplified to the following equation 4.7.

$$NPV = yearly\,payments \cdot \sigma - investment \tag{4.7}$$

The annuity value σ is calculated as in the following equation 4.8, r being the interest rate and T the operational lifetime of the production plant.

$$\sigma = \frac{(1+r)^T - 1}{(1+r)^T \cdot r} \tag{4.8}$$

The NPV is calculated by the revenue R^P of selling pretreated biomass and the cost for biomass C^B, transport C^T, and utilities C^U as well as the investment for the biorefinery C^I.

$$maximize\,NPV = \left(R^P - C^B - C^T - C^U\right) \cdot \sigma - C^I \tag{4.9}$$

The revenue for pretreated biomass is calculated as in equation 4.10 by multiplying the market price of pretreated biomass p^{PB} with the total produced amount of pretreated biomass m_j^{PB} at location j.

$$R^{PB} = \sum_{J=1}^{J} p^{PB} \cdot m_j^{PB} \tag{4.10}$$

The price of biomass includes cultivating, handling, harvesting etc. and a profit margin. Therefore, the biomass price c_b^B per biomass type b, is multiplied with the harvested biomass amount $m_{b,i}^B$ at location i and results in total biomass cost C^B (see equation 4.11).

$$C^B = \sum_{b=1}^{B} \sum_{i=1}^{I} c_b^B \cdot m_{b,i}^B \tag{4.11}$$

Total transport cost C^T consist of a fix term $c_b^{t,fix}$ and a variable term $c_b^{t,var}$. The fixed transport cost $c_b^{t,fix}$ include personal cost and depreciation for the vehicles. The variable transport cost $c_b^{t,var}$ are mostly distance-related fuel cost. The total transport cost C^T are calculated by multiplying the specific transport cost with the amount of biomass after storage $m_{b,i,j}^{SB}$ and the transport distance d from the harvesting field to the biorefinery, where the biomass is processed to pretreated biomass. This work assumes that the storage at the biorefinery occurs without storage losses for two reasons. First, biomass is stored at the biorefinery after being dried to ensure a constant quality on site, hence losses have already occurred beforehand. Second, the biorefinery operates Just-in-Time and does not have large storage capacities and storage duration. Consequently, total transport cost can be expressed as follows (see equation 4.12).

$$C^T = \sum_{b=1}^{B} \sum_{i=1}^{I} \sum_{j=1}^{J} m_{b,i,j}^{SB} \cdot \left(c_b^{t,var} \cdot d_{i,j} + c_b^{t,fix} \right) \tag{4.12}$$

Utilities are needed to process raw biomass to pretreated biomass. Considered utilities are electricity, work, heat and water as well as other auxiliaries. The necessary amount and states of utilities depend on the process conditions, which vary across the biomass types. The stored biomass $m_{b,i,j}^{SB}$ is multiplied with the variable production cost c_b^{ut} per biomass. According to equation 4.13 this results in the total utility cost C^U.

$$C^U = \sum_{b=1}^{B} \sum_{i=1}^{I} \sum_{j=1}^{J} c_b^{ut} \cdot m_{b,i,j}^{SB} \tag{4.13}$$

Lastly, investment C^I can be estimated by the linearized function deducted in the previous section 4.2.1. They are predefined by capacity and investment sections from input data and can estimated by the equation 4.14.

$$C^I = \sum_{i=1}^{I} \sum_{g=2}^{G} \left(s_g \cdot \omega_{j,g} + y_g \cdot \mu_{j,g} \right) \tag{4.14}$$

4.2.2.2 Constraints

The objective function is subject to the following constraints on biomass potential, storage losses, biomass conversion and capacity constraints.

The amount of biomass $m^B_{b,i}$ that is utilized per year needs to be lower or equal than the total amount harvested $A_{b,i}$ in that year per location i and biomass b as stated in equation 4.15.

$$m^B_{b,i} \leq A_{b,i} \qquad \begin{array}{l} \forall b \in B \\ \forall i \in I \end{array} \tag{4.15}$$

On the one hand, biorefineries operate continuously throughout the year. On the other hand, crop residues are only harvested within one to three months in the fall. Hence, the majority of the biomass needs to be stored. This work assumes that these storages are close to the harvesting sites. The factor λ_b represents the storage degradation after harvest. Therefore, the maximum amount of biomass from the storage to the biorefineries $m^{SB}_{b,i,j}$ is less or equal than the harvest $m^B_{b,i}$ (see equation 4.16). Consequently, more biomass needs to be harvested than is actually available for conversion to pretreated biomass. But for the harvest also collecting, handling and storage cost need to be assessed. The biomass cost of the objective function are respective to the harvested and not utilized biomass.

$$\sum_{j=1}^{J} m^{SB}_{b,i,j} \leq m^B_{b,i} \cdot (1 - \lambda_b) \qquad \begin{array}{l} \forall b \in B \\ \forall i \in I \end{array} \tag{4.16}$$

Different yields α_b of pretreated biomass can be achieved depending on the utilized biomass. The amount of pretreated biomass m_j^{PB} at each production plant at location j is related to the type and amount of the transported biomass $m_{b,i,j}^{SB}$ to that location. The biomass conversion is modeled as in equation 4.17.

$$m_j^{PB} \leq \sum_{b=1}^{B} \sum_{i=1}^{I} \alpha_b \cdot m_{b,i,j}^{SB} \qquad \forall j \in J \qquad (4.17)$$

The following constraints are defined for the estimation of investment and utility cost of the production capacities. The sum of stored biomass $m_{b,i,j}^{SB}$ defines the capacity of the production plant modeled by the capacity variable $\omega_{j,g}$ as shown in equation 4.18. The capacity variable $\omega_{j,g}$ needs to fulfill the upper (equation 4.19) and lower boundaries (see equation 4.20) of the respective capacity intervals, which are defined by the given bases.

$$\sum_{b=1}^{B} \sum_{i=1}^{I} m_{b,i,j}^{SB} = \sum_{g=2}^{G} \omega_{k,g} \qquad \forall j \in J \qquad (4.18)$$

$$\omega_{j,g} \leq n_g \cdot \mu_{j,g} \qquad \forall j \in J \quad \forall g \in 2,...,G \qquad (4.19)$$

$$\omega_{j,g} \geq n_{g-1} \cdot \mu_{j,g} \qquad \forall j \in J \quad \forall g \in 2,...,G \qquad (4.20)$$

For every production site only one capacity interval can be chosen by summarizing the binary variable $\mu_{j,g}$ to maximum 1 as in equation 4.21, while the variable $\mu_{j,g}$ is defined as a binary variable in equation 4.22 .

$$\sum_{g=2}^{G} \mu_{j,g} \leq 1 \qquad \forall j \in J \qquad (4.21)$$

$$\mu_{j,g} \in 0,1 \qquad \forall j \in J \quad \forall g \in G \qquad (4.22)$$

For the remaining decision variables non-negativity constraints need to be implemented as in equation 4.23.

$$m^{B}_{b,i}, m^{SB}_{b,i,j}, m^{PB}_{j}, \omega_{k,g} \geq 0 \qquad \begin{array}{c} \forall b \in B \\ \forall i \in I \\ \forall j \in J \\ \forall g \in G \end{array} \qquad (4.23)$$

4.3 Technical sub-model

In this section, the technical sub-model is introduced. The main in- and output data is depicted in figure 4.4. The approach and the needed data will be explained in detail below.

The technical sub-model provides the technical input data for the integrated model. This includes yields of the processes, energy and utility demand and the overall mass balances. These mass balances are also the basis for the estimation of investments and production cost. In the technical sub-model, the processes of the biorefineries and conversions of pretreated biomass to chemicals are simulated and assessed techno-economically.

At first, relevant technologies, which will be considered in the process simulation, need to be defined. This depends on many factors. One main factor is the considered region, where the biomass conversion plant will be installed. The chosen region may already determine the available biomass as feedstock due to climate, soil and geographical restrictions (see Lewandowski and Wilhelm [205]) as the biomass cultivation is strongly dependent on nutrients, moisture and temperature. The biomass potential has an influence on the chosen technology due to the following reasons: processes are bound to minimum and maximum production capacities; in case only a limited amount of biomass is available, certain technologies may not be feasible.

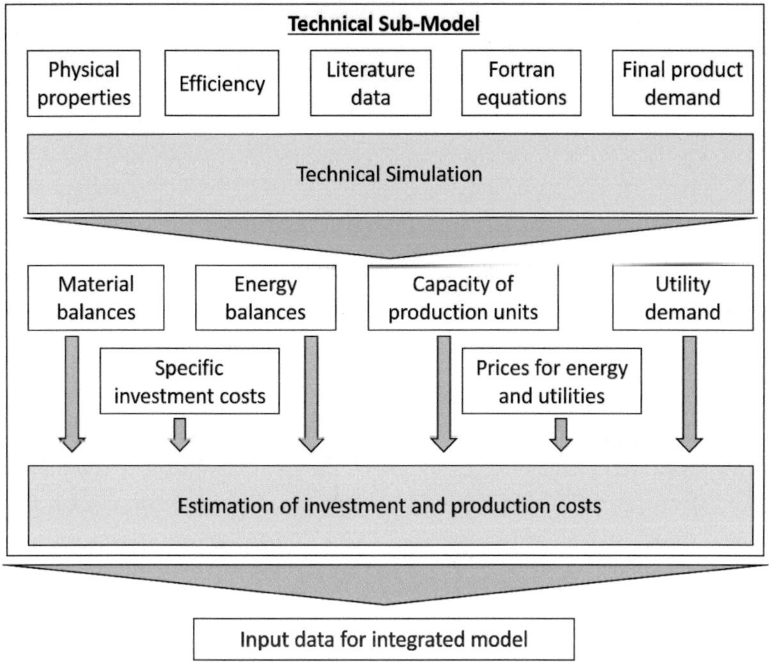

Figure 4.4: Block diagram of the technical sub-model

Some types of biomass are better suitable for certain processes, whilst others can be used more efficiently in other processes. Additionally, the final product, which will be produced from biomass, needs to be defined. Both influence the possible processing routes. By-products might have an influence on the economics of the concept as they also create revenue, however they are not the core decision factor for capacity and technology.

As described by Meyer [227], a technology in this sense does not refer to a single equipment, but a set of technologies. The dimension of the plant and processing parameters, such as temperature, pressure or residence time, need to be defined for the evaluation of material and energy flow balances.

The defined process routes can be assessed based on either literature data or data given by industry. Therefore, each process step as well as the needed equipment is defined.

In a second step, all processes are simulated in AspenPlus® V9 from AspenTech. This flowsheeting program is one of the most known and used software for the design and assessment of production processes. Different properties and stream classes need to be defined depending on the type of process, feedstocks, utilities, etc. AspenPlus® V9 has a user interface and the possibility to include user specific information through FORTRAN, Microsoft Excel, Matlab, etc. interfaces. AspenPlus® V9 includes a large variety of different databanks (see AspenTech [24]). These contain the data for the material characteristics to enable the modelling of thermodynamic and kinetic values. PURE35, SOLIDS, ASPENPCD and INORGANIC are some of these databanks implemented in AspenPlus® V9. These are chosen for the simulation of biorefineries and the conversion of biomass to biochemicals. These databanks include the majority of standard materials such as alcohols, acids, organics, inorganics. As the simulations are based on biomass, the BIODFMS3-databank by the NREL [257] is added. This databank mainly focuses on biorefineries and includes components such as glucose, lignin, cellulose, etc. These components are specific for biomass and need to be implemented in the simulation.

As a first step in simulation development, a component list is defined, which includes all for the simulation relevant chemicals. The material streams are built up as vectors. They include the considered components with the respective mass shares. Energy and enthalpy streams are defined by their direction of flow and amount. All material and energy streams are balanced with their input and output streams to or from a module.

In AspenPlus® V9 different calculation methods can be used to simulate the thermodynamic properties of the material and energy streams. These can be applied to the overall system or just to single streams. Such properties define solid or conventional processes or mixed streams MIXED. Solid streams CISOLID can be implemented with particle size distributions (PSD) as CIPSD. This is relevant for mills, hammers etc. to calculate the energy demand for grinding the feedstock. Solid streams CISOLID cannot be dissolved to liquids, but remain as solid particles in solution. The thermodynamic properties can also be used by approximation systems such as UNIFAC, Redlich-Kwong or NRTL. These approximation systems describe activity coefficients of equilibria.

Humbird et al. [162] assume the reference size of the pretreatment biorefineries to have a capacity of 2200 dry tons per day. Humbird et al. [162] have calculated a biorefinery of that size in detail. The capacity of the conversion plants to biochemicals is provided as parameter for the integrated model, and, hence also for the technical simulations. The production process can be divided into three main steps: pretreatment, conversion and purification. These steps can combined at one location or can be subdivided and done at individual locations. Hence, the processes can be combined and simulated as such as follows:

- pretreatment (P0)
- conversion (P1)
- purification (P2)
- chemical production (P12 (P1+P2))
- total production process (P0 + P12)

Splitting up processes can reduce technical risks and lead to a higher flexibility within the value chain. In contrast, if multiple process steps take place at one location, the system can benefit from heat integration effects and reduce the total energy demand.

The five different process configurations as described above are simulated in AspenPlus® V9 for different biomass types. The chosen biomass influences the yields of the process as, especially the microorganisms in biochemical processes are very sensible to chemical composition. In case of n biomass types $5 \cdot n$ processes are simulated.

For the simulations, literature values are taken into consideration as no experimental or reported data from existing conversion plants are available. Literature values include mostly laboratory results. As no other data is available, these sets will be the basis for the simulations.

This work defines the efficiency of processes $\eta_{p,bp}$ by the amount of the final products and respective by-products $\dot{m}_{(by)product}$ multiplied with their energetic value $H_{u,(by)product}$ related to the biomass energy input $\dot{H}_{fuelinput}$ (see equation 4.24). This approach is mainly applicable for assessing the energetic efficiency of the process.

$$\eta_{p,bp} = \frac{\dot{m}_{product} \cdot H_{u,product} + \sum_{byproducts} \dot{m}_{byproduct} \cdot H_{u,byproduct}}{\dot{H}_{fuelinput}} \tag{4.24}$$

Equation 4.24 is valid beyond energetic efficiencies, and can also be formulated for production yields on a mass balance defined as in equation 4.25.

$$\varepsilon_{p,bp} = \frac{\dot{m}_{product} + \sum_{byproducts} \dot{m}_{byproduct}}{\dot{m}_{fuelinput}} \tag{4.25}$$

Simulation results reveal mass and energy flow balances. These results are used not only for efficiency calculations and utility demand estimation. The material flows define the capacity of each equipment.

In the second step of the techno-economic assessment, the mass and energy flow balances are used for economic calculations. The capacity of each unit is the basis for investment estimations. Literature or industry data is the basis to estimate total plant investment. As described in section 3.6.1, literature data is adapted to different year and size, using price adaption and size degression factors. These factors ensure a more precise investment estimation. The size degression factors includes the needed amount of material for a larger or smaller unit as well as the complexity of the equipment. The price adaption factor such as the CEPCI index, models variable market prices due to inflation, personnel cost etc. In this work, the CEPCI factor is the preferred price adaption factor as it is based on U.S. dollars. Both, the literature data and the case study, are based on U.S. dollars. Hence, the CEPCI should lead to more reality near values. The investment estimations are used as input data for the objective function of the integrated model. The chosen biomass and technology influence the investment essentially.

The material and energy flow balances are the basis for the estimation of production cost (incl. utility and personnel cost). The amount of utilities, energy, biomass, etc. multiplied with the respective cost result in the production cost of the production plant. High utility demands and low yields, leading to high biomass demands, implicate high production cost.

The results of the technical sub-model compare the efficiencies of different biomass and technologies as well as the respective investments and cost. These are used as input data for the integrated model. In detail, the output of the technical sub-model is process yields, utility and biomass demand, investment and production cost.

4.4 Risk sub-model

In this section, the risk sub-model will be presented. The basic setup of the risk sub-model is depicted in figure 4.5. Input for the risk sub-model are the identified risks in biomass value chains. The output of the model, risk cost and scenario definitions, are used as input of the integrated model.

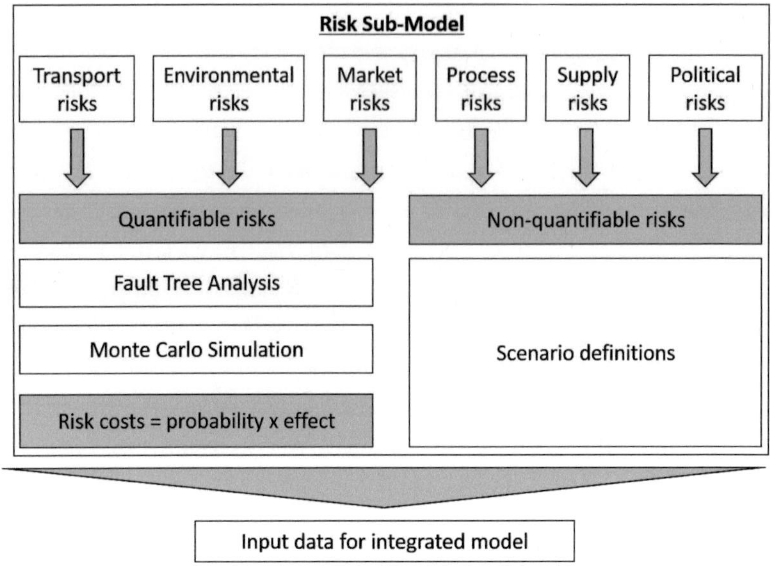

Figure 4.5: Block diagram of the risk sub-model

As described in section 3.7, the risk analysis is performed in three steps:

1. identification
2. assessment
3. mitigation

The **risk identification** is based on extensive literature research. Currently, only few publications could be found that summarize the risks, which can occur in biomass value chains. Bairamzadeh et al. [34] published a large amount of possible risks without going much into detail. Until now, risks are often only partly addressed in literature (see section 3.8.2). The aim of this work is to include as many uncertainties as could be identified. Hence, two different methods are applied to identify relevant risks in this work.

On the one hand, risks, which are named in location planning models under uncertainty (see section 3.8), are used for risk assessment. On the other hand, expert interviews and discussions are performed to include uncertainties, which are not mentioned in literature. Experts are defined by Bogner [53] as people, which – based on specific practical knowledge – create the possibility to structure a certain field sensuous and guiding for others. The experts for this approach should be selected due to their long experience in the field of biomass procurement and processing. They identify risks, which have occurred in their past or which are critical in their opinion. Even though a large variety of risks in biomass value chains can be concluded from literature and these discussions, the list of identified risks (see section 5.5) does not intend to be exhaustive. Depending on the scope of the value chain, the considered region, the biomass, technologies and technology readiness levels etc., different uncertainties can be identified.

The **risk assessment** of the identified uncertainties is the second step. Thus, the likelihood and the consequences are, if applicable, estimated by the following approaches. In general, the risks are distinguished into quantifiable and non-quantifiable uncertainties. Non-quantifiable risks are uncertainties, which cannot be addressed through probability functions. The **quantifiable risks** are assessed by historical data, by physical calculations or other approaches to estimate failures in biomass value chains. Historically, Poisson distribution functions have been used for modelling of independent events, such as in Ayyub [28]. Mathematically, risk occurrence is an integer event, since it can - by nature - only happen or not, e.g. modeled in multiples of $\{0, 1\}$. The Poisson distributions are applied for all quantifiable risks is this work. The distribution functions are modeled by applying **Fault Tree Analysis** to the defined data. This top-down approach is applicable as main events, which can be monetarily quantified, can be defined. These main events are caused by basic events. Multiple risks and uncertainties can be summed up by AND and/or OR gates to the main events. Depending on the identified risks more or less central risks can be defined.

The likelihood of an event describes how often the event occurs within a year. Two approaches exist to deal with the likelihood of an event. The location planning can either be performed by choosing adequate values from the distribution functions such as a "best case", "worst case" and "business-as-usual" scenario. Or the distribution functions are implemented by Monte Carlo Analysis. **Monte Carlo Analysis** will automatically choose random values of the distribution function. The integrated model will run as often as random values from the distribution function were chosen. In case that for all random numbers the same location is chosen by the model, the results are robust and the value chain configuration seems insensible to the modeled risk category. The Monte Carlo Analysis is the more realistic approach, as the variety and randomness of events can be analyzed. Consequently, it is implemented in this work.

After assessing the probabilities of risk events, the consequences need to be estimated. The consequences of the occurring risks shall be calculated using historical prices, the capacity of transport volumes or facilities, data on process failures etc. The consequences of failure are the difference of the current value and the losses, which will occur in case the risks will take place. This might, for instance, be the value of final product, which is destroyed by a fatal transport accident or the additional cost for biomass in case of rising demand or weather effects. In this work, for all clustered risks (done by FTA), the consequences are estimated. The calculation of the consequence cost in this work are based on historic data and the expertise of companies.

The integrated model includes quantifiable risks as risk cost, namely consequences multiplied with the likelihood of an event (see section 3.7.4).

In case the results of the different Monte Carlo runs show deviations in the value chain design, appropriate measures need to be applied to mitigate the uncertainties. These are for instance additional storage capacities. Depending on the source of uncertainty, which leads to non-robust results, other suppliers or transport modes might need to be taken into account at slightly higher cost. The proposition of a **risk mitigation** strategy is the third step in risk analysis.

All uncertainties, which cannot be either estimated by historical values or risks based on given physical restrictions, are assumed to be **non-quantifiable**. They cannot be modeled by Monte Carlo simulations, but need to be taken into account using scenario analysis. The scenario analysis will not provide a prospective of future happenings, but will show, which effect non-quantifiable risks have on the design of the value chain. These scenarios show extreme cases, which might have a large effect on the overall value chain. The definition of the scenarios largely depend on the regions and the identified risks. In section 6.7 possible extreme events are defined and applied to the case studies in this work. The scenarios are calculated for all case studies by the integrated model. The value chain setups might vary from the original setup. The results need to be interpreted to enable reasonable recommendations for the value chain setup. Unlike the risk cost, the scenarios are not directly used as input data for the integrated model. Nevertheless, the definitions lead to changed prices and other parameters. These are varied in the integrated model and lead to interpretable results.

4.5 Integrated model for optimizing the location and logistics of future biochemical plants under consideration of uncertainties

Finally, the integrated model, which combines the results of all sub-models will be presented in this section. The approach of the model is derived from the presented constraints of section 3.9. The general setup of the integrated model is depicted in figure 4.6.

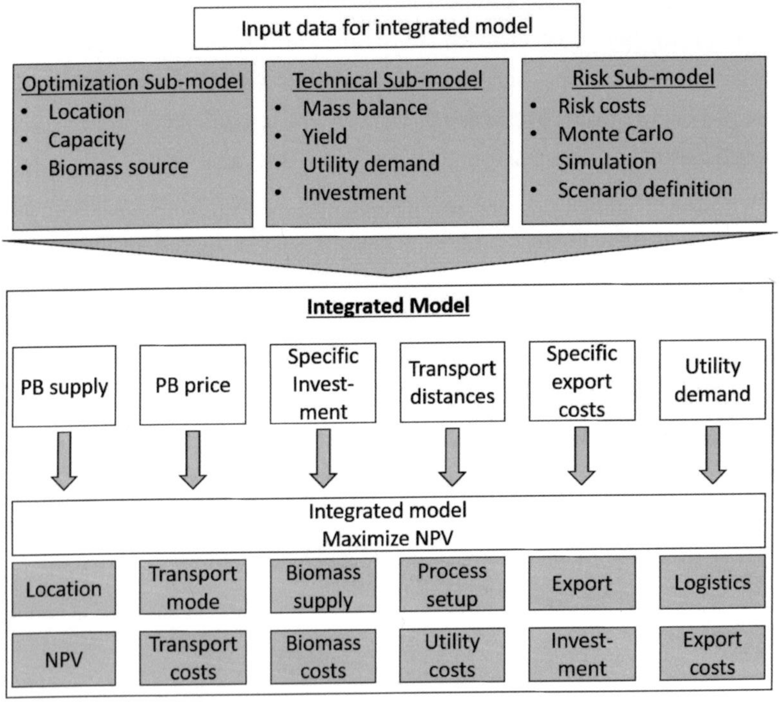

Figure 4.6: Block diagram of the integrated model

The integrated model provides decision support for operators and companies by estimating possible locations and the respective logistics of future plants for the conversion of pretreated biomass to biochemicals under consideration of uncertainties.

Multiple biomass are considered for producing multiple final products in a single production process. During conversion of biomass, often not only a single product but multiple byproducts are produced. The conversion yield depends on the utilized biomass and the process. The products can either be produced directly from pretreated biomass or via an intermediate. The production of the final products can be split up into two process steps: the production of the intermediate and the following processing to the final products. These can either occur at the same location or at different production sites. Accordingly, the model is defined as a two-stage production process. On the one hand, the benefit of producing the final product in a single process at one location is the integration of heat in the process and the minimized handling activities. On the other hand, separating the process steps leads to an increased flexibility and might be beneficial if the downstream processing is included in existing petro-chemical plants. This work assumes that a single company only plans to build up biochemical production plants one at a time to reduce the technical risk. Hence, multiple production plants are omitted.

Depending on the feedstock and product, transport restrictions on certain transport modes exist. These influence the logistics and chosen transport modes. In order to interchange between transport modes, multi-modal transport and transshipment is included in the model such as in Rudi et al. [309], Yie et al. [392] and Marufuzzaman et al. [217]. To change the transport mode, transport hubs are included in the model as additional locations.

Due to the above presented constraints of multi-modal transport and two-stage production, storage of products is inevitable. In case the handling of feedstock and products occurs stepwise, storage is needed to buffer amounts due to handling restrictions. Hence, the inclusion of storage capacity is necessary. The storage capacity is set fix by the production plant operators. The conversion facility can be included in existing infrastructure. Consequently, this work assumes that the storage capacities at existing production sites.

The final products can be transported to multiple markets, which are either locally or worldwide. Hence, also export ports as well as the export share per continent are included in the model. A more detailed consideration of customer is neglected. The distribution of biochemicals to the final customer is not biomass specific.

The integrated model is implemented in a decision support system. It includes the modeling in GAMS IDE 24.6.1 and solving with the CPLEX solver by IBM. For integrating the needed input data, a VBA.net user interface is created to facilitate the exchange of data. Therefore, different spreadsheets in Microsoft Excel need to be designed to handle the input parameters. The results of the three sub-models are included by setting them as input parameters in the Excel tables.

The model is built up of sets for transport, locations, feedstock, processes, utilities and risks. In the following, the sets and subsets are defined for the implementation of the integrated model. The set of edges of the network is defined by the nodes N. The network is represented by the transport of a feedstock/ intermediate/ product $f \in F$ with the transport mode $t \in T$ on a link between two nodes. The feedstock/ intermediate/ product f is characterized by the processing step $p \in P$. Possible products within the value chain are pretreated biomass $F_b \subset F \setminus (F_{int} \wedge F_z)$, intermediates $F_{int} \subset F \setminus (F_z \wedge F_b)$ and final products $F_z \subset F \setminus (F_{int} \wedge F_b)$. Biomass and intermediates are summarized to non final products $F_{nf} \subset F \setminus F_z$. Intermediate and final products are defined as $F_{iz} \subset F \setminus F_b$. The capacity H of the plant is set by a single, predefined final product $F_{fp} \subset F_z$. All other byproducts are defined as $F_{bp} \subset F_z \setminus F_{fp}$ These products are produced in different production settings. The process can either occur at a single location by the process $P12$ or can be split up in two sub-processes: $P1$ to produce an intermediate F_{int} and afterwards the final products F_z in $P2$. Hence, the final products can be produced in $P_z \subset P \setminus P1$. Similarly, pretreated biomass can be processed in $P_b \subset P \setminus P2$, solely at one site as well. The intermediate is produced and converted to the final products in $P_i \subset P \setminus P12$.

The edge between two nodes is described by the doublet (i, j) with $i, j \in N$. The supply nodes $N_s \subset N \setminus (N_t \wedge N_x)$ and destinations $N_d \subset N_{xd} \setminus N_x$ characterize the scope of the network. The origins represent the suppliers of pretreated biomass and destinations the export ports. The amount of goods can also be transported via transport hubs $N_h \subset N \setminus (N_s \wedge N_{dx} \wedge N_l)$. All production locations are defined by $N_l \subset N \setminus (N_{si} \wedge N_{dx})$. The intermediates $f \in F_{int}$ are produced at locations $N_i \subset N_l \setminus N_f$. The locations, where the final products $f \in F_z$ are produced in process $p \in P_z$ are defined as $N_f \subset N \setminus (N_h \wedge N_{dx} \wedge N_s)$. The final products are then transported either to hubs or directly to the export port $N_{hd} \subset (N_h \wedge N_d)$. All locations that the intermediate product can be transported to are defined by node $N_{ti} \subset N \setminus (N_{si} \wedge N_i)$. Amongst them are also the locations before the product is exported $N_{hf} \subset (N_f \wedge N_h)$. The different production locations of the intermediate product and the final products as well as the hubs can have distinctive sources. They are defined as follows. The sources of intermediate products are $N_{si} \subset (N_h \wedge N_s)$. Final products can be received from $N_{sf} \subset N \setminus (N_{dx} \wedge N_f)$. Hubs can be used for transshipment from many different sources $N_{sh} \subset N \setminus (N_s \wedge N_l \wedge N_{dx})$. The chemicals can either be used locally or exported. The nodes of the final utilization are defined by $N_x \subset N \setminus (N_t \wedge N_s)$. The total of export ports and the export locations are represented by the nodes $N_{dx} \subset N \setminus N_{sf}$. All nodes that can be approached after the supplier are defined as transfer nodes $N_t \subset N \setminus N_s$.

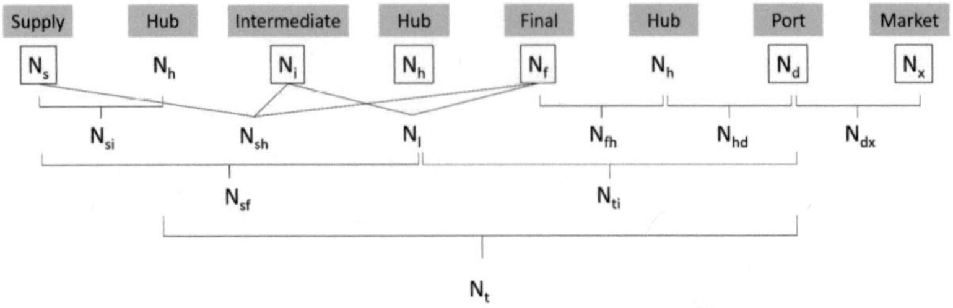

Figure 4.7: Subsets of the integrated model

The locations in the considered region without export are presented by $N_{st} \subset N \setminus N_x$. The correlations of the location subsets are depicted in figure 4.7.

Based on the above defined configurations of the model, the following decision variables $m_{f,t,i,j,p}$ include all mass streams within the value chain. These include:

- mass flow of the pretreated biomass from the supplier to the production plant
- mass flow of a possible intermediate product from one facility to another
- mass flow of the final products from a location to the export port
- mass flow of the export share of the final products to the final market

In table 4.2 all utilized sets, parameters and variables of the integrated model are displayed.

Table 4.2: Sets, parameters and variables of the integrated model

Parameter	Description	Unit
Sets		
$f, f' \in \{1,...,F\}$	feedstock	
$t, t' \in \{1,...,T\}$	transport mode	
$i, j, i' \in \{1,...,N\}$	possible locations	
$p \in \{1,...,P\}$	process	
$r \in \{1,...,R\}$	risk	
$u \in \{1,...,U\}$	utilities	
Parameters		
General parameters		
$d_{t,i,j}$	distance between location i and j with transport mode t	$[m]$
M	Big M, sufficient large number	$[-]$
Biomass and products		
$A_{f,i}$	supply of pretreated biomass f from supplier i	$[t/a]$
Economic parameters		
σ	annuity factor	$[-]$
$c_{f,t}^{T,fix}$	distance independent transport cost of feedstock f with transport t	$[\$/t]$
$c_{f,t}^{T,var}$	distance dependent transport cost of feedstock f with transport t	$[\$/(t \cdot m)]$
$c_{i,u}^{ut}$	cost of utility u at production location i	$[\$/t]$
$c_{f,i}^{PB}$	cost of pretreated biomass f at supply location i	$[\$/t]$
$c_{f,p}^{inv}$	specific investment for converting feedstock f in process p	$[\$/t]$

Table 4.2: Sets, parameters and variables of the integrated model

Parameter	Description	Unit
p_f^{FP}	price for final products f	$[\$/t]$
$c_{f,i,j}^{ex}$	export cost of a final product f from port i to destination continent j	$[\$/t]$
c_p^S	specific storage cost depending on the process p	$[\$/t]$
Process		
H	produced amount of defined final product	$[t/a]$
$\alpha_{f,f',p}$	yield of feedstock f to product f' in process p	$[-]$
$m_{f,p,u}^{ut}$	amount of utility u depending on feedstock f and process p	$[t_{ut}/t_{PB}]$
m_p^S	storage capacity depending on process p	$[t/a]$
Risk parameters		
$\pi_{f,t,i,j,p,r}$	probability of risk for each feedstock/ intermediate/ product f, transport mode t, edge i,j, process p and risk r	$[\%]$
$c_{f,t,i,j,p,r}^{risk}$	specific risk cost for each feedstock/ intermediate/ product f, transport mode t, edge i,j, process p and risk r	$[\$/t]$
Demand		
$\gamma_{f,i'}$	export share to final destination	$[-]$
Variables		
Continuous variables		
R^{FP}	total revenue of the final products	$[\$/a]$
C^x	cost of the type x (i.e. biomass, transport, investment, utilities, export, storage, risk)	$[\$/a]$
$m_{f,t,i,j,p}$	mass flow of each feedstock/ intermediate/ product f, transport mode t, edge i,j, process p	$[t/a]$

Table 4.2: Sets, parameters and variables of the integrated model

Parameter	Description	Unit
$u_{f,t,i,j,p,u}$	utility cost for each feedstock/ intermediate/ product f, transport mode t, edge i,j, process p and utility u	$[t/a]$
$r_{f,t,i,j,p,r}$	risk cost for each feedstock/ intermediate/ product f, transport mode t, edge i,j, process p and risk r	$[\$/a]$
Binary variables		
$y_{f,t,i,j,p}$	binary variable	$[0,1]$

4.5.1 Objective function

The objective of the model is to provide decision support for the setup of the overall value chain from biomass pretreatment to the export of the final products. Therefore, the net present value (NPV) of the value chain is maximized as presented in equation 4.26. The revenues of the final products R^P are subtracted by the cost for pretreated biomass C^B, transport C^T, utilities C^U, risks C^R, storage C^S and export C^E to calculate the yearly payments. The NPV is calculated by multiplying yearly payments with the annuity factor σ and the investment C^I is subtracted from them. The general approach of the NPV calculation is presented in section 4.2.2.

$$NPV = \left(R^P - C^B - C^T - C^U - C^R - C^S - C^E\right) \cdot \sigma - C^I \tag{4.26}$$

The revenues R^P of the value chain as in equation 4.27 are defined as the multiplication of the price per product p_f^{FP} with the total amount of finally sold products $m_{f,t,i,j,p}$.

$$R^P = \sum_{f=1}^{F_z} \sum_{t=1}^{T} \sum_{i=1}^{N_f} \sum_{j=1}^{N_{hd}} \sum_{p=1}^{P} p_f^{FP} \cdot m_{f,t,i,j,p} \tag{4.27}$$

The cost for pretreated biomass C^B include the processing cost as well as the price of the biomass. As different types of biomass occur in various regions and can result from contracts with certain suppliers, the cost $c_{f,i}^{PB}$ are modelled in dependence on the pretreated biomass f and location i (see equation 4.28).

$$C^B = \sum_{f=1}^{F_b} \sum_{t=1}^{T} \sum_{i=1}^{N_s} \sum_{j=1}^{N_t} \sum_{p=1}^{P} c_{f,i}^{PB} \cdot m_{f,t,i,j,p} \tag{4.28}$$

Transport cost C^T in equation 4.26 include the transport cost for pretreated biomass, intermediates, and final products depending on the transport mode. If all process steps are carried out at one location no transport of an intermediate product and, consequently, no transport cost occur. The total transport cost are made up of a fix and a variable cost share. The fix transport cost $c_{f,t}^{T,fix}$ are independent of the distance. These include cost for handling, loading, waiting times etc. The distance-dependent variable cost $c_{f,t}^{T,var}$ cover energy (gasoline) and personnel cost. The distances $d_{t,i,j}$ between i and j display the distances between sources, possible production locations, and sinks. Overall, the various products in the supply chain restrict different transport modes, required insulation of trucks or similar. Therefore, the transport cost also depend on the transported product f and the transport mode t. The total transport cost are calculated as presented in equation 4.29.

$$C^T = \sum_{f=1}^{F}\sum_{t=1}^{T}\sum_{i=1}^{N_{st}}\sum_{j=1}^{N_{st}}\sum_{p=1}^{P} m_{f,t,i,j,p} \cdot \left(c_{f,t}^{T,fix} + c_{f,t}^{T,var} \cdot d_{t,i,j}\right) \tag{4.29}$$

The investment C^I is based on the specific investment $c_{f,p}^{inv}$ per ton of input. The capacity of the plant is represented by the mass flow of the source $m_{f,t,i,j,p}$, the process p, and the chosen biomass f. The feed input and yield of the process influences the needed technologies, plant operations and the efficiency of the plant. These have an effect on the mass and energy balances, and, hence, on the dimensions of the production plant. Consequently, the investment is calculated as follows in equation 4.30.

$$C^I = \sum_{f=1}^{F_{nf}}\sum_{t=1}^{T}\sum_{i=1}^{N_{sf}}\sum_{j=1}^{N_l}\sum_{p=1}^{P} c_{f,p}^{inv} \cdot m_{f,t,i,j,p} \tag{4.30}$$

For processing biomass, utilities such as electricity, fresh and waste water, heat, enzymes, etc. are needed. This work assumes that the necessary equipment for converting raw materials such as oil, gas, coal, etc. into energy are available on site, so that no investment for this need to be taken into account. Hence, the utility cost C^U are the sum of all specific utility cost $u_{f,t,i,j,p,u}$ as presented in equation 4.31. The specific utility cost are calculated as in equation 4.42.

$$C^U = \sum_{f=1}^{F_{nf}}\sum_{t=1}^{T}\sum_{i=1}^{N_{sf}}\sum_{j=1}^{N_l}\sum_{p=1}^{P}\sum_{u=1}^{U} u_{f,t,i,j,p,u} \tag{4.31}$$

The total risk cost C^R are the sum of each risk $r_{f,t,i,j,p,r}$, that can occur on one edge of the value chain. The calculation of the risks has been described in detail in section 4.4.

$$C^R = \sum_{f=1}^{F}\sum_{t=1}^{T}\sum_{i=1}^{N_{st}}\sum_{j=1}^{N_{st}}\sum_{p=1}^{P}\sum_{r=1}^{R} r_{f,t,i,j,p,r} \tag{4.32}$$

Due to the two stage process and the risk minimization, storage is implemented at the production plant. At each location, where production occurs the feedstock as well as intermediate or final products are stored at the same location. Hence, for calculating the total storage cost, the specific storage cost $c^s_{i,p}$ are multiplied with the total amount of stored product m^s_p as in equation 4.33 and the binary factor $y_{f,t,i,j,p}$ for the total amount of locations.

$$C^S = \sum_{f=1}^{F_{iz}} \sum_{t=1}^{T} \sum_{i=1}^{N_l} \sum_{j=1}^{N_{ti}} \sum_{p=1}^{P} c^s_p \cdot m^s_p \cdot y_{f,t,i,j,p} \tag{4.33}$$

The final products are exported to different markets worldwide. Depending on the export port and the final destination, the export cost vary. Consequently, the total export cost C^E are calculated by multiplying the specific export cost $c^{ex}_{f,i,j}$ with the total amount of final product $m_{f,t,i,j,p}$, which is transported from the export port to the final destination (see equation 4.34).

$$C^E = \sum_{f=1}^{F_z} \sum_{t=1}^{T} \sum_{i=1}^{N_d} \sum_{j=1}^{N_x} \sum_{p=1}^{P_{fp}} c^{ex}_{f,i,j} \cdot m_{f,t,i,j,p} \tag{4.34}$$

4.5.2 Constraints

In the following, the restrictions such as material and energy balances of processes, transportation hubs and export ports are defined. These constraints need to be fulfilled to enable a reasonable biomass value chain.

4.5.2.1 Definition of pretreated biomass supply and demand for final product

The available amount of pretreated biomass depends on the supplier. As each supplier utilizes different biomass types and different processes, the maximum available amount $A_{f,i}$ of pretreated biomass is defined by the feedstock f and location i. This work assumes that there is only one supplier per location. Therefore, the usable amount of pretreated biomass for biochemical production is restricted by the maximum capacity of the supplier $A_{f,i}$ as presented in equation 4.35.

$$\sum_{t=1}^{T}\sum_{j=1}^{N_t}\sum_{p=1}^{P} m_{f,t,i,j,p} \leq A_{f,i} \qquad \begin{array}{l}\forall f \in F_b\\ \forall i \in N_s\end{array} \qquad (4.35)$$

As the chemical industry is bound to customers, the maximum capacity of a production site H, based on a predefined final product, is set fix by the company. Not only the customers influence the production amounts of a facility, but also economic parameters, technical risk minimization etc. Equation 4.36 defines the capacity restriction.

$$\sum_{f=1}^{F_{fp}}\sum_{t=1}^{T}\sum_{j=1}^{N_{hd}} m_{f,t,i,j,p} = \sum_{f=1}^{F_{fp}}\sum_{t=1}^{T}\sum_{j=1}^{N_{hd}} H \cdot y_{f,t,i,j,p} \qquad \begin{array}{l}\forall i \in N_f\\ \forall p \in P_z\end{array} \qquad (4.36)$$

Depending on the export location, a share of the produced amount $m_{f,t,i,j,p}$ will be transported to different export destinations and, hence, to different export ports. The share per export destination is defined by the user as $\gamma_{f,i'}$. This calculates the demand of each final destination in equation 4.37.

$$\sum_{t=1}^{T}\sum_{i=1}^{N_d}\sum_{p=1}^{P_{fp}} m_{f,t,i,j,p} = \sum_{t=1}^{T}\sum_{i=1}^{N_f}\sum_{j=1}^{N_{hd}}\sum_{p=1}^{P_{fp}} \gamma_{f,i'} \cdot m_{f,t,j,i',p} \qquad \begin{array}{l}\forall f \in F_z\\ \forall i' \in N_x\end{array} \qquad (4.37)$$

4.5.2.2 Modeling of the production processes

The process can be split in two stages. These process steps can either occur at the same location or be combined in one production facility.

In equation 4.38, the production of an intermediate product F_{int} is modeled. Incoming biomass $m_{f,t,i,j,p}$ can be converted by a yield factor $\alpha_{f,f',p}$ to an intermediate f'. This intermediate is the produced, but not yet purified biochemical.

$$\sum_{f=1}^{F_b}\sum_{t=1}^{T}\sum_{i=1}^{N_s}\alpha_{f,f',p}\cdot m_{f,t,i,j,p}=\sum_{t=1}^{T}\sum_{i=1}^{N_{hd}}\cdot m_{f',t,j,i',p'} \qquad \begin{array}{r}\forall f'\in F_{int}\\ \forall j\in N_{int}\\ \forall p,p'\in P_i\end{array} \tag{4.38}$$

In equation 4.39, the conversion of either biomass f or an intermediate to the purified biochemical and byproducts is defined by the yield of the process $\alpha_{f,f',p}$ and the mass streams $m_{f,t,i,j,p}$. In case biomass is directly converted to the purified final products, then equation 4.38 is skipped.

$$\sum_{f=1}^{F_{nf}}\sum_{t=1}^{T}\sum_{i=1}^{N_{sf}}\alpha_{f,f',p}\cdot m_{f,t,i,j,p}=\sum_{t=1}^{T}\sum_{i=1}^{N_{hd}}m_{f',t,j,i',p'} \qquad \begin{array}{r}\forall f'\in F_z\\ \forall j\in N_f\\ \forall p\in P_{sf}\end{array} \tag{4.39}$$

To minimize the risk of new technologies, a company would start with a single production facility. Consequently, the number of locations for final production is restricted to one.

$$\sum_{t=1}^{T}\sum_{i=1}^{N_f}\sum_{j=1}^{N_{hd}}\sum_{p=1}^{P_z}y_{f,t,i,j,p}=1 \qquad \forall f\in F_z \tag{4.40}$$

$$\tag{4.41}$$

The utility consumption is strongly related to the utilized biomass type, the production location and the process. The utility cost are composed of the specific price for a unit of utility $c^{ut}_{i,u}$ and are multiplied with the needed amount of utility $m^{ut}_{f,p,u}$ per ton of feedstock $m_{f,t,i,j,p}$ as in equation 4.42.

This work assumes that all residues are converted into chemicals and no excess electricity is produced.

$$u(f,t,i,j,p,u) = c^{ut}_{i,u} \cdot m^{ut}_{f,p,u} \cdot m_{f,t,i,j,p} \qquad \begin{array}{l} \forall f \in F_{nf} \\ \forall t \in T \\ \forall i \in N_l \\ \forall j \in N_{sf} \\ \forall p \in P \\ \forall u \in U \end{array} \tag{4.42}$$

4.5.2.3 Transport within the value chain

The model includes multi-modal transport of all products within the value chain. To change the transport mode, hubs are needed where the feedstock is transferred from one mode to another. The hubs are restricted by mass balances and the necessity to change the transport mode. The total mass input in a certain transport mode t needs to leave the hub on another transport mode t'.

$$\sum_{i=1}^{N_{sh}} m_{f,t,i,j,p} = \sum_{i=1}^{N_t} m_{f,t',j,i,p} \qquad \begin{array}{l} \forall f \in F \\ \forall t,t' \in T \\ \forall j \in N_h \\ \forall p \in P \end{array} \tag{4.43}$$

To fulfill material balances the amount, which is transported to the export port also needs to be shipped to the final destination (see equation 4.44).

$$\sum_{f=1}^{F} \sum_{t=1}^{T} \sum_{i=1}^{I} m_{f,t,i,j,p} = \sum_{f=1}^{F} \sum_{t=1}^{T} \sum_{j=1}^{J} m_{f,t,j,i',p} \qquad \begin{array}{l} \forall (i,j,i') \in N \\ \forall p \in P \end{array} \tag{4.44}$$

Risks $r_{f,t,i,j,p,r}$ are estimated by the probability $\pi_{f,t,i,j,p,r}$ of an event multiplied with the cost effect $c^{risk}_{f,t,i,j,p,r}$ of that risk (see equation 4.45).

$$r_{f,t,i,j,p,r} = c^{risk}_{f,t,i,j,p,r} \cdot \pi_{f,t,i,j,p,r} \cdot m_{f,t,i,j,p} \qquad \begin{array}{r} \forall f \in F \\ \forall t \in T \\ \forall (i,j) \in N \\ \forall p \in P \\ \forall r \in R \end{array} \tag{4.45}$$

The variables need to fulfill the non-negativity constraint, as no negative amounts can be transported.

$$m_{f,t,i,j,p} \geq 0 \qquad \begin{array}{r} \forall f \in F \\ \forall t \in T \\ \forall (i,j) \in N \\ \forall p \in P \end{array} \tag{4.46}$$

According to Rudi et al. [309], the Big M-method can be used to ensure that in case of at least one unit of feedstock or product the binary variable $y_{f,t,i,j,p}$ has the value one.

$$m_{f,t,i,j,p} \leq y_{f,t,i,j,p} \cdot M \qquad \begin{array}{r} \forall f \in F \\ \forall t \in T \\ \forall (i,j) \in N \\ \forall p \in P \end{array} \tag{4.47}$$

4.6 Conclusion

In this chapter, the approach for the evaluation of biomass value chains from the biomass source to the distribution of the final products was presented. Therefore, the integrated model with the input of three sub-models: optimization, technical and risk sub-model has been described.

The optimization sub-model has been developed to optimize locations of possible future biorefineries. These biorefineries pretreat biomass to sugar syrup, pyrolysis slurry or other pretreated biomass. The model optimizes not only locations but also the capacity of the biorefineries. These locations are used as supplier input for the integrated model.

The production processes are assessed according to the technical sub-model. Therefore, the processes are simulated in AspenPlus®. As a result, mass and energy balances are used to calculate needed input materials, the capacities of single units and energy demands. The output of the technical sub-model provides the input data for the conversion yields as well as investment and production cost estimations. These in turn are important input data for the integrated model.

Many risks and uncertainties occur in every biomass value chain. They are distinguished in quantifiable and non-quantifiable uncertainties. Quantifiable risks are implemented as a cost term in the integrated model and are assessed by Monte Carlo Analysis. Non-quantifiable risks cannot be fully determined and are addressed by scenario analysis (see section 5.6) of the integrated model.

Finally, the integrated model includes all the above presented input data as well as additional data. Existing pretreatment plants, export ports, multiple transport types are just examples for the above described constraints. As a result of the integrated model a single location for the production of biochemicals from pretreated biomass or two single locations in case of a split up of the process is defined. The chosen transport route is calculated including the export to overseas.

5 Determination of input parameters

In the previous chapter, the two stage approach for optimizing value chains for the production of biobased chemicals has been developed. As a result, locations and logistics of these value chains can be estimated. To prove the applicability of the developed approach, it is tested on three case studies. This model is applied to the value chain for the biochemical production of butanol and succinic acid as well as the thermochemical production of ethylene from syngas in the United States.

At first, in section 5.1 the considered biomass (corn, sugar cane, sorghum and their residues) are presented and possible locations for future conversion plants are defined. The possible locations are also a results of the optimization sub-model. Hence, the input data for the optimization are presented in section 5.1. The three case studies include either biochemical and thermochemical pathways. The biochemical processes are built up of preprocessing, depending on the biomass, conversion via fermentation and downstream processing. The preprocessing technologies include corn wet milling, sugar cane milling, sorghum milling as well as dilute acid pretreatment of agricultural residues. These processes are described in section 5.2. Thermochemical pathways preprocess lignocellulosic biomass by pyrolysis. The pyrolysis products are converted by gasification and synthesis to ethylene. The detailed process descriptions are presented in section 5.3. For the technical sub-model input data such as conversion yields, investment and production cost are needed. These are described in the respective sections.

For modeling the optimization sub-model as well as the integrated model logistical parameters are necessary. These include details on transport, storage and intermodal hubs as well as the respective cost. The data is presented in section 5.4. Not only the locations of processing sites are critical, but also the export hubs for the integrated model. Additionally, the transport distances are crucial for location planning. The respective data is presented in the same section.

A main aspect of this approach is the consideration of risks and uncertainties. These are evaluated in the risk sub-model. To understand the impact and likelihood of the risks, they need to be explained. Therefore, the considered risks for the case studies are defined in section 5.5. They have been clustered into transport, process, environmental, political, supply and market risks.

Finally, the non-quantifiable risks are addressed by a scenario analysis. These constructed scenarios are explained in section 5.6. Objective of the scenarios is to show the influence of extreme events on the location and logistics of the case studies.

The considered case studies are presented in figure 5.1. Six different biomass (corn, corn stover, sugar cane, sugar cane bagasse, sorghum and sorghum bagasse) are preprocessed. Corn wet milling, sorghum and sugar cane milling of first generation biomass as well as dilute acid pretreatment and pyrolysis of second generation biomass are the considered preprocessing technologies. Fermentation of sugar syrup to butanol (case study 1) or succinic acid (case study 2) are evaluated as biochemical production processes. The products are purified in downstream processes such as gas stripping with distillation or crystallization. Gasification (case study 3) of the pyrolysis products and the following synthesis to ethylene is the applied thermochemical pathway. Finally, all products are sold in the market. The market is either locally in the United States or parts are exported to Asia or Europe. Lignocellulosic biomass can only be transported by truck. Rail and truck transport is valid for pretreated biomass (sugar syrup and pyrolysis slurry). Due to technical difficulties, the barge transport of these products is omitted. All three transport modes (rail, truck, barge) can be used for the intermediate and final products.

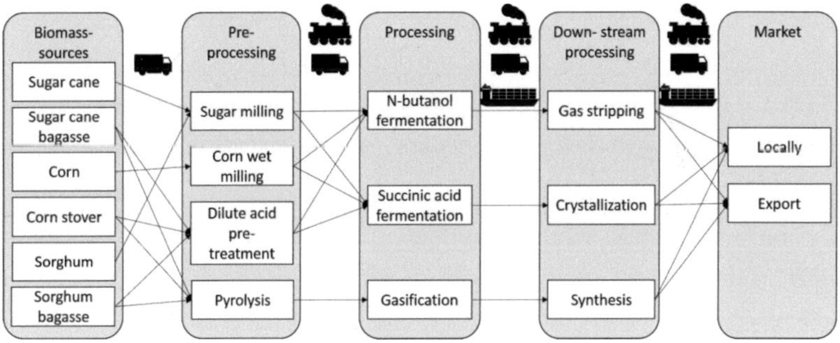

Figure 5.1: Definition of considered biomass value chains in the case study

5.1 Definition of biomass potentials and locations

The needed data regarding the supply for the optimization sub-model and the integrated model is presented in this section. The biomass potentials are estimated as feedstock supply basis for the optimization sub-model. The biomass potentials define the supply restrictions, which relate to the capacity and location of pretreatment plants. The focus of the optimization sub-model is on the residues of three major biomass in the United States. Corn, sugar cane and sorghum are the major crops in the United States (see USDA [244]). These are converted either to sugar syrup, which can be used in multiple applications such as bioethanol production or food industry or to pyrolysis products. Corn stover, bagasse, as well as sorghum residues are considered as crop residues. The input data for estimating biomass potentials is presented in section 5.1.1. The biomass residue cost are essential to estimate the capacities of biorefineries. As currently no market exists, the prices need to be estimated beforehand. The necessary input data for this is presented in section 5.1.2.

The calculated locations of biorefineries are the result of the optimization sub-model and are presented in section 5.1.3. These are possible suppliers in the integrated model. Additionally, existing pretreatment plants of first generation biomass are presented as possible suppliers. These are based on the processes of wet milling and sugar milling (see section 5.1.4). Objective of the integrated model is to propose near-optimal locations for the production of biochemicals. Hence, these considered possible locations are discussed in section 5.1.5.

5.1.1 Estimation of biomass potentials in the United States

At first, the considered biomass types in the United States are defined and their theoretic potentials identified. In the following, corn, corn stover, sugar cane, sugar cane bagasse, sorghum and sorghum bagasse are described and their chemical composition presented.

Corn

The following information is published by the US Department for Agriculture (USDA) [346]. Corn is the major crop in the U.S. and planted on more than 90 million acres of land. It is mainly cultivated in the so called "Corn Belt" in the north west, in the Heartland region. In general, corn is used in food, feed and industrial sector. In future, larger corn farms of more than 500 acres are favored. The number of small farms is declining. The technology developments in gene manipulation, fertilizers, machinery etc. have led to an increase of yields. Corn is also one of the main feedstocks for bioethanol production in the U.S. Due to the rising demand for corn, the prices rose significantly. Corn does not only have its customers in the feed and biofuel industry, but is also used for human consumption. Corn wet mills produce high-fructose corn syrup, glucose, and dextrose as well as starch and corn oil. Dry mills process corn into cereal, flour and corn meal. The price of corn is about 192 $ per ton (see Meade et al. [221]). According to Wu et al. [391], corn is composed of 61 % starch, 3.8 % corn oil, 8 % proteins, 11.2 % fiber and 16 % moisture.

The corn yields have increased significantly in the past year even though the corn acreages have remained more or less constant. Weather, GMO corn and other aspects influence corn yields. How strong the growth of corn yields is, is depicted in figure 5.2.

Corn stover

Corn stover is the residue of corn harvesting and includes stalks, leaves and cobs that remain in the field. Formerly, farmers have left the residues in the field for soil revitalization and erosion prevention. Due to developments in fertilizing and machinery, a larger amount of corn stover can be utilized for other purposes, such as the biofuel industry. Corn stover is a lignocellulosic biomass and is composed of cellulose, hemicellulose and lignin. The composition is presented in table 5.1. Corn and corn stover are harvested in autumn but are stored for a continuous processing throughout the year in wet mills or biorefineries.

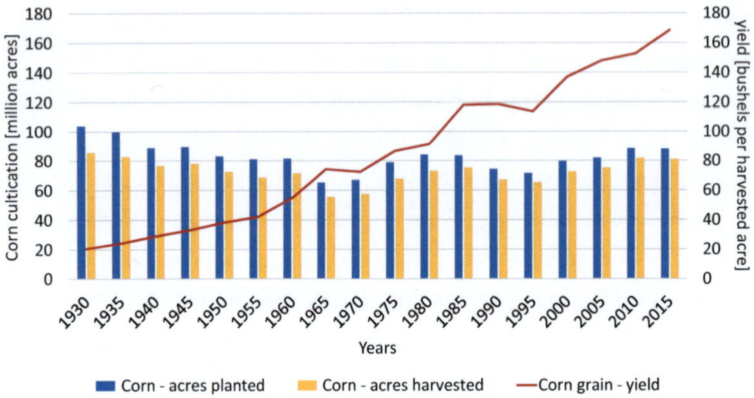

Figure 5.2: Production areas and yield of corn in the U.S. (USDA, ESR [315])

Sugar cane

Sugar cane is a tall perennial grass, which grows in tropical and subtropical climates. As sugar cane has a high moisture content, it needs to be processed as soon as possible as the sugar deteriorates over time. Sugar cane is mostly cultivated in the south of the U.S., in Louisiana, Florida and small parts of Alabama and Texas. The sugar cane of Hawaii is neglected in this study as the transport overseas is unlikely due to high transport cost. In the past thirty years, the acreages have increased from 704,000 to 885,000 acres. The sugar production rose from 2.91 million short tons, raw value (STRV) to 3.623 million STRV (see USDA [229]). The raw cane sugar price is provided by the New York Board of Trade as it is based on the price of sugar, which is delivered to New York. Within only three years the raw sugar price has ranged from 28.82 cents per pound in 2013 to 55.81 cents per pound in 2011 (see USDA [229]).

Cane field trash

When harvesting sugar cane the stalks are separated from impurities such as mud or stones. Cane field trash can either be separated directly on the field and transported on own trucks or the whole crop can be harvested (see Thorburn et al. [348]). The use of cane field trash also brings problems in the farming operations. The residue blanket normally has positive effect as it among others prevents soil erosion and water evaporation. But it also benefits the fire hazard prevention and decreases the pest infection risk. About 70 to 80 % of the harvest is left on the field, the remaining share is transported to the mill as additional energy source. Cane trash as advantages compared to bagasse: it has a similar calorific value at a lower moisture content. Cane field trash consists of tops and leaves. The average lignin content is about 17 %. Cellulose makes up for about 38 % and hemicellulose for 28 %. The share of extractives is about 13 % and ash accounts for about 4 % (see Smithers [328]).

Sugar cane bagasse

According to Pandey et al. [276], sugar cane bagasse is a major by-product in the sugar cane industry. It is composed of about 50 % cellulose, 25 % hemicellulose and 25 % lignin. The detailed composition is presented in table 5.1. Bagasse is the residue of cane stalks, which remains after sugar cane crushing and juice extraction. Currently, it is used for energy provision for the crushing processes in the sugar mill by firing it in boilers directly at the production site.

Sorghum

Sorghum seems to be an attractive crop due to its high yield potential, rapid maturation, high water-use efficiency, and drought tolerance (see Turhollow et al. [360]). Contrary, corn for example is sensitive to moisture stress, regardless of the growth stage. Sorghum is an annual grass. It is mostly grown in the Great Plains states. Kansas and Texas are the states with the highest concentration (see Kramer and Ross [187]). Sorghum consists of the sorghum head, which is mostly grains. According to Wu et al. [391] it is composed of about 70 % starch, 3.5 % oil, 11.9 % proteins, 1.8 % fibers and 1.8 % ash. The grains can be processes by dry and wet-milling processes such as corn (see Wall [377]). Additionally, the sorghum stem has a high concentration of sugars and can be compared to sugar cane.

Sorghum bagasse

Just as sugar cane bagasse, sorghum bagasse is the residue from sorghum extraction, whilst producing sorghum juice. The detailed composition is presented in table 5.1. It has a higher protein content than sugar cane bagasse and is, therefore, more suitable as animal feed (see Eggleston et al. [104]. Sugar cane and sorghum bagasse are both currently more profitable for energy conversion than for other applications (see Bennett and Anex [44]). Wright et al. [389] have analyzed the stability and different usage of sweet sorghum bagasse.

Table 5.1: Composition of biomass residues

Biomass Source	Corn stover [200]	Sorghum bagasse [16]	Sugar cane bagasse [303]
Cellulose	37.5	40.3	37
Hemicellulose	26.1	21.3	24.3
Lignin	18.9	23.2	21.5
Extractives	10	5	12
Acetate	1	2.9	-
Ash	6.4	2.6	2

Contrary to sugary and starchy biomass, lignocellulosic biomass cannot be fully utilized as they grow on the field. A certain amount needs to remain in the field to maintain a certain nutrition level and to prevent soil erosion. Hence, the available biomass potential for conversion to pretreated biomass and biochemicals needs to be estimated.

In general, biomass potentials are distinguished in theoretical, technical and economic available (see Kaltschmitt et al. [175]). Theoretical potentials are the total amount of crop residues, which accrue on the field. Technical potentials can be harvested based on the technical restrictions defined by nutrition cycles, collecting machine efficiency and soil erosion. This amount is mostly much smaller than the theoretical available potential. Nevertheless, not all technical harvestable crop residues are collectible to a competitive price. Hence, the economic potential is the amount of biomass, which is gathered without making a deficit. For detailed explanations on biomass potential estimation see section 3.4.

Detailed data for the yearly available biomass residues potentials are not available. Hence, the utilizable lignocellulosic biomass needs to be estimated by potential analysis. The ratio of straw to grain is used to approximate the residue amount. The yearly biomass grain production of corn, sorghum and sugar cane is provided for the individual counties in the United States by the U.S. Department of Agriculture (USDA) [244]. As Alaska and Hawaii are too distant from the mainland U.S. and large amounts of pretreated biomass are necessary for biochemical productions, these two states are excluded from the scope of this thesis.

Due to weather conditions, the harvest varies each year. As a basis for the model, the mean amount of harvest from 2010 to 2014 was used. These years include a very low and also a very high harvest. Therefore, they are highly suitable for modeling. Regarding the three major biomass corn, sugar cane and sorghum, 2439 counties in the considered region (east U.S.) are included in the model. In other counties either no cultivation of these crops occurs or no data exists. The calculations are based on dry metric tons. The harvested amount of corn and sorghum is displayed in bushels (bu) and short tons for sugar cane.

According to Graham [140], the ratio of corn grain to straw is almost 1:1. In the case of sugar cane 130 to 150 kg of cane field trash after harvest and 140 kg of bagasse occur per ton of sugar cane (see Dias et al. [94]). Many different sorghum types exist, which all have specific residue yields. In literature, values between 0.7 and 1.4 can be found for the ratio of straw to grain. Due to the scope of this thesis and the focus on sorghum and especially its grain a value of 0.8 is assumed.

For a sustainable residue utilization and soil conservation, a certain amount of the biomass residue needs to remain on the field. The share of residue to ensure a high concentration of organics in the soil as well as to avoid soil erosion depends on various parameters. These are for example the type of soil, the specific nutrient demand of the biomass and the weather conditions (see Ertl [107]). Soil treatment procedures often lead to a decomposition of residues to CO_2. Hence, the organic substances in the soil decrease and effects the harvesting yield. In case of less soil treatment, the residue share can reach a value of 50 %, if the soil is heavily treated then only 30 % of the straw should remain on the field. Weather related erosion, caused by rain or wind, can be avoided by a certain amount of residue on the field. The straw prevents the washing away of soil particles by rain or the ablation by wind (see Nelson [259]). These assumptions are used to estimate the usable biomass potentials.

Table 5.2: Main cultivation areas of sugarcane, corn and sorghum in the US (USDA [244])

State	Corn $[km^2]$	Sugarcane $[km^2]$	Sorghum $[km^2]$	Overall Surface of State $[km^2]$
Louisiana	-	12,300	8,928	135,382
Florida	-	15,891	-	170,304
Texas	-	1,255	137,250	695,621
Kansas	-	-	199,800	213,096
Oklahoma	-	-	17,360	181,035
Arkansas	-	-	16,005	137,732
Nebraska	1,602,050	-	13,120	200,520
South Dakota	787,360	-	9,450	199,731
Colorado	-	-	8,400	269,601
Mississippi	-	-	8,400	125,443
Iowa	2,367,400	-	-	145,743
Illinois	2,350,000	-	-	149,998
Minnesota	1,177,800	-	-	225,171
Indiana	1,084,760	-	-	94,321
Missouri	628,680	-	-	180,533
Ohio	610,720	-	-	116,096
Tennessee				

5.1.2 Estimation of biomass residue cost

The cost of the utilized biomass make up for a large share of the total cost of the value chain. Currently, mostly first generation biomass is used for the production of bioenergy, bioethanol and biochemicals. A large-scale market for second generation biomass, except for the utilization as bedding in stables or similar, does not exist yet. Hence, the prices for crop residues and bagasse need to be estimated. In the following, the needed input data for the estimations is presented.

5.1.2.1 Crop residues

Farmers consider selling biomass residues in case it is economically feasible for them. Therefore, different economic and crop production factors are included in their decision making. The price, that farmers receive for their biomass, needs to include cost for harvesting, transport from the field to the storage space and the storage itself. This also includes personnel, material and machinery cost. Taking residues from the field can also have an impact on up- and downstream activities, which are combined to agricultural utilization of the arable land.

In the following, the input data for estimating the market price of biomass residues is presented. Aim is to give incentives to the farmers to sell their residues for the conversion to biochemicals instead of leaving them on the field. Corn stover is an attractive feedstock in the U.S. due to the high potential and the good conversion properties. Hence, many approaches exist in literature, which try to estimate the corn stover price. These studies assume varying values for different harvesting, storage and transport technologies. Two very different harvesting and storage systems can be applied. Straw with a very high moisture content can be harvested just like silage and stored in plastic bags or airtight silos (see Shinners et al. [324]). The second possibility for harvesting and storing is the storage at low moisture contents.

This possibility is mostly favored in literature and is, therefore, applied for the following estimations. The harvest of straw can be performed together with the grain harvest or separately afterwards. During a joint harvest of grain and straw the number of field operations is reduced. Unfortunately, this results also in lower grain yields and a strong increase in energy demand of the harvester. The straw can be separated and transported in an extra container. This option is mostly neglected as it leads to high transportation cost due to the low density. Straw can also be pressed to bales to increase the efficiency of the transport. Unfortunately, the moisture content is often too high for direct baling. In case of wet straw the quality of the bales can decrease faster. Normally, the moisture content of straw for baling should be at most 24 % to avoid depreciation of the bales. To enable the drying of the straw it is assumed that the straw is processed in a separate step after harvest. Therefore, the residues are chopped. After drying, the straw is gathered and formed to bales. This processing enables a harvest yield of 75 to 85 % (see Milhollin et al. [230]). In a next step, the bales are transported to local storages. There they remain for up to one year, until they are transported to production plants. As biomass is harvested mostly in autumn, but is being processed all year long, the average storage time is six months. The storage conditions influence the losses within this time frame. Decreased by the cost for bale foils, which are identical for sorghum and cane field trash as well as the transport cost to the local storage, the harvesting cost add up to 12.11 $/t of corn stover. These cost are dependent on the farm area. Large straw harvest per acre result in lower specific harvesting cost. Economies of scale can be applied. As the yield of sugar cane and sorghum farms is lower than of corn, the harvesting cost are adapted accordingly. Based on the average harvesting yields of corn, sorghum and sugar cane from the years 2010 to 2014, the harvesting cost can be estimated as follows: corn stover 12.11 $/t, sorghum straw 36.51 $/t and cane field trash 9.09 $/t. In table 5.3, the cost for harvesting and local transportation are summarized.

Table 5.3: Harvesting and local transportation cost of corn stover

Source	Collection $\$/dt$	Baling $\$/dt$	Transport $\$/dt$
Argo et al. [21]	11.73		3.87
Atchison and Hettenhaus [25]	16.09		9.00
DOE [97]	12.29		4.05
Gallagher et al. [128]	4.09	5.23	3.24
Gallagher and Baumes [129]	5.35	7.26	5.72
Hess et al. [153]	4.59	12.03	2.08
Kaliyan et al. [174]	6.06	26.51	5.81
Morey et al. [237]	4.80	24.89	6.48
Sokhansanj et al. [331]	2.70	9.01	3.66
Vadas and Digman [370]	11.10		3.66
Average	16.37		5.40
minus baling foil			
Petrolia [283]	4.26		
Harvesting cost	12.11		

Together with the crop residues also the nutrients within the residues are extracted from the soil. These need to be replaced to ensure high harvesting yields in the following years. The amount of removed residues from the field depends not only on the considered crop type but also on the area. Erosion, weather, soil, harvesting techniques, etc. can influence the nutrition demand. The need for fertilizers and the additional erosion risks lead to higher biomass residue prices. Fertilizer prices depend on the residue type due to its composition.

In the following table 5.4, the price for replacing the nutrition is estimated based on the fertilizer price and the amount of nutrition needed based on the residue composition. The estimation is based on the three main nutrients potassium, phosphorous and nitrogen.

Table 5.4: Nutrient prices

Source	Unit	N	P_2O_5	K_2O	Total
Price (December 2015)					
Silva [326]	$/t	716.50	600.21	456.36	
Corn stover					
Darr et al. [90]	kg/dt	4.80	1.83	8.44	
Fixen et al. [118]	kg/dt	9.50	2.85	16.00	
Wortmann et al. [387]	kg/dt	8.50	2.00	17.00	
Morey et al. [237]	kg/dt	7.40	2.90	12.70	
Average	kg/dt	7.55	2.39	13.53	
cost	$/dt	5.41	1.44	6.18	**13.02**
Sorghum straw					
Stichler et al. [2]	kg/dt	14.77	9.85	43.56	
Cartwright et al. [70]	kg/dt	24.10	5.07	27.14	
Jones Jr. [172]	kg/dt	19.28	5.07	27.90	
Wortmann et al. [387]	kg/dt	8.50	2.00	17.00	
Average	kg/dt	16.66	5.50	28.90	
cost	$/dt	11.94	3.30	13.19	**28.43**
Cane field trash					
Suma and Savitha [336]	kg/dt	5.40	1.30	3.10	
o.V. [83]	kg/dt	3.85	0.95	2.35	
Average	kg/dt	4.63	1.13	2.73	
cost	$/dt	3.31	0.68	1.24	**5.23**

Additionally to the occurring cost for the farmer, also a profit margin needs to be considered to enhance economic incentives for the farmer. In literature, mostly a value of 6.5 to 10 $/dt is proposed (see Kaliyan et al. [174], Morey et al. [237], Sheehan et al. [321]). Brechbill et al. [59] suggest a profit share of 15 % of the harvesting cost. Not only economic factors influence the decision of farmers but also the impact of the biomass residue on the soil. This can, on the one hand, increase the farming of the acre due to rising effectiveness of fertilizers and decrease of possible germs. On the other hand, often plying the soil can lead to decreased harvests due to compressed soil (see Hess et al. [153]). Based on the above presented calculations a profit margin of 10.5 % is assumed in this model. The results of the biomass residue cost are presented in section 6.3.2.

5.1.2.2 Bagasse

Not only crop residues are considered as second generation biomass, but also processing residues from industrial conversion plants are often ligno-cellulosic biomass. These are mostly used for energy provision by combustion. The energy from bagasse combustion is larger than the demand in the mills. Surplus energy is currently used to produce electricity and sell it as benefit. Ongoing research activities support the development to use these residues for products with higher value. In this work, bagasse is an example for second generation biomass from processing. In the following, the input data for estimating prices for such biomass is presented.

The surplus energy from bagasse is priced by the amount of fossil energy, which can be replaced. The basis for comparison is the energy content of bagasse and the fossil fuel, mostly natural gas (see Paturau [277]). The energy content of bagasse strongly depends on the water content. Normally, bagasse has a moisture content of 50 %, but is mostly dried to 25 % by surplus heat of the process. As this affects the efficiency of the process, this work assumes the pre-dried bagasse.

5.1.3 Possible locations for the biorefinery plants

The following steps are performed to solve the optimization sub-model for future biorefinery locations: first of all the available biomass potential was estimated, then possible locations are pre-selected and cost assumed for the transport of residues.

The biomass potentials of corn stover, sugar cane bagasse, sorghum residues and cane field trash were calculated. As no data for residues exist these were estimated based on the grain to straw ratio. The annual yields of corn, sorghum and sugar cane are provided by the National Agriculture Statistics Service of the USDA [244] on a county basis. The production yields vary from year to year as they depend on weather conditions. In total 2439 counties were considered for the potential analysis. In the other counties either no data was available or the crops were not cultivated there.

Soil quality, climate influence, irrigation etc. affect the amount of residues which can be taken from the field. Additionally, a share of residues is already used for other purposes such as animal farming. Based on literature, it is assumed that about 35 % of each residue type can be extracted from the field (see Ertl [107]).

In total 390 potential biorefinery locations are considered in the optimization submodel. This value is based on the considered counties. If all 2439 counties are included, the computational complexity would rise immensely without adding much more detailed knowledge. Hence, only every third county is considered in the model. These were spread geographically to all counties in the respective regions in the U.S. Each location has a maximum distance of 150 miles to biomass residue supply. It is assumed that all farmers are willing to sell the residues. Consequently, all counties are considered as suppliers and 390 as production sites in the optimization sub-model.

5.1.4 Possible suppliers for the integrated model

Two different input parameters for possible locations of future biochemical production plants are defined to solve the integrated model, which has been presented in section 4.5. On the one hand, possible locations include already existing production sites of corn wet milling, sugar cane and sorghum milling plants. It is assumed that existing production plants for sugar syrup and the respective infrastructure are used for the biochemicals value chains.

Many corn wet milling plants exist in the United States. These are mostly concentrated in the "corn belt", which is located in the upper Midwest including the states of Illinois, Iowa, Nebraska, Indiana, Missouri, Kansas, North Dakota, Tennessee and Ohio. The major companies in 2017 were Tate & Lyle PLC, Cargill, Archer Daniels Midland Company (ADM), Ingredion, Roquette and Bunge (see McKeany-Flavell Company, Inc. [263]). Most of the companies do not publish their production capacity and product portfolio of each location, which can also vary according to the current market conditions. The product portfolio contains different qualities of starch and glucose syrup, gluten, etc. Additionally, in case the production capacity of corn glucose syrup is known, it is not sure how much of the produced amount can be purchased. Not only chemical companies can benefit from existing companies but also companies of the food and feed sector. They already purchase sugar and starch from these suppliers. Consequently, three different cases and product capacities are assumed in this work: in case the maximum capacity is known, 100,000 t of sugar syrup are available for purchase per year. If the capacity in unknown but the required quality is produced at that location, then the purchasable amount is set to 50,000 t per year. In case, the pretreatment already exists but does not produce the desired quality, the location is included for later calculations but is set to a quantity of zero tons. The locations and the respective purchasable amounts are summarized in the appendix in table A.6.

Sugar cane milling plants have been in operation for many years. The capacities of these mills are much smaller than of corn wet milling plants and are seldom operated by the same company. Most sugar cane milling plants are situated in the south of the U.S., mainly in Louisiana, Alabama and Florida. These production sites are used as fixed input data for the supply of sucrose syrup. It is assumed that the total potential of sugar cane is already utilized so that no additional production plants are possible. As the mills are quite small, the maximum purchasable amount is set to 50,000 t of sucrose syrup per year.

Wall [377] mentions the only large-scale sorghum wet mill in Corpus Christi, which has been built up in 1948. Unfortunately it was closed in 1970 and replaced by corn wet milling (see Inglett [164]).

On the other hand, possible future biorefinery locations as a result from the optimization sub-model are included in the integrated model. Currently, no large-scale biorefineries for the production of sugar syrup from crop residues such as corn stover, bagasse, cane field trash or sorghum residues exist. For the inclusion of these biomass types in the location planning for production sites for biochemicals, the optimization sub-model as described in section 4.2.2 is implemented. This approach optimizes possible locations of future biorefinery production facilities. The results of the optimization model can be found in section 6.3. These locations are set as supplier locations for second generation sugar syrup. The purchasable amount is defined as the maximum production capacity. It is assumed that in the building up phase of such biorefineries direct contracts for the supply of sugar syrup can be signed and, therefore, the total produced amount purchased.

The existing pretreatment plants (wet mills, sugar mills, sorghum mills) as well as the transport hubs (mostly along the Mississippi River) are depicted in figure 5.3. The sugar mills are highly concentrated in the South of Louisiana. Many corn wet mills are located in Illinois, Iowa and Indiana.

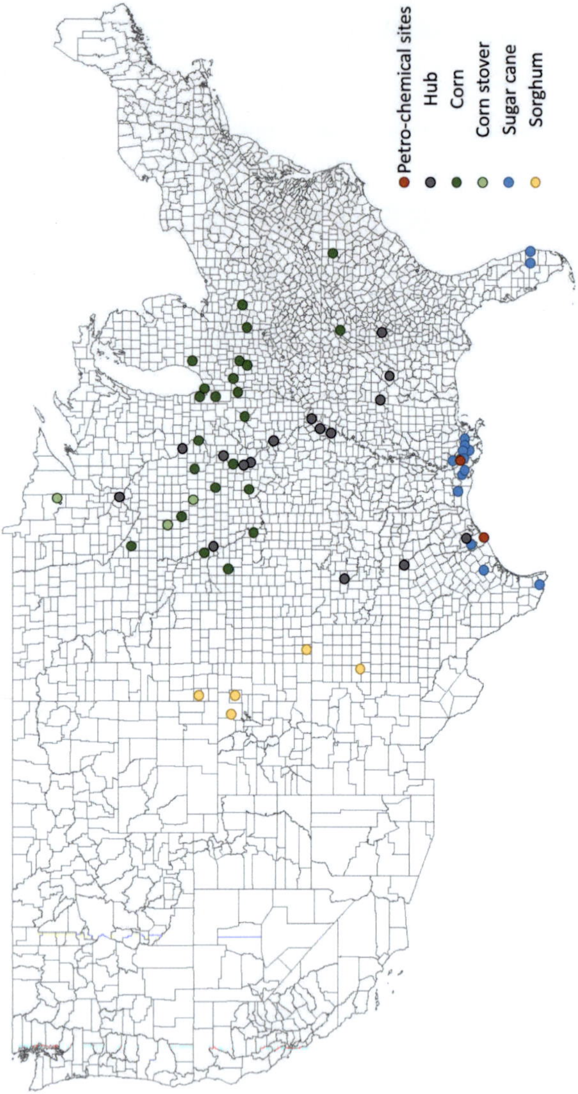

Figure 5.3: Existing pretreatment plants and transport hubs in the U.S.

5.1.5 Possible locations for the integrated model

This work considered different types of locations in the integrated model. Three possible constructs need to be discussed. Firstly, all identified locations of the suppliers (wet mill, sugar mill, biorefinery) could in theory be used for a **co-location** for the production plant of biochemicals. In order to maximize the supply safety only wet mills are considered as possible co locations. Sugar mills cannot provide large amounts of sugar syrup and are, hence, less attractive for large-scale production of biochemicals. As currently no large-scale biorefineries exist, relying on those locations is risky. Additionally, the quality and quantity of those plants are insecure. This leads to higher technology risks. Therefore, the locations of biorefineries are not included as possible final processing plants, but the first processing step P1 is possible there. This assumption is based on the idea, that joint venture contracts with biorefineries would be possible, which secures the supply. The second processing step P2 will still be preferred to at existing petro-chemical plants.

Secondly, **existing petro-chemical production plants** can be converted to biochemical sites or at least the existing infrastructure can be used, such as storage capacities, downstream processing equipment or logistics. Therefore, the locations of petro-chemical sites are considered for both, the processing steps P2 and P12 to produce the final product. The single production of the intermediate in process P1 is neglected. This work assumes that the transport of pretreated biomass to the petro-chemical plants to only produce an intermediate is not feasible.

Thirdly, a **new location** can be set up. This possibility is currently neglected in the model, as the risk of a new process is high and, as such, the location risk is minimized. Nevertheless, these locations can be added without any changes to the model in case it should be adapted to other needs.

In case of biochemical production, the above mentioned assumptions and the boundary conditions of existing and possible locations of suppliers lead to 92 locations in the integrated model for biochemical production. These include 26 wet mills and 20 sugar/sorghum mills. As a result of the optimization sub-model (see section 6.3.3), 44 locations were identified for biorefineries. Two petro-chemical production sites are included. Additionally, 30 transport hubs as well as 4 export ports are considered. In total, 126 locations are implemented in the integrated model.

The boundary conditions change for thermochemical production sites. As currently, no large-scale thermochemical processes are in operation, co-locations or new locations are identical. Hence, all 37 identified pretreatment plants by pyrolysis (see section 6.3.4) can also be treated as possible locations for the production of biochemicals via thermochemical pathway. Additionally, the two existing petro-chemical sites are included as they provide the necessary infrastructure. Again 30 transport hubs are implemented for logistical reasons. As only lignocellulosic biomass is included in case of thermochemical production, the existing wet and sugar mills are not included in the integrated model.

5.2 Process simulation and techno-economic analysis of biochemical processes

After estimating the biomass potentials and identifying possible locations for biorefineries in the previous section 5.1, the simulation of material and energy flow balances of the value chain for the production of biochemicals are shown in the upcoming sections.

In this work, three case studies are considered and evaluated. These case studies include the biochemical and thermochemical conversion of biomass to chemicals. Therefore, three process routes are defined. At first, the biochemical production of two different main chemicals is shown in this section. In the following section 5.3, the third case study of thermochemical conversion is presented.

Sugar syrup is the feedstock for biochemical conversion processes. Therefore, the production of sugar syrup by corn wet milling, sugar cane milling, and biorefineries, is presented in section 5.2.1. Then, the biochemical conversion of sugar syrup to chemicals is explained in section 5.2.2. Two biochemical processes are considered in separate case studies: butanol and succinic acid. Based on the results of the process simulation, a techno-economic analysis is conducted by estimating investments and production cost. The basis for the economic assessment is input data from literature, which is presented in section 5.2.3.

5.2.1 Production of sugar syrup in biorefineries

For the production of sugar syrup, different processes are chosen, depending on the type of biomass used. Most processes for first generation are state of the art and are already implemented within the United States. In this study, corn is converted to glucose syrup by corn wet milling. Sugar cane is crushed in mills to produce sucrose syrup. In sorghum mills the sugar is extracted from sorghum. Lignocellulosic biorefineries are not state of the art yet. Therefore, the set up of a lignocellulosic biorefinery is defined by data provided in literature. Dilute acid pretreatment seems to be the most promising technology as it leads to high hemicellulose break down and is, therefore, applied in this work. In the following the processes of corn wet milling, sugar cane milling and sorghum milling as well as dilute acid pretreatment in biorefineries, are described in more detail.

5.2.1.1 Corn Wet Milling

Corn can be processed to different qualities of glucose syrups and other byproducts either by wet or dry milling. Wet milling is especially favorable as it produces a high purity starch slurry as well as valuable byproducts such as germ meal, crude oil or animal feed. The starch slurry is utilized for syrup or high-quality dry starch production (see Blanchard [49]).

In the wet milling process, corn is broken down by physical, chemical and biological processes into starch, germ, gluten, fiber and steep liquor. The yields of the process steps depend on the range of by-products produced, the available equipment and the analysis of corn. The typical corn composition, and, hence, conversion yields, on dry matter basis are presented in table 5.5.

Table 5.5: Typical yields of the wet milling process (Blanchard [49])

Product	Yield in %
Steep liquor	6.5
Germ	7.5
Bran	12.0
Gluten	5.6
Starch	68.0
Losses (volatiles, etc.)	0.4

The following descriptions are valid for the considered corn wet milling process. Corn is first cleaned and steeped in hot 0.2 wt.-% dilute sulfur dioxide SO_2 for about 40 hours. This leads to an easier grinding, removes soluble material and simplifies the extraction of proteins and starch. These pretreatment steps lead to higher efficiency of the wet milling process as it improves the separation of the products by softening the kernel, removes soluble matter and increases the moisture content (see Ramirez et al. [297]). Before grinding corn, the water of the steeping process is removed. After steeping, corn is degermed in two stages. The lighter fraction of the germ, which contains most of the oil, is separated from the suspending starch slurry by hydro cyclones. After that the germ is dewatered, dried and the oil is extracted (see Blanchard [49]).

The heavier fraction consists of starch, gluten, fiber and fragments of kernel. These are separated from each other in various screening steps. The fiber is then dewatered and dried. The fiber-free fraction is processed in high speed nozzle centrifuges, in which the gluten is separated (see Blanchard [49]).

In the following process steps, the starch slurry is washed with fresh water and in multiple stages of hydro cyclones for purification. The grinding process consists of multiple stages, which are all carried out by disk plate grinders. After the removal of corn germs, the product stream is fed to a screen. This leads to very fine particles in the last grinding step as the larger particles are recycled to previous grinding operations. According to Blanchard [49], refiners and impact mills are used. The first is a modern version of a stone mill and is composed of two vertical steel discs, which rotate contrariwise. A 36-inch mill rotates normally at 1,800 rpm and can process about 508 tons a day with two 250 HP machines. The impact mill only has one disc, which is fixed either vertically or horizontally. The following details are based on Blanchard [49].

Germ Separation

Corn germ is produced with a high quality and an oil content of 45 to 50 %. Due to the high oil content, germ can be separated from other components by utilizing the density difference in hydro cyclones. To ensure a volume stream of 18 m^3/h (1. step), resp. 27 m^3/h (2. step), a pressure drop of 2.8 to 3.2 kg/cm^2 is necessary. The top to feed ratio also influences the separation quality. Low ratios lead to higher qualities of the germ. Afterwards, the germ is washed on three screens.

Fiber production

The bottom stream of the germ separation is cleaned from loose starch and gluten particles as well as large parts of water on a screen. The remaining solid particles are grinned in a third mill to remove the resident starch. Fibers are resistant to the grinding process. The mixture is washed with water flowing counter-currently and to separate starch and gluten from the fibers. These are dried on a screen and a screw press to a moisture content of 60 %.

Gluten

First sand and rust are removed from the mixture. The starch is concentrated in a centrifuge. By using the density difference between starch and gluten both are separated from each other by multiple disc centrifuges.

Starch

The raw starch is washed in a series of hydrocylones. The washing water is fed in a counter current manner to the starch stream. The bottom stream is led to the next centrifuge whilst the top stream is fed back to the previous one. This leads to high quality starch.

Glucose from Starch

The starch is processed to sugar by multiple steps. At first $\alpha-$amylase is added to a mixture of corn starch and water. It splits up the starch to oligosaccharides. These are then processed by $\gamma-$ amylase secreted by fungus aspergillus. Finally, 2300 liters of corn are needed to produce one ton of glucose.

In figure 5.4 the basic flow sheet of a corn wet mill is shown.

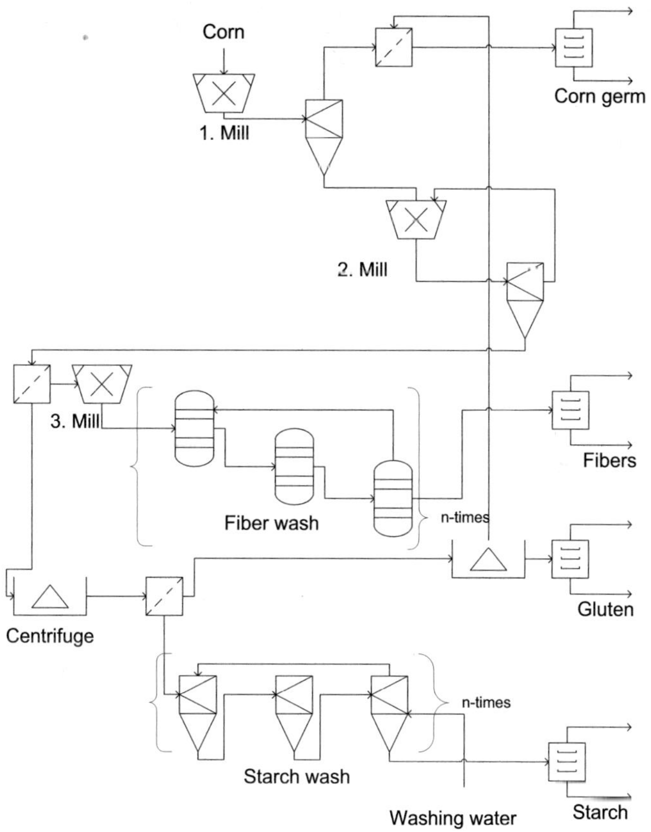

Figure 5.4: Scheme of the corn wet milling process

5.2.1.2 Sugar Mills

Pancoast and Junk [275] have gathered the most relevant data on sugar mills. The following descriptions are based on their knowledge. Sugar cane consists of 10 to 15 % of dry fiber and 85 to 90 % of juice. The processing of sugar cane consists of two steps. At first, the sugar cane stalks are cut into chips and then crushed between heavy rolls. Afterwards the dark green juice is cleared with lime (*CaO*) and heat. The impurities of the sugar juice are separated by sedimentation and vacuum filters. The now dark brown juice is evaporated in multiple stages to a solid content of about 65 %. The solution is crystallized on vacuum pans and then the molasses are separated from the crystals. In the second step, the refined sugar is produced. After washing of the crystals, the sugar is decolorized and finally crystallized. In figure 5.5, the process scheme is shown (see Bonomi et al. [3]).

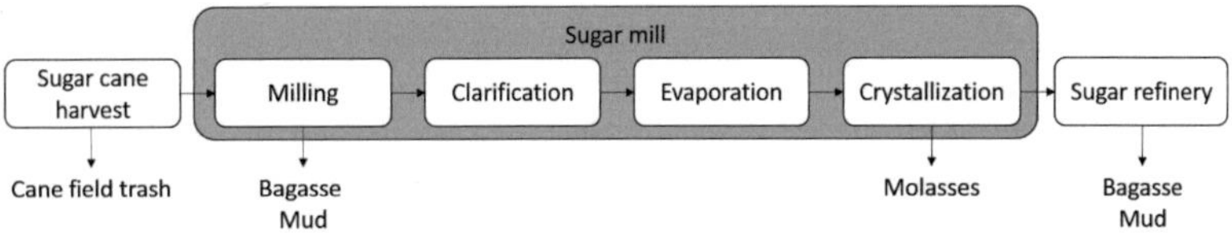

Figure 5.5: Scheme of the sugar cane processing (Meyer [227])

Extraction

The first step in sugar processing is the extraction of the sugar cane juice. The sugar cane is shredded by revolving knives, which cut the cane into chips. Once the cane is processed to chips, the sugar syrup can be pressed out of the chips. The sugar juice needs to be clarified in the following process step (see Baikow et al. [33]). In this step, the byproduct bagasse, which is the solid residue of the extraction, is produced. It can be processed as other lignocellulosic biomass. The dilute acid process to convert bagasse to sugar syrup is explained in the following section.

Clarification

For the clarification the concentration of P_2O_5 is essential for the success of the process. The level should be at least 300 ppm or else the clarification is rather poor (see Baikow et al. [33]).

Vacuum distillers

The clarified sugar syrup has a very high water content. This does not only lead to higher transport cost, but also to a higher vulnerability to quality reducing processes. Hence, the sugar juice is densified in vacuum distillers to reduce the moisture content. If sucrose is sold to the market it is mostly crystallized. As liquid sugar is used for fermentation, the crystallization step is neglected in this study and is, therefore, be explained (see Pancoast [275]).

5.2.1.3 Sorghum mills

Sorghum mills operate similar to sugar mills. At first the sorghum is milled and separated in grains and stalks. The grains are processed in a hydrolysis step to convert the starch to sugars. After centrifugation the products are separated in filter cake and sugars, which are fed to the fermentation reactor. The stalks are pressed and the sugar juice is extracted such as sugar cane. Sorghum bagasse is one product, which can be dissolved to sugar by further processing such as sugar cane bagasse. The juice can also be processed in a fermentation step such as the sugars from grains (see Wall [377]).

Grain processing

According to Wall [377], sorghum can be dry and wet-milled. Due to quality issues, wet milling is more interesting in this work. Watson [381] has summarized the wet mill processing of sorghum. It is almost identical to the corn wet milling process. At first, the grain is steeped aqueous at elevated temperatures and with small amounts of sulfur dioxide. Then, the steeped grain is milled in multiple steps to optimize the yield and purity of each component. Afterwards, the germ is separated from the endosperm by liquid cyclones. The endosperm is finally milled and washed. This results in the separation of fiber from starch and gluten. Due to the higher density of the starch, the latter can be split by differential sedimentation in a continuous centrifuge.

Stalk processing

Similar to sugar cane, the stalks are crushed by a series of mills, which results in extracting the juice from the stalks. Then, the juice is screened, heated up to 100 °C and is clarified. Afterwards it is processed in a rotary vacuum filter. The filtrated juice is then sent to a series of evaporators, which reduce the water content of the syrup.

5.2.1.4 Lignocellulosic biorefineries

For the production of sugar syrup from lignocellulosic biomass different processes exist as described in section 2.3.1. In this work, the following steps are considered: grinding, Dilute Acid pretreatment, conditioning and enzymatic hydrolysis as these result in the highest production yields. These are described in the following.

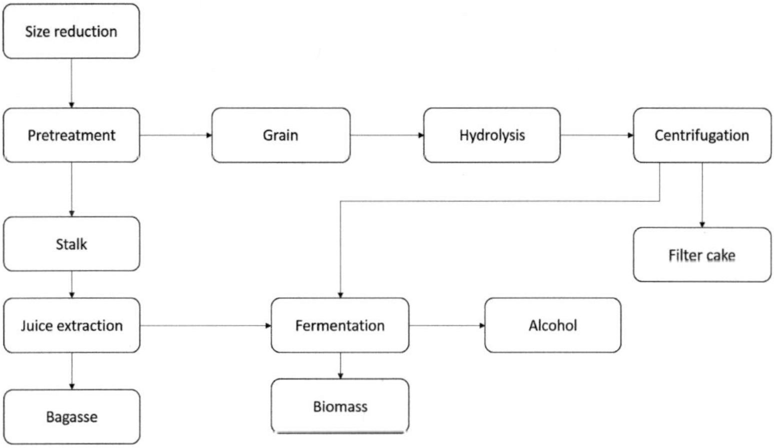

Figure 5.6: Scheme of the sorghum processing (Almodares and Hadi [16])

Grinding

Before the biochemical and physical-chemical pretreatment of biomass the feedstock needs to be grinded. By grinding the biomass the surface area and, therefore, the reactivity is increased. Mass and heat transfer limitations are minimized through the reduction of particle sizes. The needed energy for grinding varies depending on the biomass type, its moisture content, the initial particle size and the machine parameters. Hammer mills are the most common grinding machines as they need relatively low investments, they are easy to operate and produce a wide variety of particle sizes. In table 5.6 the needed specific energy depending on moisture content and particle size is presented.

Table 5.6: Energy demand for grinding biomass residues in a hammer mill (Mani et al. [213])

Material	moisture content (wt%)	average specific energy consumption (kWh/t)
Corn stover	12.0	19.84
Bagasse	20	48
Sorghum residues [a]	20	48

[a] No information on energy consumption for sorghum bagasse milling could be found, value of sugar cane bagasse assumed

Dilute Acid pretreatment and conditioning

The grinned biomass is pretreated with sulfuric acid or hydrochloric acid. According to Kumar et al. [192], the acids can support an enzymatic hydrolysis of lignocellulosic biomass to form fermentable sugars. Nevertheless, acids are toxic, corrosive and expensive and need to be recovered after the process. The acids are mostly added with a concentration of less than 4 wt %. Especially sulfuric acid seems to be very promising. It can achieve high reaction rated and convert hemicellulose to xylose and other sugars.

In this thesis aqueous sulfuric acid with a concentration of 0.75 vol.-% is used. The process is performed at 250 °F. The low temperature but comparably longer processing time is beneficial for the conversion of pentoses. Saha et al. [310] state that 92 % of the hemicelluloses can be converted to sugars but only 47 % of the cellulose is decomposed to sugar. Inhibitory product such as furfural or HMF are not produced. After the dilute acid pretreatment the hydrolysate is mixed with sodium hydroxide to neutralize the acid. The yields of Dilute Acid pre-treatment depending on the biomass type is presented in table 5.7.

Table 5.7: Yield of Dilute Acid pre-treatment depending on the biomass type

Biomass	Product	Fractional conversion (%)	Source
Corn stover	Glucose	0.065	
	Xylose	0.52	
	HMF	0.05	[295]
	Furfural	0.05	
	Acetic acid	1	
Sugar cane bagasse	Glucose	0.124	
	Xylose	0.9	
	HMF	0.05	[236]
	Furfural	0.05	
	Acetic acid	1	
Sorghum bagasse	Glucose	0.065	
	Xylose	0.775	[290]
	HMF	0.05	[399]
	Furfural	0.05	[400]
	Acetic acid	1	

Enzymatic hydrolysis

In the next step cellulose and xylan molecules are further split up via enzymatic hydrolysis in a following reactor. It is processed at 113 °F for 72 hours. According to Qureshi et al. [296], the enzymes cellulase and β-glucosidase lead to high conversion yields. Celluclast and Novozym 188 contain these enzymes. The yields of the enzymatic hydrolysis are presented in the following table 5.8.

5.2.1.5 Sugar syrup

This work considers different pretreated biomass. In this section, the different considered sugar syrups for fermentations are described. These include glucose syrup, sucrose syrup and syrup from lignocellulose.

Table 5.8: Yield of enzymatic hydrolysis depending on the biomass type

Reaction	fractional conversion (%)	Source
Corn stover		
Cellulose $\rightarrow$ *sugar*	0.65	[6]
Xylan $\rightarrow$ *Xylose*	0.38	
Sugar cane bagasse		
Cellulose $\rightarrow$ *sugar*	0.65	[6]
Xylan $\rightarrow$ *Xylose*	0.38	
Sorghum bagasse		
Cellulose $\rightarrow$ *sugar*	0.772	[280]
Xylan $\rightarrow$ *Xylose*	0.68	

Glucose syrup

A glucose syrup is defined by Hull [161] as "a purified and concentrated aqueous solution of nutritive saccharides derived from starch", and having the following characteristics:

- Dry matter of not less than 70 %
- A dextrose equivalent (DE), expressed as d-sugar, of not less than 20 % based on dry matter
- A sulphated as content of not more than 1 % on a dry basis.

DE is defined as the total reducing sugars present in a sugar syrup. It is a clear liquid with a sweet taste. Cargill [337] recommends to store sugar syrup between 130 and 140 °F to avoid crystallization.

Sucrose syrup

Sucrose syrup from sugar cane and sorghum has a high moisture content. It contains fructose and glucose to identical parts as sucrose. This sugar is also called invert sugar syrup (see Pancoast [275]). As in many publications only glucose syrup is mentioned but not the fermentation of fructose, this work assumes, that fructose cannot be metabolized by microorganisms.

Table 5.9: Sugar syrup composition in % by biomass type (Blanchard [49])

Component	Corn glucose	Sugar cane	Sorghum
Water	1.5	50	83.79
Sugars	98	46	14.24
Others	0.5	4	1.97

Lignocellulosic sugar syrup

Lignocellulose is composed of cellulose, hemicellulose and lignin. The cellulose and hemicellulose content is about 45 to 80 % (see Azadi et al. [30]). Hence, the remaining content is lignin. This is results in low sugar concentrations in the sugar syrup as lignin cannot be hydrolyzed to sugar such as cellulose and hemicellulose. Additionally, most microorganisms can ferment hexoses much better than pentoses. During pretreatment of lignocellulose, inhibitors can be produced which reduce the fermentation efficiency.

5.2.2 Production of biobased chemicals via biochemical processes

In this section, the modeled technical processes of the fermentations are described. This thesis focuses on two biochemical products: butanol and succinic acid. Both can be used as platform chemicals and be further processed to higher quality products such as plastics. Butanol has already been produced by fermentation during the First World War, but the production was ceased shortly afterwards as it was not economically feasible. In the past years, rising oil prices have led to a re-establishment of the process in commercial scale (see Green [143]). Succinic Acid is currently the most developed biochemical, which is already been operated in commercial scale worldwide (see table 2.1).

Both processes are simulated in AspenPlus for all considered biomass types. The capacity of the plants was set fix to 50,000 tons of the main final product (butanol, succinic acid). The needed biomass input was optimized respectively. Five process configurations (see section 4.3) were modeled to analyze heat integration effects.

5.2.2.1 Case study 1: Butanol Fermentation

Butanol is produced via fermentation with the co-products acetone and ethanol generally in a ratio of 3:6:1 (acetone : butanol : ethanol (ABE)). Depending on the fermentation time and the downstream processing technique also acetic acid and butyric acid are produced. The so called ABE fermentation is mostly conducted by clostridia. The most popular bacteria are *Clostridium acetobutylicum* and *Clostridium beijerinkii*. This work chooses the microorganism *Clostridium beijerinkii* as it is a hyper-butanol producing bacteria with high yields of butanol. This increases the economic feasibility of the production. Consequently, it is more favorable (see Qureshi and Blaschek [294]). The process is split up in hydrolysis/fermentation and downstream processing.

Hydrolysis and fermentation

At first, the received pretreated biomass might need to be hydrolyzed to increase the concentration of pentoses and hexoses for fermentation. After the pretreatment of biomass according to the above presented steps (milling, conversion to sugars), the fermentation is performed. The equations of the reaction from glucose $C_6H_{12}O_6$ to the products are presented in the following. For the reaction equations from xylose please refer to the table A.3 in appendix A.1.2.

Butanol (C_4H_9OH)

$$C_6H_{12}O_6 \rightarrow C_4H_9OH + 2CO_2 + H_2O \tag{5.1}$$

Acetone (C_3H_6O)

$$C_6H_{12}O_6 + H_2O \rightarrow C_3H_6O + 3CO_2 + 4H_2 \tag{5.2}$$

Ethanol (C_2H_5OH)

$$C_6H_{12}O_6 \rightarrow 2C_2H_5OH + 2CO_2 \tag{5.3}$$

Butyric Acid ($C_4H_8O_2$)

$$C_6H_{12}O_6 \rightarrow C_4H_8O_2 + 2CO_2 + 2H_2 \tag{5.4}$$

Acetic Acid ($C_2H_4O_2$)

$$C_6H_{12}O_6 \rightarrow 3C_2H_4O_2 \tag{5.5}$$

In this thesis, the fermentation with *C. beijerinckii* is chosen. This microorganism metabolizes sugar to the largest share of butanol. The products are separated from the fermentation broth by gas stripping with the help of the fermentation gases CO_2 and H_2. This downstream processing technique has the advantage that it separates the products *in situ* from the broth. Butanol has a negative effect on the fermentation yield as it acts as an inhibitor to the bacteria. Hence, the separation leads to a maximum yield of 100 % so that no residual sugar remains in the broth. The stripped gases with the products are cooled down to separate CO_2 and H_2 from ABE.

The reactors in the AspenPlus simulation are modeled by RSTOIC. The reactions are based on stoicometric reaction equations and the respective conversion factors. All utilities such as enzymes, nutrition, etc. are modeled by calculators, which are based on FORTRAN codes. These optimize the amounts based on the reference stream in the model (e.g. cellulose content of the feed). The fermentation yields based on the biomass type are displayed in table 5.10.

Table 5.10: Butanol fermentation yields depending on the biomass type

Biomass	Product	Yield in g/l	Source
Corn	Butanol	17.6	
	Acetone	8.3	[108]
	Ethanol	0.6	
Sugar cane	Butanol	9.95	
	Acetone	3.5	[214]
	Ethanol	0.4	
Sorghum[a]	Butanol	13.98	
	Acetone	8.83	[66]
	Ethanol	1.2	
Corn stover	Butanol	34.77	
	Acetone	14.04	[295]
	Ethanol	1.33	
Bagasse	Butanol	4.7	
	Acetone	9.7	[170]
	Ethanol	6.3	
Sorghum bagasse	Butanol	12.3	
	Acetone	6.1	[67]
	Ethanol	2.5	

[a] No information on *C. beijerinkcii* is available, therefore *C. acetobutylicum*

Downstream processing

Acetone, butanol, ethanol and water are led into a series of four rectification columns. At first the light volatile acetone is distilled in the first column. In the second, ethanol is separated as overhead product. Butanol and water form a heterogenic azeotrope so that a conventional separation in a fractionating column is not possible. Hence, butanol and water are first fed into a decanter and parted into a butanol rich and a water rich phase, which are then led into two distillation columns.

In figure 5.7, the basic process flow sheet for the production of ABE from corn stover is depicted.

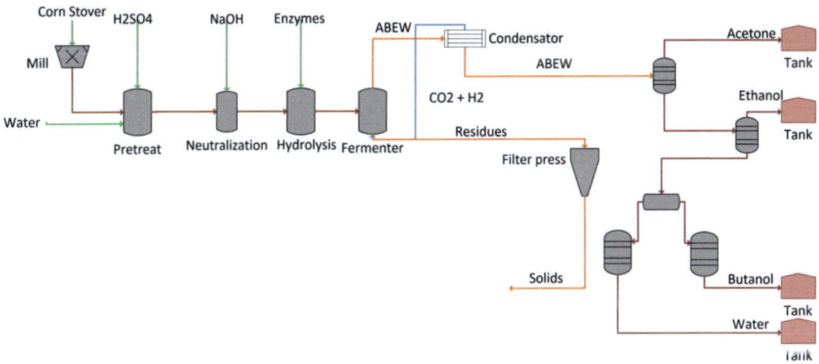

Figure 5.7: Process flow sheet for the production of ABE from corn stover

5.2.2.2 Case study 2: Succinic acid fermentation

Succinic acid fermentation is an attractive route for producing many platform chemicals such as 1,4-butanediol, tetrahydrofuran (THF) and fumaric acid. The bacteria for metabolizing sugars to succinic acid (SA) are well known as they occur in nature. Up to now *Actinobacillus succinogenes* and *Actinobacillus succininiciproducens* are the most efficient bacteria as they produce succinic acid as a major fermentation product (see Vaswani [372]).

Succinic acid ($C_4H_6O_4$) is a dicarboxylic acid (see Song and Lee [332]). According to Song and Lee [332], the demand for succinic acid might rise in the coming years at it is used in the production for biodegradable polymers. Werpy and Petersen [383] as well as Bozell and Petersen [57] refer to succinic acid being one of the top building blocks.

Hydrolysis and fermentation

Just like the previous case study, the pretreated biomass might need to be further broken down to pentoses and hexoses by enzymatic hydrolysis. Afterwards, the hydrolysate is fermented as described by Kurzrock and Weuster-Both [194]. Cell-debris and proteins are separated from the fermentation broth by ultrafiltration. Afterwards, the carboxylic acids (e.g. lactic and citric acid) are isolated from the aqueous fermentation broth via precipitation with calcium hydroxide or calcium oxide. This reaction leads to calcium salt of succinic acid, which is then filtered off and treated with sulfuric acid. The so produced gypsum ($CaSO_4$) is generated in an equimolar amount. The process of precipitation decreased the yield of the fermentation by about 15 %. Another disadvantage of this process is the high amount of calcium sulfate, which is produced but does not have any value as by-product. Additionally, a large consumption of calcium hydroxide, calcium oxide and sulfuric acid. The fermentation is performed at 37 °C and normal pressure. In the following the reaction equations for the products based on glucose is presented.

Succinic acid from glucose

$$7C_6H_{12}O_6 + 6CO_2 \rightarrow 12C_4H_6O_4 + 6H_2O \tag{5.6}$$

Succinic acid from xylose

$$7C_5H_{10}O_5 + 5CO_2 \rightarrow 10C_4H_6O_4 + 5H_2O \tag{5.7}$$

The production yields for converting different biomass types to SA is presented in table 5.11.

Table 5.11: Succinic acid production yields depending on the biomass type

Biomass	Sugar	Fractional conversion in %	Source
Corn [a]	Glucose	70	[202]
Sugar cane	Glucose	77	[167]
Sorghum	Glucose	77	[167][b]
Corn stover	Glucose	80.4	[401]
	Xylose	45	
Sugar cane bagasse	Glucose	43	[55]
	Xylose	42	
Sorghum resdiues	Glucose	43	[55][c]
	Xylose	42	

[a] No information on *A. succinogenes*available, value based on *Mannheimia succiniciproducens*
[b] No information on sorghum fermentation available, the same conversion ratio as sucrose was assumed
[c] No information on sorghum residues fermentation available, the same conversion ratio as sugar cane bagasse was assumed

Downstream processing

According to Cheng et al. [78], the downstream processing of succinic acid fermentation broth is crucial. It can make up more than 50 % of the total production cost. Separation technologies are direct crystallization, membrane separation, extraction, and *in situ* separation and others. Succinic acid has a high boiling point and is hydrophilic. Additionally, the concentration of succinic acid in the fermentation broth is with 5 to 15 % quite low. In the fermentation broth, succinic acid is only one of a large amount of components. These are succinate, water, by-products such as ethanol or acetate as well as residual sugar and salts. Therefore, the downstream process for separating succinic acid from the fermentation broth is made up of three steps. At first, the microbial cells are removed by membrane filtration or centrifugation. Secondly, impurities are removed and the primary separation of succinic acid is performed by evaporation, electrodialysis, solvent or reactive extraction or adsorption with ion exchange resin, molecular sieves, active charcoal or others. Finally, the residual succinic acid is purified by vacuum evaporation and crystallization.

In the following, the applied downstream processing technique in this work is explained. The cell biomass and impurities are removed in a first separation step. Afterwards, the pH of the fermentation broth is adjusted to 4.2 by adding 1.1 kg HCl per ton of succinic acid before the vacuum distillation is performed at 60 °C. The crystallization of succinic acid is carried out at 4 °C and 2 pH (see Lee [201]). Finally, the crystals are dried.

In figure 5.8 the process flow for the production of succinic acid from corn stover is presented.

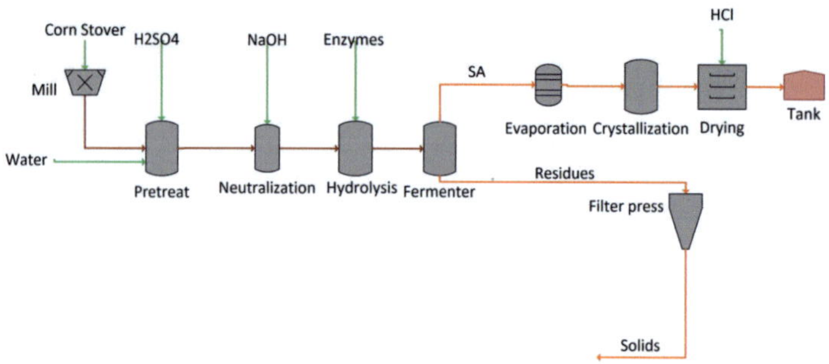

Figure 5.8: Process flow sheet for the production of succinic acid from corn stover

5.2.3 Estimation of investment and production cost

This section defines the necessary input data and assumptions for estimating investments and production cost. In the following, all necessary data for the models are presented. As no biorefinery and biochemical production plants exist, literature values need to be taken into account. The investment and production cost are first calculated for the submodel. The results of the production cost plus an additional profit margin are considered as market price for sugar syrup from biorefineries. Hence, it is used as input for the integrated optimization under uncertainty.

The production cost as well as the investment related cost are based on a time period of one year. The total project lifetime is assumed to be twenty years. In literature, different values in a range from ten (see Bergman [46]) to thirty years (see Humbird et al. [162]) can be found. Although single elements of the production process may have shorter life time expectancy, their utilization can be prolonged by maintenance and repair.

The investment data as well as the specific cost for the production cost are valid for both, butanol and succinic acid production.

5.2.3.1 Estimation of investment

As a result of the process simulations, the capacity of the single equipment can be calculated. According to section 3.6.1, the investment of the planned production plant is estimated by comparing it to reference investments of a reference unit and its capacity. Table 5.12 presents a summary of the needed equipment for converting biomass to biochemicals. In general, many requirements are valid for different fermentation process. Therefore, the values of a bioethanol production plant can be used as reference. In case the production plant is built up at a single location and is not split up into two separate processes, this work assumes that the operator can benefit from synchronizing effects. Therefore, the investments of $P12$ are only 95 % of the sum of the investments for $P1$ and $P2$.

Table 5.12: Reference cost of equipment

	cost in DOLLAR	Base capacity	year	R	installation factor	source
Storage	2,907,020	98,039 kg/h	2000	0.7	1.81	[6]
Hammer mill	370,000	50,000 kg/h	2008	0.7	1.25	[369]
Pretreatment reactor DA	13,868,680	83,333 kg/h	2009	0.6	1.5	[162]
Wet Milling	72,700,000	123,613 kg/h	2008	0.7	2	[297]
Vacuum evaporator	902,131	200,000 kg/h	2000	0.68	2.1	[6]
PressNeutralisation	82,600	410,369 kg/h	2009	0.7	2	[162]
Hydrolysis reactor	2,688,000	412,776 kg/h	2009	0.7	2	[162]
Fermentor	1,747,263	392,029 kg/h	2009	0.7	1.2	[162]
Tank fermentation broth	1,890,344	412,222 kg/h	2000	0.7	1.2	[6]
Distillation columns	2,384,900	30,379 kg/h	2009	0.6	2.4	[162]
Decanter	3,600,060	303,646 kg/h	2000	0.6	1.04	[6]
Filter press	100,000	98,039 kg/h	2000	0.6	1.25	[178]
Tank product storage	273,827	24,686 kg/h	2000	0.51	1.4	[6]
Crystallizer	20,513	25,382 kg/a	2014	0.7	2	[196]
Dryer	11,538	25,382 kg/a	2014	0.6	1.8	[196]

5.2.3.2 Estimation of production cost

Production cost are mainly variable cost. They depend on the produced amount of final product, and, hence on the needed biomass and utilities. Therefore, in order to estimate production cost, the specific cost of biomass and utilities is multiplied with the biomass and utility demand. Such utilities are energy, steam, enzymes, etc. The majority of the input data is regionally specific. As the prices and cost for feedstock, energy and other utilities depend on the state and, hence, on the location of the plant, price ranges are presented in the following table 5.13.

Table 5.13: Current prices for feedstock, energy and utilities

Feedstock/utility	Price	Source
Corn	192 $/t	[221],[368]
Sugar cane	40 $/t	[362]
Sorghum	35 $/t	[19]
Corn stover	40.66 $/t	see section 6.3.2.1
Bagasse	25 $/t	see section 6.3.2.2
Cane field trash	28.71 $/t	see section 6.3.2.1
Sorghum residues	84.64 $/t	see section 6.3.2.1
Electricity	0.05 - 0.1 $/kWh	[147]
Water	0.53 $/t	[379]
Natural gas	12.5 $/MWh	[333]
Enzymes	20 $/kg	[208]
Ammonia	450 $/t	[184]
HCl	250 $/t	[62]

For location planning and comparison of different alternatives, the maximization of the NPV is a suitable variable. In order to estimate the NPV not only the cost in a production process are necessary, but also the revenues. The assumed prices for the final products to calculate the revenues are presented in table 5.14.

Table 5.14: Current prices for final products

Product	Price	Source
Butanol	1500 $/t	[134]
Ethanol	1170 $/t	[103]
Acetone	1600 $/t	[269]
Succinic acid	2000 $/t	[199]

5.3 Process simulation and techno-economic analysis of thermochemical processes

Not only biochemical processes can be applied to produce biochemicals. Thermochemical processes such as the combination of pyrolysis for pretreatment and the conversion to chemicals via gasification and synthesis are currently discussed thoroughly. In order to compare the results of thermochemical and biochemical conversion pathways the above mentioned process is considered in the following.

Contrary to the biochemical conversion, the thermochemical processing of first generation biomass is not as economically favorable. Sugar and starch is less favored for pyrolysis due to their chemical composition (see Carpenter et al. [69]). Hence, in this case study only the biomass residues are considered: corn stover, sugar cane bagasse, sorghum residues and cane field trash.

Identical to biochemical conversion (pretreatment, fermentation, downstream processing), the thermochemical pathway is designed as a three step process: at first, biomass is pretreated by fast pyrolysis (P0) to gain biooil and biochar, the so called slurry. The transport of this slurry is more reasonable than of biomass itself as the energetic density is much higher (just as sugar syrup). After the pretreatment of biomass, the slurry can be transported to thermochemical conversion facilities. These production plants include the gasification of the slurry to syngas (P1) and afterwards the conversion of syngas by DME synthesis to ethylene and gasoline (P2). Ethylene is a platform chemical, which can be further processed to various chemicals. In the following, the processes and their parameters are described.

5.3.1 Case study 3: Production of biooil via pyrolysis

For the production of biooil from biomass residues the thermochemical process of fast pyrolysis is used. Trippe et al. [358] have assessed the fast pyrolysis of wheat straw to char, oil and gas and the further processing to syngas and ethylene. Their data is especially be used for the economic assessment. For the representation of the processes the conversion values given in table 5.15 for the different biomass types are presented.

Table 5.15: Biooil production yields depending on the biomass type

Biomass	Product	fractional conversion in %	Source
Corn stover	Oil	62	
	Char	17	[388]
	Gas	21	
Bagasse	Oil	60.4	
	Char	18	[330]
	Gas	21	
Sorghum bagasse	Oil	69.4	
	Char	13	[287]
	Gas	17.6	

The simulation of pyrolysis in AspenPlus has hardly been done in literature (e.g. Letsinsky and Palit [203]), as often too many products in unknowable concentrations occur. As this research is beyond the scope, the simulation of the pyrolysis is excluded in this work. Therefore, the basic yields as in table 5.15 have been used in the optimization sub-model. Based on the yields of pyrolysis, the locations of possible locations are optimized by the optimization sub-model. These locations are suppliers of pyrolysis slurry for syngas and ethylene production.

5.3.2 Production of biobased chemicals via thermochemical processes

After preprocessing of biomass via pyrolysis to biooil and char (P0), the slurry from oil and char is used as feedstock for the production of biochemicals. The products are gasified to synthesis gas (syngas) (P1), which is afterwards converted to ethylene (P2). In the following, the processes and the respective input data are presented. Both processes are based on the currently at the Karlsruhe Institute of Technology (KIT) developed bioliq concept (see Dahmen et al. [87]). It can convert low-value lignocellulosic biomass as straw or wood to biofuels or biochemicals. This work focuses on biochemicals, therefore the production of ethylene is considered. Ethylene can be converted to a large variety of chemicals such as polyethylene (PE), polyethylene terephthalate (PETE) or olefins.

The bioliq concept is a two-stage process (gasification and synthesis), which enables the conversion of biomass with low energy density. In this work, the capacity of the synthesis plant was set fix to 50,000 t ethylene per year. The capacity of the gasification plant was sized respectively to provide enough syngas for 50,000 t of ethylene.

Gasification of pyrolysis products to syngas

The gasification of the pyrolysis slurry has been assessed techno- economically by Trippe et al. [357]. The gasification has been modeled in AspenPlus to simulate the material and energy flow balances. Trippe et al. [357] consider entrained flow gasification as the most promising technology for the production of biochemicals from gasification. In their study a gasifier of the size of 1 GW_{th} input is assessed. Different configurations have been modeled. The authors varied the gasification agent (oxygen and oxygen/steam), operating pressures (40 and 80 bar), the $H_2 : CO$ ratio (1:1 and 2:1) and the feed composition (100 % biomass and 90 %/10 % biomass). This work considers only the following configuration: oxygen, 80 bar, $H_2 : CO$ ratio of 1:1 and 100 % biomass. The very simplified process is depicted in figure 5.9.

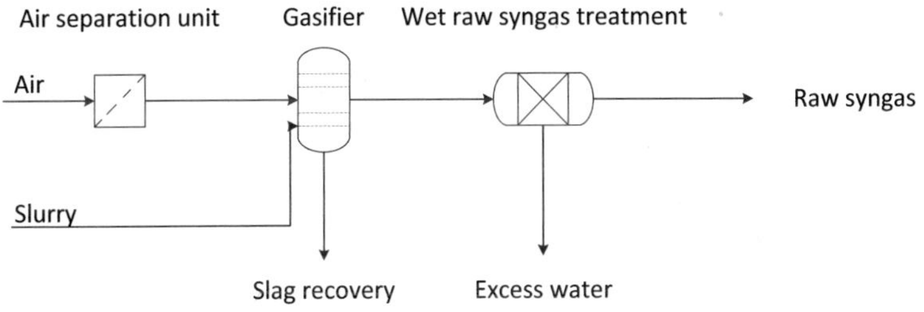

Figure 5.9: Process flow sheet for the production of syngas from slurry (Trippe et al. [357])

To produce oxygen for gasification, a cryogenic air rectification is installed. Before gasification, the slurry of the pyrolysis needs to be handled, transported, stored, and pre-heated to approximately 120 ° C. In table 5.16 the in- and output data for the gasification process is presented.

Table 5.16: Input and output data of gasification (Trippe et al. [357])

Input	
Biomass slurry $[t/h]$	192
Natural gas $[Nm^3]$	50
Power consumption $[MW_e]$	58
Output	
Syngas $[Nm^3/h]$	217,810
Usable heat $[MW]$	152
Slag $[t/h]$	15.3

The product stream from gasification consists of carbon monoxide CO, hydrogen H_2, steam H_20, carbon dioxide CO_2 and methane CH_4. In the considered process the product stream is conditioned accordingly to enable an efficient synthesis, which is described in the following section. Therefore, the product stream is dewatered and the $H_2 : CO_2$ ratio is adjusted to 1:1 for DME synthesis. In case Fischer Tropsch synthesis is applied in the next step, the respective ratio should be 2:1. Finally, other impurities (hydrogen sulfide (H_2S), carbonyl sulfide (COS), ammonia (NH_3) etc.) need to be recovered from the syngas as they can harm the catalyst, which is necessary for the synthesis.

The implementation in AspenPlus was performed by defining the stream class MIXED and including the sub-stream non-conventional (NC) with particle size distribution (PSD). Only the main components (H_2, C, CO, CO_2, H_2O, CH_4, C_2H_6, N_2 and O_2 were modeled. For further details on the definition of unit processes see Trippe et al. [357].

Production of ethylene from syngas

Trippe et al. [359] and Haro et al. [149] have analyzed the production of ethylene from syngas. After the production of syngas, it is cleaned and conditioned. The molar $H_2 : CO$ ratio needs to be $1:1$ to enable an optimized

DME conversion. The advantage of this ratio is also, that it is quite near to the natural composition of biomass-derived syngas. At a temperature of 35 ° C at 75 bar the syngas is fed into the synthesis plant. For the assessment the process alternative of 80 bars (otherwise 40 bars) is chosen. The higher pressure results in higher investments but also higher yields. The overall process flow sheet for the production of ethylene from syngas is shown in figure 5.10.

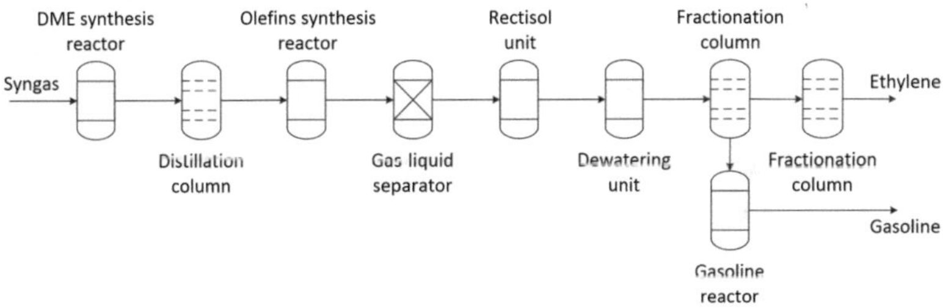

Figure 5.10: Process flow sheet for the production of ethylene f. syngas (Trippe et al. [149])

The study of Haro et al. [149] models a single step reactor. Here the methanol synthesis and *in situ* dehydration take place as in equation 5.8.

$$3CO_2 + 3H_2 \rightarrow CH_3OCH_3 + CO_2 \tag{5.8}$$

The process has been simulated in AspenPlus just as the biochemical processes for the production of butanol and succinic acid. Consequently, the results are comparable. To model hydrocarbons and light gases accurately, Haro et al. [149] applied the Soave-Redlich-Kwong (SRK) thermodynamic method and the SRK with Boston-Mathias for low pressures. The DME, olefins synthesis and gasoline reactors were modeled as yield reactors (RYield); the DME synthesis as equilibrium (REquil) and the isomerization reactor as stochiometric reactor (RStoic).

5.3.3 Estimation of investment and production cost

Haro et al. [149] provide the investment data for the basic equipment. The investment are given in million Euro of 2010. Hence, the data needs to be adapted to Dollars and the considered year of 2016 based on the capacities of the units and the scaling factors as defined by the authors. Both have used 1 GW_{th} as input capacity for gasification and the produced amount of syngas for the synthesis. The investments are the reference values for the adaption to a production capacity of 50,000 t of ethylene.

This approach is identical to Trippe et al. [356] and Haro et al. [149]. Hence, their values are comparable and applyable. The investment data is presented in table 5.17.

Table 5.17: Economic input data of thermochemical conversion

Cost Source	Pyrolysis [358]	Gasification [357]	Synthesis [149]
Capital cost $[tEUR]$	43,950	274,000	270,800
Maintenance$[tEUR/a]$	1,857	12,273	8,124
Taxes $[tEUR/a]$	439.549	2,738	5,416
Insurance $[tEUR/a]$	439.549	2,738	5,416

For water, heat and electricity cost, the same values as in table 5.13 are assumed. Additionally, a catalyst for the water gas shift reaction is necessary. This work assumes a value of 1.7 $/kg of product per year (see Trippe et al. [357]). For the calculation of the revenues in the optimization submodel and the integrated model, the sales prices of the pyrolysis products as well as of gasoline and ethylene are necessary. Pyrolysis oil can be sold for 200 $/t (see Trippe et al. [358]). Currently, the gasoline price is about 50 $/t (see EIA [163]). This work assumes an ethylene price of 675 $/t (see Waldheim [376]).

5.4 Definition of logistical parameters

In this section, the relevant logistical parameters for the optimization sub-model and the integrated model are defined. The optimization sub-model only includes truck transport due to the short, economically feasible transport distances of lignocellulosic biomass. The integrated model considers three transport modes: rail, barge and truck transport. Not only the choice of transport influences the design of the supply chain, but also the restrictions and cost of the transported material depending on the mode. In the following, the specifications of the American transport system is displayed.

With 39.5 % of all transported ton-miles of freight, rail is according to LaHood [195] the most used transport mode in the U.S. followed by truck (28.6 %) and water (12 %).

As seen in figure 5.13, truck transport of corn has the largest share in the U.S. Even though for other goods the transport via rail seems to be more reasonable, the transport distance of corn to pretreatment plants such as wet mills is too short. In general, the transport of corn has increased significantly in the past years, showing also the rising demand for corn due to biofuels and glucose syrup utilization. The transport of corn via barge does not seem to be a feasible option as most of the corn is converted within the corn belt itself. These observations are not only valid for corn but can also be transferred to other biomass types.

The development and projection of the share of different transport modes, both domestic and in total, are displayed in figure 5.11. Truck is by far the most favored transport mode and will rise in the future, but multiple modes are also expected to increase by 2040.

In the following, the different transport systems in the United States are explained.

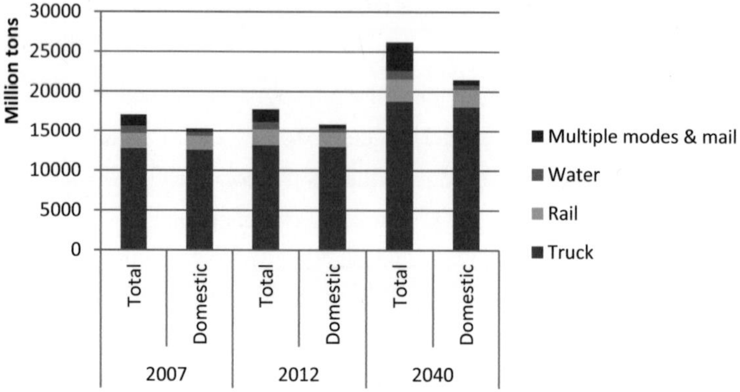

Figure 5.11: Future development of transport of corn in the U.S. (USDA, AMS [8])

5.4.1 Rail transport

The U.S. have a very dynamic freight system. Especially four companies own rail tracks and organize the transport of grains, solid and fluid products as well as chemicals on a total of 140,000 rail miles long network. These companies are BNSF (Burlington Northern Santa Fe LLC), CSX (Chessie System, Seabord System, X-Multiplicator), NS (Norfolk Southern Railway) and UP (Union Pacific Railroad). Most bulk materials such as grain and coal are transported via rail (see Federal Railroad Adminstration [115]). The amount of goods, which are transported on rail, has increased in the past years. Even though the system mileage has decreased, the ton-miles rose immensely (see Denicoff et al. [93]).

5.4.2 Barge transport

The waterways for the transportation from north to south are well established in the eastern United States. The main network for barge transport includes the Mississippi River and its waterway branches such as the Missouri River, Ohio River or Illinois River. According to the National Waterways Foundation [341], the overall commercially utilizable inland waterways system of the United States is about 12,000 miles long and includes more than 240 lock sites. It stretches from Minneapolis, Minnesota to New Orleans, Louisiana. With its connected rivers (The Illinois, Missouri, Ohio River, Arkansas and Ouachita Rivers), the whole system covers 9,000 miles (see Kruse et al. [188]). In 2005 approximately 513 million tons of domestic and coastwise freight were shipped down the Mississippi River system. Since then, transport has increased significantly.

As already seen above (see figure 5.11), barge transport is only scarcely used for grain transport. Reasons for this are not only the higher transport cost, but also the seasonality of barge transport. Especially in the north of the United States, the river navigation system is shut down due to weather and ice conditions in winter (see Meersman [222]). About 14 % of the intercity freight is transported on waterways, which is equivalent to about 624 million tons. It is especially important for the agricultural industry as more than 60 % of the nation's grain exports are handled on the waterways (see National Grain and Feed Association [141]).

5.4.3 Truck transport

Transport is the most critical element in biomass supply chains. Especially the transport of biomass feedstock from the field to the first storage area is very expensive due to the wide spread accumulation of biomass. In case of grains in the United States, many so called elevators exist. Farmers can transport their grain, mainly corn, to these facilities, which can hold between 50,000 and 5,500,000 bushels.

The assumed variable transport cost for lignocellulosic biomass are 0.25 $\frac{\$}{mi \cdot t}$ (see Brechbill et al. [59], Gallagher and Baumes [129], Sokhansanj et al. [331] a.o.). This work presumes fix transport cost of 4.85 $/t. The transport cost for pretreated biomass and chemicals for each transport mode is presented in table 5.18.

Table 5.18: Transport cost for pretreated biomass and chemicals by transport mode

Transport mode	Fixed $\frac{\$}{t}$	Variable $\frac{\$}{mi \cdot t}$	Source
truck	6.3	0.1938	
rail	35	0.056	
barge	11	0.008	[139]

5.4.4 Hubs

A hub is needed in case transport mdes are changed on route. At these facilities, the equipment is available to shift the product from one mode to the other. Depending on the total freight amount and the considered state size, more or less transport hubs exist. The state with the most hubs is Texas with 43 port terminals and 20 truck/rail facilities (see Strocko et al. [335]).

In this work, the following hubs were included. They can be accessed by truck, rail and barge, whilst not all can serve all transport modes.

- Atlanta
- Baton Rouge
- Birmingham
- Burlington
- Caruthersville
- Chicago
- Cincinnati
- Cleveland
- Dallas
- Detroit
- Dubuque
- Granite City

- Greenville
- Hannibal
- Houston
- Kansas City
- Louisville
- Memphis
- Minneapolis
- Natchez
- New Madrid
- New Orleans
- Omaha
- Quincy
- Saint Paul
- Scott City
- St. Louis
- Toledo
- Vicksburg
- West Quincy

5.4.5 Export

This work considers the four main export ports in the U.S.: New York, New Orleans, Freeport and Los Angeles. In case many ports are close to each other as e.g. Corpus Christi, South Texas, Houston and Freeport, only a single port was considered. The export is currently enabled for Asia and Europe. Due to their low industrial significance, Africa and South America are neglected in this study. Nevertheless, the inclusion is possible in the model. Distribution to the local markets is considered, but the definition of certain customers or regions have been not been included in this study. The main ports and their export shares are depicted in figure 5.12.

The export shares depend on the process and (by-)products. Bioethanol and biobased gasoline for example will be fully used in the U.S. due to their biofuel quota. The assumed export shares are summarized in table 5.19.

Each export port has its specific export rates. As New Orleans and Freeport are highly frequented, their export rates are quite high. This work assumes an export rate of 88 $/t from New Orleans and 100 $/t from Freeport. New York and Los Angeles are less busy ports. Therefore, this work assumes export rates of 60 $/t. As no values from literature could be found, these value are based on expert opinions (pers. comm.).

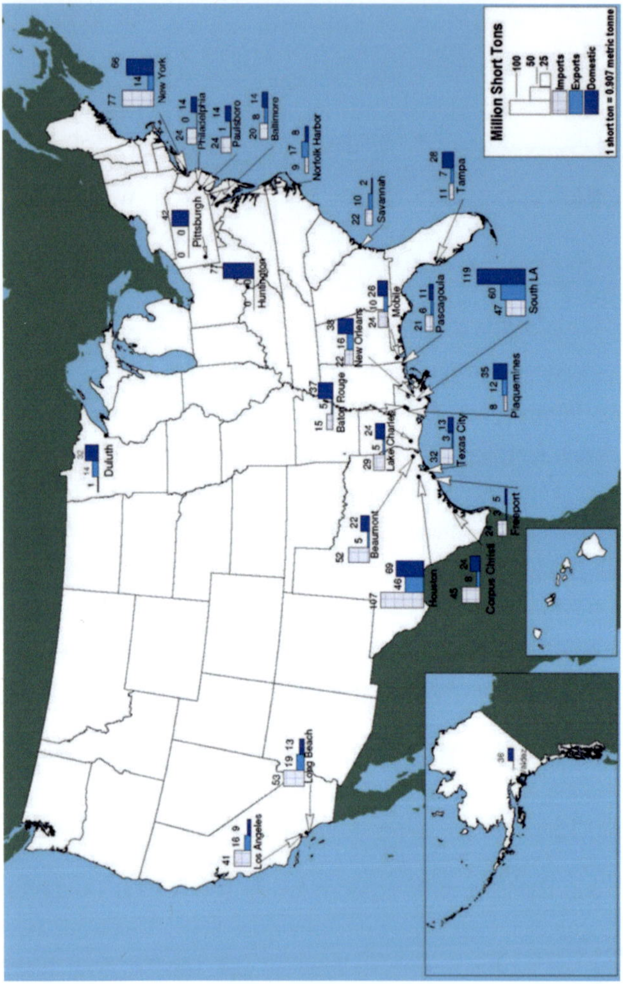

Figure 5.12: Top water ports by tonnage (Federal Highway Administration [364])

Table 5.19: Export shares depending on product and continent

Case study	Product	Local	Europe	Asia
1	Butanol	0.23	0.35	0.42
	Acetone	0.23	0.35	0.42
	Ethanol	1	-	-
2	Succinic acid	0.23	0.35	0.42
3	Ethylene	0.23	0.35	0.42
	Gasoline	1	-	-

5.4.6 Transport distances

For optimizing the location of biochemical plants and the respective logistics, the transport distances between the potential locations, the supply nodes and demand sinks are essential. The transport cost depend on the type of transport and the transport distances. Therefore, all distances between the locations need to be estimated for each transport mode. Rail, barge and truck have their own networks. Hence, the transport distances vary from transport mode to transport mode.

As many locations are considered in this model, the manual calculation of transport distances is time consuming. Consequently, two different approaches were applied to estimate the truck and rail transport distances. For truck transport, Google Maps is used as database. To download the transport distances, the coordinates of each location is necessary. It is used as input for a Python code in Anacoda. With two given coordinates, the code calculates the distances between those nodes as also applied in Zimmer et al. [404].

To estimate rail distances, the given GIS data from the U.S. Department of Transport [354] on all nodes and edges of the U.S. rail system is used. With the cost-distance calculation in ArcGIS10 the rail distances can be calculated accurately.

For the barge transport, distances the values provided by the U.S. Army Corps of Engineers [365] have been analyzed and the differences between the locks result in the barge transport distances.

5.5 Risk Analysis

In this section, the risk analysis and its input data are presented. At first, the risks have been identified based on discussions with experts from industry and by literature research (see section 3.8.2). The experts were part of a joint project with the chemical industry and included partners from purchasing, engineering and logistics. A recent literature review by Bairamzadeh et al. [34] already includes a large variety of general risks. Unfortunately, they do not go very much into detail. Hence, the identified risks in this work are more detailed and specific to the case studies. Nevertheless, the list below is not intended to by exhaustive. In general, the identified risks are clustered as defined in section 3.7.5 in transport, process, environmental, political, supply and market risks. The specific risks are described in detail and the utilized data for analysis are displayed. The presented risks are especially relevant for biomass value chains of corn, sugar cane, sorghum as well as their residues for the production of the biochemicals in the United States. Some risks may be also considered for other biomass in other regions and other final products, but many risks are specific for this application.

The risks were identified for biomass value chains from biomass cultivation to the transport to the final port as defined in figure 5.1. This work does not include risks for the export of products. The identified risks are based on the current state of the art and do not include risks, which might occur based on future setting. Nevertheless, uncertainties of future developments based on the current view are identified.

5.5.1 Transport risks

Transport risks include multiple different uncertainties but are all dependent on the utilized transport mode. In this work, three transport types are considered: rail, barge and truck. The specifics of the infrastructure network are presented in section 5.4. In the following, the identified uncertainties are assessed for each transport mode. The main identified uncertainties are: accidents, congestion, strikes, restrictions due to sugar syrup and time delays caused by the utilization of multiple transport modes connected by transport hubs. Especially in the United States, the historical data for transport modes are well documented. Consequently, many data is available for risk assessment. For estimating the likelihood of risks in transportation, all risks are analyzed for all transport modes. The respective historical data were gathered for each relevant state in the considered region. Hence, twenty states for three transport modes were investigated for each risk.

The consideration of uncertainties in the transport sector is crucial as the domestic transport of corn as increased immensely in the past years as presented in figure 5.13.

From 1984 to 2013, the total transported amount of corn has increased threefold. Truck transport has risen the most. It is the most favored transport mode for corn. The main reason for this is the lacking railway network to every farmer and the short transport distances to the next processing plant. Barge and rail transport has remained more or less constant in the past years. In the following, the different transport risks are explained.

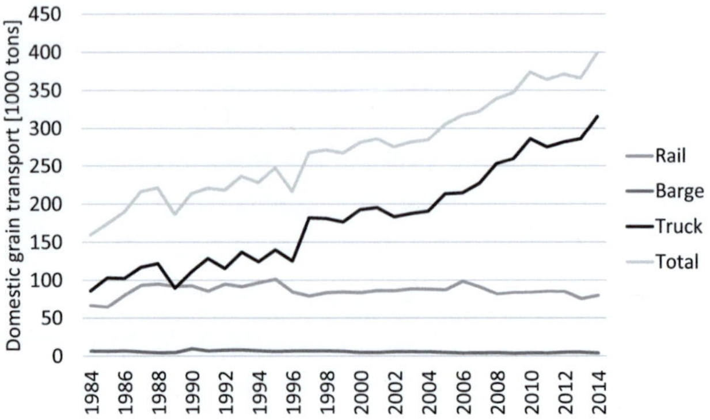

Figure 5.13: Development of domestic transport of corn in the U.S. (USDA, AMS [8])

5.5.1.1 Accidents

Accidents are reported quite thoroughly by the Federal Motor Carrier Safety Administration for truck [114], the Federal Railroad Administration [266] for rail and the National Transportation Safety Board [258] for barge. The accidents and their history are presented in the following.

Rail

The Office of Safety Analysis of the Federal Railroad Administration [266] gathers all rail accidents by state and rail company from 1975 onward. This data provides the accidents on all railroads in the United States. All accidents of the largest rail companies (BNSF, UP, CSX and NS) in the relevant states were considered in the analysis. For estimating the probability of rail accidents, the average amount was calculated based on the available years. As the different states have different rail distances, the number of rail accidents need to be normalized to the distance of each state. In states with longer rail miles the probability of an accident is higher. Therefore, the amount of accidents is divided by the rail miles in the respective state. In figure 5.14, the rail accidents are in the past years are displayed by state.

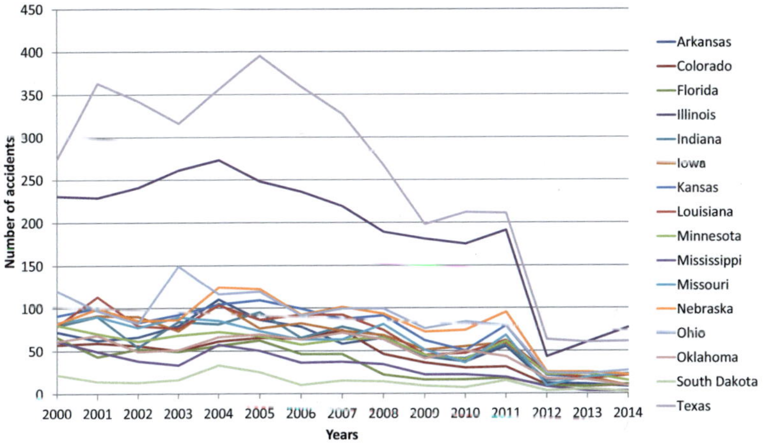

Figure 5.14: Rail accidents by rail mile (Office of Safety Analysis [266])

Truck

The National Highway Traffic Safety Administration (NHTSA) has gathered data on truck accidents in the United States (see NHTSA [252] [253] [255] [254] [251] [250] [249] [248]). For the years 1993 to 2013 these accidents have been analyzed. The number of accidents are clearly dependent on the economy. In the time after the crash of 2008 the truck accidents have decreased immensely as not as many goods needed to be transported in those years. With rising economy, the accidents also increased again. Evidently, more accidents occur in larger states with more traffic (e.g. see Texas). Hence, the probabilities of accidents were normalized by the area of each state. Not all reported accidents were considered. This work only analyzed the accidents of large trucks in highways. Small truck accidents on field roads were excluded from the analysis.

These do not have the large influence (neither probabilities nor consequence) to be considered in this work. The truck accidents of the past years are displayed by state in figure 5.15.

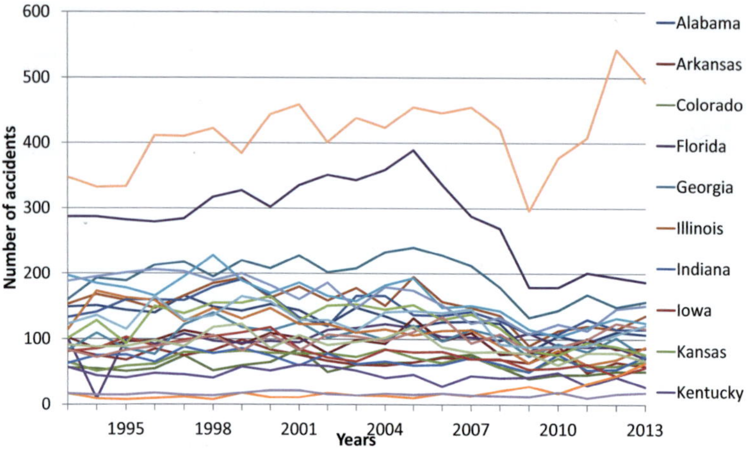

Figure 5.15: Truck accidents by highway mile (NHTSA [255])

Barge

Barge accidents are rare. Mostly, accidents are directly dependent on the river level. The Mississippi River is the main waterway from the corn belt to the southern ports. In figure 5.16, the historical river levels are displayed. Even though barge transport is highly weather related, the fatalities are much lower compared to other transport modes. On a per ton mile basis, there is only one fatality in the marine sector for every 22.7 in the rail or 155 fatalities in the highway sector (see Texas Transportation Institute [341]). The reason for this is also the low amount of barge on the Mississippi River compared to the high frequency of trucks on highways. Although a truck can hold much less goods than barge, the amount of corn transported by truck is much higher (see figure 5.13). Myers [242] describes an accident in 2014 as a barge accident caused oil spill. Another oil spill occurred in 2013 near Vicksburg (see Mohr [235]). Two separate accidents due to floods on the Mississippi and Ohio rivers caused the closure of the rivers (see Plume [288]). These are only a few examples for barge accidents.

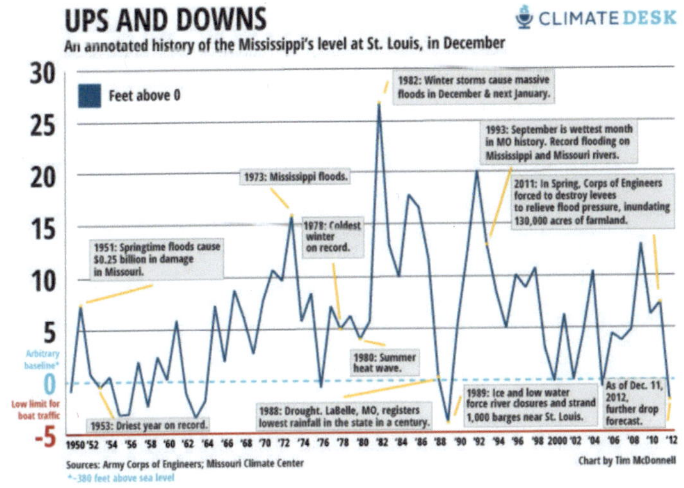

Figure 5.16: History of Mississippi's level at St. Louis (McDonnell [219])

5.5.1.2 Congestion

Congestion is affected by different aspects in the transport sector and is monitored by the U.S. Department of Transportation [112]. It occurs if the available capacity of a transport system (in this thesis mainly the highway system) is lower than the actual traffic demand. Influencing factors for congestion are: bottlenecks, traffic incidents, work zones, bad weather, poor traffic signal timing and special events. The effect of congestion is often not as dramatic as accidents but can cause delays, which are not planned in Just-in-Time production.

Rail

In the past years the amount of transported grain, oil and coal have increased significantly in the United States (see The AgriNews [15]). As a consequence, congestion occurs more and more often. Mostly oil companies have the upper hand so that farmers and elevators can wait for thirty and more days for a rail car to arrive. This leads to a shift of rail transport to barges (see Meersman [222]).

Additionally to the rising demand for oil and coal, also an increasing amount of grains leads to bottlenecks in the Upper Midwest. Especially the harvest of 2013/2014 caused delays in Minnesota, Montana, North Dakota and South Dakota (see USDA [79]). These states also lack an access to barge transport and can therefore not elude. Currently, the rail system operates near full capacity, which is risky in case other incidents such as severe weather occur. Consequently, it is assumed, that rail congestion will further increase in future.

Truck

Due to rising freight demands, the congestion of trucks spreads from urban areas to larger stretches in also urban areas. According to the Federal Highway Administration [113], congestion will increase by 2035. Highway segments with more than 10,000 trucks per day are expected to rise to more than 10,000 miles for slow traffic and an additional 23,000 miles for stop-and-go-traffic. This development is caused by an increased freight volume. According to the Department of Transportation [112], truck congestion only lead to a mean delay of a few minutes. Nevertheless, the development of tardiness will increase by 2035 (see figure 5.17 and figure 5.18) and are, hence, included in this work.

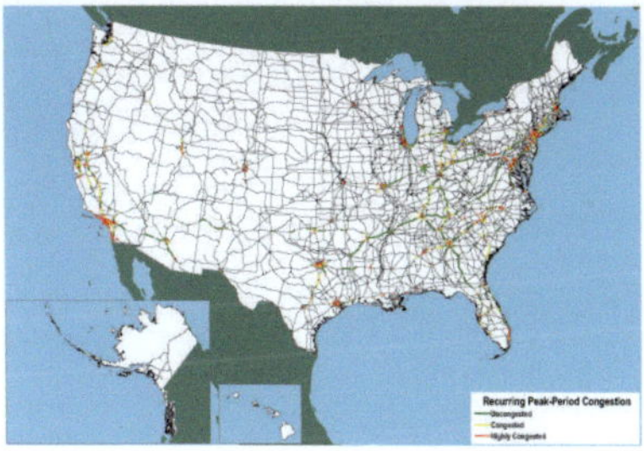

Figure 5.17: Congestion 2002 (FHA [112])

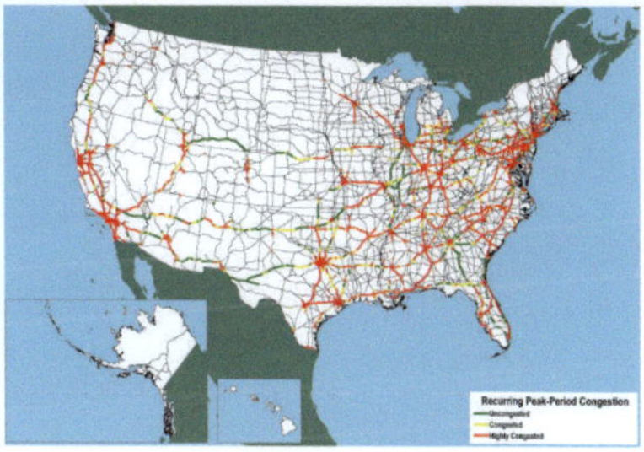

Figure 5.18: Congestion 2035(FHA [112])

Barge

Congestion in barge transport occurs once multiple vessels arrive at the same time at a port although they are normally scheduled throughout the week. Additionally, the size of container ships is constantly increasing, leading to longer loading times are space issues. Due to lock operations and an aging infrastructure the inland waterways cause bottlenecks. In 2007, 31 % of the 520,000 vessels were delayed on average by 30 to 90 minutes. Environmental risks such as floods, droughts, storm or ice can cause additional congestion (see Federal Highways Administration [113]).

5.5.1.3 Strike

Depending on the country and the existing labor unions, the risk of strikes varies. In the United States, the number of strikes has decreased immensely. As shown in figure 5.19, the total strikes, including sectors, which are irrelevant for this study (e.g. teachers and hospitals), occur seldom in the past years. Therefore, the risk of strikes seems negligible and are not further modeled with probabilities in this work. Nevertheless, the failure of a single transport mode due to strikes or similar needs to be considered. Hence, this risk is modeled as a scenario (see section 5.6.5). Strikes cannot only occur in the transport sector but also in production (see Arnesen [22]). This can lead to shutdowns of the plant.

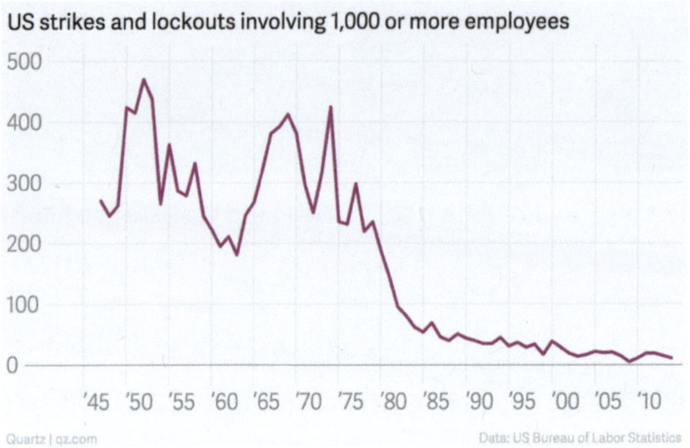

Figure 5.19: Number of U.S. strikes and locouts involving 1000 or more employees (Matts [284], Office of Compensation and Working Conditions [265])

5.5.1.4 Restrictions for transporting pretreated biomass

Due to the crystallization characteristics of sugar syrup, the transport distance and, hence, time is restricted to the ambient temperature. Sugar syrup can be transported in insulated containers via truck or rail, but not in vessels. In barge transport the risk of crystallization and contamination is too high as the vessels cannot be insulated, heated and cleaned as required. For more details on crystallization of sugar syrup see section 5.5.5.1. These restrictions do not only apply to sugar syrup but also to pyrolysis slurry. It does not crystallize when it gets too cold, but too long transportation times and a lack of mixer can lead to sedimentation (see section 5.5.5.1).

5.5.2 Process risks

In this section, process risks, which occur in chemical industry in general and especially whilst using biomass as feedstock are described. Gunukula et al. [145] have discussed the effect of platform technologies for the production of biochemicals for risk reduction. Often, facilities are designed to produce a single main product. These are extremely prone to technological and market risks as they cannot swap products in case the demand decreases. If the intermediate product can be combined by bio- and chemical-catalysis and be further processed to other chemicals, then the financial risk might decrease and profitability of the investment will rise. The considered process risks in this work are utility demand, varying yields, shutdown of production plants, color of the product, and technical storage risks.

5.5.2.1 Utility demand

The processes for converting biomass to chemicals vary depending on the feedstock. In most cases, this leads to varying utility demands. This can have a positive effect if for example less water is needed for the fermentation but can also mean an increase of energy in case of additional downstream processing steps. The varying utility demand is included in the model by simulation of different biomass sources. The quality of biomass cause varying compositions of the pretreated biomass. However, these risks are reduced by supplier contracts and are, therefore, minimized. Consequently, this risk is not further analyzed in this work.

5.5.2.2 Process stability and varying yields

This section analyzes the process stability and varying yields resulting from different feedstocks and process conditions for biochemical and thermochemical processes.

Fermentation and other biochemical processes

Fermentation yields strongly depend on the performance of the microorganisms. Mainly, the sugar composition and the presence of inhibitors in the fermentation broth will affect the efficiency of fermentations. Other production factors such as pressure, temperature, etc. also influence the fermentation yield but are more easily to control. Especially sugars syrups from biorefineries of lignocellulosic biomass contain not only C6 sugars as sugar but also C5 sugars (e.g. xylose), which are often not as easy to metabolize. Hence, the choice of biomass influences the production yield. The influence is quantified by the simulations in AspenPlus and is used as input parameter for the integrated model.

Thermochemical processes

Thermochemical processes are not as sensible to the biomass or pretreated biomass composition, especially the lignin content (see Boateng et al. [52]). Nevertheless, high ash content will cause slag in the gasifier, which can reduce the overall efficiency. Additionally, varying qualities can lead to different $H_2 : CO$ ratios, which need to be buffered by the catalyst and cause additional cost. Consequently, varying biomass qualities can lead to additional processing times, maintenance, and cost.

5.5.2.3 Shutdown

In case of weather risks, especially hurricanes/tornadoes or heavy storms, or in case of an outage of the electricity supplier shutdowns of the production site might occur. Often, an emergency generator will be used to overcome the outage. Short-time shutdowns can be handled quite easily, but the electricity net can also be harmed by severe weather and power lines can be cut. In these cases the production will halt, which might result in varying fermentation yields and product destruction. Additionally, strikes can cause a shutdown if the production plant as no worker will arrive to run the plant. This results in less product and unsatisfied customers.

5.5.2.4 Color

Corn syrups normally have a „water white“color. The color might change depending on the processing as well as storage and transport conditions. Influencing factors for the formation of color changes in corn syrups are time, temperature, pH and SO_2 concentration. Corn syrups caramelize during heating causing the development of dark brown colors and the production of inhibitors. The formation of 5-(hydroxymethyl)-2-furaldehayde and 2-(2-hydroxyacetyl)-furan during excessive heating at 80°C have an influence on the color. The optical density and spectrophotometer are used to measure and classify the color development(see Pancoast [275]).

Granulated sugars develop colors as well. When stored at room temperature of 20 °C the color development is very slowly. If the ambient temperature exceeds 50 °C then color will develop more rapidly. Colors in the feedstock will also lead to color in the product. The color needs to be eliminated by additional processing steps, which result in higher production cost (see Pérez et al. [281]).

5.5.2.5 Technical storage risks

The storage of biomass and sugar syrup needs special care. The storage and transport tanks need to be disinfected and sealed. Such as in biochemical conversion to chemicals, the contamination with microbes leads to the degradation of the feedstock. In case sugar, or biomass in general, is in contact with microbes during storage, it is converted to ethanol, biogas, fermentation gases, and similar. Hence, it cannot be converted to final products anymore. To reduce storage losses the treatment and handling of biomass and sugar syrup as well as the storage tanks is essential. The minimization of storage times reduces the risk of storage degradation (see Kumar and Kalita [191]).

Long storage times just as long transport times lead to sedimentation of pyrolysis slurry. Additional energy is needed to stir up the slurry. In the worst case, the slurry cannot be reused and needs to be disposed (see Nicoleit [261]).

5.5.3 Environmental risks

This section defines the specific environmental risks, which occur in the biomass relevant states in the United States. The environmental risks include mainly extreme weather conditions, which immensely affect the harvest. Other environmental risks are insects and fungi. These risks are described in the following.

5.5.3.1 Weather

Weather risks include all extreme events that can harm the harvest. Some weather conditions do not only affect the biomass itself but also the transport system, production or supply. In the following the risks, which occur on mainland U.S. for corn, sugar cane, sorghum and their residues. Some weather risks might have a more severe impact on some biomass than others. Especially residues might be affected more positively by weather events than the grain itself as the energy of the crop will not focus on the grain anymore but the residue is still produced. The main weather risks, that affect the crop are hail, drought, hurricane/tornado, temperatures, and blizzards.

Hail

Hail is defined by the The National Severe Storms Laboratory of the National Oceanic and Atmospheric Administration (NOAA) [343] as "a form of that occurs when updrafts in thunderstorms carry raindrops upward into extremely cold areas of the atmosphere where they freeze into balls of ice". The ice balls can destroy the harvest, so that the grain is not fully grown. On the other hand, the straw share can still be utilized for sugar syrup production in biorefineries or pyrolysis slurry. The top ten states with hail damages are Texas, Illinois, Colorado, Missouri, Nebraska, South Carolina, Pennsylvania, Iowa, South Dakota and Kansas. The historic data of the past 50 years has been analyzed and probabilities based on the Poisson distribution have been calculated.

Drought

According to the NOAA [245], drought is the "deficiency in precipitation over an extended period". In the U.S. drought is measured by the Palmer Drought Severity Index (PDSI). Especially in the past years heavy droughts became more and more frequent. The variability of interannual precipitation causes not only variations in crop yields but also in quality. In 1988 a severe drought occurred in the U.S. Midwest. The temperatures were comparably high from early spring on throughout the summer with reduced precipitation. Hence, the crop yields dropped by 37 %, which required a congressional bailout for farmers of a billion dollars. Between 1989 and 2012, 90 % of crop loss indemnity payments were caused by extreme weather events (equivalent to $ 80 billion) of which drought accounted alone to 40 % of the payments (see Rosenzweig et al. [308]). The drought in 2012 was one of the most severe droughts in the past decade. Especially states with a high corn acreage were affected by the drought. Louisiana and Alabama with high sugar cane production had rather wet weather, which resulted in high yields. The past 50 years have been analyzed and Poisson distributions of drought severity are included in the integrated model. Nevertheless, some droughts are very severe and cannot be portrayed in probabilities. Therefore, the severe drought of 2012 is modeled by a scenario (see section 5.6.2) to show the influence of such risks. In figure 5.20, the precipitation ranks of the drought in 2012 are displayed.

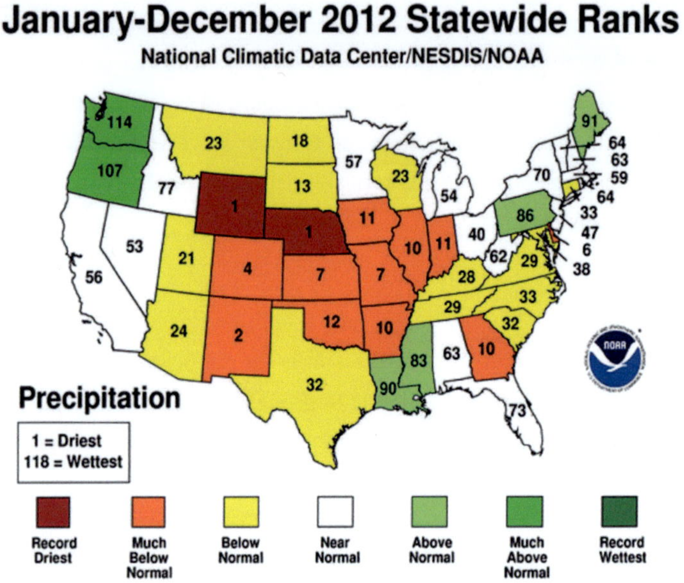

Figure 5.20: Precipitation ranks of 2012 drought in the U.S. (NOAA [246])

Heavy rainfall and precipitation

According to farmers in the corn belt and the USDA [63], corn yield was extremely high in 2014 due to wet weather on the one hand. This lead to a decrease by 13 % of corn prices compared to the previous year, which was already 40 % lower than the years before. On the other hand, heavy rainfalls can lead to floods or fouling of the crop roots. The past 50 years have been analyzed regarding extreme heavy rainfalls and included by Poisson distribution in the integrated model.

Hurricane/Tornadoes

Hurricanes are defined as tropical cyclones with a maximum wind speed of 74 mph. This term is mostly used in the Northern Hemisphere. Typhoon is more known for the Pacific regions (see National Hurricane Center [256]).

Tornadoes are "narrow, violently rotating columns of air that extend from the base of a thunderstorm to the ground" (see National Severe Storms Laboratory [344]). Tornadoes occur more in the north and hurricanes more in the south of the U.S., due to the closeness of water. Both severe storms combine heavy wind and rain, which can destroy the harvest. Especially tornadoes are very regional, hence, the probability of destruction is lower compared to hurricanes (see Central Pacific Hurricane Center [73]).

This work treats hurricanes and tornadoes equally in terms of harvest destruction. The probabilities of hurricane/tornadoes based on the historical values of the past 50 years are included in the integrated model (see NOAA [247]).

Temperatures

On the one hand, at temperatures below 10°C corn will not sprout. These temperatures are normally reached between late April and early May in the corn belt. On the other hand, too high temperatures will cause the sprouts to burn. The data for the past 50 years is provided by the NOAA [247].

Blizzards

Blizzards mostly occur in winter time. As the grain is already harvested in autumn and the new seed will not be brought out until spring blizzards hardly affect the crop itself. Nevertheless, the biomass as well as the products are processed and transported throughout the year. Blizzards cause on the one hand frozen streets, tracks and rivers, which results in a transport chaos. On the other hand it also influences production itself as frozen power lines might lead to shutdowns. Therefore, the likelihood of severe blizzards based on the historic values by the NOAA [247] is included in the model.

5.5.3.2 Natural Risks

Natural risks include all risks, which are evident in nature but are not referred to weather risks. These can be caused by severe weather events but are not defined as such (e.g. floods) (see Merz [224]).

Floods

Flood risks affect the biomass cultivation as well as the transport of goods on rivers. For example in 1993 the Mississippi River flooded. 15 million acres of farmland were hit, especially Nebraska, Iowa and Michigan. More than 50 people died and an economic damage of more than 15 billion dollars occurred (see Larson [198]). Not only farm land was affected but the flood had a large impact on transportation. Barge traffic stopped for about two months on the Missouri and Mississippi River. According to Larson [198], two major events have an influence on floods: significant rainfall and wet soil conditions. Milly et al. [231] forecast that rainfall is likely to become less frequent but with more intense causing more extreme floods.

Crop pests

Crop pests include insects, mites and some species of wood lice (see Capinera et al. [68]). Many different insects can harm the crop and result in reduced harvest yields. Depending on the biomass and the considered region the insects vary. Especially in dry and warm periods the corn root worm can damage the crop. Genetically modified corn organisms have been developed by companies such as Monsanto, Dow Chemicals or DuPont to be resistant to pests and to herbicides (see ISAAA [264]). GMO-corn produces a protein, which should harm the corn root worm (*Diabrotica spp.*) but be harmless to people and animals. Unfortunately, the corn root worm has grown to be resistant to these proteins. Especially the major corn regions in the Midwest (Illinois, Iowa, Nebraska and Minnesota) are affected of this development. Farmers fear that without a soil insecticide the yields and harvest could be much lower and lead to financial drawbacks. In the past years the root worm has cost more than billion dollars in expenses and lost harvest (see Crop Science United States [86]). The rootworm-protected corn from Monsanto only allowed 0.2 % of the total corn acreage to be unexpectedly damaged (see Factiva [109]).

5.5.4 Political risks

In this section the considered political risks in the biomass value chain is described. The risks are based on the political situation in 2017. It is not possible to propose a likelihood of a certain political event, as they depend on the people and other circumstances. Hence, this work does not estimate probabilities for political risks. Nevertheless, some of these risks have severe consequences to biomass value chains. Therefore, these are modeled as scenarios as described in section 5.6. The political uncertainties include the decision of policy makers based on stakeholder and public perception to ban the utilization of GMO biomass. Politicians can also decide to foster incentives for the utilization of lignocellulosic biomass. Not only the production of biomass but also the use of the final product, mainly bioethanol in the United States can be pushed and a quote for biofuel production can be set.

5.5.4.1 Non-GMO biomass

The influence of GMO (gene manipulated organisms) feedstock on the yield and hence on the availability and cost for the production of biobased products is tremendous. GMO feedstocks are more resistant to insects, tolerant to herbicides and have varieties of stacked genes (see Owen [274]).

Even though GMO feedstocks have a higher yield, which contributes to nourishment of the world and the fulfillment of the bioethanol quota, the production is highly discussed among the public. The acceptance due to sustainability issues as well as unknown effects on biodiversity and other organisms is declining in the population. Consequently, the topic is highly discussed in politics. This could lead to the ban of GMO biomass (see Frankfurter Allgemeine Zeitung [243]).

The acreage of GMO corn has increased significantly in the U.S. in since 2000. Depending on the state, the share of GMO corn has increased from around 20 to 30 % to more than 90 %. The strongest rise could be found for Indiana where currently 88 % of the corn acreage was gene manipulated in 2014/2015. Compared to 2000, this is an increase of 800 %. But the share of GMO areas has decreased slightly from 2013/2014 to the following year for almost all states (see USDA [10] [11][12] [13]). In figure 5.21, the development of GMO corn in the respective states is depicted.

Sugar cane on the other hand is currently not modified genetically in the large-scale due to the complexity of its genome. Hence, the risk of political quotas, which forbid the growth GMO sugar cane is non existent (see Arruda [23]). As sorghum is a very drought resistant feedstock, the demand for GMO grain is not identified. Hence, sorghum is not directly affected by a political decision (see Bergin [45]). The influence of non-GMO corn could have a significant influence on the biomass value chain. As the likelihood of such a development cannot be quantified, this work includes this work by scenario analysis in section 5.6.3.

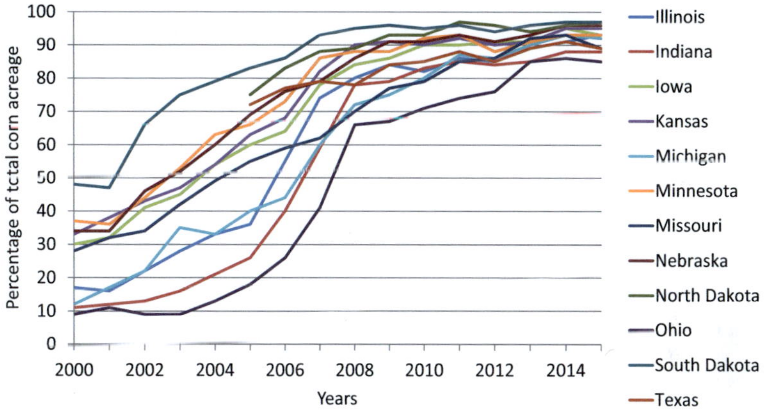

Figure 5.21: Percentage of GMO corn acreage in the U.S. (USDA [9])

5.5.4.2 Incentives for lignocellulosic biomass

Due to quality reasons of the sugar syrup the utilization of lignocellulosic biomass is up to now not realized in industrial size. Sugar and starchy biomass result in a sugar syrup, which contains mainly hexoses and only few to none pentoses. Many microorganisms metabolize C6 sugars much better and, hence result in a higher yield and efficiency of the fermentation. As high yields also result in a higher economic feasibility many companies prefer to use first generation biomass. Nevertheless, especially corn-based bioethanol is more and more under pressure of the "food and tank" debate. According to Chen and Smitz [77], especially government policies have a large influence on the commercialization of cellulosic biofuels. In case government decides to give incentives for the use of lignocellulosic biomass the profits can increase for sugar syrups from biorefineries. Consequently, the choice of feedstock might shift from first to second generation biomass.

This work assumes an incentive of 50 % as it is comparably established for biodiesel (see Alternative Fuels Data Center [17]). As the decision of policy makers cannot be described as a probability, this risk is modeled as scenario (see section 5.6.4).

5.5.4.3 Quota for bioethanol production

According to the Second Renewable Fuel Standard, which was announced in 2007 as part of the Energy Independence Act [339], the aim of the United States is to produce 136 billion liters of biofuels annually. 61 billion liters of which must be based on cellulosic sources. However, it also sets a maximum of 57 billion liters of corn based ethanol. Without governmental support this might not be feasible in the near future (see Chen and Smith [77]).

Abrams et al. [4] claim that even though public policies for biomass promotion are substantial for the development of the woody biomass energy sector, the effectiveness of them remains unclear. Many of the state level support policies are in conflict with federal regulatory policies and lead to additional cost and uncertainties.

This work assumes, that the aim of the Second Renewable Fuel Standard can be met and will increase the competition for biomass. This will result in increasing prices. These influences cannot be quantified by probabilities, hence, the developments are shown by scenario calculations in section 5.6.4.

5.5.5 Supply risks

As in many other supply chains, biomass supply is one of the most critical aspects. In case biomass or one of its downstream products cannot be supplied, all following steps lack their feedstock. In the following, the considered supply risks of the defined biomass supply chain in the United States are explained. These include utilization risks of the feedstock, uncertainties in harvesting seasons, supplier outage and storage.

5.5.5.1 Risks affecting the utilization of pretreated biomass

After producing pretreated biomass (sugar syrup and pyrolysis slurry) the transport and supply is sensible to ambient conditions. Sugar syrup can crystallize or caramelize, color can develop during storage and inhibitors can affect the syrup quality. Pyrolysis slurry can sediment, which reduces the efficiency of the utilization.

Crystallization of sugar syrup

Corn glucose syrup is produced in corn wet mills, in biorefineries from lignocellulosic biomass such as corn stover or bagasse or as an intermediate product in sugar mills. If sugar syrup cools down below 130 to 140 °F, which is about 55 °C (see Sweeteners Regional Offices [337]), it crystallizes and forms a solid state. The crystallized sugar syrup is not pumpable so that it needs to be reheated, which can then, cause caramelization and other risks. These lead to additional cost for the transport and timing problems. According to information given by a large corn syrup producer, the corn sugar syrup is transported in vacuum isolated tanks to prevent crystallization. The tank temperature decreases by 1 °F every four days. Consequently, a tank can be stored for about half a year before crystallization occurs (private information). This of course depends on the outside temperature, the material of the tank as well as the starting temperature of the sugar syrup. In order to prove the information by the source, the duration of crystallization is calculated according to the following equation 5.9.

$$\frac{1}{Bi} = \frac{\lambda}{\alpha \cdot L} \tag{5.9}$$

The Biot number Bi is a dimensionless value, which is used for thermodynamic calculations. With λ being the thermal conductivity, α the heat transfer coefficient and L the characteristic length of the heat transfer, the cooling down of a truck by ambient temperature can be calculated. See the appendix A.1.3 for more details. As most supply chains, especially in the United States, are shorter than the maximum calculated distance, the risk of crystallization does not seem essential. Furthermore, not only the probability of crystallization is low but also the effect of a crystallized tank. Hence, this work does not model the the time dependency of crystallization in detail but considers the mean risk.

Caramelization of sugar syrup

Yildiz [176] defines caramelization as "the degradation of sugars in the absence of amino acids and proteins by heating them over their melting point and thereby causing color and flavor changes." Caramelization can lead to the production of unpleasant compounds within the sugar syrup, which influence the downstream processes and the final product quality due to color and inhibitors. During caramelization inhibitors such as furfural, 5-hydroxymethyl furfural (HMF), weak acids, and phenolic compounds are produced by the degradation of sugar.

Color

The color of the sugar syrup itself does not have a direct impact on the fermentation process itself. If colored products are envisaged, then this caramelization effect does not induce a risk. Otherwise, if clear white chemicals are produced, then the formation of color leads to a risk.

Color is formed by nonenzymatic glycation, the so called Maillard Reaction, which was observed in 1912. During the reaction the reducing-sugars of the carbonyl groups react with the amino groups of amino acids, polypeptides, proteins, enzymes etc. to a brown pigment called melanoidin. The type of sugar has a large influence on the browning of the Maillard Reaction. Products from glucose react faster to brown pigments as from fructose. Also, shorter sugars, e.g. xylose have a higher reactivity than longer sugars. Temperature has the highest impact on the Maillard Reaction. If temperature rises by 10 K then the browning rate is two to three fold. Temperature also affects the composition of the products of the Maillard Reaction. Bozkurt et al. [58] found that the browning rate increased by 3.2 times whilst changing the reaction temperature from 55 to 65 °C.

Inhibitors

As already described in section 2.3.2.1, inhibitors can be produced during preprocessing of mainly second generation biomass. These inhibitors are for example furfural, hydroxymethylfurural, phenols, acids, aldehydes and alcohols. Especially biochemical processes are sensible to these chemicals. Therefore, the preprocessed biomass needs to be conditioned accordingly. In case this is not done in a sufficient manner, the fermentation can either process less efficiently or not at all (see Pienkos and Zhang [286] and Joensson et al. [171]). Consequently, lower efficiencies cause additional feedstock demand.

Sedimentation of pyrolysis slurry

The slurry composition of biooil and biochar influences the stability of the suspension. Nicoleit [261] has analyzed the stability of the pyrolysis slurry and proposed a constant stirring of the slurry to avoid sedimentation. Once the slurry is fully sedimented it is almost impossible to stir it up. Hence, the container cannot be used for further processing.

5.5.5.2 Uncertainties in harvesting season

Harvesting seasons depend on the weather conditions throughout the year. Firstly, if the soil is still too frozen and wet then the seed cannot be brought out to the field. This delays the harvesting. Also, if the season is too dry or cold then the crop cultivation time is longer. On the one hand, an early harvest leads to an overfull stock at storage locations and an efficient storage management is necessary. On the other hand, in case of a late harvest shortages in the supply may occur (see Xie et al. [392], Rentizelas et al. [301]). These are uncertainties, which are not biomass or location dependent. In order to manage these risks, the storage capacity should be optimized accordingly, both at the farmers location and the conversion facilities. Additionally, the possibility to import pretreated biomass from other continents need to be considered. As storage and biomass import are not optimized in this work, these uncertainties are not included in the model.

5.5.5.3 Supplier cannot supply

It might occur that the supplier cannot provide the pretreated biomass. This risk could have multiple causes. The supplier might shut down his production due to strikes, blackouts, etc. He might also need to pause his production because of lacking biomass supply due to rising demand or weather related risks. The effect of this risk depends on the storage management of the company. If still enough feedstock is available, then the supply for the fermentation is still ensured. A lack of supply can cause additional cost for the production of biochemicals. The operator needs to choose another supplier, which is either more expensive or will cause additional transport cost to ensure a continuous production. Alternatively, he could also optimize his storage capacity to overcome some days without new supply. The most reasonable solution seems to be a location close to a many suppliers.

5.5.5.4 Economic storage risk

Storage can be a source for risk mitigation but also risk occurrence. During storage, the raw biomass can deterioate but also pretreated biomass can crystallize or sediment respectively. The storage capacity depends on many different factors. Additional storage is therefore chance and risk at once. Large storage capacities are expensive, but can buffer on the one hand supply risks. On the other hand, in case of deterioration, large storage capacities lead to large losses. Its optimization is essential and should be considered carefully. This is beyond the scope of this work and is therefore not included in the integrated model. Rentizelas et al. [301] for example have developed a model, that optimizes storage capacities.

5.5.6 Market risks

This section analysis the market risks, which occur in biomass to biochemicals value chains. Market risks mostly focus on the demand for final products. This can affect either the demand for the biochemical itself or for a competing product such as biofuels. Additionally, varying market prices can influence the profitability of the value chain. These risks are described in the following.

5.5.6.1 Demand for biobased chemicals

The demand for biomass based chemicals have different impacts. Higher demands lead to a higher demand for the feedstock. This, in turn, results in higher prices of pretreated biomass. Consequently, the own value chain and production would be more expensive. On the one hand, if other chemical companies produce the same product, the market can decrease and the prices are more competitive. On the other hand, this might persuade the customers to increase their the willingness to pay more for biobased chemicals (see Carus et al. [71]). Currently, only few facilities for the production of biobased chemicals exist. For example, DuPont and Tate & Lyle have installed a biobased propanediol plant in Loudon (see DuPont and Tate & Lyle [99]). This work assumes that the majority of other companies would also tend to build up biobased chemical plants in the corn belt. This would increase the demand and, hence, the price of corn based glucose syrup. This risk has similar effects as any scenario, which reduces the corn availability. Consequently, it is not separately considered as scenario.

5.5.6.2 Demand for bioethanol

The production of bioethanol is strongly related to the oil prices, the rising demand for fuels in the transport sector and the quota for bioethanol as shown above. An increasing demand for bioethanol leads to rising biomass prices and a lack of supply in the worst case. Hence, the production prices for biochemicals rise and the economic feasibility is questionable. Currently, a large number of bioethanol plants exist in the United States. The locations are depicted in figure 5.22. These plants are currently based on corn, therefore, they are mainly located in the corn belt. Political decisions (see section 5.5.4) can lead to more lignocellulosic bioethanol, which could release additional corn syrup potential for biochemicals.

5.5.6.3 Market price

Biochemicals may replace petrochemical products structurally or functionally (see Gunukula et al. [145]). Low market prices for petrochemical products results in a decreased interest of the customers in biobased chemicals. Many of them are not willing to pay a high benefit for a more sustainable product as it decreases their margin.

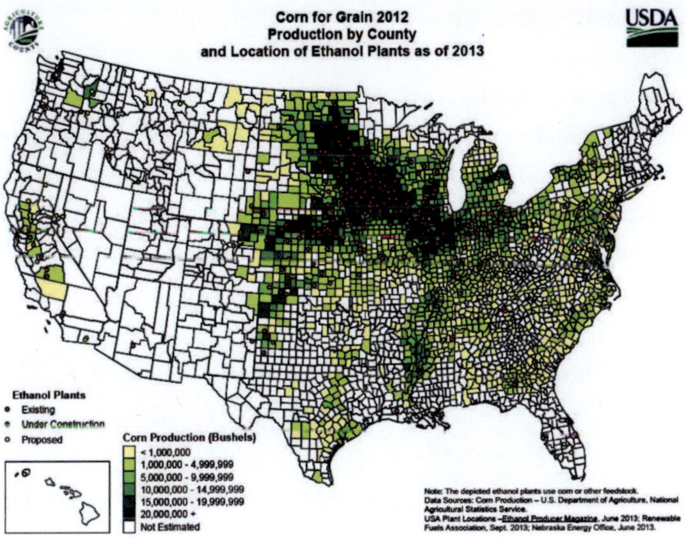

Figure 5.22: Existing bioethanol plants in the U.S. (USDA [14])

5.6 Scenario construction

The developed approach in this work includes quantifiable and non- quantifiable risks. In case of quantifiable risks the likelihood and consequences of the risks can be estimated based on historical data as described in section 4.4. Non-quantifiable risks are modeled by scenarios, which show the effect of these risks on the design of the biomass value chain.

In this section, the basics for the construction and input data of different scenarios are defined. The model as presented in section 4.5 is calculated with varying input parameters, which are explained in the upcoming sections.

5.6.1 Basic scenario

The basic scenario focuses on the business as usual (BAU) without including non-quantifiable risks. This scenario only includes the quantifiable risks, which are described above. The values of the basic scenario are given by a year without any outstanding occurrences, such as a severe drought or fertility, which influences the biomass yield. No additional, unforeseeable disruptions of the logistics occur. The politics have not changed compared to the year 2016, hence no additional incentives or similar have been implemented. All used input is presented in this chapter. The three case studies butanol, succinic acid, and ethylene are analyzed. It is assumed that the preprocessing of sorghum can be integrated in factories, which are similar to sugar cane mills. Hence, it is assumed, that the investment are comparable and the values of sugar cane mills are applied.

5.6.2 Scenario 1: Drought 2012

Drought has a large influence on biomass availability. Sorghum is a very drought tolerant crop. Extreme weather events do not have a large impact on the sorghum yield. Corn grain is more sensitive to water availability. On the other hand, although the grain is not fully grown, the straw of the different biomass types is still available.

In the year 2012, the drought in the U.S. was very severe. This led to a sudden increase of the corn prices. Whilst the corn belt had very little rain, the precipitation increased in Louisiana. Even though water scarcity was a crucial point in 2012, sugar yields of sugar cane in Louisiana were on record-high (see Gautreaux [132]). Hence, the sugar cane, and, therefore, sucrose and bagasse prices were comparably low.

After the severe drought in 2012, Emerson et al. [106] have analyzed the effect of drought on the chemical composition and yield of corn stover. They have shown, that the drought had only a small influence on the corn stover yield, but affected other grasses. As only corn stover, bagasse/cane field trash and sorghum bagasse are included in this model, only the corn stover results are considered in this work. Rippey [305] has described and analyzed the drought of 2012 on agriculture. The National Centers for Environmental Information (NCEI) have estimated the damage of the 2012 drought to about $30 billion. In 2012, about 65 % of continental U.S. was affected by drought. The Palmer Drought Index measures the severity of drought by their duration. The drought of 2012 was the most severe according to the PDI. The drought reduced the corn crop yield by more than 25 %. As sorghum is more drought resistant, its yield was reduced by only 9 %. In table 5.20, the altered biomass prices for the drought 2012 are presented. Other values such as process yields, investments, transport cost and routes remain as defined for the basis scenario. The results of scenario 1 are analyzed in section 6.7.1.

Table 5.20: Changed prices for scenario 1

Biomass	Price in $/t
Corn	600
Corn stover	275
Sugar cane	400

5.6.3 Scenario 2: Customers neglect GMO based feedstocks

Currently, in the U.S. the corn is gene manipulated. This leads to very high productivity and harvesting yields. Not only the corn to crop ratio is higher, but also the resistance against natural risks such as drought, crop pests or insects. This makes the corn more robust against outer influences. On the other hand gene manipulated crops are discussed more and more often. Especially in case of first generation biomass, which is used not only for energy and biochemical feedstock provision but also for food and feed, the critics are rising. The consequences of gene manipulated organisms on the human organism are unsure. In other countries such as e.g. Germany, the use of gene manipulated crops is even forbidden (see German Federal Government [293]). As the discussions are also rising in the U.S., the cultivation of GMO corn can be neglected by customers to buy a sustainable product. If conventional corn is grown, then the overall yield will decline. Assuming the same demand for corn and a decreased supply will lead to rising prices. However, not only are the prices influenced directly, but also the sensitivity of the crops to risks. Insects or droughts will harm crops to a larger extent than it would affect GMO corn. This might influence the yield and price. Hence, this work assumes that the cultivation of non-GMO corn will lead to half of the yield and, consequently, to double the price. Reducing the harvest also results in less available biomass potential. This will have a negative effect on the production capacities. This scenario assumes, that only half of the capacity of the base scenario is available at each corn supplier location. For calculating the second scenario the following data in table 5.21 is assumed.

Table 5.21: Changed input values for scenario 2

Biomass	Price in \$/t
Corn	700
Corn stover	550
Sugar cane	400

5.6.4 Scenario 3: Incentives for lignocellulosic bioethanol

According to Chen and Smith [77], different factors have an influence on the use of lignocellulosic biomass for ethanol. The three main drivers for launching lignocellulosic bioethanol are governmental policies, added value from non-fuel co-products as well as the reduction of carbon emissions and volatile oil prices. Despite this, the high production cost compared to corn-grain ethanol, the policy uncertainties and the competition with petro-fuel inhibit the commercialization of ligno-cellulosic ethanol.

This scenario assumes that the price of pretreated lignocellulosic biomass is subsidized by 50 % by governmental incentives. Hence, the input cost for corn stover, sugar cane residues and sorghum residues are reduced to 50 % of the former value. For the scenario calculations the values of table 5.22 are applied.

Table 5.22: Changed input values for scenario 3

Biomass	Price in $/t
Corn	350
Corn stover	137.5
Sugar cane	400

5.6.5 Scenario 4: Influence of transport disruption on the choice of logistics

Supply chain disruptions of a certain route can be caused by floods, strikes or other disturbances. Even though these events have been considered during the decision process of the location, these events demand for short-term adaption of the logistics. These can be alternative suppliers, transport routes with longer distances or the change of transport mode.

Due to sudden events the proposed logistics as calculated by the base scenario cannot be used. Under these circumstances the route and, possibly, the transport mode needs to be adapted. In the scenario 4, the expected route will be disrupted. The effect on the chosen biomass, transport cost and route will be recalculated. The chosen transport mode as from the results of the base scenario will be changed. Hence, the transport is not feasible anymore due to different possible reasons. These are strikes, sudden floods, earthquakes or similar. The model is adapted accordingly and the possibility of transport is neglected. Two different types of scenarios are considered regarding this point of view. In scenario 4a, only a short term disruption is considered. Hence, the location of the conversion facilities is fix and other suppliers might be chosen. Scenario 4b discusses the alternative setup in case the normally chosen transport route is not available for a longer period or not for the chosen feedstock.

5.6.6 Scenario 5: Increased conversion yields from second generation biomass

Currently, the conversion yields from second generation biomass are much lower than of first generation biomass. Also, the conversion of fructose and xylose is much lower than of fructose. Reason for this is the low sugar content of the fermentation broth and the lacking ability of the microorganisms to metabolize multiple sugars, especially also sugars from hemicellulose. This scenario assumes higher conversion yields from second generation biomass as well as of sucrose by applying the same fractional conversion to pentoses as for hexoses. The prices of this scenario are the same as of the basis scenario.

5.7 Conclusion

Biomass value chains depend on many different input parameters. Data on biomass potentials, biomass quality and composition as well as biomass cost are needed to estimate the supply for biochemical plants. For the conversion of biomass to biochemicals, data on conversion yields, energy demand, utilities, etc. are used to estimate the efficiency of the production. Additionally, cost for transport, utilities, export, investment and production are necessary. The relevant input data for the integrated model as well as the sub-models has been presented in the previous sections. This work considers six biomass types (corn, sugar cane, sorghum, corn stover, sugar cane bagasse, and sorghum residues). These biomass are pretreated either by corn wet milling, sugar cane milling, dilute acid pretreatment or pyrolysis. The pretreated biomass (sugar syrup and pyrolysis slurry) is then converted either biochemically to butanol and succinic acid as well as thermochemically to ethylene as three case studies. These processes are applied to the region of the western United States. In total 142 resp. 137 locations were included as suppliers, hubs and production locations. Three different transport modes (truck, rail, barge) are used to transport biomass, pretreated biomass, intermediate products and the final products. The considered risks as well as the analyzed data for probability estimations were displayed. Uncertainties, which cannot be quantified, were identified. Five scenarios have been proposed and described to model the most crucial uncertainties. These data are the basis for the integrated model and the three sub-models. The approaches are carried out and the results are presented in the following chapter.

6 Value chains for the production of biochemicals in the United States and other results of the model application

In the previous chapter, the input data is defined for the calculation of the case studies based on the developed approach. The integrated model includes the results of the optimization, technical, and risk sub-model. The results of the technical sub-model are discussed in section 6.1 for biochemical conversion pathways and in section 6.2 for thermochemical pathways. In the following section 6.3, the results of the optimization sub-model are presented for two cases: sugar for biochemical fermentation and pyrolysis slurry for thermochemical gasification and synthesis. In section 6.4, the results of the risk sub model are discussed. The results of the integrated model are presented in section 6.5 for all three case studies. In section 6.6, sensitivity analysis for different input parameters are performed and interpreted. The integrated model are undergone scenario calculations to show the dependency of the results from different non-quantifiable uncertainties. These are discussed in section 6.7. The chapter closes with a conclusion in section 6.8.

In the following, the raw biomass (corn, corn stover, sugar cane, bagasse, sorghum, and sorghum residues) are named as simplification instead of writing "corn based glucose syrup" or "sugar cane syrup". Except in the case of the pretreatment processes, these references always recall the pretreated and not the raw biomass.

6.1 Results of the technical sub-model for biochemical pathways

In the technical sub-model for biochemical processes, the conversion of biomass residues to sugar via dilute acid pretreatment as well as the existing corn wet milling, sugar milling, and sorghum milling are considered. The biochemical conversion of sugars to butanol as well as succinic acid have been modeled in case study one and two. These processes were simulated in AspenPlus. In the following sections, the results of these simulations as well as the techno-economic assessment are presented for both case studies. The results include the efficiency of the conversion to sugar syrup and to biochemicals, the energy and utility demand, the plant capacity as well as the estimation of investment and production cost. At first, the results of the technical sub-model for the conversion of biomass residues to sugars is presented in section 6.1.1. Afterwards, in the sections 6.1.2 and 6.1.3, the efficiencies and cost of the case studies one (butanol) and two (succinic acid) are discussed.

This work distinguishes between six processes based on the respective biomass types. Hence, the following processes are discussed:

P-C	corn
P-SC	sugar cane
P-SO	sorghum
P-CS	corn stover
P-SCB	sugar cane bagasse
P-SR	sorghum residues

The milling processes are also simulated in AspenPlus to show heat integration effects with the conversion processes to chemicals. At this point, the detailed evaluation of the processes is neglected. Ramirez [297] has already simulated a corn wet mill in detail and evaluated it techno-economically. This work is based on his simulations. Bonomi et al. [3] have published results of simulations of a sugar cane biorefinery. The sugar milling is adapted to their results. This work utilizes real market data for sugar cane syrup and corn glucose syrup. Therefore, the production cost and investment are not as relevant as input data. Nevertheless, to compare different pretreatment technologies economically, the investments have been estimated based on the desired capacity for producing 50,000 tons of butanol or succinic acid. The results are included in the investments of the case studies. For details, see sections 6.1.2 and 6.1.3.

6.1.1 Evaluation of biorefineries for sugar syrup production

In this section, the performance of biorefineries for the production of sugar syrup for the biochemical conversion to biochemicals is discussed. The technologies, as described in section 5.2.1, are applied for the production of sugar syrup. The efficiency as well as economic feasibility of the sugar production are evaluated and are presented in the following sections.

6.1.1.1 Efficiency of sugar production

The efficiency of conversion depends on the biomass type. The size of the production plant is optimized based on the circumstances in the U.S. These include the available biomass potentials, the transport cost and the economies of scale of the respective production plants. The AspenPlus simulations provide the material and energy flow balances of the processes. Based on the material balances, the efficiency of the conversion of biomass residues to fermentable sugars can be calculated. The results are shown in table 6.1.

Table 6.1: Efficiency of sugar production depending on biomass type

Biomass	Yield in %
Corn stover	61.98
Sugar cane bagasse	55.15
Sorghum residues	59.45

Sugar cane bagasse and sorghum residues have a higher lignin content than corn stover. Therefore, the sugar yield from corn stover is higher. The efficiency of sugar production correlates directly with the cellulose and hemicellulose content. Nevertheless, the yields are all in the same order of magnitude between 55 and 62 %.

6.1.1.2 Investment of biorefineries

The variable production cost by biomass type are summarized in table 6.2. Glucose cost and electricity revenues depend on the biomass as these rely on the chemical composition. The conversion of sorghum residues is more complex (see Theerarattananoon et al. [345]). Nevertheless, the reaction conditions can be optimized at additional cost. Hence, 2 $/t are added to the variable production cost.

The investment of biorefineries to convert biomass residues to sugars are calculated. Humbird [162] published reference values of a 2000 tons per day biorefinery of the year 2000. This work estimates the investment of 2016 by applying CEPCI indexes.

Humbird [162] assumes that the biomass is transported to the facility already washed and shredded. Therefore, additionally handling cost defined by Aden et al. [6] are included. The results shown below in table 6.3.

Table 6.2: Variable production cost of biorefineries by biomass($/t)

Utilities	CS	SCB	SR
Sulfuric acid		2.78	
Ammonia		8.15	
Glucose for enz. prod.	31.26	34.86	30.18
Other materials		1.43	
Waste treatment		2.85	
Electricity	-8.79	-7.94	-7.88
Surcharge			2
Total	37.68	42.13	39.51

Table 6.3: Investment of sugar production from lignocelluose

Investment	in t$ 2016
Direct cost	
Handling	10,188
Pretreatment	33,622
Enzym. hydrolysis	19,969
Enzym. production	18,645
Solid recovery	7,438
Storage	1,926
Boiler	67,244
Utilities	7,030
Total investment	166,100
Indirect cost	120,600
Fixed capital	286,700
Current assets	14,300
TCI	301,000

6.1.2 Evaluation of butanol production

Based on the simulation of the ABE (acetone, butanol, ethanol) fermentation, as described in section 5.2.2.1, the production yields depending on the biomass types are evaluated. These are used as input data for the integrated model. The efficiency and economic feasibility influence the performance of the biomass value chain and decide, which type of biomass and, therefore, location are chosen.

6.1.2.1 Efficiency of butanol production

The efficiency of butanol fermentation depends on the type of biomass, which is metabolized by the bacteria *C. beijerinckii*. The results for each process is presented in figure 6.1.

ABE fermentation produces not only butanol, but also the by-products ethanol and acetone. Both can be sold to the market and are, therefore, valuable products. Hence, they are also included in the efficiency calculations. The yield of the different processes is calculated on a mass basis by biomass as biomass utilization rate (see equation 4.25). As seen in figure 6.1, the process based on corn glucose syrup is the most efficient. About 35 % of the input biomass is converted to ABE. Other products such as water, CO_2 and H_2, are not included in the efficiency calculations. Even though sorghum and sugar cane syrups also have high sugar contents, the utilization is much lower. This work assumes that fructose cannot be metabolized to biochemicals due to a lack of data on the fructose conversion by the *C. beijerinckii*. The sugar syrup (mostly sucrose) consists of 50 % fructose in the sugars. If fructose would be fermentable, the biomass utilization would double, but would still be lower than the conversion rate of corn syrup. This assumption reduces the production yield estimations. Additionally, sugar syrups from sugar cane and sorghum have higher water contents in the feed. This also leads to lower conversion yields on a mass basis.

The biomass utilization of the three biomass residue syrups (corn stover, sugar cane bagasse, sorghum residues) is in the same order of magnitude. The efficiency based on those biomass types is about 4 to 8 %. The biomass utilization of sorghum residue is the highest as sorghum residue still contains large amounts of sugar although the lignin content is. The cellulose content of sorghum residues is higher compared to corn stover and sugar cane bagasse due to the low extractives content and lower hemicellulose concentrations. The ratios of ABE differ depending on the biomass. The share of butanol is rather low in case of sorghum and sorghum residues, whereas the acetone share is high for those two biomass types. The highest butanol share is found for corn and corn stover. This results from high shares of glucose in the sugar syrup. *C. beijerinckii* preferably convert glucose to chemicals. Butanol is the focus of production in this work. Hence, biomass, which produce large shares of butanol, are preferred. Based on the results of the efficiency calculations, corn glucose syrup is the most favorable feedstock for the production of ethanol, acetone and butanol.

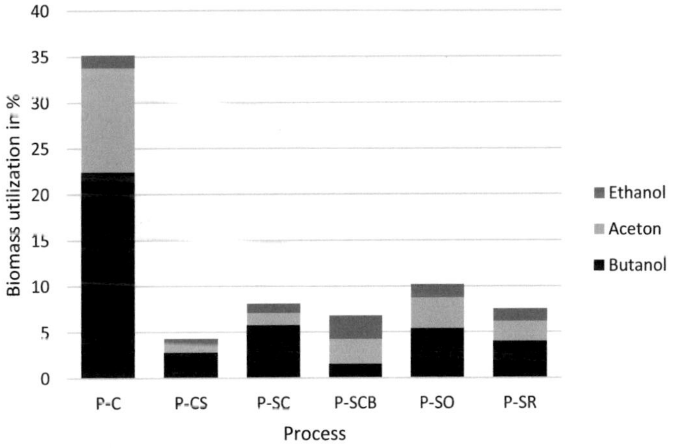

Figure 6.1: Efficiency of biomass utilization for butanol production

The utility demand depends on the process and, therefore, on the biomass type (see figure 6.2). The main utilities are water and heat. Ammonia, enzymes, and electricity are also utilized. Due to its large water content, sugar syrup from sugar cane bagasse leads to large waste water streams. Additionally, according to Jonglertjunya et al. [170], butanol is not the main product in this fermentation. Hence, also large amounts of water are produced in fermentation. In case of biomass of the first generation, much less waste water is produced, due to the high butanol selectivity. In total, the most utilities are needed for corn stover and sugar cane bagasse processes. Process routes based on sorghum and corn sugar syrup need the least. Low utility demands lead to low variable production cost.

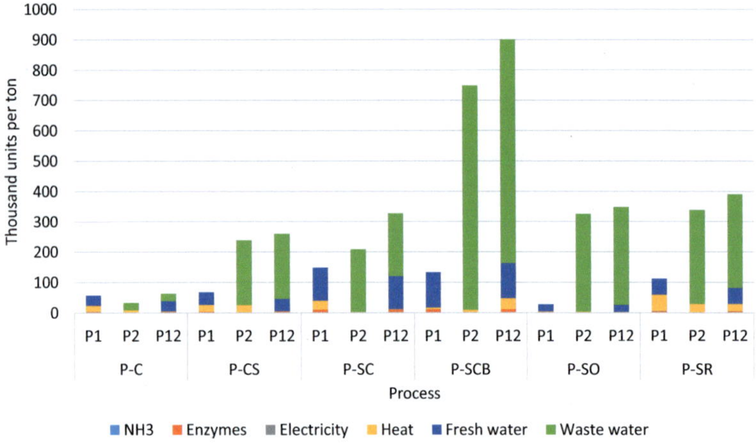

Figure 6.2: Utility demand of butanol production

6.1.2.2 Investment of butanol production

In this section, the results of the economic assessment of butanol production from different sugar syrups are analyzed. The results are displayed in figure 6.3. The investment for the six different processes based on the six biomass types are comparably similar for all processes except for the sugar cane bagasse. The majority of the investment is about 60 million dollars. Only the production of butanol from sugar cane is only 40 million dollars. For utilizing sugar cane bagasse almost thrice of the investment is necessary (175 million dollars). Due to the low butanol yield and the high water content, the units are much larger to produce the same amount of butanol as in the other process simulations.

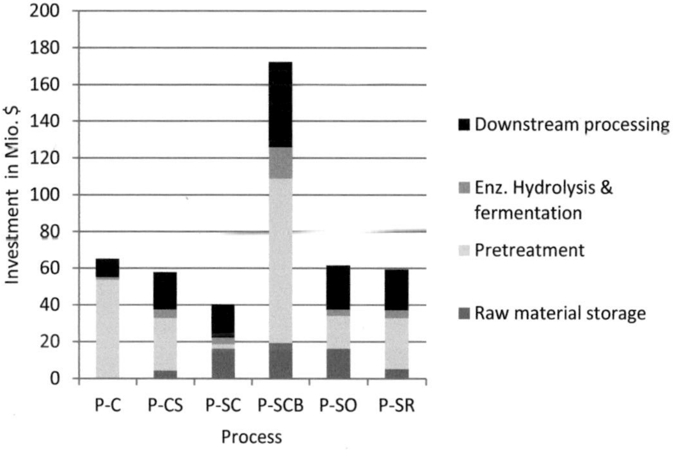

Figure 6.3: Investment of butanol production by biomass type

The expensive pretreatment of lignocellulosic biomass results in the largest share of investment for the dilute acid pretreatment compared to sugar and sorghum milling. Corn milling is the most expensive of the first generation biomass pretreatment. This facility produces four products (starch, fiber, germ, gluten). The separation in high quality products is complex. This leads to the high investments. For more comparable results, the investments should be related to the amount of product. This would reduce the investment related to starch.

In case of sugar cane bagasse, the conversion ratio to butanol is very low. Hence, large amounts of bagasse are needed to produce the same amount of butanol as in the other processes. This results in large production capacities for the pretreatment. Consequently, these investments are much higher compared to the other processes.

The above presented values are the joint investment for process P1 and P2. Nevertheless, this work assumes that the operator can benefit from lower engineering and personnel cost in case both processes are built at the same location. Consequently, the investment of P12 is only 95 % of the total investment of P1 and P2.

Although the investment of sugar cane based butanol production is lower, the high yield of corn based glucose syrup is that high, that it is presumably the preferred feedstock.

6.1.3 Evaluation of succinic acid production

In this section, the production of succinic acid by fermentation is evaluated techno-economically. The following sections show the results of the yield calculations and the estimation of investments. Contrary to ABE fermentation, no valuable by-products are produced to increase efficiency and profitability of the value chain.

6.1.3.1 Efficiency of succinic acid production

The efficiency of succinic acid production is estimated for each biomass type based on the material balances from AspenPlus. The results are depicted in figure 6.4. As corn syrup has a high concentration of glucose, the biomass utilization is the highest based on corn starch. The succinic acid conversion factors from corn hydrolysate is above 94 %. The other two processes based on first generation biomass are less efficient. The low concentration of sugars and the higher ratio of non-glucose sugars result in lower efficiencies for all other biomass types. The water content of these syrups is much higher. This leads to a higher mass input than for corn syrup. Additionally, sugar cane and sorghum have high concentrations of fructose from sucrose. Second generation biomass also consists of high lignin and xylose fractions, which reduces the efficiency. These fractions are not or to a lesser extent convertible than cellulose. Cellulose, which can be converted to glucose, only makes up for about one third of the syrup. This work assumes, that lignin is not separated from the sugar syrup. Additional processing steps or other production processes such as Organosolv processes can be considered to resolve the lignin problem. Nevertheless, corn syrup is the feedstock of choice for biochemical processes.

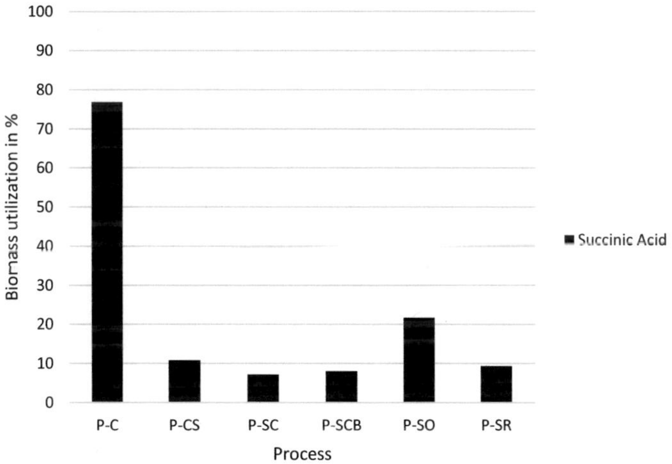

Figure 6.4: Efficiency of biomass utilization for succinic acid production

Not only the efficiency depends on the biomass type, but also the utility demand. In figure 6.5, the utility demand by process, biomass type and utility is depicted. Sugar syrup is hydrolyzed and fermented in P1. For this, enzymes, ammonia, CO_2, heat, and water is needed. In P2, the downstream processing, only heat and HCl is necessary for crystallization. Waste water occurs in the second processing step. P-C is not only the most efficient, but also needs the least utilities. P-SCB on the other hand has large waste water amounts due to the large water content in the feedstock.

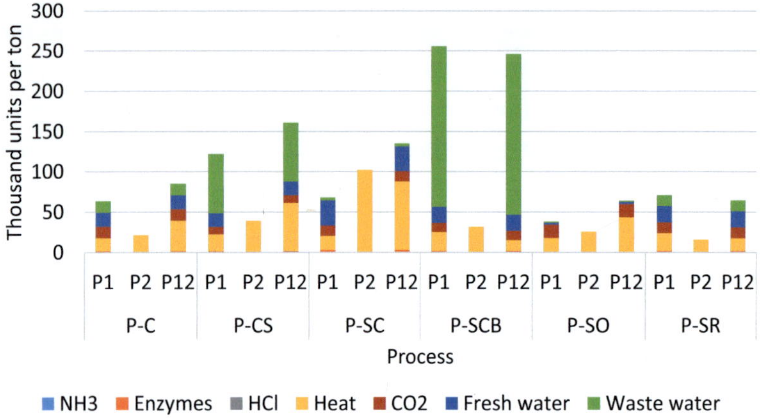

Figure 6.5: Utility demand of succinic acid production

6.1.3.2 Investment of succinic acid production

The investment of succinic acid production from sugar syrup is analyzed in this section. The results are displayed in figure 6.6. Just as explained in the previous section, this work assumes that the investment of P12 is only 95% of the total investment of P1 and P2. The investment includes all relevant units from biomass pretreatment to the final product. Due to the high pretreatment demand in the wet mill, the investment for pretreating corn to corn starch and glucose syrup respectively is the highest of all six processes. The high efficiency of corn syrup conversion leads to comparatively low investments for the fermentation and downstream processes. High yields result in lower needed inputs for the same output. Hence, the overall material flows are less. Low material flows lead to low unit capacities and, hence, investments. The investments for second generation biomass such as corn stover, sugar cane bagasse and sorghum residues are higher for the fermentation and downstream processes. This is in regard to the higher water contents based on the pretreatment technology and also due to lower yields. Second generation biomass also consist of C5 sugars, which reduce the efficiency. The corn based process route is the most expensive but results in the highest yields. The optimization will show, which of these parameters is predominant to influence the chosen location. Sorghum also seems to be a favorable feedstock due to the low investment and the second highest production yields.

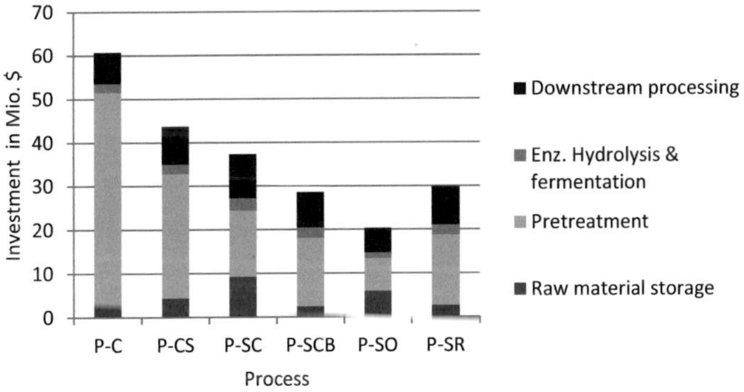

Figure 6.6: Investment of succinic acid production by biomass type

6.2 Results of the technical sub-model for thermochemical pathways

In this section, the results of the technical sub-model for estimating the efficiency and economic feasibility of thermochemical conversion plants from biomass to biochemicals are presented.

This third case study considers the thermochemical production via pyrolysis and gasification as well as synthesis to ethylene. In this case study, only lignocellulosic biomass (corn stover, sugar cane bagasse and sorghum residues) is considered.

6.2.1 Evaluation of fast pyrolysis conversion

The simulation of pyrolysis in AspenPlus is not feasible. The thermochemical processes of pyrolysis are very complex and not well understood by literature yet (see Trippe et al. [358]). Therefore, it was modeled as described by Trippe et al. [358]. The process dries biomass to 8 % water content. This work assumes steel balls as heat carriers and a three-stage product recovery. The conversion factors for the biomass sources was presented in section 5.3.1.

According to Trippe et al. [358] this results in 43.95 million euro. The reference investment was defined for the year 2010. Therefore, the investment is recalculated to the year 2016 by CEPCI values (see equation 6.1).

$$C^I_{pyr} = 33 \cdot \frac{541.7}{541.8} \cdot \left(\frac{x}{617{,}000}\right)^{0.7} mio\$ \tag{6.1}$$

The investments are variable and depend on the capacity x. Due to the economies of scale, the dependency is non-linear and has a size degression factor of 0.7. The investment is implemented as linearized investments as presented in section 4.2.1. Based on the estimated 35 EUR per MWh, this work assumes a selling price of 200 $ per ton of pyrolysis slurry.

6.2.2 Evaluation of syngas production and synthesis

In this section, the production of syngas from pyrolysis products is evaluated technically and economically. The results of the efficiency calculations and investment estimations are described in the following.

6.2.2.1 Efficiency of syngas production and synthesis

The efficiencies of the gasification and synthesis are calculated based on the mass flow balances. These are provided by the simulations in AspenPlus. 54.27 tons of syngas are produced from 192.75 tons of pyrolysis slurry per hour. Hence, the overall conversion factor is 28 %. The 54.27 tons are then converted to 6.25 tons per hour of ethylene. This results in a conversion factor of 0.115.

The gasification efficiencies are in the same order of magnitude as of the direct combustion of biomass. Haykiri-Acma et a. [151] have analyzed the latter and came to results of 20 to 30 %.

6.2.2.2 Investment of syngas production and synthesis

The investments are based on the data published by Trippe et al. [357] and Haro et al. [149]. According to Trippe et al. [357], the investments for a gasification plant of 145.88 t/h are about 274 million euro in 2010. With the CEPCI values, dollar/euro conversion and the capacities of the reference gasification plant and the gasification plant for 50,000 tons of ethylene, the investment is calculated as in equation 6.2.

$$C^I_{gas} = 251.84 \cdot \frac{541.7}{541.8} \cdot \left(\frac{434,782}{1,021,160}\right)^{0.7} mio\$ \qquad (6.2)$$
$$= 138.5 mio\$$$

The approach for estimating the investment of synthesis plants is identical to the investment calculation of the gasification plant (see equation 6.3). The reference plant presented by Haro et al. [149] has a capacity of 18.2 t/h and a reference investment of 270.8 million euro.

$$C^I_{synt} = 203.53 \cdot \frac{541.7}{541.8} \cdot \left(\frac{50,000}{127,400}\right)^{0.7} mio\$ \qquad (6.3)$$
$$= 105.73 mio\$$$

This work assumes, that the operator can benefit from infrastructure and learning effects of 5 % in case both, gasification and synthesis, are built at the same location. Hence, the overall facility needs an investment of 238.95 million dollars (see equation 6.4).

$$C^I_{DME} = \left(C^I_{gas} + C^I_{synt}\right) \cdot 0.95 \qquad (6.4)$$
$$= 238.95 mio\$$$

6.3 Results of the optimization sub-model

Contrary to wet mills and sugar mills, biorefineries to produce pretreated biomass from biomass residues do not exist yet. Therefore, the optimization sub-model aims at proposing future biomass pretreatment facility locations. Different input data are necessary for this. First, this section presents the results of the biomass potential analysis (see section 6.3.1). Second, the cost estimation of biomass residues (see section 6.3.2) are shown. The results of the optimization sub-models for both case studies (sugar syrup and pyrolysis slurry) are discussed. The locations of possible suppliers were optimized based on the model described in section 4.2. The locations for sugar production in biorefineries are defined in section 6.3.3. Section 6.3.4 determines the locations of pyrolysis facilities.

6.3.1 Usable biomass potentials in the U.S.

This section presents the results on the usable biomass potentials in the U.S. for the production of pretreated biomass in biorefineries. These are the basis for the supplier locations and capacities of future biorefineries. The biomass potential analysis is performed as described in section 3.4 with the input data described in section 5.1.1. This work assumes that 35 % of the biomass are available for the conversion to pretreated biomass.

The available biomass potential for each county in the U.S. is depicted in figure 6.7. These include 2273 biomass counties. As expected, the majority of usable biomass potential is located in the corn belt. Corn stover is the primary biomass residues for biorefineries. Other biomass residues are not as highly concentrated. Of the 2273 counties, 390 are chosen as possible locations for biorefineries. The maximum distance between these is 150 miles. The locations are widely spread across the eastern U.S. and are mostly concentrated where large biomass potentials exist. The usable biomass potentials as well as the possible locations are depicted in figure 6.7. The price for these residues needs to be estimated, as they currently remain on the field and are not used in large scale production plants. Hence, no market prices are available for implementation in the optimization sub-model. The estimation of biomass residue cost is performed in the following section 6.3.2.

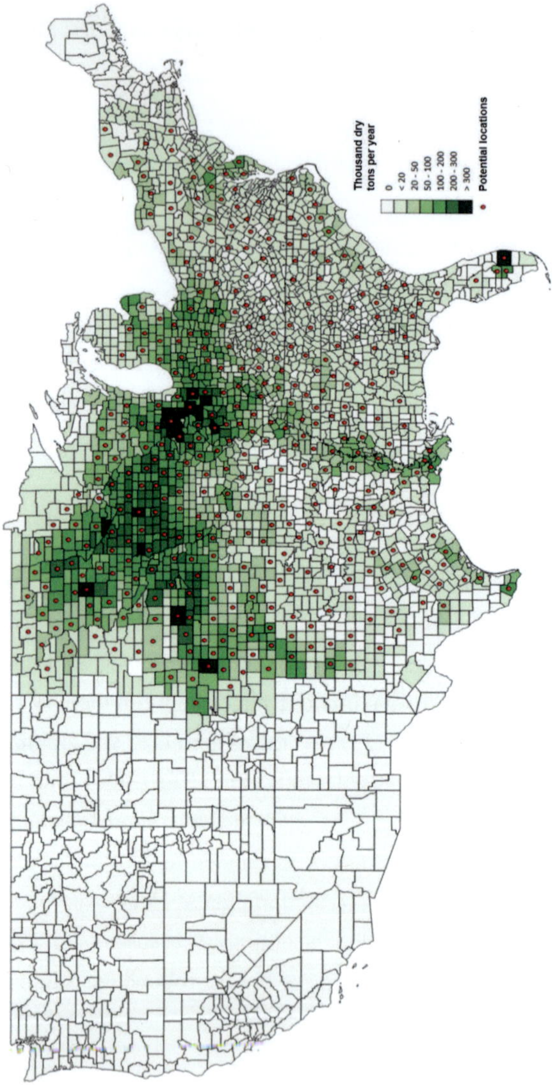

Figure 6.7: Available biomass potentials and possible locations for pretreatment plants in the U.S.

6.3.2 Estimation of biomass residue cost

In this section, the results of the estimated crop residue and bagasse cost are presented. As these feedstocks are currently not used in large scale biochemical plants, the prices need to be estimated based on the data presented in section 5.1.2. The estimation is performed for both, crop residues (see section 6.3.2.1) and bagasse (see section 6.3.2.2). The results of the cost estimations are used as input for the optimization sub-model.

6.3.2.1 Crop residue cost

Based on the data given for harvesting, baling, transport, storage, and fertilization in section 5.1.2.1, the total cost for biomass residues (corn stover, cane field trash, sorghum bagasse) for their utilization in biorefineries is estimated. The results are displayed in table 6.4.

Table 6.4: Estimated biomass residues cost in $ per ton

	CS	CFT	SR
Harvest	12.11	36.51	9.09
Round bale foil	4.26	4.26	4.26
Transport to local storage	5.4	5.4	5.4
Storage	2	2	2
Fertilizer	13.02	28.43	5.23
Bonus	3.86	8.06	2.73
Total	40.66	84.64	28.71

Harvesting of the residues as well as the fertilizer for removed nutrients have the largest influence on the crop residue cost. Hence, cane field trash is the most expensive and sorghum residues are the cheapest.

6.3.2.2 Bagasse cost

Based on the approach as presented in section 5.1.2.2, the price of bagasse was estimated. A natural gas price of 3 $ per thousand cubic feed lead to a bagasse price of about 42 $/t (see table 6.5).

Sugar and sorghum mills run only three months per year. During the remaining months, energy conversion from bagasse would cause production cost, which reduce the value of bagasse (see Kent et al. [179]). Hence, this work assumes a value of 25 $/dt. This price includes storage cost.

Table 6.5: Estimation of bagasse cost from natural gas cost

	Natural gas		Bagasse	
Lower Heating Value	983	BTU/cft	7447	kJ/kg
	1037	kJ/cft	12595	kJ/kg
Boiler efficiency	80	%	72	%
Net energy	830	MJ/Mcft	11701	MJ/dt
Price	3	$/Mcft	42	$/dt

6.3.3 Results of the optimization sub-model for biorefineries

The model is implemented in GAMS IDE 24.6.1 and is solved with the CPLEX Solver of IBM. Due to its long calculation times, a regret of 4 % of the optimal solution is admitted. Different scenarios are calculated. For the utilization in the integrated model only the results of the base case are considered. 95.73 % of the available biomass can be converted to 55 million tons of sugar syrup. Of the possible 390 locations, 44 were chosen for a production plant. A map of the proposed locations is depicted in figure 6.8. The detailed listing of locations including their sugar syrup production is displayed in the appendix A.4.

Table 6.6: Main results of the optimization sub-model for sugar production

Result	Value
Net present value billion $	33.71 billion $
Produced sugar syrup	55.18 mio t per year
Number of production plants	44
Mean transport distance	64.31 miles
Utilized corn stover	97.61 %
Utilized sorghum residues in	13.33%
Utilized sugar cane residues	95.38 %

In table 6.6, the main results of the optimization sub-model are summarized. Sorghum residues are only utilized by 13.33 %. Due to high harvesting and fertilizing cost it is not attractive for utilization. The share of total transport cost make up for about 21 % of the total cost. Biomass cost are the most expensive part of the value chain and add up to 42 %. The remaining 37 % can be assigned to the variable production cost. In total about 55 million tons of sugar syrup is produced in biorefineries.

6.3.4 Results of the optimization sub-model for pyrolysis

In this section, the results of the optimization sub-model for the pretreatment of biomass by pyrolysis are displayed. This work assumes that both, pyrolysis oil and char are used in the gasification plant. Hence, no revenues for by-products are included. In total, for a selling price of 200 $/t (see section 6.2.1) of slurry 37 possible pretreatment plants are calculated by the sub-model. A detailed listing of the locations and their pyrolysis slurry capacity is presented in the appendix A.5. The results of the model are very sensible to the selling price. In case the price rises or declines by 7.5 % either only 27 or 305 plants are installed.

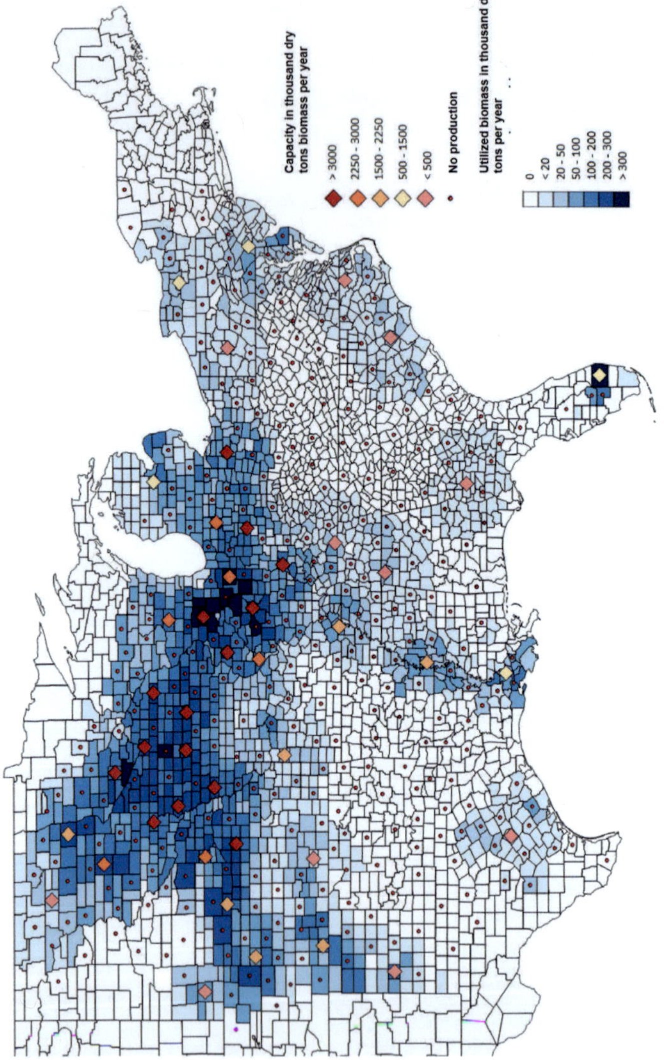

Figure 6.8: Utilized biomass potentials and chosen locations for biorefineries

In figure 6.9, the utilized biomass potentials and the chosen locations for pyrolysis plants is shown.

In case of pyrolysis, sorghum residues are not used. The mean transportation difference is a lot lower. The biomass residues are only transported 15.81 miles on average. Only about 5 million tons of slurry are produced per year. Nevertheless, the NPV is higher than in case of sugar syrup. The results are summarized in table 6.7.

Table 6.7: Main results of the optimization sub-model for pyrolysis

Result	Value
Net present value	161.22 billion $
Produced slurry	4.8 mio. t per year
Number of production plants	37
Mean transport distance	15.81 miles
Utilized corn stover	95 %
Utilized sorghum residues	0 %
Utilized sugar cane residues	93.5 %

6.4 Results of the risk sub-model

In this section, the results of the risk sub-model are presented. The results include the calculations of probabilities (see section 6.4.1) and consequences (see section 6.4.2). Finally, risk matrices show, which uncertainties are the most and the least crucial in biomass value chains (see section 6.4.3). This work identifies three main risks:

- process variation
- feedstock price
- transport delays

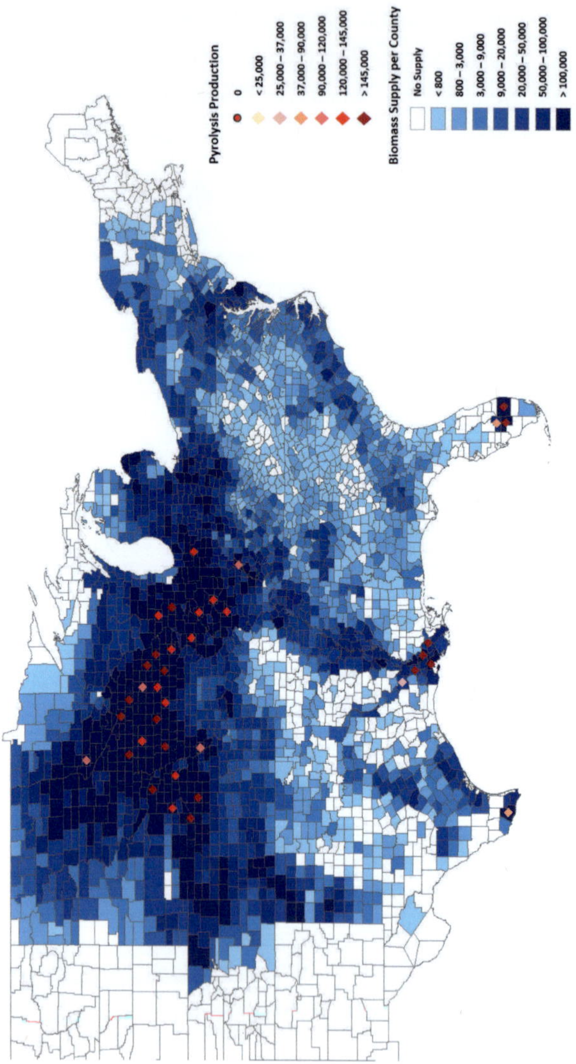

Figure 6.9: Utilized biomass potentials and chosen locations for pyrolysis

Process variation describes the deviation of the final products from the optimal process conditions. This can either be the case regarding the quality, quantity or time issues. Risks, which could influence variation of the process are inhibitors, caramelized sugar syrup, or failed reactions due to microorganisms. A low feedstock quality leads to low fermentation yields. Process variations result in unsatisfied customers and additional cost.

The second main risk is variation in **feedstock prices**. Especially weather risks or other natural risks such as insects can have a large effect on the price of the feedstock. Not only natural risks but also increasing demand for the feedstock or non-GMO crop can lead to increasing feedstock prices. Feedstock cost make up for the majority of the value chain cost. An increase in feedstock prices question the economic feasibility of the overall value chain. In case customers are willing to pay higher prices for the final products, the influence is negligible, but otherwise, the profit is reduced drastically.

Transport delays can have the most causes. Transport risks such as accidents or congestion have the largest influence on transport delays, but also natural risks such as floods lead to transport delays. Process related delays such as the crystallization of sugar syrup delay the transport as the sugar needs to be warmed up before it can be used. Also the sedimentation of pyrolysis slurry leads to transport delays as the slurry needs to be stirred up before utilization. Transport delays lead to a lack of supply either on the supply or demand side. Finally, this causes unsatisfied customers and, hence, additional cost.

6.4.1 Probabilities

In order to estimate the risk cost for the integrated model, the likelihood of their occurrence needs to be calculated. This was done based on the data of section 5.5 with a Fault Tree Analysis. The FTA is performed for all three main risks. In the following figure 6.10, the Fault Tree for the feedstock prices is presented. Within this Fault Tree, also the Fault Trees of transportation and process failures are included. These are depicted by separate FTAs as shown by the triangles in the sugar syrup Fault Tree. The inclusion of these Fault Trees would cause a decrease of visibility. Therefore, they are presented in the appendix A.3.

The circles at the bottom of the Fault Tree depict the basic events, such as weather, process specifications, accidents, etc. These basic events are combined by AND and OR gates, which define the dependencies of these events. The selection of AND and OR gates are discussed with experts. The probabilities for quantifiable risks are calculated according to the calculation routines described in section 3.7.3.3. Based on the FTA, equations can be defined, with which the overall likelihood of the main risk event can be calculated and used as input in the integrated model. In the following, the calculations of the probabilities of the three main risks are presented. They are performed for biochemical pathways based on sugar syrup and for thermochemical pathways based on pyrolysis slurry.

6.4.1.1 Biochemical pathways

The risk of **process variation** is influenced by unplanned maintenance as it reduces the operating hours and, hence, the yearly output. The presence of inhibitors in the fermentation broth might reduce the production yield. The lack or quality of enzymes could also influence the fermentation yields as it reduces the available amount of fermentable sugars. Varying process temperatures, which can be affected by ambient temperatures, lead to decreased yields due to the temperature sensitivity of microorganisms. In case of crystallization and caramelization of the pretreated biomass (esp. sugar syrups), the final products may have reduced quality (e.g. color). Additionally, energy is needed to warm up crystallized sugar syrup.

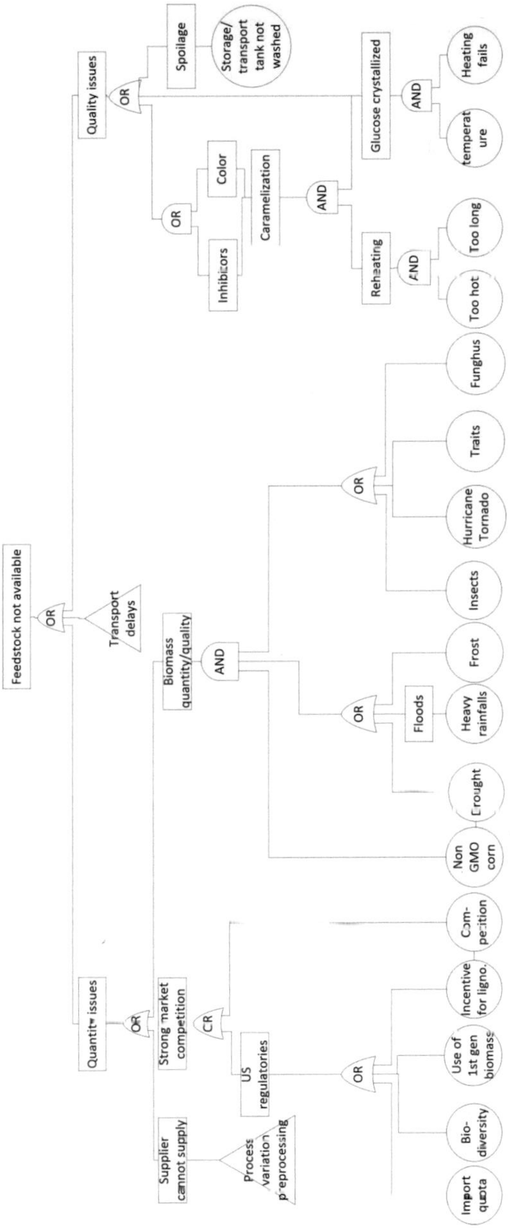

Figure 6.10: Fault Tree for varying feedstock prices

The estimation of the probability of varying processes $P(vp,b)$ is presented in equation 6.5 based on the existing AND and OR gates in the FTA.

$$
\begin{aligned}
P(pv,b) = & \\
& \pi(unplanned\,maintenance) + \pi(inhibitors) + \pi(enzymes) \\
& + \pi(temperature) + \pi(crystallization) + \pi(caramelization) \\
& - \pi(unplanned\,maintenance) \cdot \pi(inhibitors) \cdot \pi(enzymes) \\
& \cdot \pi(temperature) \cdot \pi(crystallization) \cdot \pi(caramelization) \qquad (6.5)
\end{aligned}
$$

Delayed transports are a crucial risk in supply chains. If a transport does not arrive on time, this leads to lacking feedstocks and, hence, the process cannot produce the final products. This is especially critical if not enough raw material is stored. Transport delays are affected by weather risks and transport risks. Weather risks such as tornadoes/hurricanes, blizzards and floods, can lead to disruptions in infrastructure. Therefore, other, more flexible transport modes (e.g. trucks), might need to be used. This leads to increased transport cost and longer transport times. Depending on the transport mode, different transport risks can occur. These are congestion, strikes or accidents. Congestion and strike result in transport delays, accidents might even cause spillage, and, hence also destruction of the transported good. The likelihood of transport delays $P(td,b)$ can be estimated as presented in equation 6.6.

$$
\begin{aligned}
P(td,b) = & \\
& \pi(tornado) + \pi(blizzard) + \pi(floods) \\
& + \pi(congestion) + \pi(accidents) + \pi(crystallization) \\
& - \pi(tornado) \cdot \pi(blizzard) \cdot \pi(floods) \\
& \cdot \pi(congestion) \cdot \pi(accidents) \cdot + \pi(crystallization) \qquad (6.6)
\end{aligned}
$$

Feedstock prices are influenced by the market itself but also by the availability of the feedstock. Especially natural risks affect the harvesting yields, and, hence, the availability of biomass. Tornadoes/hurricanes, hail, frost, increased precipitation, drought, blizzards as well as insects or fungus decrease the harvesting yields. Low harvests lead to high feedstock prices. The likelihood of higher feedstock prices P(fp,b) can be calculated according to equation 6.7.

$$
\begin{aligned}
P(fp,b) = & \\
& \pi(tornado) + \pi(hail) + \pi(frost) + \pi(precipitation) \\
& + \pi(drought) + \pi(blizzard) + \pi(insects) + \pi(funghus) \\
& + \pi(tornado) + \pi(crystallization) + \pi(caramelization) \\
& - \pi(tornado) \cdot \pi(hail) \cdot \pi(frost) \cdot \pi(precipitation) \\
& \cdot \pi(drought) \cdot \pi(blizzard) \cdot \pi(insects) \cdot \pi(funghus) \\
& \cdot \pi(tornado) \cdot \pi(crystallization) \cdot \pi(caramelization)
\end{aligned} \tag{6.7}
$$

6.4.1.2 Thermochemical pathways

The likelihoods of the three main risks not only need to be calculated for biochemical pathways but also for the conversion of pyrolysis slurry by gasification and synthesis to ethylene. The main risks and many of the influencing factors are identical to the biochemical risks. Nevertheless, there are some minor differences. Therefore, the calculation of the probabilities are presented in the following. In case of process variation risks P(pv,t) as shown in equation 6.8, the same factors are summarized by AND and OR gates as in case of biochemical processes. The main difference is, that slurry does not crystallize or caramelize. Nonetheless, it can sediment. This causes the same risks as the crystallization: time delays and quality issues.

$$
\begin{aligned}
P(pv,t) = &\\
&\pi(unplanned\,maintenance) + \pi(inhibitors) + \pi(slag)\\
&+\pi(sedimentation) + \pi(temperature)\\
&-\pi(unplanned\,maintenance) \cdot \pi(inhibitors) \cdot (sedimentation)\\
&\cdot\pi(temperature) \cdot \pi(slag)
\end{aligned}
\tag{6.8}
$$

Transport delays $P(td,t)$ of thermochemical products are also dependent on the sedimentation of the pyrolysis slurry and are adapted accordingly (see equation 6.9).

$$
\begin{aligned}
P(td,t) = &\\
&\pi(tornado) + \pi(blizzard) + \pi(floods)\\
&+\pi(congestion) + \pi(accidents) + \pi(sedimentation)\\
&-\pi(tornado) \cdot \pi(blizzard) \cdot \pi(floods)\\
&\cdot\pi(congestion) \cdot \pi(accidents) \cdot +\pi(sedimentation)
\end{aligned}
\tag{6.9}
$$

The calculation of the feedstock price risk $P(fp,t)$ is identical to biochemical pathways. Just the same adaption as for process variation needs to be made: slurry does not crystallize or caramelize but can sediment (see equation 6.10).

$$
\begin{aligned}
P(fp,t) = &\\
&\pi(tornado) + \pi(hail) + \pi(frost) + \pi(precipitation)\\
&+\pi(blizzard) + \pi(insects) + \pi(funghus)\\
&+\pi(tornado) + \pi(sedimentation)\\
&-\pi(tornado) \cdot \pi(hail) \cdot \pi(frost) \cdot \pi(precipitation)\\
&\cdot\pi(blizzard) \cdot \pi(insects) \cdot \pi(funghus)\\
&\cdot\pi(tornado) \cdot \pi(sedimentation)
\end{aligned}
\tag{6.10}
$$

6.4.2 Consequences of the occurring risks

The consequences of are estimated for each of the three main risks and each case study. They depend on the type of feedstock/intermediate/product, the transport mode, and the process. The type of feedstock/intermediate/product influence the value of loss, which influence the revenues and cost. The transport mode defines the volume of feedstock/intermediate/product, that is being transported. In case of process variation not the volume of the transport mode, but of the reactor is the value defining volume. The product of both, lost volume and value of that volume describes the risk consequences. In the following, the estimation of the consequences is described in detail.

The risk consequences are estimated based on historical data. For the loss by transport delays caused by strikes, accidents, etc. the value of lost feedstock is calculated by the volume in the transport mode and its value. Regarding the risk of feedstock at alternative cost, the difference between mean and maximum biomass feedstock cost of recent history is chosen. Which cost are applied depend on the risk and the involved products.

Process variation includes the quality and amount variability of the final product. The most crucial risk is the destruction of a complete fermentation broth, which is assumed to be about one truck load (25t). In case of destruction of the final product, the cost do not only include the final products itself, but also the value for the feedstock. If the final product cannot be sold to generate value, the price for the feedstock was paid regardless. Consequently, the consequence of process variation $C(pv)$ is the volume of the reactor $v(reactor)$ multiplied with the value of the pretreated biomass $c(pretreated\ biomass)$ and of the final products $c(final\ products)$ as presented in equation 6.11.

$$C(pv) = v(reactor) \cdot (c(pretreated\ biomass) + c(final\ products)) \tag{6.11}$$

Transport delays can have different causes. Accidents, congestion or strikes are sources for this risk. In case the transport is delayed, this might result in a lack of feedstock/intermediate/final product. This leads to an interruption of production or the final customer cannot be supplied. Therefore, transport delay risk have the consequence $C(td)$ of the value of the product within the transport mode and of the final products (see equation 6.12).

$$\begin{aligned} C(td) &= v(transport\ mode) \cdot c(transported\ good) \\ &\quad + v(reactor) \cdot c(final\ product) \end{aligned} \tag{6.12}$$

The consequence of **feedstock prices** are only dependent on the feedstock type. The products in the biomass value chain are clustered into three different groups. This work assumes that the prices of final products and intermediates are directly dependent on the biomass price. In order to not double count the effect of increased feedstock prices, the consequence of this risk is set to zero for intermediates and final products. This work distinguishes between biomass of the first and second generation. Sugary and starchy biomass are directly affected by other risks. Based on historical data corn prices can rise by \$150 per ton. Hence, this consequence is assumed for first generation biomass. Crop residues have a price of about one third compared to corn. Consequently, an additional risk consequence of \$50 per ton of second generation biomass is assumed (see equation 6.13).

$$C(fp) = \begin{cases} \$150 & \text{for corn, sugar cane, sorghum} \\ \$50 & \text{for corn stover, sugar cane bagasse,} \\ & \text{sorghum residues} \\ \$0 & \text{for intermediates, final products} \end{cases} \tag{6.13}$$

6.4.3 Risk matrix

In this section, the risks depending on the feedstock/ intermediate/ product as well as on the state and transport mode are discussed. The risks differ by technology and are therefore presented below for butanol, succinic acid and ethylene. The risks are displayed in two different figures. For all case studies 3D diagrams show the dependency on feedstock/intermediate/final product as well as on the state and transport mode. In these figures, the risks are depicted as the multiplied values of consequences and likelihood of events. The second chart shows the risk matrix as single combinations of probabilities and effects. These diagrams show the difference between risks with high likelihood and low consequences and vice versa. The black bars depict the risk of process variation. Transport delays are displayed by red bars and feedstock prices are presented by green bars. On the x-axis the feedstock/ intermediate/ product are distinguished. The y-axis displays the states and the respective transport mode (truck, rail, barge). The z-axis determines the risk of feedstock prices, process variation and transport delays.

As the consequence of feedstock price variation was set zero for intermediates and final products, the green bars are only applicable for the different biomass types. The risk of varying feedstock prices is immensely high for truck and rail transport. As the transport of sugar syrup and pyrolysis slurry in barge was omitted, the feedstock risk does not apply for this transport mode. Transport delays are especially crucial in case of large vessels. Hence, the risk of transport delays have the largest consequences for rail and barge transport. This risk is negligible for truck transport.

6.4.3.1 Case study 1: Biochemical production of butanol

As explained above and proven in the following figure (see figure 6.11), feedstock price risks are only applicable for the biomass types. These risks are the highest in the biomass value chain. Especially, as feedstock risks often dependend on natural risks, which are hard to mitigate compared to transport risks. The process and transport risks depend on the value of the considered product and the respective volume. Due to the small transport volumes, truck transports are not as risky as rail or barge. Some states are more prone to risks than others. Illinois, Nebraska and Iowa for example have higher feedstock risks than Louisiana.

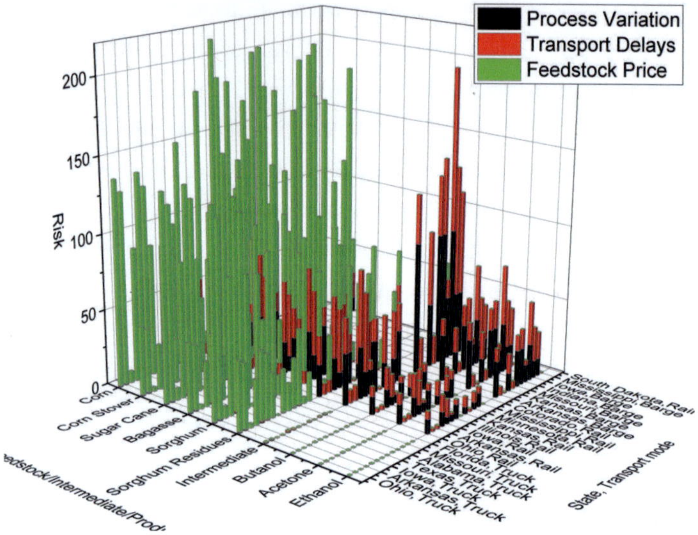

Figure 6.11: 3D risk matrix of the identified risks of butanol

In figure 6.11, the risk is multiplied by consequence and likelihood. This already provides a decision basis to see which states, transport modes and feedstock/intermediate/final products have the largest risks. Nevertheless, the measures depending on the likelihood and consequence are different. Risks with low probability of occurrence but high consequences are hard to influence and mitigate.

High probability risks with low consequences can easily be avoided. Therefore, the differentiation between high and low likelihoods as well as high and low consequences is essential for risk mitigation. This differentiation was performed in figure 6.12. Especially barge transport delays cause high consequences but are quite rare. Variations in feedstock prices on the other hand almost always occur, but their consequences are often negligible.

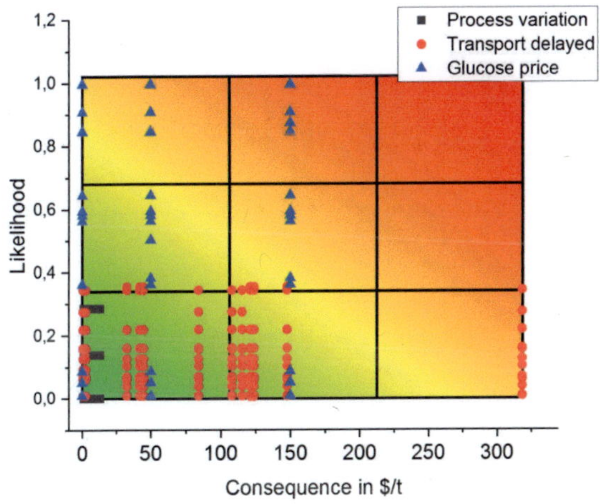

Figure 6.12: Risk matrix of the identified risks of butanol

6.4.3.2 Case study 2: Biochemical production of succinic acid

In case of succinic acid, the figures are quite similar. The main difference is the higher value of succinic acid, but no by-products are considered. The 3D risk matrix depicts the multiplied consequences and probabilities depending on feedstock/intermediate/product as well as state and transport mode in figure 6.13. The transport delays and process variations include the influence of the value of succinic acid as well as of the feedstocks.

Consequently, process variations are in the same order of magnitude as feedstock prices. The likelihood of feedstock price variations is much higher. Values of almost 100 % can occur due to the FTA approach. As all possible natural risks are summarized by OR gates, a variation in feedstock price will occur every year. The risk matrix is displayed in figure 6.14.

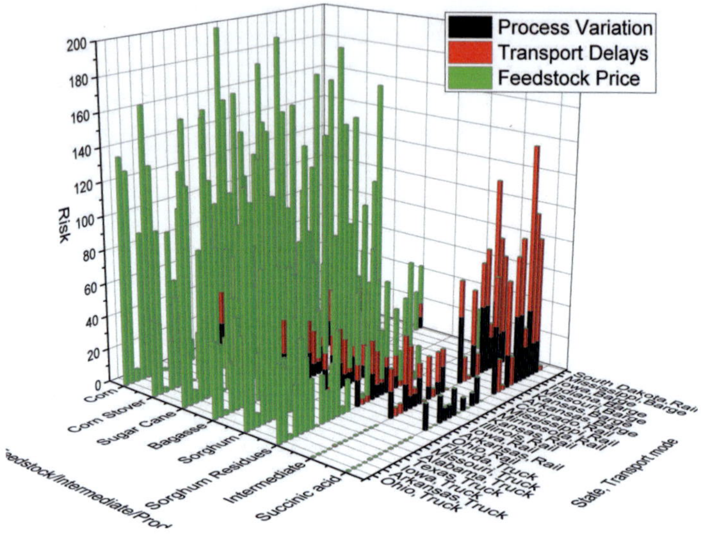

Figure 6.13: 3D risk matrix of the identified risks of succinic acid

6.4.3.3 Case study 3: Thermochemical production of ethylene

In figure 6.15, the multiplied risks by feedstock/intermediate/final product is presented. Due to the low value of gasoline, the risks are not as high as in the case of butanol or succinic acid. Feedstock price risks are the highest risk in case study 3. Transport risks are the highest for barge and rail transport due to the high consequences resulting from large transport capacities.

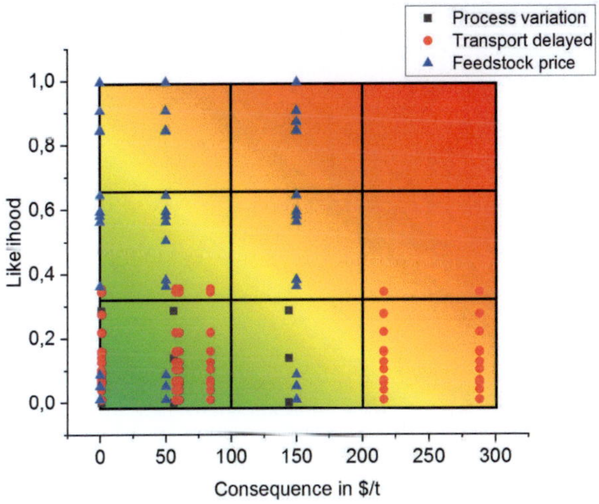

Figure 6.14: Risk matrix of the identified risks of succinic acid

The products ethylene and gasoline have lower values than butanol and succinic acid. Therefore, the consequences depicted in figure 6.16 are a lot lower. Also, only crop residues are considered in this case study. Hence, the maximum loss is $50 per ton. The likelihood of feedstock variation is identical to the other case studies.

6.5 Results and system configurations of the integrated model

In this section, the results of the integrated model with and without considering uncertainties are presented. The comparison of both shows, if uncertainties in general have an influence on the biomass value chain. As only a single random probability is chosen, the effects can vary depending on the case study.

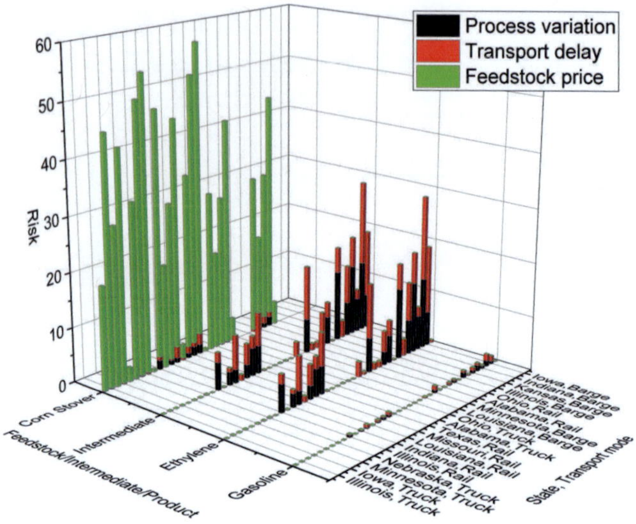

Figure 6.15: 3D risk matrix of the identified risks of ethylene

6.5.1 Results without uncertainties

Not only the effect of varying probabilities, but also the presence of risks in the model need to be considered. Therefore, the results of the integrated model with and without risks are analyzed in the following. The corresponding results of the risk analysis is presented in section 6.5.

6.5.1.1 Case study 1: Biochemical production of butanol

In this first case study, butanol is produced from corn syrup, which was pretreated in wet mills. These wet mills are all already existing suppliers. As only maximum 100,000 tons of corn syrup can be supplied by one wet mill to one customer, three suppliers are necessary to provide the 222,694 tons for the production of 50,000 tons of butanol.

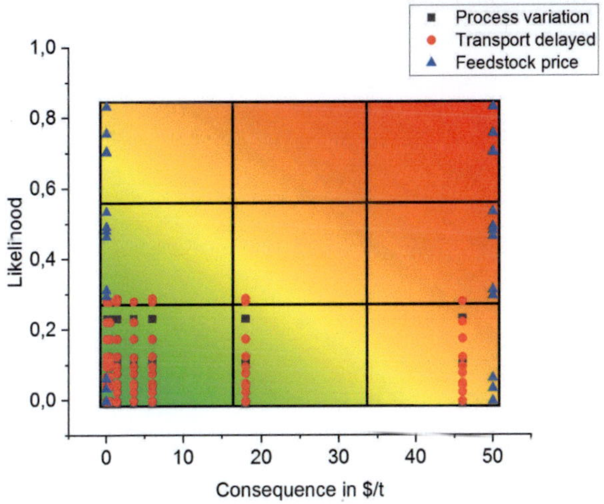

Figure 6.16: Risk matrix of the identified risks of ethylene

The chosen suppliers are Cedar Rapids, Clinton and Sycamore. The suppliers transport corn syrup by truck to Clinton. The final products butanol, acetone and ethanol are produced in Clinton. From there they are transported by barge to the export port New Orleans. Locally used products are transported there by truck, all exports to Asia and Europe are shipped there by barge. This work assumes that ethanol is not exported in order to fulfill the national biofuel quota in the U.S. The results of the integrated model without uncertainties for case study 1: butanol is presented in table 6.8. The results are also depicted for geographical orientation in a map of the U.S. in figure 6.17.

Table 6.8: Product flows for the production of butanol

Product	From	To	Transport	Amount [t/a]
Corn	Cedar Rapids	Clinton	Truck	100,000
Corn	Clinton	Clinton	Truck	100,000
Corn	Sycamore	Clinton	Truck	22,694
Butanol	Clinton	New Orleans	Barge	50,000
Acetone	Clinton	New Orleans	Barge	26,341
Ethanol	Clinton	New Orleans	Barge	4,273
Butanol	New Orleans	Asia	Barge	20,800
Acetone	New Orleans	Asia	Barge	10,958
Butanol	New Orleans	local	Truck	17,500
Acetone	New Orleans	local	Truck	9,219
Ethanol	New Orleans	local	Truck	4,273
Butanol	New Orleans	Europe	Barge	11,700
Acetone	New Orleans	Europe	Barge	6,164

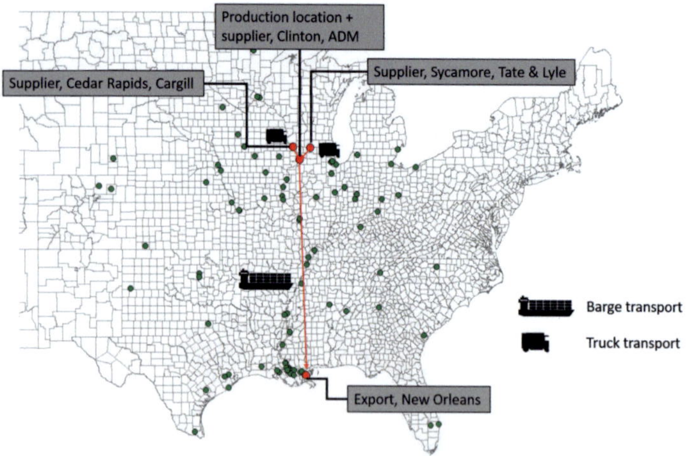

Figure 6.17: Suppliers and production of butanol

6.5.1.2 Case study 2: Biochemical production of succinic acid

As in case study 1 above, case study 2 also is calculated with and without uncertainties. The setup of the value chain is quite simple. Due to the high conversion efficiency, only a single supplier is necessary to provide corn syrup (77,400 tons) to the fermentation to succinic acid. Both, supplier and production site, are situated in Keokuk. From Keokuk, 50,000 tons of succinic acid (SA) are transported by barge to New Orleans and are exported from there to Asia and Europe and are sold locally.

Table 6.9: Product flows for the production of succinic acid without uncertainties

Product	From	To	Transport	Amount [t/a]
Corn	Keokuk	Keokuk	-	77,400
SA	Keokuk	New Orleans	Barge	50,000
SA	New Orleans	Asia	Barge	20,800
SA	New Orleans	Europe	Barge	11,700
SA	New Orleans	Local	Truck	17,500

The closeness to the Mississippi River compensates for the lack of additional suppliers close to Keokuk. However, if the supplier cannot supply, the feedstock and transport cost will increase. The results of the model is presented in table 6.9. The results are also depicted for geographical orientation in a map of the U.S. in figure 6.18.

6.5.1.3 Case study 3: Thermochemical production of ethylene

In this section, the setup of the biomass value chain for the production of ethylene from biomass is presented. The results are shown in table 6.10. Due to the low conversion factors, eleven suppliers of pyrolysis products are necessary.

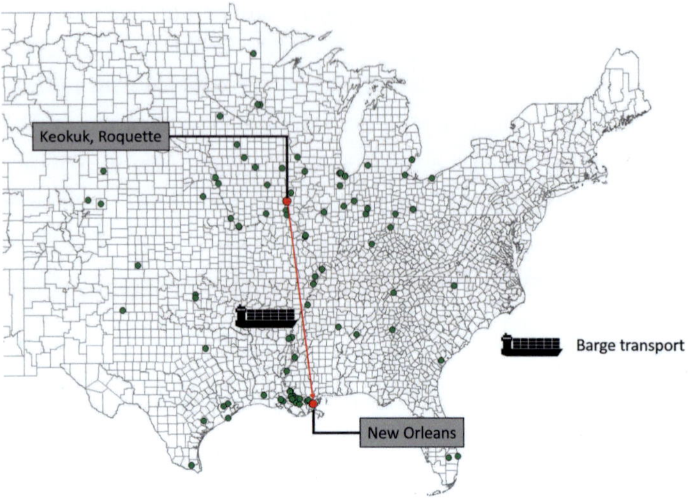

Figure 6.18: Suppliers and production of succinic acid

Floyd is chosen as main production location and is supplied by corn stover based sugar syrup from Benton, Blue Earth, Cedar, Clay, Fayette, Floyd, Freeborn, Grundy, Crawford, Nobles and Stephenson County. The latter three are accessed by rail, the others by truck. The final products are sold to the market via New Orleans port. The results of the base scenario are depicted in figure 6.19 for a better understanding of the local surroundings.

6.5.2 Results with uncertainties

The configuration of the value chain according to the base scenario of the integrated model is presented in this section. At first the different system configurations for the production of butanol and succinic acid as well as ethylene from pyrolysis and gasification are described in the following. The input data for the integrated model is presented in chapter 5.

Table 6.10: Product flows for the production of ethylene without uncertainties

Product	From	To	Transport	Amount [t/a]
Corn stover	Benton	Floyd	Truck	127,022
Corn stover	Blue Earth	Floyd	Truck	145,320
Corn stover	Cedar	Floyd	Truck	145,320
Corn stover	Clay	Floyd	Truck	145,320
Corn stover	Fayette	Floyd	Truck	144,221
Corn stover	Floyd	Floyd	-	134,593
Corn stover	Freeborn	Floyd	Truck	145,320
Corn stover	Grundy	Floyd	Truck	142,766
Corn stover	Crawford	Floyd	Rail	142,044
Corn stover	Nobles	Floyd	Rail	145,320
Corn stover	Stephenson	Floyd	Rail	135,549
Ethylene	Floyd	New Orleans	Truck	50,000
Gasoline	Floyd	New Orleans	Truck	54,783
Ethylene	New Orleans	Europe	Barge	11,700
Ethylene	New Orleans	Local	Truck	17,500
Ethylene	New Orleans	Asia	Barge	20,800
Gasoline	New Orleans	local	Truck	54,783

6.5.2.1 Case study 1: Biochemical production of butanol

The results of the first case study regarding the value chain configuration as well as the logistics is presented in this section. The product flows of the value chain to produce butanol are shown in table 6.11.

The risks influence the value chain setup for butanol production. The results are based on the worst case probabilities (highest likelihood) of the Poisson functions. Contrary to the basc scenario without uncertainties, Clinton is not the production location anymore. Based on the worst case, Lafayette is the best possible location under the given circumstances. Lafayette is supplied by Marshall and Indianapolis with corn glucose syrup. From Lafayette, the products are transported to New Orleans for export.

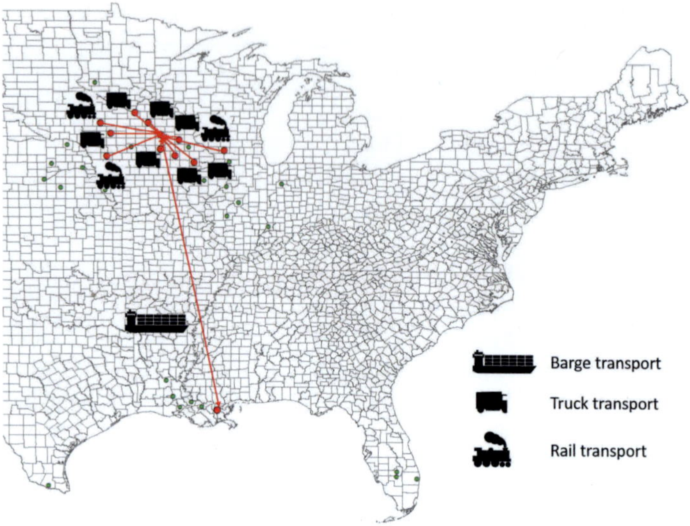

Figure 6.19: Suppliers and production of ethylene

Table 6.11: Product flows for the production of butanol with uncertainties

Product	From	To	Transport	Amount [t/a]
Corn	Marshall	Lafayette	Truck	100,000
Corn	Lafayette	Lafayette	-	100,000
Corn	Indianapolis	Lafayette	Truck	22,694
Butanol	Lafayette	New Orleans	Barge	50,000
Acetone	Lafayette	New Orleans	Barge	26,341
Ethanol	Lafayette	New Orleans	Barge	4,273
Butanol	New Orleans	Asia	Barge	20,800
Acetone	New Orleans	Asia	Barge	10,958
Ethanol	New Orleans	local	Truck	4,273
Butanol	New Orleans	local	Truck	17,500
Acetone	New Orleans	local	Truck	9,219
Butanol	New Orleans	Europe	Barge	11,700
Acetone	New Orleans	Europe	Barge	6,164

If uncertainties are considered, the risk cost rise. The change of location from Clinton to Lafayette does not have an influence on transport or biomass cost. However, Clinton in located in Illinois and Lafayette in Indiana. It seems that Illinois is a state with higher risks due to traffic and weather.

6.5.2.2 Case study 2: Biochemical production of succinic acid

Contrary to the base scenario, the production location is not Keokuk but Clinton. It is supplied also from there and succinic acid is transported to New Orleans for export to Asia, Europa and the local markets. The product flows of the value chain to produce succinic acid are presented in table 6.12. Although Keokuk can benefit from the closeness to the Mississippi River, the location is prone to multiple risks. The transport via barge does not have a economic alternative. Additionally, Keokuk is located in a state, which is affected by multiple weather risks. As no additional supplier is near, risk mitigation is complex. The uncertainties influence the choice of location.

Table 6.12: Product flows for the production of succinic acid with uncertainties

Product	From	To	Transport	Amount [t/a]
Corn	Clinton	Clinton	-	77,400
SA	Clinton	New Orleans	Barge	50,000
SA	New Orleans	Asia	Barge	20,800
SA	New Orleans	Europe	Barge	11,700
SA	New Orleans	Local	Truck	17,500

6.5.2.3 Case study 3: Thermochemical production of ethylene

The product flows of the value chain to produce ethylene and gasoline are presented in table 6.13.

If risks are considered in the value chain calculations, the setup varies from the previous result of the basis scenario. The uncertainties lead to a change in feedstock choices and shift from north to south. Freeport is the production location of choice instead of Floyd. It is supplied with sugar syrup from bagasse from Iberia, St. James, and St. Landry. Additionally, sugar syrup based on corn stover is transported to Freeport from Blue Earth, Freeborn, Macon, Montgomery, Stephenson, Tazewell, Warren, and White. Of course, the closest port, Freeport, is used for export.

Table 6.13: Product flows for the production of ethylene with uncertainties

Product	From	To	Transport	Amount [t/a]
Bagasse	Iberia	Freeport	Truck	145,320
Bagasse	St.James	Freeport	Truck	145,320
Bagasse	St.Landry	Freeport	Truck	145,320
Corn stover	BlueEarth	Freeport	Rail	128,101
Corn stover	Freeborn	Freeport	Rail	145,320
Corn stover	Macon	Freeport	Rail	136,845
Corn stover	Montgomery	Freeport	Rail	129,062
Corn stover	Stephenson	Freeport	Rail	145,320
Corn stover	Tazewell	Freeport	Rail	145,320
Corn stover	Warren	Freeport	Rail	145,320
Corn stover	White	Freeport	Rail	141,547
Ethylene	Freeport	Freeport Port	Truck	50,000
Ethylene	Freeport Port	local	Truck	17,500
Ethylene	Freeport Port	Asia	Barge	20,800
Ethylene	Freeport Port	Europe	Barge	11,700
Gasoline	Freeport	Freeport Port	Truck	54,783
Gasoline	Freeport Port	local	Truck	54,783

6.5.3 Comparison of economic results

In table 6.14, the results of the economic parameters are compared for all three case studies, with and without the consideration of risk.

In all cases, the consideration of risks reduces the NPV. Values, which do not variate with changing logistics, remain identical to the results without risks. These include revenues, utility, storage, and export cost as well as investments. Biomass, transport, and risk cost are affected by the inclusion of uncertainties. In case study 1 and 2, the optimal biomass does not change. Therefore, the biomass cost remain. Mainly, the suppliers shift to other states and, hence, locations. This results in an increase of transport cost. Risks have a crucial effect especially on ethylene production. Due to eleven suppliers, the transport distances are high. Consequently, feedstock prices and transport delays have a large influence. Succinic acid is hardly affected as it only depends on a single supplier.

Table 6.14: Comparison of economic parameters of the three case studies

	B[a]	B-R[a]	SA[b]	SA-R[b]	E[c]	E-R[c]
NPV in mio. $	258	153	556	555	-3617	-3994
Revenue in mio. $	119		100		35	
Cost in mio. $						
Biomass	77	77	27	27	342	350
Transport	5.2	14.4	1.5	1.62	68	82
Risk	-	3.25	-	0.02	-	30.2
Utility	0.1		0.59		20	
Storage	0.32		0.32		0.32	
Export	4.3		4.4		2.9	
Investment	10.8		8.7		236	

[a] B: butanol, B-R: butanol with risks
[b] SA: succinic acid, SA-R: succinic acid with risks
[c] E: ethylene, E-R: ethylene with risks

6.6 Sensitivity analysis of the influence of economic parameters and risks

In the following sections, the influence of economic parameters and uncertainties are analyzed. The main economic parameters are transport, export, biomass, and utilities. The effects of single parameters on the value chain configuration will be shown by choosing adequate parameter variations.

Often, investments have an influence on the capacity of the production plant (see Schwaderer [314]), but this work currently does not consider capacity optimization. Hence, the variation of investment would only have an effect on the NPV, but not on the setup of the value chain. Also the prices for the final products, hence the revenues, will not have an influence on the value chain. Only parameters, which are location specific, are crucial to the setup of the value chain. The influence of risks on the value chain configuration and their probability are analyzed by Monte Carlo Simulations. Based on random values of the distribution function and multiple model runs, the effect of risks is presented.

6.6.1 Transport cost and transport routes

Transport cost have a large effect on the biomass value chain. Not only do they influence the profitability of the production, but also the configuration of the value chain and the choice of transport mode. In the following, the transport mode cost are varied. Currently, the transport by rail is the most expensive as the total amount of transported goods is significantly lower than in case of barge. The share of transport cost of the overall value chain depends on the process. Due to increasing transport along the rivers, it is assumed that the transport cost will also rise for barge transport. Hence, in the following analysis the influence of rising barge transport cost or sinking rail cost respectively, on the biomass value chain, the logistics and the location will be investigated.

6.6.1.1 Case study 1: Biochemical production of butanol

The transport is sensitive to varying transport cost. These make up for about 15% of the total biobased value chain for butanol production. This work assumes, that truck is too expensive for long distances. Hence, only rail and barge transport cost were varied. In case both transport cost are identical, the location with the shortest distance to the export port is chosen. As the location is now independent on the river access, the production shifts in case of butanol from Clinton to Decatur. The results are displayed in table 6.15.

Table 6.15: Product flows for the production of butanol with varying transport cost

Product	From	To	Transport	Amount [t/a]
Identical rail and barge cost				
Corn	Decatur	Decatur	-	100,000
Corn	Lafayette	Decatur	Rail	100,000
Corn	Indianapolis	Decatur	Rail	22,695
Butanol	Decatur	New Orleans	Rail	50,000
Acetone	Decatur	New Orleans	Rail	10,958
Ethanol	Decatur	New Orleans	Rail	4,273
Rail cost: 20$/t fix, 0.02$/(tm)				
Corn	Keokuk	Keokuk	-	100,000
Corn	Eddyville	Keokuk	Rail	100,000
Corn	Cedar Rapids	Keokuk	Rail	22,695
Butanol	Keokuk	New Orleans	Barge	50,000
Acetone	Keokuk	New Orleans	Barge	10,958
Ethanol	Keokuk	New Orleans	Barge	4,273

In the second case, the rail transport cost, both fix and variable, are about the mean of the previous rail and the current barge fix and variable cost.

These cost lead to the above presented setup. The shorter transport distance by barge from Keokuk is now feasible, as the transport cost to Keokuk from Eddyville and Cedar Rapids are now lower compared to the basis scenario. Comparing the overall transport cost, the transport in the basis scenario cost 5.173 mio. $. The location at Keokuk reduces the transport cost to 5.019 mio. $. In case the rail transport is at the same cost as barge transport, the transport cost are reduced to 3.5 mio. $.

6.6.1.2 Case study 2: Biochemical production of succinic acid

Variations in transport cost might have a crucial influence on the setup of the value chain. Transport cost make up for about 5 % in the succinic acid value chain. In case rail and barge would have the same fix and variable transport cost, the location of the supplier and production plant of succinic acid would change. Loudon is closer to New Orleans. Hence, Loudon is chosen as a new location. It does not have an influence, if the rail and barge cost are low or high, as long as they are less than truck transport cost in the long run. River access is not needed anymore. Due to the single supplier, the location of succinic acid production is quite flexible. The changed setup is depicted in table 6.16.

Table 6.16: Product flows for the production of succinic acid with varying transport cost

Product	From	To	Transport	Amount [t/a]
Corn	Loudon	Loudon	-	77,400
SA	Loudon	New Orleans	Barge	50,000

6.6.1.3 Case study 3: Thermochemical production of ethylene

Ethylene production and transport is sensible to rail transport cost. In case the transport cost for rail are reduced to a fix share of 20 $/t and a variable share of 0.02 $/(tm), rail is preferred. Consequently, all transports are performed with rail. Freeport is now the production location of choice. Compared to the other two case studies, transport cost make up for the largest share with 16 % in this case study. The results are summarized in table 6.17.

Table 6.17: Product flows for the production of ethylene with varying transport cost

Product	From	To	Transport	Amount [t/a]
Bagasse	Iberia	Freeport	Rail	145,320
Bagasse	St.James	Freeport	Rail	145,320
Bagasse	St.Landry	Freeport	Rail	145,320
Corn stover	Delaware	Freeport	Rail	131,067
Corn stover	Floyd	Freeport	Rail	134,593
Corn stover	Freeborn	Freeport	Rail	145,320
Corn stover	Grundy	Freeport	Rail	142,766
Corn stover	Stephenson	Freeport	Rail	145,320
Corn stover	Tazewell	Freeport	Rail	144,658
Corn stover	Warren	Freeport	Rail	145,320
Corn stover	Webster	Freeport	Rail	127,791
Ethylene	Freeport	Freeport	Truck	50,000
Gasoline	Freeport	Freeport	Truck	54,782

6.6.2 Export shares

In this section, the influence of export shares cost on the value chain design is analyzed. Therefore, export factors for different products are analyzed.

6.6.2.1 Case study 1: Biochemical production of butanol

Even though export shares were set to 100 % to Europe, the port of choice was not New York but remained New Orleans. This work assumes, that New York can only be approached by rail and truck. These transport modes are too expensive for long distance transport. Therefore, barge transport down the Mississippi River is preferred compared to the export from New York, even though the export cost from there are lower. In case of butanol, the variation of export shares does not have an influence.

6.6.2.2 Case study 2: Biochemical production of succinic acid

Export does not show a sensitivity in case study 2. Due to the same reasons as case study 1, succinic acid is always exported from New Orleans. An increase of export cost in New Orleans, lead to a shift of export from New Orleans to Freeport.

6.6.2.3 Case study 3: Thermochemical production of ethylene

In case of case study 3, barge transport is only implemented between transport hubs. The transport to New York can also be performed by rail just as to New Orleans. The export cost to Europe are lower than from New Orleans. This work assumes at this point, that 100 % of ethylene is exported to Europe. This leads to a shift in the value chain setup. Gasoline is still transported to New Orleans, but due to the lower export cost from New York to Europe, ethylene is transported to New York instead of New Orleans.

6.6.3 Biomass cost

Different approaches exist to test the dependency of the value chain on biomass prices. Not only the prices influence the setup, but also the yields. Biomass with high yields is often preferred due to lower transport and biomass prices as less input is needed. Nevertheless, only biomass prices are varied in this sensitivity analysis. The price of biomass depends not only on the type of biomass, but also on the availability within a season and the demand for the biomass. In case of weather extremes the price can increase significantly (see section 6.7). The influence of biomass cost on the setup of the value chain for the production of biochemical is analyzed in this section. As the overall configuration and system boundaries influence the results, the sensitivity analysis is performed for all three case studies. The results are presented in the following.

6.6.3.1 Case study 1: Biochemical production of butanol

Biomass cost are an important parameter for the production of butanol. They announce for more than 75 % of the total value chain cost. Two different parameter variations were considered in this sensitivity analysis. At first, the cost for sugar syrup based on lignocellulosic biomass is reduced to see the shift from first to second generation resources. In a second step, the price of corn based glucose syrup is increased to analyze the influence on other sugary biomass. The results are summarized in table 6.18.

In case lignocellulosic sugar prices are reduced to only 35 $/t, bagasse based sugar syrup is chosen as additional feedstock from Iberville Parish. Nevertheless, corn is still the feedstock of choice. The production location is in the corn belt, in Lafayette.

In case corn price is increased by more than 500 %, the production location shifts to Geismar and the main suppliers are New Iberia, Belle Rose, Jeanerette, Paincourtville and Raceland for sugar cane syrup.

6.6.3.2 Case study 2: Biochemical production of succinic acid

The prices of sugar syrup from lignicellulosic biomass have to sink to about 35 $/ton to become economically feasible. The supplier changes to Macon County. From there the sugar syrup is transported to Decatur as displayed in table 6.19.

Table 6.18: Product flows for the production of butanol with varying biomass prices

Product	From	To	Transport	Amount [t/a]
2nd gen. sugar syrup price: 35 $/t				
Corn	Lafayette	Lafayette	-	100,000
Corn	Decatur	Lafayette	Truck	81,418
Bagasse	Iberville Parish	Lafayette	Rail	605,700
Butanol	Lafayette	N. Orleans	Barge	50,000
corn glucose syrup price: 1800$/t				
Corn	Loudon	Geismar	Rail	100,000
Sugar cane	New Iberia	Geismar	Truck	50,000
Sugar cane	Belle Rose	Geismar	Truck	50,000
Sugar cane	Jeanerette	Geismar	Truck	50,000
Sugar cane	Paincourtville	Geismar	Truck	50,000
Sugar cane	Raceland	Geismar	Truck	605,700
Butanol	Geismar	N. Orleans	Barge	50,000

Biomass prices are essential in succinic acid production. They make up for more than 75 % of the value chain cost. In case not the price of second generation biomass is reduced, but the price for corn glucose syrup is increased to 1800 $/t, then sorghum is the feedstock of choice. The production location is now in Kansas City and is also supplied with corn glucose syrup from there. Additionally, sugar syrup from sorghum from Overland Park, Plainview and Colwich is used to produce succinic acid (see table 6.19). Due to the low investments and comparably high production yields based on sorghum, this feedstock seems to be an interesting alternative to corn.

6.6.3.3 Case study 3: Thermochemical production of ethylene

The sensitivity analysis of biomass cost for the case study 3 is not as complex. Only two biomass types are considered as feedstock for pyrolysis and, therefore, for the production of ethylene. Up to a bagasse sugar price of 200 $/t, corn stover is the preferred feedstock.

Table 6.19: Product flows for the production of succinic acid with varying biomass prices

Product	From	To	Transport	Amount [t/a]
2nd gen. sugar syrup price: 35$/t				
Corn stover	Macon County	Decatur	Truck	534,760
corn glucose syrup price: 1800$/t				
Corn	Kansas City	Kansas C.	-	35,953
Sorghum	Plainview	Kansas C.	Rail	50,000
Sorghum	Colwich	Kansas C.	Rail	50,000
Sorghum	Overland Park	Kansas City	Rail	50,000

In case the sugar syrup price from bagasse sinks below 190 $/t, the value chain setup shifts from corn stover to sugar cane bagasse. The results are identical to the scenario 2 (see section 6.7.2). Biomass cost are not as crucial to the value chain as in the previous case studies. In case of ethylene, they only account for about 66 % of the total value chain cost.

6.6.4 Utility cost

The influence of water, energy and other utility cost on the overall value chain design are analyzed in this section. Depending on the process, partly large amounts of utilities are needed. The biomass type and process influences the needed amount of utilities. In case the location is integrated in already existing production plants the energy demand can be lowered. This might have a great effect on the chosen locations. Therefore, the influence of utility cost at different locations is analyzed in the following section for each case study.

6.6.4.1 Case study 1: Biochemical production of butanol

In the case study of butanol, the basis scenario results in Clinton as the main production location. Cedar Rapids and Sycamore are close by and supply Clinton with corn glucose syrup. The influence of variable utility cost depending on the location were tested in this sensitivity analysis. Although the utility cost were set zero for the next closest location Cedar Rapids, the production location remained in Clinton. The latter location has the advantage, that is directly located at the Mississippi River. Therefore, the transport cost are low. A shift in the location would lead to much higher transport cost, which reduces the profitability of the overall value chain. The transport cost have a higher share of the overall value chain cost. Hence, the utility cost do not have a large influence on the butanol value chain.

6.6.4.2 Case study 2: Biochemical production of succinic acid

For the second case study, the utility cost of different locations were varied. As Clinton seems to be a robust location (it is often chosen as location in case study 1), the utility cost are decreased there. In case of a co-location plant, a contract might be possible to buy certain utilities to a reduced price. Enzymes or nutrients need to be paid nonetheless, but other utilities such as water, carbon dioxide or heat/electricity might be used from excess utilities of the wet mill. Hence, this work assumes the cost for these utilities to be half the size as in the basis scenario for Clinton. This small adaption of the model input data leads to a change of the value chain setup. Indeed, Clinton is chosen as location as supplier and production location. The results of case study 2 are sensible to variations of utility cost at certain locations. Nevertheless, not all locations can be influenced by utility cost adaption. All utility cost at the locations Geismar and Freeport were set to zero. This work assumes that also enzymes and nutrients could be received to special prices at large scale chemical production sites. These locations were not chosen although the cost were changed dramatically. The results are presented in table 6.20.

Table 6.20: Product flows for the production of succinic acid with varying utility cost

Product	From	To	Transport	Amount [t/a]
Corn	Clinton	Clinton	-	77,400
SA	Clinton	New Orleans	Barge	50,000

6.6.4.3 Case study 3: Thermochemical production of ethylene

In case of ethylene, two different variations were chosen for sensitivity analysis. At first, the utility prices in Freeport were set to zero for heat and electricity, assuming, that the production can benefit from the existing petrochemical plant. Second, the utility prices at the former location Floyd were increased by 20 %. Both cases led to a shift in the biomass value chain. As heat and electricity are the major cost in thermochemical processes, the production is shifted to Freeport. The case study is very sensible to utility cost. Already an increase by 20 % resulted in a new production location close to Floyd, in Lee. The results are summarized in table 6.21.

6.6.5 Uncertainties

The influence of the identified risks and uncertainties on the value chain and the logistics are analyzed in this section. Therefore, the integrated model is run with a Monte Carlo simulation. This work performs 100 trial runs with varying risk events. These risk events are based on a probability function and random numbers for these events. The random numbers are calculated by the random function in Microsoft Excel. These assume values, which are in the same order of magnitude as the risk events.

Table 6.21: Product flows for the production of ethylene with varying utility cost

Product	From	To	Transport	Amount [t/a]
Corn stover	BlueEarth	Freeport	Rail	145,320
Corn stover	Clay	Freeport	Rail	145,320
Corn stover	Delaware	Freeport	Rail	131,067
Corn stover	Floyd	Freeport	Rail	134,593
Corn stover	Freeborn	Freeport	Rail	145,320
Corn stover	Grundy	Freeport	Rail	142,766
Corn stover	Nobles	Freeport	Rail	144,658
Corn stover	Stephenson	Freeport	Rail	145,320
Corn stover	Tazewell	Freeport	Rail	145,320
Corn stover	Warren	Freeport	Rail	145,320
Corn stover	Webster	Freeport	Rail	127,791
Corn stover	Benton	Lee	Truck	127,022
Corn stover	BlueEarth	Lee	Truck	145,320
Corn stover	Delaware	Lee	Truck	131,067
Corn stover	Fayette	Lee	Truck	144,221
Corn stover	Lee	Lee	Truck	145,320
Corn stover	Macon	Lee	Truck	136,845
Corn stover	Stephenson	Lee	Truck	145,320
Corn stover	Tazewell	Lee	Truck	145,320
Corn stover	Warren	Lee	Truck	145,320
Corn stover	Freeborn	Lee	Rail	144,274
Corn stover	Grundy	Lee	Rail	142,766
Ethylene	Lee	New York	Truck	50,000
Gasoline	Lee	New Orleans	Truck	54,782

For each Monte Carlo run, a new random number is used. Due to the long calculation times of the model not more than 100 trials have been implemented and analyzed. The approach can be extended without much effort to perform more model runs. The benefit of more model runs on more accurate results needs to be proven. For this first analysis 100 are sufficient. The results of the Monte Carlo Analysis for all three case studies are presented in the following sections.

6.6.5.1 Case Study 1: Monte Carlo Analysis

In 93 test runs, the same location (Clinton) as in the basis scenario was selected (see figure 6.20). Seven of the 100 runs, hence 7 % of the test series, resulted in different value chain setups. The alternative locations were in 5 test runs Blair (see table 6.22), in one Bedford Park (see table 6.23) and in another one Lafayette (see table 6.24).

In case Blair is the chosen location, Fort Dodge and Columbus are additional suppliers. The feedstock corn is transported by truck. The final products are transported from Blair to New Orleans for export just as in the basis scenario. Therefore, the further transport is not presented in the table.

Table 6.22: Monte Carlo Simulation: Blair as alternative location

Product	From	To	Transport	Amount [t/a]
Corn	Fort Dodge	Blair	Truck	72,694
Corn	Blair	Blair	-	100,000
Corn	Columbus	Blair	Truck	50,000
Butanol	Blair	New Orleans	Barge	50,000
Acetone	Blair	New Orleans	Barge	26,341
Ethanol	Blair	New Orleans	Barge	4,273

Bedford Park is supplied from Lafayette, Hammond and Bedford Park by Truck and from Marshall by rail. After the production of ABE in Bedford Park, the products are transported to New Orleans and sold to the markets from there.

Table 6.23: Monte Carlo Simulation: Bedford Park as alternative location

Product	From	To	Transport	Amount [t/a]
Corn	Marshall	Bedford Park	Rail	22,694
Corn	Lafayette	Bedford Park	Truck	100,000
Corn	Hammond	Bedford Park	Truck	50,000
Corn	Bedford Park	Bedford Park	-	50,000
Butanol	Bedford Park	New Orleans	Barge	50,000
Acetone	Bedford Park	New Orleans	Barge	26,341
Ethanol	Bedford Park	New Orleans	Barge	4,273

Lafayette is the fourth chosen location. It was selected in one model run. Lafayette is supplied by itself and by Indianapolis and Marshall by truck. The final products are transported to New Orleans to be exported from there.

Table 6.24: Monte Carlo Simulation: Lafayette as alternative location

Product	From	To	Transport	Amount [t/a]
Corn	Marshall	Lafayette	Truck	100,000
Corn	Lafayette	Lafayette	-	100,000
Corn	Indianapolis	Lafayette	Truck	22,694
Butanol	Lafayette	New Orleans	Barge	50,000
Acetone	Lafayette	New Orleans	Barge	26,341
Ethanol	Lafayette	New Orleans	Barge	4,273

The alternative locations were especially chosen for very low random numbers. The probabilities for risky events are the highest for low numbers.

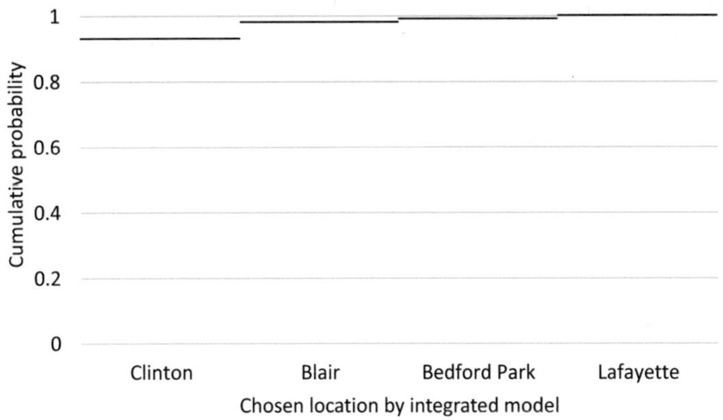

Figure 6.20: Cumulative frequency of the Monte Carlo runs for butanol

These lead to high risk cost. They exceed other cost of the value chain. Consequently, in these cases, the risk cost have larger impact on the value chain. Clinton seems to be a location, which is prone to risks. Blair is located in Nebraska and is the second preferred location. Illinois seems to be a risky state for biomass value chains according to the results above.

6.6.5.2 Case Study 2: Monte Carlo Analysis

Succinic acid often needs only a single supplier due to higher yields. Hence, only two value chain setups are defined by the integrated model. Of the 100 Monte Carlo runs, 80 % resulted in Keokuk as the supplier and production location as in the basis scenario without risks. In the remaining 20 % Clinton was chosen for both, supplier and production (see table 6.25).

Table 6.25: Monte Carlo Simulation: Clinton as alternative location

Product	From	To	Transport	Amount [t/a]
Corn	Clinton	Clinton	-	77,400
SA	Clinton	New Orleans	Barge	50,000

The results lead to the same interpretation as for butanol. The alternative location Clinton is chosen for low random numbers. For these low numbers, the probabilities are the highest. The risk cost are higher than other cost. Therefore, they have a larger influence on the results. Keokuk is located in Iowa, Clinton in Illinois. The results lead to the conclusion, that value chains in Iowa are more prone to risks. The weather extremes occur more often in Iowa than in Illinois. They have a larger influence on the value chain than transport or process risks. Not only the exposure to risks, but also the closeness of alternative suppliers (see butanol results) lead to the decision, that Clinton should be the preferred location. Despite the results of the majority of the Monte Carlo Simulations (80 % for Keokuk), Clinton is more robust and reduces risks.

The cumulative frequency function of the 100 Monte Carlo runs for succinic acid is presented in figure 6.21.

6.6.5.3 Case Study 3: Monte Carlo Analysis

Of the 100 Monte Carlo runs, only six runs led to overall four different setups for case study 3. The main production location is Floyd. Other locations are Freeport, Fayette and Lee. Hence, the majority of the production locations are in the corn belt close to biomass as corn stover. The main reason is that a lot of pyrolysis slurry is needed and the most suppliers are located in the corn belt.

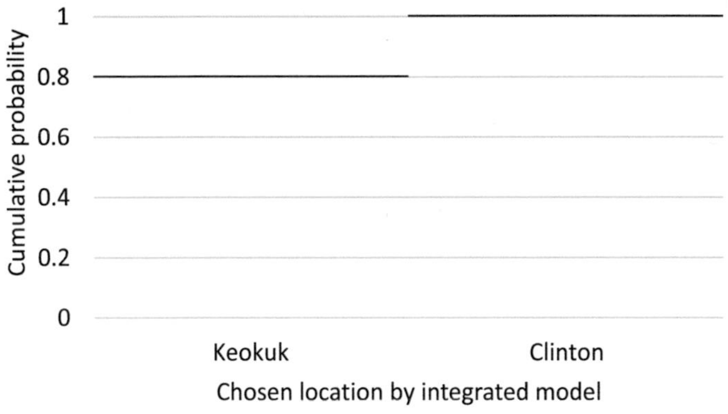

Figure 6.21: Cumulative frequency of the Monte Carlo runs for SA

The alternative locations minimize Iowa as supplier. Fayette is also in Iowa but more to the south, so that it has an additional supplier from Florida. Lee is located in Illinois and Freeport in Texas. All three locations are chosen in two cases.

The setup for Lee is presented in table 6.26. Lee is situated in Illinois. Although this state is often neglected Lee is chosen due to the reduced uncertainties in this one Monte Carlo run (very high number).

Even though Fayette is in the same state as Floyd, it includes less suppliers from Minnesota and Iowa but adds suppliers from Florida and Illinois (see table 6.27).

Two different setups for Freeport as alternative location exist (see table 6.28). In the first setup, most of the supply is provided from corn stover. The second setup includes more bagasse based suppliers.

The cumulative frequency function of the 100 Monte Carlo runs for succinic acid is presented in figure 6.22.

Table 6.26: Monte Carlo Simulation: Lee as alternative location

Product	From	To	Transport	Amount [t/a]
Corn stover	Benton	Lee	Truck	127,022
Corn stover	Cedar	Lee	Truck	145,320
Corn stover	Delaware	Lee	Truck	131,067
Corn stover	Fayette	Lee	Truck	144,221
Corn stover	Lee	Lee	-	145,320
Corn stover	Macon	Lee	Truck	136,845
Corn stover	Stephenson	Lee	Truck	145,320
Corn stover	Tazewell	Lee	Truck	145,320
Corn stover	Warren	Lee	Truck	145,320
Corn stover	Clay	Lee	Rail	144,274
Corn stover	Grundy	Lee	Rail	142,766

Table 6.27: Monte Carlo Simulation: Fayette as alternative location

Product	From	To	Transport	Amount [t/a]
Corn stover	Blue Earth	Fayette	Truck	145,320
Corn stover	Cedar	Fayette	Truck	145,320
Corn stover	Clay	Fayette	Truck	145,320
Corn stover	Delaware	Fayette	Truck	131,067
Corn stover	Fayette	Fayette	-	144,221
Corn stover	Floyd	Fayette	Truck	134,593
Corn stover	Freeborn	Fayette	Truck	145,320
Corn stover	Grundy	Fayette	Truck	142,766
Corn stover	Lee	Fayette	Truck	128,228
Corn stover	Stephenson	Fayette	Truck	145,320
Corn stover	Warren	Fayette	Truck	145,320

Table 6.28: Monte Carlo Simulation: Freeport as alternative location

Product	From	To	Transport	Amount [t/a]
Bagasse	Iberia	Freeport	Truck	145,320
Bagasse	Cedar	Freeport	Truck	145,320
Corn stover	Delaware	Freeport	Rail	131,067
Corn stover	Freeborn	Freeport	Rail	145,320
Corn stover	Grundy	Freeport	Rail	142,354
Corn stover	Macon	Freeport	Rail	136,845
Corn stover	Montgomery	Freeport	Rail	129,062
Corn stover	Stephenson	Freeport	Rail	145,320
Corn stover	Tazewell	Freeport	Rail	145,320
Corn stover	Warren	Freeport	Rail	145,320
Corn stover	White	Freeport	Rail	141,547
Bagasse	Iberia	Freeport	Truck	145,320
Bagasse	St. James	Freeport	Truck	145,320
Corn stover	St. Landry	Freeport	Truck	145,320
Corn stover	Blue Earth	Freeport	Rail	128,101
Corn stover	Freeborn	Freeport	Rail	145,320
Corn stover	Macon	Freeport	Rail	136,845
Corn stover	Montgomery	Freeport	Rail	129,062
Corn stover	Stephenson	Freeport	Rail	145,320
Corn stover	Tazewell	Freeport	Rail	145,320
Corn stover	Warren	Freeport	Rail	145,320
Corn stover	White	Freeport	Rail	141,547

6.7 Scenario calculations

The results of the different scenarios are presented and discussed in this section. The scenarios are defined as presented in section 5.6. The set up of the value chain varies depending on the configuration of the scenario.

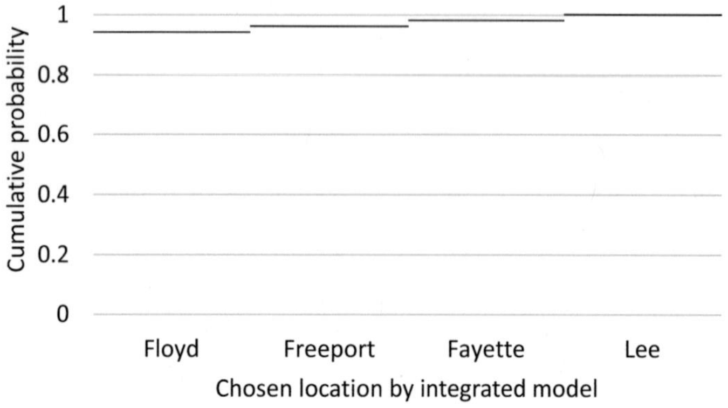

Figure 6.22: Cumulative frequency of the Monte Carlo runs for ethylene

The considered scenarios are the following: drought of 2012, the neglect of GMO based feedstocks, incentives for the utilization of lignocellulosic biomass, transport disruptions in the value chain, and increased production yields. As the quantifiable risks are not the focus of this analysis, the Monte Carlo Analysis is neglected for the scenario calculations. Therefore only results for one risk value is calculated for all three case studies.

6.7.1 Scenario 1: Drought 2012

The results of the three case studies under consideration of scenario 1 are discussed in this section. Years with heavy drought have increased in the past. The drought of 2012 was a severe drought in the U.S.. The boundary conditions for this scenario is described in section 5.6.2.

6.7.1.1 Case study 1: Biochemical production of butanol

The grain to residue ratio is influenced in case of drought. The amount of corn stover remains the same, but the grain yield is decreased. Other crops, such as sugar cane and sorghum are more drought resistant or are cultivated in areas, which are not effected by drought. Hence, only the price of corn increased during the drought of 2012. Consequently, the supplier changes to other feedstocks in case of a drought. This might also lead to an alternative location for the production of the final products. Nevertheless, if only a single year of drought occurs, it is not feasible to change the overall setup of the value chain. In future, drought years could occur more often, which can lead to this alternative scenario.

The results for the scenario 1 of the case study 1 is presented in table 6.29.

Table 6.29: Product flows for the production of butanol in scenario 1

Product	From	To	Transport	Amount [t/a]
Corn	Cedar Rapids	Clinton	Truck	100,000
Corn	Clinton	Clinton	-	100,000
Corn	Sycamore	Clinton	Truck	22,694
Butanol	Clinton	New Orleans	Barge	50,000
Acetone	Clinton	New Orleans	Barge	26,341
Ethanol	Clinton	New Orleans	Barge	4,273

Even though the price for corn, and therefore glucose syrup, has increased, it is still the preferred feedstock. The yield from glucose is very high. Hence, less feedstock and, consequently, suppliers are needed, compared to the other feedstocks. This keeps the transport cost at a minimum. Consequently, the setup of the value chain is the same as in the basis scenario. The profit of that year decreases due to the increased feedstock cost by about 44 mio $.

6.7.1.2 Case study 2: Biochemical production of succinic acid

Despite the rising corn price, the high yield of corn to succinic acid still results in an identical value chain set up as the basis scenario. Hence, Keokuk is still the location of choice for producing the succinic acid. The results for the scenario 1 of the case study 2 is presented in table 6.30. The additional cost for glucose syrup are 15 mio. $.

Table 6.30: Product flows for the production of succinic acid in scenario 1

Product	From	To	Transport	Amount [t/a]
Corn	Keokuk	Keokuk	-	77,400
SA	Keokuk	New Orleans	Barge	50,000

6.7.1.3 Case study 3: Thermochemical production of ethylene

The results for the scenario 1 of the case study 3 is presented in table 6.31. The price of corn stover is identical to the basis scenario, but bagasse price, and hence the sugar price from bagasse, was decreased by $20 as the sugar cane price was also lower in 2012. Even though the price of bagasse is decreased, corn stover is still the feedstock of choice. The transport cost are too high to benefit from the $20 lower bagasse price. Consequently, the setup of the value chain is equivalent to the basis scenario. As the corn stover price has not changed, the profit of this setup remains the same.

Table 6.31: Product flows for the production of ethylene in scenario 1

Product	From	To	Transport	Amount [t/a]
Corn stover	Benton	Floyd	Truck	127,022
Corn stover	Blue Earth	Floyd	Truck	145,320
Corn stover	Cedar	Floyd	Truck	145,320
Corn stover	Clay	Floyd	Truck	145,320
Corn stover	Fayette	Floyd	Truck	144,221
Corn stover	Floyd	Floyd		134,593
Corn stover	Freeborn	Floyd	Truck	145,320
Corn stover	Grundy	Floyd	Truck	142,766
Corn stover	Crawford	Floyd	Rail	142,044
Corn stover	Nobles	Floyd	Rail	145,320
Corn stover	Stephenson	Floyd	Rail	135,549
Ethylene	Floyd	New Orleans	Truck	50,000
Gasoline	Floyd	New Orleans	Truck	54,783

6.7.2 Scenario 2: Customers neglect GMO based feedstocks

GMO feedstocks produce not only more harvest, but are also more resistant to risks such as insects, drought etc. This work assumes, that by forbidding GMO based feedstocks, the yields decrease by half. Less feedstock results in reduced production capacities for pretreated biomass. Hence, each supplier can only sell half the pretreated biomass than originally. The amount of suppliers is expected to increase due to a constant demand for pretreated biomass. In this section, the results of the three case studies under consideration of scenario 2 will be discussed. A more detailed description of the scenario is presented in section 5.6.3.

6.7.2.1 Case study 1: Biochemical production of butanol

Due to the low harvesting yields, in total seven suppliers are needed, from which the full amount of pretreated biomass is used. To minimize transport cost, the location with the most adjacent suppliers is chosen for producing ABE. The final products are then transported by barge to the export port.

The results for the scenario 2 of the case study 1 is presented in table 6.32.

Table 6.32: Product flows for the production of butanol in scenario 2

Product	From	To	Transport	Amount [t/a]
Corn	Sycamore	Clinton	Truck	25,000
Corn	Eddyville	Clinton	Truck	47,695
Corn	Cedar Rapids	Clinton	Truck	50,000
Corn	Clinton	Clinton	-	50,000
Corn	Keokuk	Clinton	Truck	50,000
Butanol	Clinton	New Orleans	Barge	50,000
Ethanol	Clinton	New Orleans	Barge	2,980
Acetone	Clinton	New Orleans	Barge	25,325

Additionally to the suppliers Clinton, Cedar Rapids and Sycamore, the suppliers Eddyville and Keokuk are included to deliver enough sugar syrup. The transport cost increase by 2.4 mio. $ due to the additional two suppliers. Not only the harvesting yields are expected to decrease but also the corn prices, and hence, the glucose syrup price will increase. This leads to higher feedstock cost of double the original cost.

6.7.2.2 Case study 2: Biochemical production of succinic acid

As now less feedstock is available at the supplier locations, more suppliers need to be considered. The transport distance is the restrictive variable. Hence, a location for the production of the final product is chosen, where the sum of all transports is minimized. Clinton is now the production location of choice. As already seen in case study 1, it is adjacent to multiple other suppliers. The lacking amount of feedstock is provided by Cedar Rapids. Succinic acid is then transported via barge to the export port of New Orleans. The results for the scenario 2 of the case study 2 is presented in table 6.33.

Table 6.33: Product flows of the succinic production in scenario 2

Product	From	To	Transport	Amount [t/a]
Corn	Cedar Rapids	Clinton	Truck	27,400
Corn	Clinton	Clinton	-	50,000
SA	Clinton	New Orleans	Barge	50,000

Both, transport and feedstock cost increase for the scenario. Cedar Rapids is very close to Clinton and Clinton is directly situated at the Mississippi River. Hence, the transport cost only increase by about $500,000.

6.7.2.3 Case study 3: Thermochemical production of ethylene

In case GMO feedstock is neglected, corn yields will decrease immensely. Corn yield will only be half of the current yields. Not only corn yield decreases but also of corn stover. The prices of sugar syrup from corn stover is doubled. This results in a shift towards the utilization of sugar cane residues. The results for the scenario 2 of the case study 3 is presented in table 6.34. The production location is no longer set up in Floyd and supplied by corn stover biorefineries. In this scenario, the location of choice is Geismar in Louisiana. It is preferably supplied by bagasse based pyrolysis slurry. As not enough sugar syrup is available in the south, additional suppliers of the corn belt are used. They transport the corn stover based pyrolysis slurry by rail to Geismar. As the total supply decreases for corn stover, more suppliers are needed as in the basis scenario.

Table 6.34: Product flows of the ethylene production in scenario 2

Product	From	To	Transport	Amount [t/a]
Bagasse	Hendry	Geismar	Truck	145,320
Bagasse	Iberia	Geismar	Truck	145,320
Bagasse	Palm Beach	Geismar	Truck	145,320
Bagasse	Rapides	Geismar	Truck	36,984
Bagasse	St. James	Geismar	Truck	145,320
Bagasse	St. Landry	Geismar	Truck	145,320
Corn stover	Cedar	Geismar	Rail	70,549
Corn stover	Crawford	Geismar	Rail	71,022
Corn stover	Fillmore	Geismar	Rail	72,660
Corn stover	Grundy	Geismar	Rail	71,383
Corn stover	Hall	Geismar	Rail	71,383
Corn stover	Hidalgo	Geismar	Rail	73,761
Corn stover	Lee	Geismar	Rail	72,660
Corn stover	Macon	Geismar	Rail	68,422
Corn stover	Tazewell	Geismar	Rail	72,660
Corn stover	Warren	Geismar	Rail	72,660
Corn stover	White	Geismar	Rail	70,773
Ethylene	Geismar	New Orleans	Barge	50,000
Gasoline	Geismar	New Orleans	Barge	54,782

6.7.3 Scenario 3: Incentives for the production of lignocellulosic bioethanol

In this section, the results of the three case studies under consideration of scenario 3 are discussed. The input data is varied according to the description indicated in section 5.6.4. Consequently, the prices of lignocellulosic biomass are lowered due to 50 % incentives by politics.

6.7.3.1 Case study 1: Biochemical production of butanol

The results for the scenario 3 of the case study 1 is presented in table 6.35. Even though the price of lignocellulosic biomass was reduced by 50 %, still corn is chosen as the favored feedstock. The high conversion yields lead to the same setup and, therefore, cost and revenues as in the basis scenario. Cedar Rapids, Clinton and Sycamore are chosen as the suppliers and Clinton as production location of the joint process P12.

Table 6.35: Product flows for the production of butanol in scenario 3

Product	From	To	Transport	Amount [t/a]
Corn	Cedar Rapids	Clinton	Truck	100,000
Corn	Clinton	Clinton	-	100,000
Corn	Sycamore	Clinton	Truck	22,694
Butanol	Clinton	New Orleans	Barge	50,000
Acetone	Clinton	New Orleans	Barge	26,341
Ethanol	Clinton	New Orleans	Barge	4,273

6.7.3.2 Case study 2: Biochemical production of succinic acid

Even though the cost for lignocellulosic biomass are 50 % less, the production yields are high for glucose syrup. Hence, corn is still the feedstock of choice for the biomass value chain. Consequently, the setup of the value chain does not deviate from the basis scenario. Therefore, the cost and revenues remain unaltered as well. The results for the scenario 3 of the case study 2 is presented in table 6.36.

6.7.3.3 Case study 3: Thermochemical production of ethylene

As all relevant cost in this case study are reduced by 50 %, this scenario does not have an influence on the setup of the value chain for ethylene production.

Table 6.36: Product flows for the production of succinic acid in scenario 3

Product	From	To	Transport	Amount [t/a]
Corn	Keokuk	Keokuk	-	77,400
SA	Keokuk	New Orleans	Barge	50,000

The overall feedstock cost are reduced by half. Hence, the biomass cost are only 170 mio.$. The results for the scenario 3 of the case study 3 is presented in table 6.37.

Table 6.37: Product flows of the ethylene production in scenario 3

Product	From	To	Transport	Amount [t/a]
Corn stover	Benton	Floyd	Truck	127,022
Corn stover	Blue Earth	Floyd	Truck	145,320
Corn stover	Cedar	Floyd	Truck	145,320
Corn stover	Clay	Floyd	Truck	145,320
Corn stover	Fayette	Floyd	Truck	144,221
Corn stover	Floyd	Floyd	-	134,593
Corn stover	Freeborn	Floyd	Truck	145,320
Corn stover	Grundy	Floyd	Truck	142,766
Corn stover	Crawford	Floyd	Rail	142,044
Corn stover	Nobles	Floyd	Rail	145,320
Corn stover	Stephenson	Floyd	Rail	135,549
Ethylene	Floyd	New Orleans	Truck	50,000
Gasoline	Floyd	New Orleans	Truck	54,783

6.7.4 Scenario 4: Influence of transport disruption on the choice of logistics

In this section, the results of the three case studies under consideration of scenario 4 will be discussed. Depending on which transport mode (rail or barge) was used in the basis scenario, the possible transport modes are defined in scenario 4. The logistics and setup of the value chain will change. Two different types of transport disruptions are considered in scenario 4 and are discussed in the following sections.

6.7.4.1 Scenario 4a: Short-term disruption of a transport

Scenario 4a analyzes short-term disruptions of transport modes. The locations, which are chosen in the basis scenario, are set fix. The suppliers and export ports are variable.

Case study 1: Biochemical production of butanol

Clinton is the production location in the basis scenario. The final products ABE are transported via barge to New Orleans and sold to different markets from there. In this scenario, the facility is still located in Clinton, but barge transport is omitted. The results for the scenario 4a of the case study 1 is presented in table 6.38. Now that the barge transport is forbidden, ethanol is transported to New York. Ethanol has an export share of 0 and is fully used in the local market to fulfill the bioethanol quota. The rail transport distance is closer to New York. The remaining products are transported by rail to New Orleans and exported from there.

Case study 2: Biochemical production of succinic acid

Barge transport was possible in the basis scenario. In this scenario 4a, barge transport is omitted. This changes the chosen transport mode of the value chain. As the final production location cannot be changed in this scenario, the results remain the same as in the basis scenario. Keokuk can provide enough supply for the production of succinic acid.

Table 6.38: Setup of the butanol production in scenario 4a

Product	From	To	Transport	Amount [t/a]
Corn	Sycamore	Clinton	Truck	22,695
Corn	Clinton	Clinton	-	100,000
Corn	Cedar Rapids	Clinton	Truck	100,000
Butanol	Clinton	New Orleans	Rail	50,000
Butanol	New Orleans	Europe	Barge	11,700
Butanol	New Orleans	local	Truck	17,500
Butanol	New Orleans	Asia	Barge	20,800
Acetone	Clinton	New Orleans	Truck	25,325
Acetone	New Orleans	Europe	Barge	5,926
Acetone	New Orleans	local	Truck	8,864
Acetone	New Orleans	Asia	Barge	10,535
Ethanol	Clinton	New York	Truck	2,979
Ethanol	New York	local	Truck	2,979

Nevertheless, succinic acid is transported to New Orleans by rail. This setup increased the transport cost almost fourfold. The results for the scenario 4a of the case study 2 is presented in table 6.39.

Table 6.39: Product flows of the succinic production in scenario 4a

Product	From	To	Transport	Amount [t/a]
Corn	Keokuk	Keokuk	-	77,400
SA	Keokuk	New Orleans	Rail	50,000

Cast study 3: Thermochemical production of ethylene

Floyd was set as fix production location in this scenario 4a, as in the result of the basis scenario. The transport by rail is omitted. Hence, all transports are performed by truck. Regardless, the same suppliers are chosen by the model. The results for the scenario 4a of the case study 3 is presented in table 6.40.

Table 6.40: Product flows for the production of ethylene in scenario 4a

Product	From	To	Transport	Amount [t/a]
Corn stover	Benton	Floyd	Truck	127,022
Corn stover	Blue Earth	Floyd	Truck	145,320
Corn stover	Cedar	Floyd	Truck	145,320
Corn stover	Clay	Floyd	Truck	145,320
Corn stover	Crawford	Floyd	Truck	142,044
Corn stover	Fayette	Floyd	Truck	144,221
Corn stover	Floyd	Floyd	-	134,593
Corn stover	Freeborn	Floyd	Truck	145,320
Corn stover	Grundy	Floyd	Truck	142,766
Corn stover	Nobles	Floyd	Truck	145,320
Corn stover	Stephenson	Floyd	Truck	135,549
Ethylene	Floyd	New Orleans	Truck	50,000
Gasoline	Floyd	New Orleans	Truck	54,783

6.7.4.2 Scenario 4b: Long-term disruption of a certain transport mode

Scenario 4b considers the long-term neglect of a certain transport mode. Depending on the results of the basis scenario a certain transport mode was chosen to be avoided. The results are discussed in the following.

Case study 1: Biochemical production of butanol

The results of scenario 4b do not differ from the scenario 4a. Even though the location is flexible, the integrated model defines Clinton as the production location. Reason therefore, is the closeness of two other suppliers. This reduces the transport cost from suppliers to production plant.

Table 6.41: Product flows for the production of butanol in scenario 4b

Product	From	To	Transport	Amount [t/a]
Corn	Cedar Rapids	Clinton	Truck	100,000
Corn	Clinton	Clinton	-	100,000
Corn	Sycamore	Clinton	Truck	22,694
Butanol	Clinton	New Orleans	Rail	50,000
Acetone	Clinton	New Orleans	Barge	26,341
Ethanol	Clinton	New Orleans	Barge	4,273

Case study 2: Biochemical production of succinic acid

In case of succinic acid, barge was the optimal transport mode. As the production location can be changed in this scenario, the overall setup of the value chain is adapted. Corn is used as it has the highest production yield. Loudon is directly connected to the railway system and has the shortest distance to the port in New Orleans, from which the final product is exported to overseas.

Table 6.42: Product flows of the succinic production in scenario 4b

Product	From	To	Transport	Amount [t/a]
Corn	Loudon	Loudon	-	77,400
SA	Loudon	New Orleans	Rail	50,000

Case study 3: Thermochemical production of ethylene

The location was flexible in scenario 4b, but the transport by rail was omitted completely. Regardless these changes, Floyd remains the chosen location for the production. The setup is presented in table 6.43.

Table 6.43: Product flows for the production of ethylene in scenario 4b

Product	From	To	Transport	Amount [t/a]
Corn stover	Benton	Floyd	Truck	127,022
Corn stover	Blue Earth	Floyd	Truck	145,320
Corn stover	Cedar	Floyd	Truck	145,320
Corn stover	Clay	Floyd	Truck	145,320
Corn stover	Crawford	Floyd	Truck	142,044
Corn stover	Fayette	Floyd	Truck	144,221
Corn stover	Floyd	Floyd	-	134,593
Corn stover	Freeborn	Floyd	Truck	145,320
Corn stover	Grundy	Floyd	Truck	142,766
Corn stover	Nobles	Floyd	Truck	145,320
Corn stover	Stephenson	Floyd	Truck	135,549
Ethylene	Floyd	New Orleans	Truck	50,000
Gasoline	Floyd	New Orleans	Truck	54,783

6.7.5 Scenario 5: Increased conversion yields from second generation biomass

In this section, the results of the three case studies under consideration of scenario 5 are discussed. Assuming that research can increase the conversion factors of alternative biomass sources the production yields are adapted. The yield of sugar cane and sorghum are increased to the yield of corn. Additionally, the conversion rates from sugar cane bagasse and sorghum residues are set to the same rates as from corn stover.

6.7.5.1 Case study 1: Biochemical production of butanol

Even though the conversion yields are increased significantly, corn syrup is still the feedstock of choice. This has two reasons. Firstly, the suppliers Cedar Rapids and Sycamore are close to Clinton. Hence, the transport cost are comparably low. Secondly, corn syrup price remains constant in this scenario. It is lower than the syrup prices of sorghum and sugar cane. Consequently, the setup of scenario 5 is identical to the basis scenario. The results for the scenario 5 of the case study 1 is presented in table 6.44.

Table 6.44: Product flows of the butanol production in scenario 5

Product	From	To	Transport	Amount [t/a]
Corn	Cedar Rapids	Clinton	Truck	100,000
Corn	Clinton	Clinton	Truck	100,000
Corn	Sycamore	Clinton	Truck	22,694
Butanol	Clinton	New Orleans	Barge	50,000
Acetone	Clinton	New Orleans	Barge	26,341
Ethanol	Clinton	New Orleans	Barge	4,273

6.7.5.2 Case study 2: Biochemical production of succinic acid

The results for the scenario 5 of the case study 2 is presented in table 6.45. The conversion yields are adapted as described above. Nevertheless, the setup of the value chain is identical to the basis scenario. The biomass cost are higher than the transport cost. Corn syrup is less expensive than sorghum and sugar cane syrup. Consequently, corn is still the feedstock of choice.

Table 6.45: Product flows of the succinic production in scenario 5

Product	From	To	Transport	Amount [t/a]
Corn	Keokuk	Keokuk	-	77,400
SA	Keokuk	New Orleans	Barge	50,000

6.7.5.3 Case study 3: Thermochemical production of ethylene

Even though the conversion yields from corn stover and bagasse based pyrolysis slurry are identical, a location in the corn belt is still favored. As the prices for the slurry are identical, the only influencing factor are the transport distances. These are directly related to the amount and location of the suppliers. Not enough bagasse based pyrolysis slurry suppliers exist in the south. Hence, the location is built in Floyd and supplied by Benton, Blue Earth, Cedar, Clay, Fayette, Floyd, Grundy, Crawford and Stephenson county. The results for the scenario 5 of the case study 3 is presented in table 6.46.

Table 6.46: Product flows of the ethylene production in scenario 5

Product	From	To	Transport	Amount [t/a]
Corn stover	Benton	Floyd	Truck	127,022
Corn stover	Blue Earth	Floyd	Truck	145,320
Corn stover	Cedar	Floyd	Truck	145,320
Corn stover	Clay	Floyd	Truck	145,320
Corn stover	Fayette	Floyd	Truck	144,221
Corn stover	Floyd	Floyd	-	134,593
Corn stover	Freeborn	Floyd	Truck	145,320
Corn stover	Grundy	Floyd	Truck	142,766
Corn stover	Crawford	Floyd	Rail	142,044
Corn stover	Nobles	Floyd	Rail	145,320
Corn stover	Stephenson	Floyd	Rail	135,549
Ethylene	Floyd	New Orleans	Truck	50,000
Gasoline	Floyd	New Orleans	Truck	54,783

6.7.6 Comparison of economic results

In this section, the setup results of the five scenarios are compared for each case study. For the specific setup please see the previous sections.

The five scenarios are compared to the basis scenario S0. The cost for utilities, storage, export as well as the revenues and the investments are identical for all scenarios. Reasons are that the same amount of products are sold from the same export port to the same markets. Additionally, the process configuration does not change. Hence, the utility demand and, consequently, utility cost are identical. The setup also influences the investment. The main influence on the NPV is the biomass and transport cost.

6.7.6.1 Case study 1: Biochemical production of butanol

The economic results of the scenarios are depicted in table 6.47. In the following, the influence of the scenarios on the economic performance of the system is analyzed and compared. The NPV of almost all scenarios is positive. Consequently, the investment in this value chain is economically feasible. Only scenario S2 leads to a negative NPV. In case GMO corn is forbidden, prices explode and additional suppliers are needed. This does not only increase the biomass cost but also the transport cost. The use of non-GMO corn leads to the closure of such a production plant. Even incentives of 50 % for lignocellulosic biomass do not alter the setup and the economic feasibility of the value chain. The conversion efficiency of corn glucose syrup is too high. Rising corn prices as in scenario S1 due to weather risks have no impact on the value chain but reduce the profit.

Table 6.47: Value chain cost of butanol production of the different scenarios

cost in $ bio	S0	S1	S2	S3	S4	S5
NPV	258	-222	-432	258	256	258
Revenue	119					
Biomass	77	133	156	77	77	77
Transport	5.2	5.2	7.6	5.2	10.3	5.2
Risk	0.309	0.309	0.252	0.309	0.297	0.309
Utility	0.099					
Storage	0.32					
Export	4.3					
Investment	10.8					

The process setup does not change throughout the scenario calculations. Hence, the utility, storage, export cost as well as the investment remain constant in all scenarios. As the capacity of the production plant is set fix and the biomass type does not change in the scenarios, the revenues are identical. The high revenues result from the additional by-products which generate profits. Without the consideration of these by-products, the value chain would not be economical feasible.

6.7.6.2 Case study 2: Biochemical production of succinic acid

The production of succinic acid is in all scenarios feasible. This process generates high revenues due to the high market price of succinic acid. It is very efficient and has therefore low biomass demands. This leads to low transportation cost. Although GMO restrictions result in reduced biomass supply and high prices, the process is economically feasible. As not many suppliers are needed, the risks are low. Succinic acid fermentation does not produce other by-products. This, and the high conversion rates from corn glucose syrup, result in low investments. Succinic acid seems to be a product, which is highly recommendable for large-scale production.

Table 6.48: Value chain cost of succinic acid production of the different scenarios

cost in $ bio	S0	S1	S2	S3	S4	S5
NPV	556	389	319	556	528	556
Revenue				100		
Biomass	27	46	54	27	27	27
Transport	1.5	1.5	2	1.5	4.8	1.6
Risk				0		
Utility				0.59		
Storage				0.32		
Export				4.4		
Investment				8.7		

As in case study 1, the process setup is identical for all scenarios. Consequently, utility, storage, and export cost as well as revenues and investments are equal in all scenarios.

6.7.6.3 Case study 3: Thermochemical production of ethylene

The most significant difference to the other two case studies is the negative NPV in all scenarios. The production of ethylene from pyrolysis slurry via gasification and synthesis does not seem economically feasible at the time. Compared to butanol and succinic acid production, the investments are high but the revenues are low. Ethylene and gasoline are products of lower value than butanol or succinic acid. Especially gasoline needs to compete with petrol. Additionally, thermochemical processes have high energy demands. This leads to high utility cost.

To produce ethylene from pyrolysis slurry, many suppliers are needed due to the low conversion yield on a mass basis. This results in high transport cost, which in turn, reduces the profit of the value chain. The results of the different scenarios are presented in table 6.49.

Table 6.49: Value chain cost of ethylene production of the different scenarios

cost in $ bio	S0	S1	S2	S3	S4	S5
	S0	S1	S2	S3	S4	S5
NPV	-3,617	-3,617	-6,176	-2,163	-3,620	-2,367
Revenue				35		
Biomass	342	342	603	171	342	342
Transport	68	68	105	68	68	68
Risk	0.046	0.131	0.119	0.046	0.018	0.046
Utility	19.5	19.5	19.6	19.5	19.5	19.5
Storage				0.32		
Export				2.9		
Investment				237		

6.8 Conclusion

The results of the model runs are presented in this chapter. At first, the sub-models are applied to generate the necessary input data for the integrated model. All three case studies (butanol, succinic acid, ethylene) are simulated in AspenPlus. The material and energy balances are used to estimate investments and calculate the conversion efficiencies of the processes.

Based on the estimated biomass potentials, the optimization sub-model is applied to two case studies to produce pretreated biomass (sugar syrup and pyrolysis slurry). The results of the optimization sub-model are used as suppliers for the integrated model.

All identified risks and uncertainties are analyzed. The FTA approach leads to a clustering of all uncertainties to three quantifiable main risks. Probabilities and consequences are estimated for these main risks and depicted in risk matrices. Feedstock prices are the highest risk that occurs in biomass value chains. Transport risks of large vessels such as barge is the second crucial risk. Monte Carlo simulations are implemented in the integrated model to assess these risks. The influence of non-quantifiable risks is discussed based on five predefined scenarios

Although some locations are the preferred location based on the extreme scenarios, risks can exceed the influence of biomass cost. Biomass cost is the primary influence value in the scenario calculations, but are even less than the risk cost in the Monte Carlo Simulations.

The setup of most value chains is quite robust. Due to the high yield of biochemicals from corn glucose syrup, it is the most favored feedstock. The production yield based on corn glucose syrup is often more than threefold compared to other. Additionally, many suppliers exist in the corn belt. Hence, multiple suppliers for a single biochemical plant are often close together. This reduces supply risks and transport cost. The cost of barge transport is the cheapest for long distances. As all ports are in many cases more than 1000 miles away, the transport mode of choice is barge. Consequently, the facilities close to the Mississippi River are preferred.

Biomass cost make up for the largest share of the overall value chain. In the case studies, the share was between 66 and 75 %. Transport cost are the second most crucial cost share with about 15 %.

Based on the case studies, the preferred locations are most likely in the corn belt. Depending on the risks, the location can even shift to the south as droughts and other natural risks are less likely in Texas or Louisiana. Sorghum and sugar cane are also more resistant to risks. In many cases, Clinton was the location of choice for production processes based on corn glucose syrup. Consequently, it seems to be the most robust location for the production of chemicals based on biochemical conversion.

7 Conclusion

The model itself as well as the results are critically reflected and discussed in chapter 7.1. Also the application of the model to real world problems and the transferability to other problems are analyzed. A conclusion and an outlook are presented in chapter 7.2.

7.1 Discussion and application

In the following section 7.1.1, the developed approach is discussed. The results are summarized and analyzed in section 7.1.2. The application of the approach is discussed in section 7.1.3.

7.1.1 Discussion of the developed approach

This work has developed a two stage approach, which includes three sub-models and an integrated model. Objective of this work is to provide a decision support tool for the location and logistics optimization of value chains for the production of biobased chemicals under uncertainties. This approach can be applied to different case studies and research questions by varying input parameters. Most of the identified risks can be found in other regions. Nevertheless, the risk assessment needs to be performed individually for each application. In all cases, the input data for the three sub-models and the integrated model needs to be recalculated. Results and conclusions for the above presented case studies might vary depending on the boundary conditions (other biomass, regions, processes and cost).

The following reviews will discuss the single models: optimization, technical, and risk sub-model as well as the integrated model.

7.1.1.1 Optimization sub-model

The optimization sub-model has been developed as capacity and biomass optimization model. Based on precalculated biomass potentials and non-linear investment curves, the approach optimizes future locations and capacities of biomass conversion plants. Sugar syrup or pyrolysis slurry are products of these pretreatment plants.

Many different technologies can be applied to pretreat biomass. Their use depends on the type of biomass and the desired pretreatment product. This work has considered only a single technology for each, biochemical and thermochemical conversion, which is applicable for the production of sugar syrup, resp. pyrolysis slurry. The operator needs to preselect the technologies and the necessary input data. The inclusion of a technology optimization would support the decision of the operator.

The optimization sub-model is based on non-linear investment functions. These functions describe the economies of scale of investments. They need to be linearized to include them in the MILP model. The user defines a certain amount of support points to describe the linear functions. More support points lead to more accurate results. This work has defined only five points to enhance the calculation times.

7.1.1.2 Technical sub-model

The simulation of the pretreatment facilities has been based on a single reference plant, but not on the actual plant capacity. The results might deviate from the simulated values. Due to variable capacities in the optimization sub-model, the simulation of the true capacities is not feasible. The utility demand and efficiencies could be approached by simulating multiple capacities and finding a regression function based on the capacity.

No biorefineries for the conversion of biomass residues to high value sugar syrups exist. Therefore, the validation of the model has not been possible. The existing biochemical plants are based on first generation biomass. Their location is often not only based on the available biomass potentials, but also by already existing petrochemical plants. Up to now, the decision of possible locations are also based on strategic reasons and not only based on hard facts such as cost and raw material supply.

Due to the restricted data on large scale biochemical plants, the used data for the model application is based on publications, which have tested different process variations at laboratory scale. Hence, the utilization of these values for large scale plants is questionable. Especially in case of biochemical conversion with microorganisms such as bacteria, the efficiency strongly depends on the sugar concentration and composition in the fermentation broth, the downstream processing mode, the chosen microorganism, etc.

This work has simulated the technical process for the assessments in the technical sub-model. The processes have been implemented in AspenPlus. Unfortunately, AspenPlus is still developing appropriate tools for the simulation of batch processes. Especially fermentations are often batch processes and, therefore, time dependent and discrete. Hence, the quality of simulation might be reduced. Nevertheless, AspenPlus is a well-known and accepted flowsheeting simulation program. Its application is sufficient for first estimations.

The efficiencies of the processes are calculated on a mass basis, which is currently, the most interesting measure as long as the economic feasibility is assured. The overall efficiency of the process, also regarding energetic parameters, is currently becoming more and more important. In terms of sustainability, the process needs to be technically and economically feasible and efficient. Therefore, not only the mass, but also the energy balances should be considered more carefully.

7.1.1.3 Risk sub-model

The risk model presents the identification of risks along biomass value chains. In order to assess these risks, the estimation of probabilities and consequences of risks based on historic events has been performed. The likelihood of the events has been described as Poisson distribution. These risks have been summarized by Fault Tree Analysis to quantifiable main events. The cost, which accrue in case the risk occurs, are included in the objective function of the integrated model. The variability of the distribution function has been considered by applying Monte Carlo analysis. Although many aspects are included in the approach, time and event dependencies are not yet considered due to complexity reasons. Additionally, risks can correlate with each other. For example, heavy rains can lead to floods, which in turn result in barge transport delays. The description and calculation of the correlations between risks are very complex. Due to the large amount of considered risks in this work, the correlation analysis is not included. Hence, correlations such as Markov chains are neglected in this work.

Risks can be time dependent and especially occur multiple years in a row. Normally for example, dry periods alternate with wet seasons. In case of global warming, multiple drought years could occur in a row. As the storage might decrease or be fully consumed, the supply risks could increase with each additional drought year. Scenarios on weather developments have not been included in this work.

7.1.1.4 Integrated model

The integrated model enables the use of multiple biomass types. The conversion yields as well as the investments are based on the biomass. The input depends on the conversion yield and leads to the capacity of the facility. The investments have been estimated for production plants of a single biomass. Hence, the applicability of this approach to a mixed plant is questionable. Not only the investment but also the conversion yield might be influenced by the mix of feedstock input. Currently, no data on mixed plants are available to provide realistic input data for these critical aspects. From a technical point of view, it does not seem realistic, that multiple biomass plants are feasible at the same efficiency as single feedstock facilities. Due to the complexity of the problem, this work needed to simplify the problem regardless of the knowledge of this critical point. As soon as better data is published and available, the respective input data should be adapted.

A risk mitigation strategy could be the accurate storage capacity. This work has assumed a fix storage capacity. Nevertheless, the optimization of the needed storage capacity depending on the risk likelihood and consequence would be an additional value for the operator. The optimization of the storage capacity is complex. Many risks are time dependent and restrict storage itself as well. For example, in case a barge transport is three days delayed, then the storage needs to hold the production volume for three days. Still, pretreated biomass, e.g. sugar syrup or pyrolysis products, can deteriorate during storage. In this work, sugar syrup can crystallize or slurry can sediment. Consequently, storage is also prone to risks, which need to be considered in the optimization of storage capacities.

7.1.2 Discussion of the results

The results of the sub-models and the integrated model are summarized and interpreted in this section.

7.1.2.1 Optimization sub-model

Two case studies have been considered in the optimization sub-model: production of sugar syrup by dilute acid pretreatment and slurry by fast pyrolysis. Both are based on lignocellulosic biomass such as corn stover, sugar cane bagasse and sorghum residues. The approach optimizes locations and capacities of future biorefineries. In case of sugar syrup, 44 locations were found. Almost all residues were utilized to produce the sugar syrup. The model calculated 37 locations for the production of pyrolysis slurry. Both products are sensible to the investment functions and the product prices. Only an increase of about 7 % of the final product price led to 305 locations instead of only 37 in case of pyrolysis. Therefore, the results need to be considered carefully. Due to the high available potential of corn stover, the majority of the locations are situated in the corn belt.

7.1.2.2 Technical sub-model

The three case studies (butanol, succinic acid, ethylene) have been simulated in AspenPlus. The results cannot be validated with existing plants, as so far only few biochemical plants exist. Unfortunately, they do not publish their processing data. Only literature data was available for this analysis.

Baral et al. [41] have analyzed the conversion of biomass to butanol via ABE fermentation. According to them, the efficiency is about 11 %. The results of this work show a lower conversion yield of 8.8 %. Nevertheless, the results are in the same order of magnitude.

Vaswani [372] has estimated the total capital investment of succinic acid production via fermentation. His results are about 123.1 million dollars for a 37,500 t/year plant. This leads to a specific succinic acid price of 2.86 $/kg. This is higher than the current market price of 2 $/t for petro-based succinic acid. The investments of Vaswani [372] is about tenfold the value of the estimations in this work. Unfortunately, his calculations are not very detailed. Therefore, no comparison on the assumptions and results could be performed.

In general, corn based glucose syrup led to the highest efficiencies in both, butanol and succinic acid fermentation. Due to the fermentability of glucose, these feedstocks were preferred.

Corn stover was the feedstock of choice in case of the thermochemical pathway. According to Trippe [356], the market price needs to be at least 1.5 $/liter. Currently, the ethylene and gasoline prices are much lower. Hence, the revenues do not cover the investments and production cost. Consequently, the NPV is below zero and the investment is not feasible.

7.1.2.3 Risk sub-model

The results of the risk sub-model have been based on historic data. The U.S. government departments offer many officially available data banks to different topics. Accident, weather or crop cultivation statistics are provided for each year and state at the least. These available sources were used to estimate the probabilities. As different reference values are applied by presenting these data, they needed to be adapted to enable a generic approach. Nevertheless, this work had to make many assumptions, which can deviate from reality. Additionally, historic events cannot predict the future. Especially historic weather data will not provide certain information on future events. Therefore, some scenario calculations should be performed for extreme events.

The distribution functions have been performed with a Monte Carlo simulation. For this, random numbers for all risks have been assumed to enable a comparable data basis. Nevertheless, the values were in a certain range. Higher numbers are more applicable for accidents than for hurricane days per year. This led to very low possibilities in some cases, which could underestimate the results.

The basic risks have been summarized by Fault Tree Analysis (FTA) to three main risks: transport delays, feedstock price variations and process variations. As no correlations between the risks were analyzed, the FTA led in some cases to probabilities of more than 100 %. Especially weather risks have been added together due to the OR gates. Assuming a single random number, one of the weather events are very likely to occur in a year and lead to feedstock price variations. This is actually a fact, as feedstock prices are very fluctuating.

Low random numbers led to variations in the value chain. Hence, the risks have an influence on the setup. Uncertainties need to be considered in case of new investments to reduce possible risks beforehand.

7.1.2.4 Integrated model

In most cases, corn is considered the primary feedstock of choice. High conversion factors influence the location and suppliers the most. Due to the low efficiencies from second generation biomass, these are hardly chosen. Their prices need to be reduced by 90 % in order to change the feedstock.

Some locations are very robust to risks and cost variations such as utility or biomass prices. Only transport cost have a large influence on the value chain and the logistics. Clinton was in many scenarios the preferred location and seems to be robust against transport, utility, and biomass cost changes. It was also often the preferred location considering risks.

The scenario calculations of extreme events has proven that these often have a large influence on the value chain and need to be considered carefully.

7.1.3 Application

The approach has been applied for six biomass types, first and second generation biomass, which are cultivated in the United States. Each feedstock has been converted by three technologies to biochemicals. These have been modeled by case studies. The location planning models included three transport modes, hubs, storage and the export of the final products. The uncertainties were calculated based on existing statistics in the considered region and represent real world problems. Hence, the approach provides decision support for realistic value chains in a defined region.

The decision support system can be applied not only to the above presented parameters, but can be seen as a generic approach for multiple problems. In general, different transport modes, biomass, risks, technologies, etc. can be implemented. The model can be adapted to other transport, biomass and utility cost as well as investment and production cost. The suppliers, possible locations and export hubs can be individualized. Nevertheless, the transport distances per transport mode need to be adapted. These depend on the region, the predefined locations and the available transport modes.

Uncertainties, their occurrence, probabilities and consequences, strongly depend on the value chain and need to be carefully reconsidered in case the model is applied to other value chains. The risks need to be identified from scrap. Of course, the identified risks in this work can be used as basis, but they do not claim completeness.

This work focuses on biochemicals. Nevertheless, the approach is also applicable for bioenergy and biofuel processes. Some risks might be identical, but need to be reconsidered (e.g. quota for bioenergy/biofuel). In case of bioenergy, the assessment of the production process efficiency needs to be redefined. This work has assessed the efficiency on mass basis. In case of bioenergy, the more reasonable indicator is the energy content (e.g. lower heating value (LHV) of biomass).

7.2 Conclusion and outlook

This final section concludes this work and presents an outlook on further possible research.

7.2.1 Conclusion

This work has developed an approach for decision support for location planning of biomass value chains for the production of biochemicals. Biomass value chains are prone to multiple risks. Their economic and technical feasibility depend on many input factors. This work has proposed a two stage approach to include the majority of the influencing factors. In three sub-models, optimization, technical, and risks, the necessary input data for the integrated model have been calculated and analyzed.

7.2.1.1 Optimization sub-model

Currently, conversion facilities for first generation biomass are state of the art but only few biorefineries for the pretreatment of lignocellulose exist. These can supply the production of biobased chemicals with the respective feedstock. In order to include these in the approach, an optimization sub-model has been developed. The optimization sub-model optimizes future biorefinery locations based on lignocellulosic biomass residues. This work has developed a capacity and feedstock optimization problem. The non-linear economies of scale of the plant capacity have been approximated based on investment curves. Biomass is transported by truck to the pretreatment facility. This work has considered two different technologies and, therefore, pretreated feedstocks. Dilute Acid pretreatment converts lignocellulosic biomass to sugars for biochemical conversion. Fast pyrolysis is used to produce pyrolysis slurry (biooil and biochar) as feedstock for thermochemical processes. Based on the biomass potentials of corn stover, sorghum residues and sugar cane bagasse, 44 biorefineries for sugar or 37 pyrolysis locations were selected by the model. The price of the pretreated biomass has a large influence on the amount of opened facilities. Already an increase of 7.5 % of the slurry price led to 305 locations. Incentives on the price of pretreated lignocellulosic biomass could result in a large increase of pretreatment facilities.

7.2.1.2 Technical sub-model

The technical sub-model has been used to simulate the conversion processes from biomass to sugar or pyrolysis slurry and for the conversion from pretreated biomass to chemicals. The results of the simulations have been used to estimate production cost, especially of utilities, and investments. These provide input data for the integrated model. Corn resulted in the highest conversion yields of biochemical processes. It contains the highest concentration of glucose, which is metabolized best by microorganisms. Other biomass of the first generation, such as sugar cane and sorghum, also consist of fructose. The conversion rates are unknown for sucrose and have been therefore neglected in this work. Lignocellulosic biomass contains large amounts of hemicellulose and, hence, xylose as well as lignin. These led to reduced efficiencies. Nevertheless, due to high pretreatment cost, the price of corn is rather high. Succinic acid for example has quite large yields of almost 80 % based on corn glucose syrups but investments of about 60 mio. dollars.

7.2.1.3 Risk sub-model

The risk sub-model has identified quantifiable and non-quantifiable risks in biomass value chains. The quantifiable risks, such as transport risks (e.g. accidents, congestion) or weather risks (e.g. drought, hurricane) haven been estimated based on historical data. All identified risks have been summarized to three main risks by Fault Tree Analysis: process variation, transport delay, and feedstock prices. These have been be described by Poisson distributions. The integrated model has included the probability functions by Monte Carlo Analysis. Although the risk for a single risk event was low, the sum of all possible risks, which have an influence on the main risks was in some cases almost 100 %. Therefore, these risks need to be considered carefully. The non-quantifiable risks have been modeled by scenario analysis. These events could not be described by historical data as they are often very extreme (e.g. extreme drought in 2012) or are influenced by mankind (e.g. policies). These risks had the largest influence on the biomass value chain. Therefore, extreme scenarios are inevitable to be considered.

7.2.1.4 Integrated model

The choice of biomass depended on the conversion yields. The efficiency of the process had the greatest influence on the setup of the value chain. Corn was the preferred biomass for fermentations. The high glucose concentrations of corn glucose syrup has led to the highest conversion yields in case of biochemical processes. Microorganisms can metabolize hexoses more easily. Consequently, the efficiencies of sugar syrup from sugar cane, sorghum and biomass residues, have been much lower. Only very high corn cost resulted in a switch in feedstock supply.

Processes were more likely to operate at the same location. Splitting up processes in conversion and downstream processes did not seem feasible due to increased transport cost and utility demands. Additionally, this work assumed, that joint locations reduces the engineering and personnel cost.

Often, a single supplier was not sufficient for the provision of pretreated biomass for the conversion to biochemicals. A production location, which is close to multiple suppliers can increase supply security and, hence, reduce the risk of supply outages. Therefore, even if only a single supplier was needed (as in case study 2), the operator should consider to choose a location close to multiple suppliers. This is also proposed based on the Monte Carlo simulation. Case study 2 showed a high probability of 20 % to change the production location compared to the other case studies (case study 1: 7 %, case study 3: 6 %).

Barge transport was the most efficient for long distances. As the final products needed to be transported to the ports for export, the transport distances were very long. Especially, if corn wet mills were selected as co-location, the products need to be transported from the central corn belt to the coast for export. Nonetheless, barge transport risks have high consequences, which might occur. Hence, locations, which are not restricted to barge transport should be considered.

The developed approach provides decision support to operators of chemical plants based on biomass and other stakeholders. New production plants are strategic decisions, which need to be carefully accessed. This problem is very complex due to many influencing factors. The operators can utilize the approach to plan such facilities and the overall value chain. With the help of the approach, many different scenarios and regions can be evaluated. This can lead to a more profound result. Nevertheless, the effort to gather all relevant data for the models is very time consuming and complex.

7.2.2 Outlook

Although this work includes multiple characteristics of biomass value chains and risks, many possible targets exist to extend more aspects in the approach.

7.2.2.1 Optimization sub-model

The optimization sub-model is a capacity and location optimization model, which takes different biomass types into account. Nevertheless, many additional aspects can be considered in the approach. Currently, the biomass potentials are modeled as a total sum of available feedstock. The usable potentials are non-linearly restricted by harvesting cost, technical possibilities and ecological restrictions. In order to estimate, which share of the potential should be harvested, biomass supply can be modeled by non-linear supply cost curves.

The biomass transport is currently enabled only by truck. For long distances in the corn belt, also rail transport is feasible. The optimization sub-model could be further developed not only as location optimization but also as a logistics model.

Furthermore, the optimization sub-model currently assumes that the applicator of the model is aware of the best available technique (BAT) and implements the necessary data. As multiple technologies exist to pretreat biomass, the optimization of the utilized method should be considered. The efficiency and economic feasibility depends on the capacity and, therefore, on the biomass potentials. Consequently, the applied technology needs to be optimized. Additionally, the investment is currently only estimated based on a reference capacity. As the size of the conversion facility is optimized, the conversion yields, investments and variable production cost might deviate from the optimal value. Hence, correlation functions between these factors and the capacity should be implemented instead of fix values in order to lead to more accurate results.

7.2.2.2 Technical sub-model

The simulation for the technical sub-model is currently implemented in AspenPlus. The application of AspenPlus is currently optimized for continuous processes. However, biochemical processes are often batch processes. In future research, other software tools such as Chemadis, SuperPro Designer, etc. should be tested. The results of the simulations should be compared and validated with real production data.

The current simulations could not be validated with real world data of large scale conversion plants. Companies are very strict with disclosing process data of their facilities. Nevertheless, a cooperation with a chemical company should be envisaged to validate the models.

Besides the simulation results, research needs exist to further develop the efficiency of biochemical conversion of ligocellulosic biomass. Bacterial strains need to be developed that can convert other sugars than glucose more efficiently. Thermochemical conversion processes are not well understood. Especially pyrolysis processes can currently not be simulated. Hence, the knowledge of the processes further need to be extended.

7.2.2.3 Risk sub-model

Currently, multiple risks are considered and modeled. Nevertheless, the risks are considered individually. In many cases, correlations between these risks exist. For example, heavy rains correlate with floods and therefore barge accidents. Also, drought and heavy rain are unlikely to occur in the same month. Consequently, the identification and consideration of correlations between risks leads to a more precise result. This work focuses on the identification of most risks along the biomass value chain as well as many other parameters. Hence, the analysis of correlations is beyond the scope but should be considered in future research.

Additionally, not all possible risks are included in the approach. This work assumes that the demand for biobased chemicals is fix. However, many factors influence the demand for biochemicals. Multiple operators, fluctuating customers, varying market conditions can lead to shifting demands. These demand variations influence the biomass demand and, hence, the location of suppliers and production. In literature, demand variations are often modeled by stochastic programming. As this approach is beyond the scope of this work, it was neglected. In further research it should be considered. The approach should be tested, if it can be adapted to stochastic programming.

7.2.2.4 Integrated model

The integrated model has been developed as location and logistic planning model. This work considers three case studies: two biochemical conversion plants (n-butanol and succinic acid) and one thermochemical production pathway (DME via pyrolysis). A general approach has been developed, which can be applied to other processes (e.g. propanediol, itaconic acid, bioenergy, etc.) as well. In future research, also other processes can be assessed with this approach. Although this work focuses on biochemicals, the approach is also applicable for bioenergy and biofuels. The general idea and setup of the approach can also be transferred to other research fields.

The case studies focused on the United States and the major biomass resources there. The general approach can also be applied to other regions and biomass types. Europe, for example, might lead to very different results as many smaller countries exist and the biomass is far less concentrated. The input data needs to be adapted to the regional specifics. Especially, transport distances, locations, biomass potentials, existing plants, all other regional aspects, need to be reassessed and included in the sub-models and integrated model.

The integrated model currently focuses on economic parameters. However, biomass value chains also aim at reducing emissions and increasing sustainability by producing “green chemicals”. Therefore, not only the economic optimization of value chains, but also the consideration of ecologic factors by multi-objective optimization should be implemented. The locations and logistical concepts might deviate from the current setup and lead to pareto-optimal results.

8 Summary

Due to limited fossil resources, the importance and improvement of a bio-economy has increased more and more in the past years. Biomass based value chains are very complex and depend on many different factors. Currently, research focuses on supply and demand risks of biofuel and bio-energy networks or parts of the supply chain. Nevertheless, the inclusion of the full scope of sugary/starchy as well as lignocellulosic biomass from cultivation to the production of biochemicals for the final market could not be found in literature. Consequently, in this work a decision support approach for location and logistics planning has been developed and applied to the production of chemicals from biomass considering uncertainties.

The decision support approach consists of an integrated model and three sub-models. The optimization sub-model optimizes the location and capacities of pretreatment plants, which convert lignocellulosic biomass to processable feedstocks. The technical sub-model assesses conversion processes techno-economically by flowsheeting simulations. Production yields, utility demands, production costs and investments are the main results of the technical sub-model. The risk sub-model identifies and assesses risks and uncertainties that can occur along biomass value chains. Beside the results of the three sub-models, the integrated model also considers various cost, transport restrictions, existing infrastructures and suppliers, etc. The integrated model, designed as a Mixed Integer Linear Programming model, allows modeling of multiple biomass, multiple transport modes, intermediate processes and uncertainties. In this work, three case studies are analyzed with this model, two biochemical and one thermochemical conversion in the United States. As a result, the integrated model proposes a nearly optimal location and the respective logistical network for the production of bio-based chemicals.

The results are strongly related to the biomass price, the conversion yields and transport modes. In general, uncertainties have an impact on the setup of the value chain. Especially non-quantifiable risks have a large influence on the value chain and should therefore be considered carefully before decision-making. Although this work aims at modeling problems based on real world data, the results need to be revised carefully. All relevant data is based on literature and could not be validated with reality. Nevertheless, the presented model is a first approach to assess multiple problems of complex biomass value chains.

A Appendix

A.1 Appendix 1

A.1.1 Unit processes in AspenPlus

Table A.1: List of the most common unit processes in AspePlus Simulation (AspenTech manual [289])

Unit	Label	Process unit	Description
	Mixer	stream mixer	merge and mixing of multiple material and energy streams
	FSplit	stream split	split of material and energy streams in multiple sub streams
	SSplit	cyclone	separation of solids from fluids
	SEP	component separation	separation of the feed in multiple output streams based on flow rates or split factors
	Flash	vacuum evaporator	separation by utilizing the saturation equilibrium
	Heater	heat exchanger	inducing and dissipating heat

	Decanter	decanter	separation of phases of in each other insoluble mixtures
	RStoic	stoichiometric reactor	reactions based on stoichiometric definitions in form of reaction equations
	Compr	compressor or turbine	pressure change of gases and vapors
	Pump	pump	pressure increase of fluids
	RadFrac	rectification column	separation of a fluid in two/three components
	Crusher	mill	modeling of hammer mills, impact mills etc.
	CCD	counter stream decanter	multistage solid wash
	Screen	screen	solid-solid separation with screens
	HyCyc	hydroyyclone	solid-fluid separation
	CFuge	centrifuge	solid-fluid separation
	ClChng	manipulator	change of stream classes

A.1.2 Conversion factors of biomass processing

Table A.2: Conversion factors of pretreatment (Saha et al. [310])

Number	Reaction equation	Dilute Acid in %
1	$Cellulose + H_2O \rightarrow Glucose(Monomer)$	6.5
2	$Cellulose \rightarrow Glucose(Oligomer)$	0.7
3	$Xylan \rightarrow Xylose(Oligomer)$	52
4	$Xylan + H_2O \rightarrow Xylose$	2
5	$Xylan \rightarrow Furfural + 2H_2O$	0.01
6	$Mannan + H_2O \rightarrow Mannose$	52
7	$Mannan \rightarrow Mannose(Oligomer)$	2
8	$Manan \rightarrow HMF + 2H_2O$	0.01
9	$Galactan + H_2O \rightarrow Galactose(Monomer)$	52
10	$Galactan \rightarrow Galactose(Oligomer)$	2
11	$Galactan \rightarrow HMF + 2H_2O$	0.01
12	$Arabinan + H_2O \rightarrow Arabinose(Monomer)$	52
13	$Arabinan \rightarrow Arabinose(Oligomer)$	2
14	$Arabinan \rightarrow Furfural + 2H_2O$	0.01
15	$Acetat \rightarrow Aceticacid$	100
16	$Xylan + H_2O \rightarrow DEGRAD$	5
17	$Lignin \rightarrow LIGNSOL - 1$	5
18	$Arabinan + H_2O \rightarrow DEGRAD$	5

Table A.3: Conversion rates of hydrolysis and fermentation of ABE (Qureshi et al. [296])

Number	Reaction equation	Yield in %
Hydrolysis		
1	$Cellulose + H_2O \rightarrow Glucose(Monomer)$	65
2	$Xylan + H_2O \rightarrow Xylose(Monomer)$	38
Fermentation		
	Glucose	
1	$Glucose \rightarrow Butanol + 2CO_2 + H_2O$	58.2
2	$Glucose + H_2O \rightarrow Acetone + 3CO_2 + 4H_2$	24.5
3	$Glucose \rightarrow 2\,Ethanol + 2CO_2$	1
4	$Glucose \rightarrow Butyricacid + 2CO_2 + 2H_2$	0
5	$Glucose \rightarrow 3Aceticacid$	0
	Xylose	
1	$3Xylose \rightarrow 2.5\,Butanol + 5CO_2 + 2.5\,H_20$	58.2
2	$Xylose \rightarrow 2Aceton + 2CO_2 + 2H_2$	4.5
3	$3Xylose \rightarrow 5\,Ethanol + 5CO_2$	17
4	$3Xylose \rightarrow 2.5\,Butyricacid + 5CO_2 + 2.5\,H_2$	0
5	$2Xylose \rightarrow 5\,Aceticacid$	0

A.1.3 Cooling down of glucose syrup during truck transport

During transport, glucose syrup, or any other sugar syrup, cools down. The cool down curve depends on the ambient temperature, the driving velocity as well as on the insulation of the container and its materials. All presented values are based on VDI Wärmeatlas [378]. No detailed data is available on the containers. According to experts (pers. comm.) the containers are vacuum insulated. No values could be found on vacuum, therefore an insulation of glass wool was assumed for the calculations. Additionally, this work assumes, that the containers are made of steel. For the heat transfer the following steps were identified:

- air - steel (as)
- steel - glass wool (sw)
- glass wool - steel (ws)
- steel - glucose syrup (sg)

Consequently, the following equation has been developed:

$$\sum \frac{1}{Bi} = \frac{1}{Bi_{as}} + \frac{1}{Bi_{sw}} + \frac{1}{Bi_{ws}} + \frac{1}{Bi_{sg}} \tag{A.1}$$

This work assumes, that already contact with a cold steel wall will cause crystallization. Hence, the last Biot value can be neglected and will not be included in the calculations of the following equation.

$$= \frac{\lambda_s}{\alpha_{as} \cdot L} + \frac{\lambda_w}{\alpha_{sw} \cdot L} + \frac{\lambda_s}{\alpha_{ws} \cdot L} \tag{A.2}$$

$$= \frac{50}{80 \cdot 0.01} + \frac{0.04}{150 \cdot 0.1} + \frac{50}{150 \cdot 0.01} \tag{A.3}$$

$$= 95.83 \tag{A.4}$$

$$Bi = 0.01 \tag{A.5}$$

According to the Wärmeatlas, this results in Fourier numbers of 15, which in turn is about 1°C per 4 days. Experts say, that a container looses about 1°F per 4 days. Considering, that vacuum and not glass wool insulated containers are used, these values are comparable.

A.2 Appendix 2

A.2.1 Biomass utilization and sugar production of the optimization sub-model

Table A.4: Biomass capacity and sugar production: results of the optimization sub-model

County	State	Biomass utilization dt/year	Sugar production dt/year
Lauderdale County	AL	329,404	204,164
Palm Beach County	FL	1,175,319	691,758
Terrell County	GE	333,385	206,632
Iroquois County	IL	2,844,541	1,763,046
Lee County	IL	3,506,270	2,173,186
Macon County	IL	3,506,270	2,173,186
Pike County	IL	2,336,093	1,447,807
Warren County	IL	3,506,270	2,173,186
Hamilton County	IN	3,033,092	1,879,910
Knox County	IN	3,074,948	1,905,725
Kosciusko County	IN	2,527,977	1,566,840
Grundy County	IO	3,506,270	2,173,186
Plymouth County	IO	3,253,439	2,016,482
Pottawattamie County	IO	3,506,270	2,173,186
Webster County	IO	3,506,270	2,173,186
Cheyenne County	KS	2,109,673	1,306,452
Kingan County	KS	472,656	292,952
Stevens County	KS	2,075,325	1,282,815
Simpsons County	KE	481,982	298,732
Iberville Parish	LA	1,132,817	669,945

Table A.4: Biomass capacity and sugar production: results of the optimization sub-model

County	State	Biomass utilization dt/year	Sugar production dt/year
Midland County	MI	1,328,616	823,476
Blue Earth County	MN	3,506,270	2,173,186
Fillmore County	MN	3,246,338	2,012,080
Kandiyohi County	MN	3,438,380	2,131,108
Washington County	MS	1,550,638	960,874
Cass County	MO	1,537,923	953,183
New Madrid County	MO	1,575,456	976,292
Boone County	NE	2,816,402	1,745,572
Dawson County	NE	2,235,726	1,385,466
Fillmore County	NE	3,376,384	2,091,473
Morrill County	NE	383,823	237,894
Yates County	NY	552,499	342,439
Hertford County	NC	492,103	305,006
Robeson County	NC	475,970	295,006
Cass County	ND	2,023,501	1,254,166
Wells County	ND	335,251	207,788
Wyandot County	OH	3,506,270	2,173,186
Armstrong County	PE	383,517	237,704
Chester County	PE	1,259,057	780,361
Brown County	SD	2,272,228	1,408,318
Minnehaha County	SD	3,278,204	2,031,829
Bastrop County	TX	489,383	303,320
Castro County	TX	419,751	260,162
Dane County	WI	2,450,409	1,518,763

A.2.2 Biomass utilization and pyrolysis oil production of the optimization sub-model

Table A.5: Biomass capacity and slurry production: results of the optimization sub-model

County	State	Capacity of biomass dt/year	Oil production dt/year
Glades County	FL	81,621	56,482
Hendry County	FL	210,000	145,320
PalmBeach County	FL	210,000	145,320
Macon County	FL	197,752	142,044
Montgomery County	FL	186,505	131,067
Stephenson County	FL	210,000	144,220
Tazewell County	FL	210,000	134,593
Warren County	FL	210,000	142,766
Lee County	IL	210,000	145,320
Knox County	IN	167,007	94,073
White County	IN	204,547	127,790
Benton County	IO	183,558	145,320
Cedar County	IO	210,000	136,845
Clay County	IO	210,000	129,061
Crawford County	IO	205,266	145,320
Delaware County	IO	189,403	145,320
Fayette County	IO	208,411	145,320
Floyd County	IO	194,498	115,568
Grundy County	IO	206,309	141,546
Story County	IO	135,943	127,022
Webster County	IO	184,668	145,320
Iberia County	LA	210,000	145,320

Table A.5: Biomass capacity and slurry production: results of the optimization sub-model

County	State	Capacity of biomass dt/year	Oil production dt/year
Iberville Parish	LA	210,000	145,320
Rapides County	LA	53,444	36,983
St.James County	LA	210,000	145,320
St.Landry County	LA	210,000	145,320
BlueEarth County	MI	210,000	145,320
Freeborn County	MI	210,000	145,320
Nobles County	MI	210,000	145,320
Stevens County	MI	158,487	109,673
Atchison County	MO	141,213	97,720
Boone County	NE	199,167	137,824
Cedar County	NE	210,000	145,320
Dodge County	NE	173,662	120,174
Fillmore County	NE	210,000	145,320
Hall County	NE	210,000	145,320
Hidalgo County	TX	106,590	73,760

A.2.3 Existing pretreatment plants in the U.S.: corn, sugar cane and sorghum

Table A.6: Existing corn wet mills, sugar cane mills, sorghum mills

City	Feedstock	Assumed sugar syrup capacity dt/year
Atchison	Corn	50,000
Bedford Park	Corn	50,000
Belle Glade	Sugar Cane	50,000
Belle Rose	Sugar Cane	50,000
Blair	Corn	100,000
Campus	Sorghum	50,000
Cedar Rapids	Corn	100,000
Clewiston	Sugar Cane	50,000
Clinton	Corn	100,000
Columbus	Corn	50,000
Colwich	Sorghum	50,000
Crete	Sugar Cane	50,000
Danville	Sugar Cane	50,000
Dayton	Corn	50,000
Decatur	Corn	100,000
Eddyville	Corn	100,000
Fort Dodge	Corn	100,000
Franklin	Sugar Cane	50,000
Hammond	Corn	50,000
Indianapolis	Corn	50,000
Jeanerette	Sugar Cane	50,000
Kankakee	Sugar Cane	50,000

Table A.6: Existing corn wet mills, sugar cane mills, sorghum mills

City	Feedstock	Assumed sugar syrup capacity dt/year
Keokuk	Corn	100,000
Keyes	Sorghum	50,000
Lafayette	Corn	100,000
Lakeland	Sugar Cane	50,000
Loudon,IL	Corn	100,000
Marshall	Corn	100,000
New Iberia	Sugar Cane	50,000
Sagamore	Corn	50,000
North Kansas City	Corn	50,000
Orangeville	Corn	50,000
Overland Park	Sorghum	50,000
Paincourtville	Sugar Cane	50,000
Plainview	Sorghum	50,000
Port Wentworth	Sugar Cane	50,000
Raceland	Sugar Cane	50,000
Santa Rosa	Sugar Cane	50,000
St. Martinville	Sugar Cane	50,000
Stockton	Corn	50,000
Stockton	Sorghum	50,000
Sycamore	Corn	50,000
Thibodeaux	Sugar Cane	50,000
Wahpeton	Corn	50,000
West Palm Beach	Sugar Cane	50,000
White Castle	Sugar Cane	50,000
Winston-Salem	Corn	50,000

A.3 Appendix 3

A.3.1 Fault Tree of transport delays

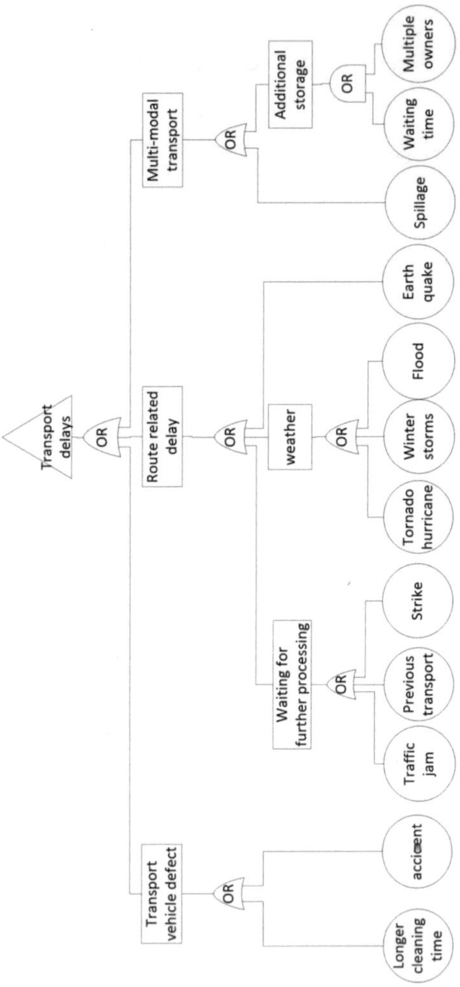

Figure A.1: Fault Tree of transport delays

A.3.2 Fault Tree of process variations

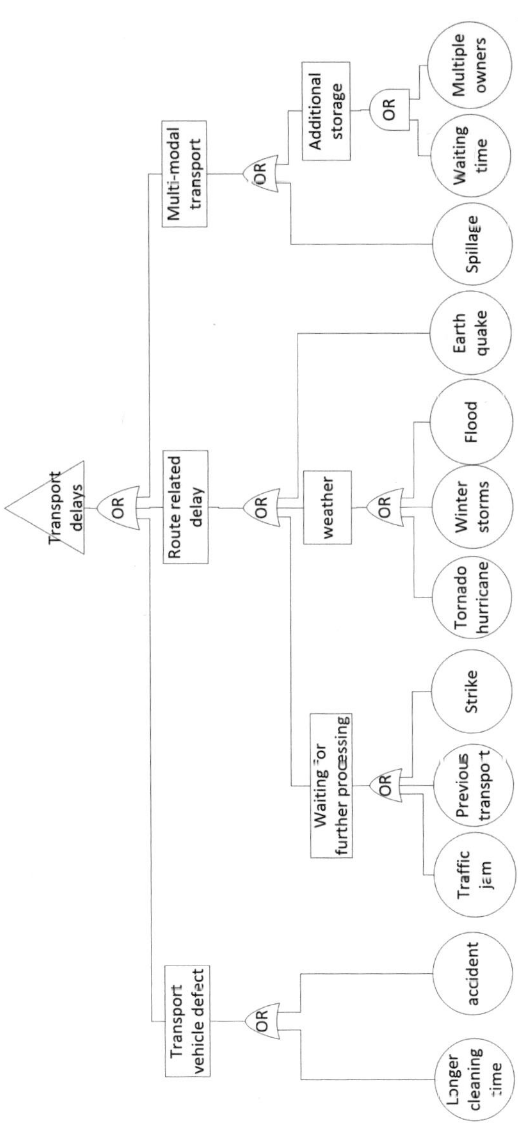

Figure A.2: Fault Tree of process variations

Bibliography

[1] BASF SE (Hrsg.): *Renewable all-rounder.* http://www.intermediates.basf.com/chemicals/topstory/basfia-succiniciproducens

[2] STICHLER, C. (Hrsg.) ; MCFARLAND, M. L. (Hrsg.) ; COFFMAN, G. G. (Hrsg.): *Irrigated and Dryland Grain Sorghum Production South and Southwest Texas.* 1997

[3] BONOMI, A. H. (Hrsg.) ; CAVALETT, O. H. (Hrsg.) ; CUNHA, M. P. d. H. (Hrsg.) ; LIMA, M. A. P. H. (Hrsg.): *Virtual Biorefinery : An Optimization Strategy for Renewable Carbon Valorization.* http://swbplus.bsz-bw.de/bsz455219125cov.htmhttp://dx.doi.org/10.1007/978-3-319-26045-7. Version: 1st ed. 2016, 2016 (Green Energy and TechnologySpringerLink : Bücher)

[4] ABRAMS, J. ; BECKER, D. ; KUDRNA, J. ; MOSELEY, C. : Does policy matter? The role of policy systems in forest bioenergy development in the United States. In: *Forest Policy and Economics* 75 (2017), 41-48. http://dx.doi.org/10.1016/j.forpol.2016.12.007. – DOI 10.1016/j.forpol.2016.12.007. – cited By 0

[5] ADAMS, J. ; ROSS, A. ; ANASTASAKIS, K. ; HODGSON, E. ; GALLAGHER, J. ; JONES, J. ; DONNISON, I. : Seasonal variation in the chemical composition of the bioenergy feedstock Laminaria digitata for thermochemical conversion. In: *Bioresource technology* 102 (2011), Nr. 1, S. 226–234

[6] ADEN, A. ; RUTH, M. ; IBSEN, K. ; JECHURA, J. ; NEEVES, K. ; SHEEHAN, J. ; WALLACE, B. ; MONTAGUE, L. ; SLAYTON, A. ; LUKAS, J. : Lignocellulosic Biomass to Ethanol Process Design and Economics Utilizing Co-Current Dilute Acid Prehydrolysis and Enzymatic Hydrolysis for Corn Stover / National Renewable Energy Laboratory. 2002. – Forschungsbericht

[7] AESCHELMANN, F. ; CARUS, M. u. a. ; INSTITUTE nova (Hrsg.): *Bio-based Building Blocks and Polymers in the World*. 2015

[8] AGRICULTURAL MARKETING SERVICE: *Transportation of U.S. Grains: A Modal Share Analysis*. `http://www.ams.usda.gov/services/transportation-analysis/data`. Version: 2016

[9] AGRICULTURAL STATISTICS BOARD ; UNITED STATES DEPARTMENT OF AGRICULTURE (USDA) (Hrsg.): *Crops Areas Planted*. `http://www.ers.usda.gov/data-products/adoption-of-genetically-engineered-crops-in-the-us.aspx`

[10] AGRICULTURAL STATISTICS BOARD ; UNITED STATES DEPARTMENT OF AGRICULTURE (USDA) (Hrsg.): *Crops Area Planted 20112012*. `http://usda.mannlib.cornell.edu/usda/nass/Acre/2010s/2012/Acre-06-29-2012.pdf`. Version: June 2012

[11] AGRICULTURAL STATISTICS BOARD ; UNITED STATES DEPARTMENT OF AGRICULTURE (USDA) (Hrsg.): *Crops Area Planted 20122013*. `http://usda.mannlib.cornell.edu/usda/nass/Acre/2010s/2013/Acre-06-28-2013.pdf`. Version: June 2013

[12] AGRICULTURAL STATISTICS BOARD ; UNITED STATES DEPARTMENT OF AGRICULTURE (USDA) (Hrsg.): *Crops Area Planted 20132014*. `http://usda.mannlib.cornell.edu/usda/nass/Acre/2010s/2014/Acre-06-30-2014.pdf`. Version: June 2014

[13] AGRICULTURAL STATISTICS BOARD ; UNITED STATES DEPARTMENT OF AGRICULTURE (USDA) (Hrsg.): *Crops Area Planted*

20142015. http://usda.mannlib.cornell.edu/usda/nass/Acre/2010s/2015/Acre-06-30-2015.pdf. Version: June 2015

[14] AGRICULTURE, U. S. D.: Corn for Grain 2012, Production by County and Location of Ethanol Plants as of 2013 / United States Department of Labor. Version: 2017. https://www.osha.gov/dts/osta/otm/otm_iv/otm_iv_5.html. – Forschungsbericht

[15] AGRINEWS, T. : *Rail congestion costs farmers.* http://www.mgfa.org/content/Rail%20congestion%20costs%20farmers%2010.10.14.pdf. Version: 2010

[16] ALMODARES, A. ; HADI, M. R.: Production of bioethanol from sweet sorghum: A review. In: *African Journal of Agricultural Research* 4 (2009), Nr. 9, S. 772 – 780

[17] ALTERNATIVE FUELS DATA CENTER ; U.S. DEPARTMENT OF ENERGY (Hrsg.): *Federal Laws and Incentives for Biodiesel.* https://www.afdc.energy.gov/fuels/laws/BIOD/US. Version: 2017

[18] AMANN, M. ; BEHRENS, S. ; BETZ, S. ; BODE, C. ; BUSCHER, U. ; CORSTEN, H. ; DIRUF, G. ; ESSIG, M. ; GÖSSINGER, R. ; GÖTZE, U. ; JANKER, C. G. ; JONEN, A. ; KAJÜTER, P. ; KALUZA, B. ; KÄSCHEL, J. ; KLEMPT, P. ; KOCH, D. J. ; KRYSTEK, U. ; KUMMER, S. ; LACKES, R. ; LASCH, R. ; LINGNAU, V. ; MIEKE, C. ; MIKUS, B. ; MIRSCHEL, S. ; POLLMEIER, I. ; REESE, J. ; ROLLBERG, R. ; SIEPERMANN, M. ; SPECHT, D. ; STEVEN, M. ; SUDY, I. ; WAAGE, M. ; WAGNER, S. M. ; WEISSENBERGER-EIBL, M. ; WELS, A. ; WERNERS, B. ; WINKLER, H. ; WINTER, D. H. ; ZSCHORN, L. ; VAHRENKAMP, R. (Hrsg.) ; SIEPERMANN, C. (Hrsg.): *Risikomanagement in Supply Chains.* Erich Schmidt Verlag, 2007

[19] AMOSSON, S. ; GIRASE, J. ; BEAN, B. ; ROONEY, W. ; BECKER, J. : Economic analysis of sweet sorghum for biofuels production in the

Texas high plains. In: *Texas A&M Agrilife Extention, Amarillo, TX* (2013)

[20] AN, H. ; WILHELM, W. E. ; SEARCY, S. W.: A mathematical model to desgn a lignocellulosic biofuel supply chain system with a case study based on a region in Central Texas. In: *Bioresource Technology* 102 (2011), S. 7860 – 7870

[21] ARGO, A. M. ; TAN, E. C. ; INMAN, D. ; LANGHOLTZ, M. H. ; EATON, L. M. ; JACOBSON, J. J. ; WRIGHT, C. T. ; MUTH, D. J. ; WU, M. M. ; CHIU, Y.-W. u. a.: Investigation of biochemical biorefinery sizing and environmental sustainability impacts for conventional bale system and advanced uniform biomass logistics designs. In: *Biofuels, Bioproducts and Biorefining* 7 (2013), Nr. 3, S. 282–302

[22] ARNESEN, E. : *Encyclopedia of US labor and working-class history*. Bd. 1. Taylor & Francis, 2007

[23] ARRUDA, P. : Genetically modified sugarcane for bioenergy generation. In: *Current Opinion in Biotechnology* 23 (2012), Nr. 3, 315 - 322. `http://dx.doi.org/https://doi.org/10.1016/j.copbio.2011.10.012`. – DOI https://doi.org/10.1016/j.copbio.2011.10.012. – ISSN 0958–1669. – Energy biotechnology, Environmental biotechnology

[24] ASPEN TECH (Hrsg.): *Physical Property Methods and Models: Reference Manual*. Aspen Tech, 1998

[25] ATCHISON, J. E. ; HETTENHAUS, J. R.: Innovative methods for corn stover collecting, handling, storing and transporting / National Renewable Energy Lab., Golden, CO (US). 2003. – Forschungsbericht

[26] AVEN, T.-. : *Risk analysis*. Second edition. Wiley (MyiLibrary). `http://lib.myilibrary.com?id=825467`. – ISBN 978–1–119–05780–2

[27] AWUDU, I. ; ZHANG, J. : Stochastic production planning for a biofuel supply chain under demand and price uncertainties. In: *Applied Energy* 103 (2013), S. 189 – 196

[28] AYYUB, B. M.: *Risk analysis in engineering and economics*. Bd. 579. Chapman & Hall/CRC Boca Raton, FL, 2003

[29] AZADEH, A. ; ARANI, H. V. ; DASHTI, H. : A stochastic programming approach towards optimization of biofuel supply chain. In: *Energy* 76 (2014), S. 513 – 525

[30] AZADI, P. ; INDERWILDI, O. R. ; FARNOOD, R. ; KING, D. A.: Liquid fuels, hydrogen and chemicals from lignin: A critical review. In: *Renewable and Sustainable Energy Reviews* 21 (2013), 506 - 523. `http://dx.doi.org/https://doi.org/10.1016/j.rser.2012.12.022`. – DOI https://doi.org/10.1016/j.rser.2012.12.022. – ISSN 1364–0321

[31] BAI, Y. ; HWANG, T. ; KANG, S. ; OUYANG, Y. : Biofuel refinery location and supply chain planning under traffic congestion. In: *Transportation Research* 4 (2011), S. 162 – 175

[32] BAI, Y. ; LI, X. ; PENG, F. ; WANG, X. ; OUYANG, Y. : Effects of Disruption Risks on Biorefinery Location Design. In: *Energies* 8 (2015), S. 1468 – 1486

[33] BAIKOW, V. E.: *Manufacture and refining of raw cane sugar*. Bd. 2. Elsevier, 1982

[34] BAIRAMZADEH, S. ; SAIDI-MEHRABAD, M. ; PISHVAEE, M. : Modelling different types of uncertainty in biofuel supply network design and planning: A robust optimization approach. In: *Renewable Energy* 116 (2018), 500-517. `http://dx.doi.org/10.1016/j.renene.2017.09.020`. – DOI 10.1016/j.renene.2017.09.020. – cited By 0

[35] BAJPAI, P. : *Pretreatment of Lignocellulosic Biomass for Biofuel Production.* 2016

[36] BALAMAN, Ş. Y. ; SELIM, H. : Multiobjective optimization of biomass to energy supply chains in an uncertain environment. 33 (2014), S. 1267–1272

[37] BALAMAN, Ş. Y. ; SELIM, H. : A network design model for biomass to energy supply chains with anaerobic digestion systems. In: *Applied Energy* 130 (2014), S. 289–304

[38] BALAMAN, Ş. Y. ; SELIM, H. : A decision model for cost effective design of biomass based green energy supply chains. In: *Bioresource technology* 191 (2015), S. 97–109

[39] BALAMAN, S. ; MATOPOULOS, A. ; WRIGHT, D. ; SCOTT, J. : Integrated optimization of sustainable supply chains and transportation networks for multi technology bio-based production: A decision support system based on fuzzy epsilon-constraint method. In: *Journal of Cleaner Production* (2017). `http://dx.doi.org/10.1016/j.jclepro.2017.11.150`. – DOI 10.1016/j.jclepro.2017.11.150. – cited By 0; Article in Press

[40] BALDUCCI, P. J. ; ROOP, J. M. ; SCHIENBEIN, L. A. ; DESTEESE, J. G. ; WEIMAR, M. R.: Electric Power Interruption Cost Estimates for Individual Industries, Sectors, and US Economy / Pacific Northwest National Laboratory (PNNL), Richland, WA (US). 2002. – Forschungsbericht

[41] BARAL, N. R. ; SLUTZKY, L. ; SHAH, A. ; EZEJI, T. C. ; CORNISH, K. ; CHRISTY, A. : Acetone-butanol-ethanol fermentation of corn stover: current production methods, economic viability and commercial use. In: *FEMS Microbiology Letters* 363 (2016), Nr. 6, fnw033. `http://dx.doi.org/10.1093/femsle/fnw033`. – DOI 10.1093/femsle/fnw033

[42] BEERBÜHL, S. S.: *Herstellung von Ammoniak unter Berücksichtigung fluktuierender Elektrizitätspreise*, Diss., 2014

[43] BEN-TAL, A. ; NEMIROVSKI, A. : Robust optimization – methodology and applications. In: *Mathematical Programming* 92 (2002), Nr. 3, 453–480. http://dx.doi.org/10.1007/s101070100286. – DOI 10.1007/s101070100286. – ISSN 1436–4646

[44] BENNETT, A. S. ; ANEX, R. P.: Farm-gate production costs of sweet sorghum as a bioethanol feedstock. In: *Transactions of the ASABE* 51 (2008), Nr. 2, S. 603–613

[45] BERGIN, N. ; STAR, L. J. (Hrsg.): *US growers move towards sorghum due to its non-GMO appeal.* http://www.gmwatch.org/en/news/archive/2014/15823-us-growers-move-towards-sorghum-due-to-its-non-gmo-appeal. Version: 2014

[46] BERGMAN, P. C. ; KIEL, J. H.: Torrefaction for biomass upgrading. In: *Proc. 14th European Biomass Conference, Paris, France* Bd. 2005, 2005, S. 17–21

[47] BIOAMBER INC. ; BIOAMBER INC. (Hrsg.): *BioAmber announces opening of world's largest succinic acid plant in Sarnia.* http://investor.bio-amber.com/2015-08-06-BioAmber-announces-opening-of-worlds-largest-succinic-acid-plant-in-Sarnia

[48] BIOAMBER INC. ; BIOAMBER INC. (Hrsg.): *BioAmber Signs Its First Succinic Acid Take-or-Pay Contract.* http://investor.bio-amber.com/2014-05-01-BioAmber-Signs-Its-First-Succinic-Acid-Take-or-Pay-Contract

[49] BLANCHARD, P. H.: *Technology of corn wet milling and associated processes.* Amsterdam [u.a.] : Elsevier, 1992 (Industrial chemistry library ; 4). – ISBN 0–444–88255–3

[50] BLANNING, R. W.: The functions of a decision support system. In: *Information & management* 2 (1979), Nr. 3, S. 87–93

[51] BLOOM, J. ; WIRE, B. (Hrsg.): *FSI Announces Opening of Aspartic Acid Facility in Taber, Alberta*. http://www.businesswire.com/news/home/20090922005218/en/FSI-Announces-Opening-Aspartic-Acid-Facility-Taber

[52] BOATENG, A. ; WEIMER, P. ; JUNG, H. ; LAMB, J. : Response of thermochemical and biochemical conversion processes to lignin concentration in alfalfa stems. In: *Energy & fuels* 22 (2008), Nr. 4, S. 2810–2815

[53] BOGNER, A. ; LITTIG, B. ; MENZ, W. : *Interviews mit Experten: eine praxisorientierte Einführung*. Springer-Verlag, 2014

[54] BOHLE, H.-G. : Vulnerability article 1: vulnerability and criticality. In: *IHDP Newsletter Update* (2001)

[55] BORGES, E. R. ; PEREIRA, N. : Succinic acid production from sugarcane bagasse hemicellulose hydrolysate by Actinobacillus succinogenes. In: *Journal of Industrial Microbiology & Biotechnology* 38 (2011), Aug, Nr. 8, 1001–1011. http://dx.doi.org/10.1007/s10295-010-0874-7. – DOI 10.1007/s10295–010–0874–7. – ISSN 1476–5535

[56] BORGHESI, A. ; GAUDENZI, B. : *Risk Management*. 2013

[57] BOZELL, J. J. ; PETERSEN, G. R.: Technology development for the production of biobased products from biorefinery carbohydrates-the US Department of Energys Top 10 revisited. In: *Green Chemistry* 12 (2010), 539-554. http://dx.doi.org/10.1039/B922014C. – DOI 10.1039/B922014C

[58] BOZKURT, H. ; GÖĞÜŞ, F. ; EREN, S. : Nonenzymic browning reactions in boiled grape juice and its models during storage. In: *Food Chemistry* 64 (1999), Nr. 1, S. 89–93

[59] BRECHBILL, S. C. ; TYNER, W. E. ; ILELEJI, K. E.: The economics of biomass collection and transportation and its supply to Indiana cellulosic and electric utility facilities. In: *BioEnergy Research* 4 (2011), Nr. 2, S. 141–152

[60] BRETHAUER, S. ; STUDER, M. H.: Biochemical conversion processes of lignocellulosic biomass to fuels and chemicals–A review. In: *CHIMIA International Journal for Chemistry* 69 (2015), Nr. 10, S. 572–581

[61] BRIDGWATER, A. : Renewable fuels and chemicals by thermal processing of biomass. 91 (2003), S. 87 – 102

[62] BROWN, B. ; ICIS (Hrsg.): *US HCl market range grows on short supply and high prices*. https://www.icis.com/resources/news/2014/11/03/9834809/us-hcl-market-range-grows-on-short-supply-and-high-prices/. Version: 2014

[63] BUNGE, J. : *U.S. Farmers Are Up to Their Ears in Corn*. online. http://www.mvttc.com/news_details.php?id=183. Version: August 2014

[64] BURSTEIN, F. a. ; HOLSAPPLE, C. W. (Hrsg.): *Handbook on Decision Support Systems 1 : Basic Themes*. Springer Berlin Heidelberg (International Handbooks Information SystemSpringerLink : Buecher). http://dx.doi.org/10.1007/978-3-540-48713-5. – ISBN 978-3-540-48713-5

[65] In: CACHON, G. P. ; NETESSINE, S. : *Game Theory in Supply Chain Analysis*. Springer US. – ISBN 978-1-4020-7953-5, 13–65

[66] CAI, D. ; WANG, Y. ; CHEN, C. ; QIN, P. ; MIAO, Q. ; ZHANG, C. ; LI, P. ; TAN, T. : Acetone-butanol-ethanol from sweet sorghum juice by an immobilized fermentation-gas stripping integration process. In: *Bioresource*

Technology 211 (2016), 704 - 710. http://dx.doi.org/https://doi.org/10.1016/j.biortech.2016.03.155. – DOI https://doi.org/10.1016/j.biortech.2016.03.155. – ISSN 0960–8524

[67] CAI, D. ; ZHANG, T. ; ZHENG, J. ; CHANG, Z. ; WANG, Z. ; QIN, P. yong ; TAN, T. wei: Biobutanol from sweet sorghum bagasse hydrolysate by a hybrid pervaporation process. In: *Bioresource Technology* 145 (2013), 97 - 102. http://dx.doi.org/https://doi.org/10.1016/j.biortech.2013.02.094. – DOI https://doi.org/10.1016/j.biortech.2013.02.094. – ISSN 0960–8524. – Special Issue: {IBS} 2012 & Special Issue: {IFIBiop}

[68] CAPINERA, J. L.: *Encyclopedia of entomology*. Springer Science & Business Media, 2008

[69] CARPENTER, D. ; WESTOVER, T. L. ; CZERNIK, S. ; JABLONSKI, W. : Biomass feedstocks for renewable fuel production: a review of the impacts of feedstock and pretreatment on the yield and product distribution of fast pyrolysis bio-oils and vapors. In: *Green Chem.* 16 (2014), 384-406. http://dx.doi.org/10.1039/C3GC41631C. – DOI 10.1039/C3GC41631C

[70] CARTWRIGHT, R. D. ; COBLENTZ, W. K. ; ESPINOZA, L. ; GARDISSER, D. ; GREENE., J. : Grain Sorghum Production Handbook / Cooperative Extention Service University of Arkansas. 2004. – Forschungsbericht

[71] CARUS, M. ; EDER, A. ; BECKMANN, J. : GreenPremium prices along the value chain of biobased products. In: *Industrial Biotechnology* 10 (2014), Nr. 2, S. 83–88

[72] CASTILLO-VILLAR, K. ; EKSIOGLU, S. ; TAHERKHORSANDI, M. : Integrating biomass quality variability in stochastic supply chain modeling and optimization for large-scale biofuel production. In: *Journal of Cleaner Production* 149 (2017), 904-918. ht

tp://dx.doi.org/10.1016/j.jclepro.2017.02.123. – DOI 10.1016/j.jclepro.2017.02.123. – ISSN 09596526. – cited By 0

[73] CENTRAL PACIFIC HURRICANE CENTER ; NATIONAL OCEANIC AND ATMOSPHERIC ADMINISTRATION (Hrsg.): *Hurricanes and Tornadoes*. http://www.prh.noaa.gov/cphc/pages/FAQ/Hurricanes_vs_tornadoes.php. Version: 2018

[74] CHARLES R KENNEDY, J. : Political risk management: A portfolio planning model. In: *Business Horizons* 31 (1988), Nr. 6, 26 - 33. http://dx.doi.org/http://dx.doi.org/10.1016/0007-6813(88)90020-1. – DOI http://dx.doi.org/10.1016/0007–6813(88)90020–1. – ISSN 0007–6813

[75] CHAUVEL, A. : *Manual of economic analysis of chemical processes: feasibility studies in refinery and petrochemical processes*. McGraw-Hill Companies, 1981

[76] CHEN, C.-W. ; FAN, Y. : Bioethanol supply chain system planning under supply and demand uncertainties. In: *Transportation Research* Part E 48 (2012), S. 150 – 164

[77] CHEN, M. ; SMITH, P. M.: The U.S. cellulosic biofuels industry: Expert views on commercialization drivers and barriers. In: *Biomass and Bioenergy* 102 (2017), 52 - 61. http://dx.doi.org/https://doi.org/10.1016/j.biombioe.2017.05.002. – DOI https://doi.org/10.1016/j.biombioe.2017.05.002. – ISSN 0961–9534

[78] CHENG, K.-K. ; ZHAO, X.-B. ; ZENG, J. ; WU, R.-C. ; XU, Y.-Z. ; LIU, D.-H. ; ZHANG, J.-A. : Downstream processing of biotechnological produced succinic acid. In: *Applied Microbiology and Biotechnology* 95 (2012), Aug, Nr. 4, 841–850. http://dx.doi.org/10.1007/s00253-012-4214-x. – DOI 10.1007/s00253–012–4214–x. – ISSN 1432–0614

[79] CHIEF ECONOMIST, O. of t. ; AGRICULTURAL MARKETING SERVICE the: Rail Service Challenges in the Upper Midwest: Implications for Agricultural Sectors, Preliminary Analysis of the 20132014 Situation / United States Department of Agriculture. 2015. – Forschungsbericht

[80] CLARK, E. : Valuing political risk. In: *Journal of International Money and Finance* 16 (1997), Nr. 3, 477 - 490. http://dx.doi.org/http://dx.doi.org/10.1016/S0261-5606(97)00008-9. – DOI http://dx.doi.org/10.1016/S0261–5606(97)00008–9. – ISSN 0261–5606

[81] COCHRANE, H. : Economic loss: myth and measurement. In: *Disaster Prevention and Management: An International Journal* 13 (2004), Nr. 4, S. 290–296

[82] COMES, M. : *Decision Maps for Distributed Scenario-Based Multi-Criteria Decision Support*, Diss., 2011

[83] http://agritech.tnau.ac.in/org_farm/orgfarm_sugar.html

[84] COPELAND, B. ; BRITANNICA, E. (Hrsg.): *Artificial intelligence*. https://www.britannica.com/technology/artificial-intelligence. Version: 2018

[85] CRICHTON, D. : The risk triangle. In: *Natural disaster management* (1999), S. 102–103

[86] CROP SCIENCE UNITED STATES ; BAYER GLOBAL (Hrsg.): *Recognizing Corn Rootworm Risks*. https://www.cropscience.bayer.us/learning-center/articles/recognizing-corn-rootworm-risks. Version: 2017

[87] DAHMEN, N. ; ABELN, J. ; EBERHARD, M. ; KOLB, T. ; LEIBOLD, H. ; SAUER, J. ; STAPF, D. ; ZIMMERLIN, B. : The bioliq process for

producing synthetic transportation fuels. In: *Wiley Interdisciplinary Reviews: Energy and Environment* 6 (2017), Nr. 3

[88] DAL-MAS, M. ; GIAROLA, S. ; ZAMBONI, A. ; BEZZO, F. : Strategic design and investment capacity planning of the ethanol supply chain under price uncertainty. In: *Biomass and Bioenergy* 35 (2011), S. 2059 – 2071

[89] DANI, S. : Predicting and managing supply chain risks. In: *Supply Chain Risk*. Springer, 2009, S. 53–66

[90] DARR, M. ; WEBSTER, K. ; BRITTANY ; SCHAU, D. ; EXTENSION, I. S. U. (Hrsg.) ; OUTREACH (Hrsg.): *Nutrient removal when harvesting corn stover*. https://crops.extension.iastate.edu/nutrient-removal-when-harvesting-corn-stover-0. Version: 2014

[91] DE LEÓN, V. ; CARLOS, J. : *Vulnerability: a conceptional and methodological review*. UNU-EHS, 2006

[92] DELGADO, M. ; VERDEGAY, J. L. ; VILA, M. : A general model for fuzzy linear programming. In: *Fuzzy Sets and systems* 29 (1989), Nr. 1, S. 21–29

[93] DENICOFF, M. R. ; PRATER, M. E. ; BAHIZI, P. ; AGRICULTURE, U. S. D. (Hrsg.): *Corn Transportation Profile*. 2014

[94] DIAS, M. O. ; JUNQUEIRA, T. L. ; CAVALETT, O. ; CUNHA, M. P. ; JESUS, C. D. ; ROSSELL, C. E. ; MACIEL FILHO, R. ; BONOMI, A. : Integrated versus stand-alone second generation ethanol production from sugarcane bagasse and trash. In: *Bioresource technology* 103 (2012), Nr. 1, S. 152–161

[95] In: DIECKMANN, C. ; EDELMANN, W. ; KALTSCHMITT, M. ; LIEBETRAU, J. ; OLDENBURG, S. ; RITZKOWSKI, M. ; SCHOLWIN, F. ; STRÄUBER, H. ; WEINRICH, S. : *Biogaserzeugung und -nutzung*. 3. Springer Berlin Heidelberg, 2016, S. 1609–1755

[96] In: DIECKMANN, C. ; HARTMANN, H. ; KALTSCHMITT, M. ; RESSEL, J. B.: *Transport, Trocknung, Konservierung und Lagerung*. 3. Springer Berlin Heidelberg, 2016, S. 493–578

[97] DOE, U. ; ENERGY, U. D. (Hrsg.): *Bioenergy technologies office: Multi-year program plan*. 2015

[98] DUERRE, P. : New insights and novel developments in clostridial acetone/butanol/isopropanol fermentation. In: *Applied Microbiology and Biotechnology* 49 (1998), S. 639 – 648

[99] DUPONT TATE & LYLE BIO PRODUCTS COMPANY, L. ; DUPONT TATE & LYLE BIO PRODUCTS COMPANY, L. (Hrsg.): *Zemea Propanediol - A New Bio-Derived Glycol for Household Cleaning and Liquid Detergent Applications*. http://www2.dupont.com/Bio-based_Propanediol/zh_TW/assets/downloads/HI&I%20PRESENTATION%20-06-02-2011.pdf. Version: unknown

[100] EAVES, J. ; EAVES, S. : Renewable corn-ethanol and energy security. In: *Energy Policy* 35 (2007), Nr. 11, S. 5958–5963

[101] EBADIAN, M. ; SOWLATI, T. ; SOKHANSANJ, S. ; SMITH, L. T. ; STUMBORG, M. : Development of an integrated tactical and operational planning model for supply of feedstock to a commercial-scale bioethanol plant. In: *Biofuels, Bioproducts and Biorefining* 8 (2014), Nr. 2, S. 171–188

[102] EBADIAN, M. ; SOWLATI, T. ; SOKHANSANJ, S. ; STUMBORG, M. ; TOWNLEY-SMITH, L. : A new simulation model for multi-agricultural biomass logistics system in bioenergy production. In: *Biosystems Engineering* 110 (2011), S. 280 – 290

[103] ECONOMIC RESEARCH SERVICE ; UNITED STATES DEPARTMENT OF AGRICULTURE (Hrsg.): *U.S. Bioenergy Statistics: Fuel ethanol, corn and gasoline prices, marketing*

year. https://www.ers.usda.gov/data-products/us-bioenergy-statistics/. Version: 2017

[104] EGGLESTON, G. ; COLE, M. ; ANDRZEJEWSKI, B. : New commercially viable processing technologies for the production of sugar feedstocks from sweet sorghum (Sorghum bicolor L. Moench) for manufacture of biofuels and bioproducts. In: *Sugar tech* 15 (2013), Nr. 3, S. 232–249

[105] EKSIOGLU, S. D. ; ACHARYA, A. ; LEIGHTLEY, L. E. ; ARORA, S. : Analyzing the design and management of biomass-to-biorefinery supply chain. In: *Computers & Industrial Engineering* 57 (2009), S. 1343 – 1352

[106] EMERSON, R. ; HOOVER, A. ; RAY, A. ; LACEY, J. ; CORTEZ, M. ; PAYNE, C. ; KARLEN, D. ; BIRRELL, S. ; LAIRD, D. ; KALLENBACH, R. u. a.: Drought effects on composition and yield for corn stover, mixed grasses, and Miscanthus as bioenergy feedstocks. In: *Biofuels* 5 (2014), Nr. 3, S. 275–291

[107] ERTL, D. : *Sustainable corn stover harvest.* 2013

[108] EZEJI, T. C. ; QURESHI, N. ; BLASCHEK, H. P.: Production of acetone butanol (AB) from liquefied corn starch, a commercial substrate, using Clostridium beijerinckii coupled with product recovery by gas stripping. In: *Journal of Industrial Microbiology & Biotechnology* 34 (2007), Nr. 12, 771–777. http://dx.doi.org/10.1007/s10295-007-0253-1. – DOI 10.1007/s10295–007–0253–1. – ISSN 1476–5535

[109] FACTIVA ; WEST HAWAII TODAY (Hrsg.): *War on cornfield pest sparks clash over insecticide.* 2014

[110] FALCONE, M. A. ; LOPES, H. S. ; SANTOS COELHO, L. dos: Supply chain optimisation using evolutionary algorithms. In: *International*

Journal of Computer Applications in Technology 31 (2008), Nr. 3-4, S. 158–167

[111] FANG, Z. ; QI, X. : *Production of Platform Chemicals from Sustainable Resources*. Springer, 2017

[112] FEDERAL HIGHWAY ADMINISTRATION ; U.S. DEPARTMENT OF TRANSPORTATION (Hrsg.): *Describing the Congestion Problem*. https://www.fhwa.dot.gov/congestion/describing_problem.htm. Version: 2017

[113] FEDERAL HIGHWAY ADMINISTRATION ; U.S. DEPARTMENT OF TRANSPORTATION (Hrsg.): *Freight and Congestion*. https://www.fhwa.dot.gov/congestion/describing_problem.htm. Version: 2017

[114] FEDERAL MOTOR CARRIER SAFETY ADMINISTRATION ; U.S: DEPARTMENT OF TRANSPORTATION (Hrsg.): *Large Truck and Bus Crash Facts*. https://www.fmcsa.dot.gov/safety/data-and-statistics/large-truck-and-bus-crash-facts. Version: 2017

[115] FEDERAL RAILROAD ADMINISTRATION ; U.S. DEPARMENT. OF TRANSPORTATION (Hrsg.): *Freight Rail Today*. https://www.fra.dot.gov. Version: 2017

[116] FIELD, C. B. ; BARROS, V. R. ; MASTRANDREA, M. ; MACH, K. J. ; ABDRABO, M.-K. ; ADGER, N. ; ANOKHIN, Y. ; ANISIMOV, O. ; ARENT, D. ; BARNETT, J. u. a.: Summary for policymakers. In: *Climate change 2014: impacts, adaptation, and vulnerability. Part a: global and sectoral aspects. Contribution of working group II to the fifth assessment report of the intergovernmental panel on climate change* 1 (2014), S. 1–32

[117] FIORENTINO, G. ; RIPA, M. ; ULGIATI, S. b.: Chemicals from biomass: technological versus environmental feasibility. A

review. In: *Biofuels, Bioproducts and Biorefining* 11 (2017), Nr. 1, 195-214. `http://dx.doi.org/10.1002/bbb.1729`. – DOI 10.1002/bbb.1729. – cited By 0

[118] FIXEN, P. E. u. a.: Potential biofuels influence on nutrient use and removal in the US. In: *Better Crops* 91 (2007), Nr. 2, S. 12–14

[119] FOREIGN AGRICULTURAL SERVICE ; UNITED STATES DEPARTMENT OF AGRICULTURE (Hrsg.): *Sugar: World Markets and Trade*. 2016

[120] FORMENTI, L. R. ; NØRREGAARD, A. ; BOLIC, A. ; HERNANDEZ, D. Q. ; HAGEMANN, T. ; HEINS, A.-L. ; LARSSON, H. ; MEARS, L. ; MAURICIO-IGLESIAS, M. ; KRÜHNE, U. u. a.: Challenges in industrial fermentation technology research. In: *Biotechnology journal* 9 (2014), Nr. 6, S. 727–738

[121] FORRESTER, J. W.: System dynamics, systems thinking, and soft OR. In: *System dynamics review* 10 (1994), Nr. 2-3, S. 245–256

[122] FOULDS, L. ; WILSON, J. : Scheduling operations for the harvesting of renewable resources. In: *Journal of food engineering* 70 (2005), Nr. 3, S. 281–292

[123] In: FRIEDL, A. ; MILTNER, A. ; NEULING, U. ; KALTSCHMITT, M. : *Fermentative Alkoholerzeugung und -nutzung*. 3. Springer Berlin Heidelberg, 2016, S. 1501–1607

[124] FRÖHLING, M. : *Zur taktisch-operativen Planung stoffstrombasierter Produktionssysteme: Dargestellt an Beispielen aus der stoffumwandelnden Industrie*, Diss., 2005

[125] FROMBO, F. ; MINCIARDI, R. ; ROBBA, M. ; SACILE, R. : A decision support system for planning biomass based energy production. In: *Energy* 34 (2009), Nr. 3, S. 362–369

[126] FUNKE, A. ; NIEBEL, A. ; RICHTER, D. ; ABBAS, M. ; MÜLLER, A.-K. ; RADLOFF, S. ; PANERU, M. ; MAIER, J. ; DAHMEN, N. ; SAUER, J. : Fast pyrolysis char - Assessment of alternative uses within the bioliq concept. In: *Bioresource Technology* 200 (2016), 905 - 913. http://dx.doi.org/https://doi.org/10.1016/j.biortech.2015.11.012. – DOI https://doi.org/10.1016/j.biortech.2015.11.012. – ISSN 0960–8524

[127] GACHET, A. : A New Component in the Classification of DSS Development Tools. In: *Journal of Decision Systems* 12 (2003), Nr. 3-4, S. 271–281

[128] GALLAGHER, P. ; DIKEMAN, M. ; FRITZ, J. ; WAILES, E. ; GAUTHER, W. ; SHAPOURI, H. u. a.: Biomass from crop residues: cost and supply estimates. In: *Agricultural Economic Report-Economic Research Service, US Department of Agriculture* (2003), Nr. 819

[129] GALLAGHER, P. W. ; BAUMES, H. : Biomass supply from corn residues: Estimates and critical review of procedures. (2012)

[130] GAO, J. ; YOU, F. : Design a sustainable supply chain under uncertainty using life cycle optimisation and stochastic programming. In: *Chemical Engineering Transactions* 61 (2017), 151-156. http://dx.doi.org/10.3303/CET1761023. – DOI 10.3303/CET1761023. – cited By 0

[131] GARY PERILLOUX ; LOUISIANA ECONOMIC DEVELOPMENT (Hrsg.): *LED, Myriant Corporation Highlight Progress of Bio-Based Chemical Plant In Northeast Louisiana.* http://www.myriant.com/media/press-releases/led-myriant-corporation-highlight-progress-of-bio-based-chemical-plant-in-northeast-louisiana.cfm

[132] GAUTREAUX, C. ; AGCENTER, L. (Hrsg.): *Louisiana: SUgarcane Crop Poised to Beark Record.* http://agfax.com/2017/12/

19/louisiana-sugarcane-crop-poised-to-break-record/. Version: 2017

[133] GEBRESLASSIE, B. H. ; YAO, Y. ; YOU, F. : Design under uncertainty of hydrocarbon biorefinery supply chains: Multiobjective stochastic programming models, decomposition algorithm, and a Comparison between CVaR and downside risk. In: *AIChE Journal* 58 (2012), Nr. 7, 2155–2179. http://dx.doi.org/10.1002/aic.13844. – DOI 10.1002/aic.13844. – ISSN 1547–5905

[134] GESTIS-STOFFDATENBANK: *1-Butanol.* http://gestis.itrust.de/nxt/gateway.dll?f=templates&fn=default.htm&vid=gestisdeu:sdbdeu

[135] GFBIOCHEMICALS LTD. ; GFBIOCHEMICALS LTD. (Hrsg.): *GFBiochemicals - About us.* http://www.gfbiochemicals.com/company/. Version: 2017

[136] GIANNAKIS, M. ; LOUIS, M. : A multi-agent based framework for supply chain risk management. In: *Journal of Purchasing and Supply Management* 17 (2011), Nr. 1, S. 23–31

[137] GIAROLA, S. ; BEZZO, F. ; SHAH, N. : A risk management approach to the economic and environmental strategic design of ethanol supply chains. In: *Biomass and Bioenergy* 58 (2013), S. 31 – 51

[138] In: GOH, M. ; MENG, F. : *A Stochastic Model for Supply Chain Risk Management Using Conditional Value at Risk.* 2009

[139] GONZALES, D. ; SEARCY, E. M. ; EKŞIOĞLU, S. D.: Cost analysis for high-volume and long-haul transportation of densified biomass feedstock. In: *Transportation Research Part A: Policy and Practice* 49 (2013), S. 48–61

[140] GRAHAM, R. L. ; NELSON, R. ; SHEEHAN, J. ; PERLACK, R. ; WRIGHT, L. L.: Current and potential US corn stover supplies. In: *Agronomy Journal* 99 (2007), Nr. 1, S. 1–11

[141] GRAIN, N. ; ASSOCIATION, F. ; N.N. (Hrsg.): *Importance of Waterway Transportation to U.S. Agriculture.* https://www.ngfa.org/wp-content/uploads/2013-NGFA-Waterways-Issue-Paper-_April.pdf. Version: 2013

[142] GREEN, C. ; VEEN, A. Van d.: Indirect economic damage: concepts and guidelines. In: *Evaluating flood damages: guidance and recommendations on principles and methods, FLOODsite, Report, T09-06-01* (2007)

[143] GREEN, E. M.: Fermentative production of butanol - the industrial perspective. In: *Current Opinion in Biotechnology* 22 (2011), Nr. 3, 337 - 343. http://dx.doi.org/https://doi.org/10.1016/j.copbio.2011.02.004. – DOI https://doi.org/10.1016/j.copbio.2011.02.004. – ISSN 0958–1669. – Energy biotechnology - Environmental biotechnology

[144] GUARD, U. C.: *Risk based decision making guidelines.* 2003

[145] GUNUKULA, S. ; KEELING, P. L. ; ANEX, R. : Risk advantages of platform technologies for biorenewable chemical production. In: *Chemical Engineering Research and Design* 107 (2016), S. 24 – 33

[146] HAMELINCK, C. N. ; FAAIJ, A. P. ; UIL, H. den ; BOERRIGTER, H. : Production of FT transportation fuels from biomass; technical options, process analysis and optimisation, and development potential. In: *Energy* 29 (2004), Nr. 11, S. 1743–1771

[147] HANKEY, R. ; CASSAR, C. ; LUI, J. ; WONG, P. ; ADMINISTRATION, U. E. I. (Hrsg.): *Electric Power Monthly with Data for December 2017.* https://www.eia.gov/electricity/monthly/epm_table_grapher.php?t=epmt_5_6_a

[148] HARLING, J. : Simulation techniques in operations research - A review. In: *Operations Research* 6 (1958), Nr. 3, S. 307–319

[149] HARO, P. ; TRIPPE, F. ; STAHL, R. ; HENRICH, E. : Bio-syngas to gasoline and olefins via DME - A comprehensive techno-economic assessment. In: *Applied Energy* 108 (2013), 54 - 65. `http://dx.doi.org/http://dx.doi.org/10.1016/j.apenergy.2013.03.015`. – DOI http://dx.doi.org/10.1016/j.apenergy.2013.03.015. – ISSN 0306–2619

[150] HATTI-KAUL, R. ; TOERNVALL, U. ; GUSTAFSSON, L. ; BOERJESSON, P. : Industrial biotechnology for the production of bio-based chemicals, a cradle-to-grave perspective. In: *Trends in Biotechnology* 25 (2007), Nr. 3, 119 - 124. `http://dx.doi.org/http://dx.doi.org/10.1016/j.tibtech.2007.01.001`. – DOI http://dx.doi.org/10.1016/j.tibtech.2007.01.001. – ISSN 0167–7799

[151] HAYKIRI-ACMA, H. ; YAMAN, S. : Interpretation of biomass gasification yields regarding temperature intervals under nitrogensteam atmosphere. In: *Fuel Processing Technology* 88 (2007), Nr. 4, 417 - 425. `http://dx.doi.org/https://doi.org/10.1016/j.fuproc.2006.11.002`. – DOI https://doi.org/10.1016/j.fuproc.2006.11.002. – ISSN 0378–3820

[152] HENDRICKS, K. B. ; SINGHAL, V. R.: Supply chain disruptions and corporate performance. In: *Supply Chain Disruptions*. Springer, 2012, S. 1–19

[153] HESS, J. R. ; KENNEY, K. L. ; WRIGHT, C. T. ; PERLACK, R. ; TURHOLLOW, A. : Corn stover availability for biomass conversion: situation analysis. In: *Cellulose* 16 (2009), Nr. 4, S. 599–619

[154] In: HOFBAUER, H. ; KALTSCHMITT, M. ; KEIL, F. ; MEIER, D. ; WELLING, J. : *Pyrolyse*. 3. Springer Berlin Heidelberg, 2016, S. 1183–1265

[155] In: HOFBAUER, H. ; KALTSCHMITT, M. ; KEIL, F. ; NEULING, U. ; WAGNER, H. : *Vergasung in der Gasatmosphäre*. 3. Springer Berlin Heidelberg, 2016, S. 1059–1182

[156] In: HOLLAND, F. ; WILKINSON, J. : *Process Economics*. 7. McGraw-Hill Professional, New York, N.Y. USA, 1997

[157] HOLLING, C. S.: Resilience and stability of ecological systems. In: *Annual review of ecology and systematics* 4 (1973), Nr. 1, S. 1–23

[158] HOPP, W. J. ; IRAVANI, S. M. ; LIU, Z. : Mitigating the impact of disruptions in supply chains. In: *Supply Chain Disruptions*. Springer, 2012, S. 21–49

[159] HU, H. ; LIN, T. ; WANG, S. ; RODRIGUEZ, L. : A cyber-GIS approach to uncertainty and sensitivity analysis in biomass supply chain optimization. In: *Applied Energy* 203 (2017), 26-40. `http://dx.doi.org/10.1016/j.apenergy.2017.03.107`. – DOI 10.1016/j.apenergy.2017.03.107. – cited By 4

[160] HUBBARD, D. W. ; HUBBARD, D. W. (Hrsg.): *The Failure of Risk Management: Why It's Broken and How to Fix it*. John Wiley & Sons, Inc., 2009

[161] HULL, P. : *Glucose syrups: technology and applications*. John Wiley & Sons, 2010

[162] HUMBIRD, D. ; DAVIS, R. ; TAO, L. ; KINCHIN, C. ; HSU, D. ; ADEN, A. ; SCHOEN, P. ; LUKAS, J. ; OLTHOF, B. ; WORLEY, M. ; SEXTON, D. ; DUDGEON, D. : Process Design and Economics for Biochemical Conversion of Lignocellulosic Biomass to Ethanol: Dilute-Acid Pretreatment and Enzymatic Hydrolysis of Corn Stover / National Renewable Energy Laboratory. 2011. – Forschungsbericht

[163] INDEPENDENT STATISTICS AND ANALYSIS ; U.S. ENERGY INFORMATION ADMINISTRATION (Hrsg.): *Today in Energy*. `https://www.eia.gov/todayinenergy/prices.php`. Version: 2017

[164] INGLETT, G. : *Cereals for Food and Beverages: Recent Progress in Cereal Chemistry and Technology.* Elsevier, 2012

[165] J.E.SANTIBAEZ-AGUILAR ; MORALES-RODRIGUEZ, R. ; GONZÁLEZ-CAMPOS, J. ; PONCE-ORTEGA, J. : Stochastic design of biorefinery supply chains considering economic and environmental objectives. In: *Journal of Cleaner Production* 136 (2016), 224-245. http://dx.doi.org/10.1016/j.jclepro.2016.03.168. DOI 10.1016/j.jclepro.2016.03.168. – cited By 9

[166] J.E.SANTIBANEZ-AGUILAR ; MORALES-RODRIGUEZ, R. ; GONZÁLEZ-CAMPOS, J. ; PONCE-ORTEGA, J. : Sustainable multi-objective planning of biomass conversion systems under uncertainty. In: *Chemical Engineering Transactions* 45 (2015), 367-372. http://dx.doi.org/10.3303/CET1545062. – DOI 10.3303/CET1545062. – cited By 1

[167] JIANG, M. ; DAI, W. ; XI, Y. ; WU, M. ; KONG, X. ; MA, J. ; ZHANG, M. ; CHEN, K. ; WEI, P. : Succinic acid production from sucrose by Actinobacillus succinogenes NJ113. In: *Bioresource Technology* 153 (2014), 327 - 332. http://dx.doi.org/http://dx.doi.org/10.1016/j.biortech.2013.11.062. – DOI http://dx.doi.org/10.1016/j.biortech.2013.11.062. – ISSN 0960–8524

[168] JIN DONG, J. B. a. a. a. a. ; DONG, J. ; DOODY, P. ; FAISAL, M. N. ; GOH, M. ; HILMOLA, O.-P. ; HUANG, C.-C. ; MENG, F. ; NAGURNEY, A. ; QIANG, Q. ; RITCHIE, B. ; SAGAR, N. ; SESHADRI, S. ; SLONE, R. ; SODHI, M. S. ; TANG, C. S. ; TSENG), T.-L. B. ; WANG, W. ; WU, T. ; WU, T. (Hrsg.) ; BLACKHURST, J. (Hrsg.): *Managing supply chain risk and vulnerability : tools and methods for supply chain decision makers.* 1st ed. Springer London http://swbplus.bsz-bw.de/bsz306714388inh.htm. – ISBN 978–1–84882–633–5

[169] JONG, E. de ; HIGSON, A. ; WALSH, P. ; WELLISCH, M. : Bio-based chemicals value added products from biorefineries. In: *IEA Bioenergy, Task42 Biorefinery* (2012)

[170] JONGLERTJUNYA, W. ; CHINWATPAIBOON, P. ; THAMBARAMEE, H. ; PRAYOONYONG, P. : Butanol, Ethanol and Acetone Production from Sugarcane Bagasses by Acid Hydrolysis and Fermentation Using Clostridium sp. In: *Advanced Materials Research* 931 (2014), 7, S. 1602–1607. `http://dx.doi.org/10.4028/www.scientific.net/AMR.931-932.1602`. – DOI 10.4028/www.scientific.net/AMR.931–932.1602

[171] JÖNSSON, L. J. ; ALRIKSSON, B. ; NILVEBRANT, N.-O. : Bioconversion of lignocellulose: inhibitors and detoxification. In: *Biotechnology for biofuels* 6 (2013), Nr. 1, S. 16

[172] JR., J. B. J.: *Agronomic Handbook*. 2002

[173] In: KAJÜTER, P. : *Risk Management in Supply Chains*. Erich Smidt Verlag, 2003, S. 321 – 336

[174] KALIYAN, N. ; MOREY, R. V. ; TIFFANY, D. G.: Economic and environmental analysis for corn stover and switchgrass supply logistics. In: *BioEnergy Research* 8 (2015), Nr. 3, S. 1433–1448

[175] KALTSCHMITT, M. ; HARTMANN, H. ; HOFBAUER, H. : *Energie aus Biomasse: Grundlagen, Techniken und Verfahren*. 3. Springer Verlag, 2016

[176] KARAKAS, B. ; CERTEL, M. ; MANTHEY, F. A. ; XU, Y. ; YILDIZ, F. ; ARAPOGLOU, D. G. ; LABROPOULOS, A. E. ; VARZAKAS, T. H. ; ARVANITOYANNIS, I. S. ; KIOKIAS, S. ; KURNAZ, I. A. ; CEYLAN, C. ; KARAKOC, A. ; DINELLI, G. ; MAROTTI, I. ; BOSI, S. ; GIOIA, D. D. ; BIAVATI, B. ; CATIZONE, P. ; BOYACIOGLU, D. ; NILUFER, D. ; CAPANOGLU, E. ; VELIOGLU, Y. S. ; GÖGÜS, F. ; FADTLOGLU,

S. ; SOYSAL, C. ; EKMEKCI, A. ; CIAK, M. Y. ; KARAHALIL, B. ; YILDIZ, F. (Hrsg.): *Advances in food biochemistry*. CRC press, 2009

[177] KAZEMZADEH, N. ; HU, G. : Optimization models for biorefinery supply chain network design under uncertainty. In: *Journal of Renewable and Sustainable Energy* 5 (2013), S. 053125–1 – 053125–17

[178] KAZI, F. K. ; FORTMAN, J. ; ANEX, R. ; KOTHANDARAMAN, G. ; HSU, D. ; ADEN, A. ; DUTTA, A. : Techno-Economic Analysis of Biochemical Scenarios for Production of Cellulosic Ethanol / National Renewable Energy Laboratory. 2010. – Forschungsbericht

[179] KENT, G. : The value of bagasse to an Australian raw sugar factory. (2007)

[180] KERDONCUFF, P. : *Modellierung und Bewertung von Proezsssketten zur Herstellung von Biokraftstoffen der zweiten Generation*, Universität (TH), Diss., 2008

[181] KIM, J. ; REALFF, M. J. ; LEE, J. H.: Optimal design and global sensitivity analysis of biomass supply chain networks for biofuels under uncertainty. In: *Computers and Chemical Engineering* 35 (2011), S. 1738 – 1751

[182] KIM, J. ; REALFF, M. J. ; LEE, J. H. ; WHITTAKER, C. ; FURTNER, L. : Design of biomass processing network for biofuel production using an MILP model. In: *Biomass and Bioenergy* 35 (2011), S. 853 – 871

[183] KNIGHT, F. H.: *Risk, uncertainty and profit*. Courier Corporation, 2012

[184] KNORR, B. ; FUTURES, F. (Hrsg.): *Fertilizer Outlook - Ammonia prices surge higher on Plains*. `http://www.farmfutures.com/story-weekly fortilizer-review-0-30765`. Version: 2017

[185] KOBRIN, S. J.: Political Risk: A Review and Reconsideration. In: *Journal of International Business Studies* 10 (1979), Nr. 1, 67–80. `http://dx.doi.org/10.1057/palgrave.jibs.8490631`. – DOI 10.1057/palgrave.jibs.8490631. – ISSN 1478–6990

[186] KOSTIN, A. ; GUILLÃ©N-GOSÃ¡LBEZA, G. ; MELEB, F. ; BAGAJEWICZC, M. ; JIMÃ©NEZ, L. : Design and planning of infrastructures for bioethanol and sugar production under demand uncertainty. In: *Chemical Engineering Research and Design* 90 (2012), S. 359 – 376

[187] In: KRAMER, N. W. ; ROSS, W. M.: *Cultivation of Grain Sorghum in the United States*. 1970

[188] KRUSE, C. J. ; PROTOPAPAS, A. ; OLSON, L. E. ; BIERLING, D. H.: A Modal Comparison of Domestic Freight Transportation Effects on the General Public / Texas Transportation Institute, The Texas A&M University System, College Station, Texas. 2007. – Forschungsbericht

[189] KUMAR, A. ; DEMIREL, Y. ; JONES, D. D. ; HANNA, M. A.: Optimization and economic evaluation of industrial gas production and combined heat and power generation from gasification of corn stover and distillers grains. In: *Bioresource technology* 101 (2010), Nr. 10, S. 3696–3701

[190] KUMAR, A. ; CAMERON, J. B. ; FLYNN, P. C.: Pipeline transport and simultaneous saccharification of corn stover. In: *Bioresource technology* 96 (2005), Nr. 7, S. 819–829

[191] KUMAR, D. ; KALITA, P. : Reducing postharvest losses during storage of grain crops to strengthen food security in developing countries. In: *Foods* 6 (2017), Nr. 1, S. 8

[192] KUMAR, P. ; BARRETT, D. M. ; DELWICHE, M. J. ; STROEVE, P. : Methods for Pretreatment of Lignocellulosic Biomass for Effi-

cient Hydrolysis and Biofuel Production. In: *Industrial Engineering Chemical Resources* 48 (2009), S. 3713 – 3729

[193] In: KUMMER, S. ; SUDY, I. : *Management von Transport- und Lagerrisiken in Supply Chains*. 2006

[194] KURZROCK, T. ; WEUSTER-BOTZ, D. : Recovery of succinic acid from fermentation broth. In: *Biotechnology letters* 32 (2010), Nr. 3, S. 331–339

[195] LAHOOD, R. : National Rail Plan / U.S. Department of Transportation, Federal Railroad Administration. 2010. – Forschungsbericht

[196] LAM, K. F. ; LEUNG, C. C. J. ; LEI, H. M. ; LIN, C. S. K.: Economic feasibility of a pilot-scale fermentative succinic acid production from bakery wastes. In: *Food and Bioproducts Processing* 92 (2014), Nr. 3, 282 - 290. `http://dx.doi.org/http://dx.doi.org/10.1016/j.fbp.2013.09.001`. – DOI http://dx.doi.org/10.1016/j.fbp.2013.09.001. – ISSN 0960–3085

[197] LANGHOLTZ, M. ; WEBB, E. ; PRESTON, B. L. ; TURHOLLOW, A. ; BREUER, N. ; EATON, L. ; KING, A. W. ; SOKHANSANJ, S. ; NAIR, S. S. ; DOWNING, M. : Climate risk management for the U.S. cellulosic biofuels supply chain. In: *Climate Risk Management* 3 (2014), S. 96 – 115

[198] LARSON, L. W.: The Great USA Flood of 1993. In: *Destructive Water: Water-Caused Natural Disasters - Their Abatement and Control*

[199] LAU, P. C.: *Quality Living Through Chemurgy and Green Chemistry*. Springer, 2017

[200] LEE, D. ; OWENS, V. N. ; BOE, A. ; JERANYAMA, P. : Composition of Herbaceous Biomass Feedstocks / Plant Science Department, South Dakota State University. 2007. – Forschungsbericht

[201] LEE, H. : *Development of lactic and succinic acid biorefinery configurations for integration into a thermomechanical pulp mill*, Diss., 2015

[202] LEE, P. ; LEE, S. ; HONG, S. ; CHANG, H. : Isolation and characterization of a new succinic acid-producing bacterium, Mannheimia succiniciproducens MBEL55E, from bovine rumen. In: *Applied Microbiology and Biotechnology* 58 (2002), Apr, Nr. 5, 663–668. http://dx.doi.org/10.1007/s00253-002-0935-6. – DOI 10.1007/s00253–002–0935–6. – ISSN 1432–0614

[203] LESTINSKY, P. ; PALIT, A. : Wood pyrolysis using aspen plus simulation and industrially applicable model. In: *GeoScience Engineering* 62 (2016), Nr. 1, S. 11–16

[204] In: LEWANDOWSKI, I. : *Landwirtschaftlich produzierte Biomasse*. 3. Springer Berlin Heidelberg, 2016, S. 167–247

[205] In: LEWANDOWSKI, I. ; WILHELM, C. : *Biomasseentstehung*. 3. Springer Berlin Heidelberg, 2016, S. 77–123

[206] LI, Q. ; HU, G. b.: Techno-economic analysis of biofuel production considering logistic configurations. In: *Bioresource Technology* 206 (2016), 195-203. http://dx.doi.org/10.1016/j.biortech.2016.01.101. – DOI 10.1016/j.biortech.2016.01.101. – cited By 2

[207] LI, Q. ; HU, G. : Supply chain design under uncertainty for advanced biofuel production based on bio-oil gasification. In: *Energy* 74 (2014), S. 576–584

[208] LIU, G. ; ZHANG, J. ; BAO, J. : Cost evaluation of cellulase enzyme for industrial-scale cellulosic ethanol production based on rigorous Aspen Plus modeling. In: *Bioprocess and Biosystems Engineering* 39 (2016), Jan, Nr. 1, 133–140. http://dx.doi.org/10.1007/

s00449-015-1497-1. – DOI 10.1007/s00449–015–1497–1. – ISSN 1615–7605

[209] LIU, Z. ; WANG, S. ; OUYANG, Y. : Reliable biomass supply chain design under feedstock seasonality and probabilistic facility disruptions. In: *Energies* 10 (2017), Nr. 11. http://dx.doi.org/10.3390/en10111895. – DOI 10.3390/en10111895. – cited By 0

[210] LUO, Q. ; JONES, R. N. ; WILLIAMS, M. ; BRYAN, B. ; BELLOTTI, W. : Probabilistic distributions of regional climate change and their application in risk analysis of wheat production. In: *Climate Research* 29 (2005), S. 41–52

[211] MAFAKHERI, F. ; NASIRI, F. : Modeling of biomass-to-energy supply chain operations: Applications, challenges and research directions. In: *Energy Policy* 67 (2014), 116 - 126. http://dx.doi.org/http://dx.doi.org/10.1016/j.enpol.2013.11.071. – DOI http://dx.doi.org/10.1016/j.enpol.2013.11.071. – ISSN 0301–4215

[212] In: MAHADEVAN, S. : *Monte Carlo Simulation*. 1997. – ISBN 0–8247–9793–0

[213] MANI, S. ; TABIL, L. G. ; SOKHANSANJ, S. : Grinding performance and physical properties of wheat and barley straws,corn stover and switchgrass. In: *Biomass and Bioenergy* 27 (2004), S. 339 – 352

[214] MARIANO, A. P. ; DIAS, M. O. ; JUNQUEIRA, T. L. ; CUNHA, M. P. ; BONOMI, A. ; MACIEL FILHO, R. . Butanol production in a first-generation Brazilian sugarcane biorefinery: technical aspects and economics of greenfield projects. In: *Bioresource Technology* 135 (2013), S. 316–323

[215] MARSHALL, E. ; AILLERY, M. ; MALCOLM, S. ; WILLIAMS, R. : Climate Change, Water Scarcity, and Adaptation in the U.S. Field-crop Sector / United States Department of Agriculture. 2015. – Forschungsbericht

[216] MARUFUZZAMAN, M. ; D.EKSIOGLU, S. ; HUANG, Y. E.: Two-stage stochastic programming supply chain model for biodiesel production via waste water treatment. In: *Computers & Operations Research* 49 (2014), S. 1 – 17

[217] MARUFUZZAMAN, M. ; EKSIOGLU, S. D. ; LI, X. ; WANG, J. : Analyzing the impact of intermodal-related risk to the design and management of biofuel supply chain. In: *Transportation Research* 69 (2014), S. 122 – 145

[218] MASON-JONES, R. ; TOWILL, D. R.: Shrinking the supply chain uncertainty circle. In: *IOM control* 24 (1998), Nr. 7, S. 17–22

[219] MCDONNELL, T. ; DESK, C. (Hrsg.): *Ups and Downs*. 2012

[220] MCKENDRY, P. : Energy production from biomass (part 1): overview of biomass. In: *Bioresource Technology* 83 (2002), S. 37 – 46

[221] MEADE, B. ; PURICELLI, E. ; MCBRIDE, W. ; VALDES, C. ; HOFFMAN, L. ; FOREMAN, L. ; DOHLMAN, E. : Corn and Soybean Production Costs and Export Competitiveness in Argentina, Brazil, and the United States / United States Department of Agriculture. 2016. – Forschungsbericht

[222] MEERSMAN, T. : *Rail congestion sends more grain to market on river barges.* `http://www.startribune.com/rail-congestion-sends-more-grain-to-market-on-river-barges/282788131/`. Version: November 2014

[223] MELNYK, S. A. ; RODRIGUES, A. ; RAGATZ, G. L.: Using simulation to investigate supply chain disruptions. In: *Supply Chain Risk*. Springer, 2009, S. 103–122

[224] MERZ, M. : *Entwicklung einer indikatorenbasierten Methodik zur Vulnerabilitaetsanalyse für die Bewertung von Risiken in der industriellen Produktion*, Karlsruhe Institute of Technology, Diss., 2011

[225] MESSNER, F. ; MEYER, V. : Flood damage, vulnerability and risk perception–challenges for flood damage research. In: *Flood risk management: hazards, vulnerability and mitigation measures*. Springer, 2006, S. 149–167

[226] MEYER, A. D. ; CATTRYSSE, D. ; RASINMAEKI, J. ; ORSHOVEN, J. V.: Methods to optimise the design and management of biomass-for-bioenergy supply chains: A review. In: *Renewable and Sustainable Energy Reviews* 31 (2014), Nr. Supplement C, 657 - 670. `http://dx.doi.org/https://doi.org/10.1016/j.rser.2013.12.036`. – DOI https://doi.org/10.1016/j.rser.2013.12.036. – ISSN 1364–0321

[227] MEYER, J.-C. : *Economic Evalutation of Bio-Commodity PrProduction Supply CHain Modelling, Design and Simulation*, Diss., 2015

[228] MEYER, S. : US Biofuels Analysis Under Uncertainty and Volatility in the Biofuels Industry: FAPRI Stochastic Modeling. In: *Biofuels, Food and Feed Tradeoffs Farm Foundation*. Saint Louis, Missouri, 12 - 13 April 2007

[229] MICHAEL J. MCCONNELL ; UNITED STATES DEPARTMENT OF AGRICULTURE - ECONOMIC RESEARCH SERVICE (Hrsg.): *Sugar & Sweeteners*. `https://www.ers.usda.gov/topics/crops/sugar-sweeteners/background/`

[230] MILHOLLIN, R. ; HOEHNE, J. ; HORNER, J. ; WEBER, S. ; GEORGE, C. : Feasibility of Corn Stover in Missouri. In: *University of Missouri, Commercial Agriculture Program* (2011)

[231] MILLY, P. C. D. ; WETHERALD, R. T. ; DUNNE, K. ; DELWORTH, T. L.: Increasing risk of great floods in a changing climate. In: *Nature* 415 (2002), Nr. 6871, S. 514–517

[232] MINAHAN, T. : The supply risk benchmark report. In: *Aberdeen Group, Boston, MA* (2005)

[233] MOBINI, M. ; SOWLATI, T. ; SOKHANSANJ, S. : Forest biomass supply logistics for a power plant using the discrete-event simulation approach. In: *Applied Energy* 88 (2011), S. 1241 – 1250

[234] MOBINI, M. ; SOWLATI, T. ; SOKHANSANJ, S. : A simulation model for the design and analysis of wood pellet supply chains. In: *Applied Energy* 111 (2013), S. 1239 – 1249

[235] MOHR, H. ; PRESS, T. A. (Hrsg.): *Mississippi River remains closed after barge accident.* https://www.usatoday.com/story/news/nation/2013/01/29/mississippi-river-barge-accident/1873467/

[236] MORAES ROCHA, G. J. ; MARTIN, C. ; SOARES, I. B. ; MAIOR, A. M. S. ; BAUDEL, H. M. ; ABREU, C. A. M.: Dilute mixed-acid pretreatment of sugarcane bagasse for ethanol production. In: *Biomass and Bioenergy* 35 (2011), Nr. 1, 663 - 670. http://dx.doi.org/http://dx.doi.org/10.1016/j.biombioe.2010.10.018. – DOI http://dx.doi.org/10.1016/j.biombioe.2010.10.018. – ISSN 0961–9534

[237] MOREY, R. V. ; KALIYAN, N. ; TIFFANY, D. G. ; SCHMIDT, D. R.: A corn stover supply logistics system. In: *Applied Engineering in Agriculture* 26 (2010), Nr. 3, S. 455–461

[238] MORROW, W. R. ; GOPAL, A. ; FITTS, G. ; LEWIS, S. ; DALE, L. ; MASANET, E. : Feedstock loss from drought is a major economic risk for biofuel producers. In: *Biomass and Bioenergy* 69 (2014), S. 135 – 143

[239] MOSIER, N. ; WYMAN, C. ; DALE, B. ; ELANDER, R. ; LEE, Y. ; HOLTZAPPLE, M. ; LADISCH, M. : Features of promising technologies for pretreatment of lignocellulosic biomass. In: *Bioresource technology* 96 (2005), Nr. 6, S. 673–686

[240] MULA, J. ; POLER, R. ; GARCÍA-SABATER, J. P. ; LARIO, F. C.: Models for production planning under uncertainty: A review. In: *International journal of production economics* 103 (2006), Nr. 1, S. 271–285

[241] MULLAI, A. : Risk management system–a conceptual model. In: *Supply Chain Risk.* Springer, 2009, S. 83–101

[242] MYERS, B. ; GROUP, N. M. (Hrsg.): *Barge accident on Mississippi River causes petrol spill in New Orleans*

[243] N.A. ; ZEITUNG, F. A. (Hrsg.): *Käferalarm im Mittleren Westen*

[244] NATIONAL AGRICULTURAL STATISTICS SERVICE ; UNITED STATES DEPARTMENT OF AGRICULTURE (Hrsg.): *Quick Stats.* `https://quickstats.nass.usda.gov/%20[Stand:%2024.05.2016]`. Version: 2016

[245] NATIONAL CENTERS FOR ENVIRONMENTAL INFORMATION: National Weather Service Drought Fact Sheet / National Oceanic and Atmospheric Administration. 2012. – Forschungsbericht

[246] NATIONAL CENTERS FOR ENVIRONMENTAL INFORMATION ; NATIONAL OCEANIC AND ATMOSPHERIC ADMINISTRATION (Hrsg.): *National Temperature and Precipitation Maps.* 2017

[247] NATIONAL CENTERS FOR ENVIRONMENTAL INFORMATION ; NATIONAL OCEANIC AND ATMOSPHERIC ADMINISTRATION (Hrsg.): *Storm Events Database.* `https://www.ncdc.noaa.gov/stormevents/choosedates.jsp?statefips=-999%2CALL`. Version: 2017

[248] NATIONAL HIGHWAY TRAFFIC SAFETY ADMINISTRATION: *Traffic Safety Facts 2008.* `http://www-nrd.nhtsa.dot.gov/Pubs/811158.pdf`. Version: 2010

[249] NATIONAL HIGHWAY TRAFFIC SAFETY ADMINISTRATION: *Traffic Safety Facts 2009.* http://www-nrd.nhtsa.dot.gov/Pubs/811388.pdf. Version: September 2011

[250] NATIONAL HIGHWAY TRAFFIC SAFETY ADMINISTRATION: *Traffic Safety Facts 2010.* http://www-nrd.nhtsa.dot.gov/Pubs/811628.pdf. Version: June 2012

[251] NATIONAL HIGHWAY TRAFFIC SAFETY ADMINISTRATION: *Traffic Safety Facts 2011.* http://www-nrd.nhtsa.dot.gov/Pubs/811752.pdf. Version: April 2013

[252] NATIONAL HIGHWAY TRAFFIC SAFETY ADMINISTRATION: *Traffic Safety Facts for Arkansas 2009 to 2013 Fatalities in Crashes Involving a Large Truck.* http://www-nrd.nhtsa.dot.gov/departments/nrd-30/ncsa/STSI/5_AR/2013/Arkansas_Map_8_DATA_2013.PDF. Version: 2013

[253] NATIONAL HIGHWAY TRAFFIC SAFETY ADMINISTRATION: *Traffic Safety Facts for Florida 2009 to 2013 Fatalities in Crashes Involving a Large Truck.* http://www-nrd.nhtsa.dot.gov/departments/nrd-30/ncsa/STSI/12_FL/2013/Florida_Map_8_DATA_2013.PDF. Version: 2013

[254] NATIONAL HIGHWAY TRAFFIC SAFETY ADMINISTRATION: *Traffic Safety Facts 2012.* http://www-nrd.nhtsa.dot.gov/Pubs/811868.pdf. Version: May 2014

[255] NATIONAL HIGHWAY TRAFFIC SAFETY ADMINISTRATION: *Traffic Safety Facts 2013.* http://www-nrd.nhtsa.dot.gov/Pubs/812150.pdf. Version: June 2015

[256] NATIONAL HURRICANE CENTER ; NATIONAL OCEANIC AND ATMOSPHERIC ADMINISTRATION (NOAA) (Hrsg.): *Glossary of NHC Terms.* http://www.nhc.noaa.gov/aboutgloss.shtml#t. Version: 2017

[257] NATIONAL RENEWABLE RESSOURCE LABORATORY ; U.S. DEPARTMENT OF ENERGY (Hrsg.): *NREL Biorefinery Analysis Process Models*. http://www.nrel.gov/extranet/biorefinery/aspen_models/, Abruf: 05.06.2017

[258] NATIONAL TRANSPORTATION SAFETY BOARD ; N.A. (Hrsg.): *Data & Stats*. https://www.ntsb.gov/Pages/default.aspx. Version: 2017

[259] NELSON, R. G.: Resource assessment and removal analysis for corn stover and wheat straw in the Eastern and Midwestern United States, rainfall and wind-induced soil erosion methodology. In: *Biomass and Bioenergy* 22 (2002), Nr. 5, S. 349–363

[260] NEXANT ; BUSINESS, I. C. (Hrsg.): *bio-based chemicals on the fast to commercialization*. 2012

[261] NICOLEIT, T. : *Konditionierung von biogenen Energieträgern aus den Produkten der bioliq®-Schnellpyrolyse*, Diss., 2017

[262] N.N. ; STANDARDIZATION, I. O. (Hrsg.): *ISO 31000*. 2009

[263] N.N. ; MCKEANY-FLAVELL COMPANY, I. (Hrsg.): *The U.S. Corn Wet Milling Industry*. http://www.mckeany-flavell.com/wp-content/publications/US_Corn_Wet_Milling_Study_Overview_2017.pdf. Version: 2017

[264] N.N. ; AGRI-BIOTECH APPLICATIONS, I. S. O. (Hrsg.): *GM Developers List*. http://www.isaaa.org/gmapprovaldatabase/developerlist/default.asp. Version: 2018

[265] OFFICE OF COMPENSATION AND WORKING CONDITIONS ; BUREAU OF LABOR STATISTICS (Hrsg.): *Major Work Stoppages in 2015*. www.bls.gov/wsp. Version: February 2016

[266] OFFICE OF SAFETY ANALYSIS ; FEDERAL RAILROAD ADMINISTRATION (Hrsg.): *Accident Data as reported by Railroads.* http://safetydata.fra.dot.gov/OfficeofSafety/publicsite/on_the_fly_download.aspx. Version: 2017

[267] OKABE, M. ; LIES, D. ; KANAMASA, S. ; PARK, E. Y.: Biotechnological production of itaconic acid and its biosynthesis in Aspergillus terreus. In: *Applied Microbiology and Biotechnology* 84 (2009), S. 597–606

[268] OKUYAMA, Y. : Economic modeling for disaster impact analysis: past, present, and future. In: *Economic Systems Research* 19 (2007), Nr. 2, S. 115–124

[269] ORBICHEM, T. ; N.N. (Hrsg.): *Chem-Net Facts, Chemical Market Insight and Foresight-On a single page - Aceton.* http://www.orbichem.com/userfiles/CNF%20Samples/act_13_11.pdf

[270] OSMANI, A. ; ZHANG, J. : Multi-period stochastic optimization of a sustainable multi-feedstock second generation bioethanol supply chain - A logistic case study in Midwestern United States. In: *Land Use Policy* 61 (2017), 420-450. http://dx.doi.org/10.1016/j.landusepol.2016.10.028. – DOI 10.1016/j.landusepol.2016.10.028. – ISSN 02648377

[271] OSMANI, A. ; ZHANG, J. : Stochastic optimization of a multi-feedstock lignocellulosic-based bioethanol supply chain under multiple uncertainties. In: *Energy* 59 (2013), S. 157 – 172

[272] OSMANI, A. ; ZHANG, J. : Economic and environmental optimization of a large scale sustainable dual feedstock lignocellulosic-based bioethanol supply chain in a stochastic environment. In: *Applied Energy* 114 (2014), S. 572 – 587

[273] In: OTTERLO, M. van ; WIERING, M. : *Reinforcement Learning and Markov Decision Processes*. Springer Berlin Heidelberg. – ISBN 978–3–642–27645–3, 3–42

[274] OWEN, M. D.: Current use of transgenic herbicide-resistant soybean and corn in the USA. In: *Crop Protection* 19 (2000), Nr. 8-10, S. 765–771

[275] PANCOAST, H. M. ; JUNK, W. R.: *Handbook of sugars, 2nd edition*. The AVI Publishing Company Inc,, 1980

[276] PANDEY, A. ; SOCCOL, C. R. ; NIGAM, P. ; SOCCOL, V. T.: Biotechnological potential of agro-industrial residues. I: sugarcane bagasse. In: *Bioresource technology* 74 (2000), Nr. 1, S. 69–80

[277] PATURAU, J. : ALTERNATIVE USES OP SUGARCANE AND ITS BYPRODUCTS IN AGROINDUSTRIES. (1987). http://www.fao.org/livestock/agaP/Frg/AHPP72/72-24.pdf

[278] PEIDRO, D. ; MULA, J. ; POLER, R. ; LARIO, F.-C. : Quantitative models for supply chain planning under uncertainty: a review. In: *The International Journal of Advanced Manufacturing Technology* 43 (2009), Nr. 3, 400–420. http://dx.doi.org/10.1007/s00170-008-1715-y. – DOI 10.1007/s00170–008–1715–y. – ISSN 1433 3015

[279] PEIDRO, D. ; MULA, J. ; POLER, R. ; VERDEGAY, J.-L. : Fuzzy optimization for supply chain planning under supply, demand and process uncertainties. In: *Fuzzy Sets and Systems* 160 (2009), S. 2640 – 1657

[280] PENGILLY, C. ; GARCÍA-APARICIO, M. ; DIEDERICKS, D. ; BRIENZO, M. ; GÖRGENS, J. : Enzymatic hydrolysis of steam-pretreated sweet sorghum bagasse by combinations of cellulase and endo-xylanase. In: *Fuel* 154 (2015), 352 - 360. http://dx.d

oi.org/http://dx.doi.org/10.1016/j.fuel.2015.03.072. – DOI http://dx.doi.org/10.1016/j.fuel.2015.03.072. – ISSN 0016–2361

[281] PÉREZ, J. ; MUÑOZ-DORADO, J. ; RUBIA, T. de l. ; MARTÍNEZ, J. : Biodegradation and biological treatments of cellulose, hemicellulose and lignin: an overview. In: *International Microbiology* 5 (2002), Jun, Nr. 2, 53–63. http://dx.doi.org/10.1007/s10123-002-0062-3. – DOI 10.1007/s10123–002–0062–3. – ISSN 1139–6709

[282] PETERS, M. S. ; TIMMERHAUS, K. D. ; WEST, R. E.: *Plant design and economics for chemical engineers*. Bd. 5. McGraw-Hill Boston, 2003

[283] PETROLIA, D. R.: The economics of harvesting and transporting corn stover for conversion to fuel ethanol: A case study for Minnesota. In: *Biomass and Bioenergy* 32 (2008), Nr. 7, S. 603–612

[284] PHILLIPS, M. ; QUARTZ (Hrsg.): *American labor-union strikes are almost completely extinct*. http://qz.com/342311/american-workers-have-pretty-much-stopped-using-their-most-powerful-weapon/. Version: February 2015

[285] PHILP, J. C. ; RITCHIE, R. J. ; ALLAN, J. E.: Biobased chemicals: the convergence of green chemistry with industrial biotechnology. In: *Trends in biotechnology* 31 (2013), Nr. 4, S. 219–222

[286] PIENKOS, P. T. ; ZHANG, M. : Role of pretreatment and conditioning processes on toxicity of lignocellulosic biomass hydrolysates. In: *Cellulose* 16 (2009), S. 743 – 762

[287] PISKORZ, J. ; MAJERSKI, P. ; RADLEIN, D. ; SCOTT, D. S. ; BRIDGWATER, A. : Fast pyrolysis of sweet sorghum and sweet sorghum bagasse. In: *Journal of Analytical and Applied Pyrolysis* 46 (1998), Nr. 1, 15 - 29. http://dx.doi.org/htt

p://dx.doi.org/10.1016/S0165-2370(98)00067-9. – DOI http://dx.doi.org/10.1016/S0165–2370(98)00067–9. – ISSN 0165–2370

[288] PLUME, K. ; REUTERS (Hrsg.): *Barge accidents shut parts of Mississippi, Ohio rivers.* https://www.reuters.com/article/us-usa-shipping-mississippi-river/barge-accidents-shut-parts-of-mississippi-ohio-rivers-idUSKBN1792JW

[289] PLUS, A. : *Aspen Plus User Guide*, 2000. https://web.ist.utl.pt/ist11038/acad/Aspen/AspUserGuide10.pdf

[290] POONSRISAWAT, A. ; PHUENGJAYAEM, S. ; PETSOM, A. ; TEERADAKORN, S. : Conversion of Sweet Sorghum Straw to Sugars by Dilute Acid Saccharification. In: *Sugar Tech* 15 (2013), Sep, Nr. 3, 322–327. http://dx.doi.org/10.1007/s12355-013-0235-8. – DOI 10.1007/s12355–013–0235–8. – ISSN 0974–0740

[291] POUDEL, S. R. ; QUDDUS, M. A. ; MARUFUZZAMAN, M. ; BIAN, L. ; BURCH V, R. F.: Managing congestion in a multi-modal transportation network under biomass supply uncertainty. In: *Annals of Operations Research* (2017), 1–43. http://dx.doi.org/10.1007/s10479-017-2499-y. – DOI 10.1007/s10479–017–2499–y. – ISSN 1572–9338

[292] POWER, D. J.: Decision support systems: a historical overview. In: *Handbook on Decision Support Systems 1* (2008), S. 121–140

[293] PRESSE- UND INFORMATIONSAMT DER BUNDESREGIERUNG ; DIE BUNDESREGIERUNG (Hrsg.): *Lebensmittel in Deutschland grundsätzlich gentechnikfrei.* https://www.bundesregierung.de/Content/DE/Artikel/2014/06/2013-06-12-lebensmittel-in-d-weitgehend-gentechnikfrei.html. Version: 2018

[294] QURESHI, N. ; BLASCHEK, H. : Butanol production using Clostridium beijerinckii BA101 hyper-butanol producing mutant strain and recovery by pervaporation. In: *Twenty-First Symposium on Biotechnology for Fuels and Chemicals* Springer, 2000, S. 225–235

[295] QURESHI, N. ; COTTA, M. ; SAHA, B. : Bioconversion of barley straw and corn stover tobutanol (a biofuel) in integrated fermentation and simultaneous product recovery bioreactors. In: *Food and Bioproducts Processing* 92 (2014), S. 298 – 308

[296] QURESHI, N. ; SAHA, B. C. ; HECTOR, R. E. ; HUGHES, S. R. ; COTTA, M. A.: Butanol production from wheat straw by simultaneous saccharification and fermentation using Clostridium beijerinckii: Part I—Batch fermentation. In: *Biomass and Bioenergy* 32 (2008), S. 168 – 175

[297] RAMIREZ, E. C. ; JOHNSTON, D. B. ; MCALOON, A. J. ; YEE, W. ; SINGH, V. : Engineering process and cost model for a conventional corn wet milling facility. In: *Industrial crops and products* 27 (2008), S. 91 – 97

[298] RANGANATH, B. : *System dynamics: Theory and case studies*. IK International Pvt Ltd, 2010

[299] RANISAU, J. ; OGBE, E. ; TRAINOR, A. ; BARBOUTI, M. ; ELSHOLKAMI, M. ; ELKAMEL, A. ; FOWLER, M. : Optimization of biofuel production from corn stover under supply uncertainty in Ontario. In: *Biofuel Research Journal* 4 (2017), Nr. 4, 721-729. `http://dx.doi.org/10.18331/BRJ2017.4.4.4`. – DOI 10.18331/BRJ2017.4.4.4. – cited By 0

[300] RAUSCH, A. : *Strategische Standortplanung unter Unsicherheit - Robuste Distributionsstruktur für einen Automobilzulieferer in GUS*, Universität Fredericiana zu Karlsruhe, Diss., 2006

[301] RENTIZELAS, A. A. ; TOLIS, A. J. ; TATSIOPOULOS, I. P.: Logistics issues of biomass: the storage problem and the multi-biomass supply chain. In: *Renewable and Sustainable Energy Reviews* 13 (2009), Nr. 4, S. 887–894

[302] REVERDIA ; REVERDIA (Hrsg.): *Growing Our Leadership Position in the Bio-succinic Market*. http://www.reverdia.com/technology/commercial-plants/. Version: 2015

[303] REZENDE, C. A. ; LIMA, M. A. ; MAZIERO, P. ; RIBEIRO DEAZEVEDO, E. ; GARCIA, W. ; POLIKARPOV, I. : Chemical and morphological characterization of sugarcane bagasse submitted to a delignification process for enhanced enzymatic digestibility. In: *Biotechnology for biofuels* 4 (2011), Nr. 1, S. 54

[304] RIESER, K.-P. ; BASF SE (Hrsg.): *BASF and Avantium intend to establish joint venture*. https://www.basf.com/en/company/news-and-media/news-releases/2016/03/p-16-153.html

[305] RIPPEY, B. R.: The U.S. drought of 2012. In: *Weather and Climate Extremes* 10 (2015), 57 - 64. http://dx.doi.org/https://doi.org/10.1016/j.wace.2015.10.004. – DOI https://doi.org/10.1016/j.wace.2015.10.004. – ISSN 2212–0947. – USDA Research and Programs on Extreme Events

[306] RODRÍGUEZ-GONZÁLEZ, P. A. ; FRAUSTO-HERNÁNDEZ, S. ; BRAVO-SÁNCHEZ, U. I.: Stochastic Optimization of the Strategic Planning Supply Chain of Biorefineries: Large Scale Models. Version: 2014. http://dx.doi.org/https://doi.org/10.1016/B978-0-444-63455-9.50117-3. In: KLEMES, J. J. (Hrsg.) ; VARBANOV, P. S. (Hrsg.) ; LIEW, P. Y. (Hrsg.): *24th European Symposium on Computer Aided Process Engineering* Bd. 33. Elsevier. – DOI https://doi.org/10.1016/B978–0–444–63455–9.50117–3. – ISSN 1570–7946, 1693 - 1698

[307] ROSE, A. Z.: Economic resilience to disasters. (2009)

[308] ROSENZWEIG, C. ; IGLESIAS, A. ; YANG, X. ; EPSTEIN, P. R. ; CHIVIAN, E. : Climate Change and extreme weather events. In: *Global Change & Human Health* 2 (2001), S. 2

[309] RUDI, A. ; FRÖHLING, M. ; ZIMMER, K. ; SCHULTMANN, F. : Freight transportation planning considering carbon emissions and in-transit holding costs: a capacitated multi-commodity network flow model. In: *EURO Journal on Transportation and Logistics* 5 (2014), S. 1 – 38

[310] SAHA, B. C. ; ITEN, L. B. ; COTTA, M. A. ; WU, Y. V.: Dilute acid pretreatment, enzymatic saccharification and fermentation of wheat straw to ethanol. In: *Process Biochemistry* 40 (2005), S. 3693 – 3700

[311] SAMOLADA, M. ; BALDAUF, W. ; VASALOS, I. : Production of a bio-gasoline by upgrading biomass flash pyrolysis liquids via hydrogen processing and catalytic cracking. In: *Fuel* 77 (1998), Nr. 14, 1667 - 1675. `http://dx.doi.org/https://doi.org/10.1016/S0016-2361(98)00073-8`. – DOI https://doi.org/10.1016/S0016–2361(98)00073–8. – ISSN 0016–2361

[312] SCHAETTER, F. : *Decision support system for a reactive management of disaster-caused supply chain disturbances*, Diss., 2015

[313] SCHIRA, J. : *Statistische Methoden der VWL und BWL: Theorie und Praxis*. Pearson Deutschland GmbH, 2009

[314] SCHWADERER, F. : *Integrierte Standort-, Kapazitaets- und Technologieplanung von Wertschöpfungsnetzwerken zur stofflichen und energetischen Biomassenutzung*, Karlsruher Institut für Technologie, Diss., 2012

[315] SERVICE, N. A. S. ; AGRICULTURE, U. S. D. (Hrsg.): *Charts and Maps*. `https://www.nass.usda.gov/Charts_and_Maps/Field_Crops/`. Version: 2018

[316] SHABANI, N. ; SOWLATI, T. : Evaluating the impact of uncertainty and variability on the value chain optimization of a forest biomass power plant using Monte Carlo Simulation. In: *International Journal of Green Energy* 13 (2016), Nr. 7, 631-641. http://dx.doi.org/10.1080/15435075.2014.993764. – DOI 10.1080/15435075.2014.993764. – cited By 1

[317] SHABANI, N. ; SOWLATI, T. : A hybrid multi-stage stochastic programming-robust optimization model for maximizing the supply chain of a forest-based biomass power plant considering uncertainties. In: *Journal of Cleaner Production* 112 (2016), 3285-3293. http://dx.doi.org/10.1016/j.jclepro.2015.09.034. – DOI 10.1016/j.jclepro.2015.09.034. – cited By 0

[318] SHABANI, N. ; SOWLATI, T. ; OUHIMMOU, M. ; RÖNNQVIST, M. : Tactical supply chain planning for a forest biomass power plant under supply uncertainty. In: *Energy* 78 (2014), S. 346–355

[319] SHARIFZADEH, M. ; GARCIA, M. C. ; SHAH, N. : Supply chain network design and operation: Systematic decision-making for centralized, distributed, and mobile biofuel production using mixed integer linear programming (MILP) under uncertainty. In: *Biomass and Bioenergy* 81 (2015), S. 401–414

[320] SHARMA, B. ; INGALLS, R. G. ; JONES, C. L. ; HUHNKE, R. L. ; KHANCHI, A. : Scenario optimization modeling approach for design and management of biomass-to-biorefinery supply chain system. In: *Bioresource Technology* 150 (2013), S. 163 – 171

[321] SHEEHAN, J. ; ADEN, A. ; PAUSTIAN, K. ; KILLIAN, K. ; BRENNER, J. ; WALSH, M. ; NELSON, R. : Energy and environmental aspects of using corn stover for fuel ethanol. In: *Journal of Industrial Ecology* 7 (2003), Nr. 3-4, S. 117–146

[322] SHELDON, R. A.: Green and sustainable manufacture of chemicals from biomass: state of the art. In: *Green Chemistry* 16 (2014), Nr. 3, S. 950–963

[323] SHIM, J. P. ; WARKENTIN, M. ; COURTNEY, J. F. ; POWER, D. J. ; SHARDA, R. ; CARLSSON, C. : Past, present, and future of decision support technology. In: *Decision support systems* 33 (2002), Nr. 2, S. 111–126

[324] SHINNERS, K. J. ; BINVERSIE, B. N.: Fractional yield and moisture of corn stover biomass produced in the Northern US Corn Belt. In: *Biomass and Bioenergy* 31 (2007), Nr. 8, S. 576–584

[325] SHOVEN, J. B. ; WHALLEY, J. : *Applying general equilibrium.* Cambridge university press, 1992

[326] SILVA, G. ; EXTENSION, M. S. U. (Hrsg.): *Fertilizer prices in 2015.* http://msue.anr.msu.edu/news/fertilizer_prices_in_2015. Version: 2015

[327] SMITH, K. ; PETLEY, D. N.: *Environmental hazards : assessing risk and reducing disaster.* 6. ed. London [u.a.] : Routledge, 2013. – ISBN 978–0–415–68105–6; 0–415–68105–7; 978–0–415–68106–3; 0–415–68106–5978–0–415–68105–9. – Previous ed.: 2008. - Formerly CIP Uk. - Includes bibliographical references and index

[328] SMITHERS, J. : Review of sugarcane trash recovery systems for energy cogeneration in South Africa. In: *Renewable and Sustainable Energy Reviews* 32 (2014), 915 - 925. http://dx.doi.org/https://doi.org/10.1016/j.rser.2014.01.042. – DOI https://doi.org/10.1016/j.rser.2014.01.042. – ISSN 1364–0321

[329] SODHI, M. S. ; TANG, C. S. ; HILLIER, F. S. (Hrsg.): *Managing Supply Chain Risk.* Springer, 2012

[330] SOHAIB, Q. ; MUHAMMAD, A. ; YOUNAS, M. : Fast pyrolysis of sugarcane bagasse: Effect of pyrolysis conditions on final product distribution and properties. In: *Energy Sources, Part A: Recovery, Utilization, and Environmental Effects* 39 (2017), Nr. 2, 184-190. `http://dx.doi.org/10.1080/15567036.2016.1212292`. – DOI 10.1080/15567036.2016.1212292

[331] SOKHANSANJ, S. ; KUMAR, A. ; TURHOLLOW, A. F.: Development and implementation of integrated biomass supply analysis and logistics model (IBSAL). In: *Biomass and Bioenergy* 30 (2006), Nr. 10, S. 838–847

[332] SONG, H. ; LEE, S. Y.: Production of succinic acid by bacterial fermentation. 39 (2006), S. 352 – 361

[333] STATISTICS, I. ; ANALYSIS ; U.S. ENERGY INFORMATION ADMINISTRATION (Hrsg.): *Natural Gas*. `https://www.eia.gov/dnav/ng/hist/n3035us3m.htm`. Version: 2017

[334] STICHNOTHE, H. ; MEIER, D. ; BARI, I. de: Chapter 3 - Biorefineries: Industry Status and Economics. Version: 2016. `http://dx.doi.org/https://doi.org/10.1016/B978-0-12-805165-8.00003-3`. In: LAMERS, P. (Hrsg.) ; SEARCY, E. (Hrsg.) ; HESS, J. R. (Hrsg.) ; STICHNOTHE, H. (Hrsg.): *Developing the Global Bioeconomy*. Academic Press. – DOI https://doi.org/10.1016/B978–0–12–805165–8.00003–3. – ISBN 978–0–12–805165–8, 41 - 67

[335] STROCKO, E. ; SPRUNG, M. ; NGUYEN, L. ; RICK, C. ; SEDOR, J. : Freight Facts and Figures 2013 / SAIC. 2014. – Forschungsbericht

[336] SUMA, R. ; SAVITHA, C. : Integrated sugarcane trash management: a novel technology for sustaining soil health and sugarcane yield. In: *Advances in Crop Science and Technology* (2015)

[337] SWEETENERS REGIONAL OFFICES: ClearsweetÂ® 95 Forschungsbericht

[338] TANG, C. ; TOMLIN, B. : How much flexibility does it take to mitigate supply chain risks? In: ZSIDISIN, G. A. (Hrsg.) ; RITCHIE, B. (Hrsg.): *Supply chain risk*. Springer, 2009, S. 155–174

[339] TAUERS, R. ; ENERGY, . P. Technology (Hrsg.): *The Second Renewable Fuel Standard*. https://webberenergyblog.wordpress.com/2013/03/25/the-second-renewable-fuel-standard/

[340] TAY, D. H. ; NG, D. K. ; ; TAN, R. R.: Robust Optimization Approach for Synthesis of Integrated Biorefineries with Supply and Demand Uncertainties. In: *Environmental Progress & Sustainable Energy* 32 (2013), July, Nr. 2, S. 384 – 389

[341] TEXAS TRANSPORTATION INSTITUTE ; MARAD MARITIME ADMINISTRATION (Hrsg.): *Waterways: Working for America*

[342] THAKUR, I. S.: *Environmental Biotechnology: Basic Concepts and Applications*. I.K. International Pvt. Ltd., 2006

[343] THE NATIONAL SEVERE STORMS LABORATORY ; NATIONAL OCEANIC AND ATMOSPHERIC ADMINISTRATION (NOAA) (Hrsg.): *Severe Weather 101, Hail Basics*. http://www.nssl.noaa.gov/education/svrwx101/hail/. Version: 2017

[344] THE NATIONAL SEVERE STORMS LABORATORY ; NATIONAL OCEANIC AND ATMOSPHERIC ADMINISTRATION (NOAA) (Hrsg.): *Severe Weather 101, Tornado Basics*. http://www.nssl.noaa.gov/education/svrwx101/tornadoes/. Version: 2017

[345] THEERARATTANANOON, K. ; WU, X. ; STAGGENBORG, S. ; PROPHETER, J. ; MADL, R. ; WANG, D. : Evaluation and char-

acterization of sorghum biomass as feedstock for sugar production. In: *Transactions of the ASABE* 53 (2010), Nr. 2, S. 509–525

[346] THOMAS CAPEHART ; ECONOMIC RESEARCH SERVICE, UNITED STATES DEPARTMENT OF AGRICULTURE (Hrsg.): *Corn*. https://www.ers.usda.gov/topics/crops/corn

[347] THOMPSON, P. B.: The agricultural ethics of biofuels: the food vs. fuel debate. In: *Agriculture* 2 (2012), Nr. 4, S. 339–358

[348] THORBURN, A. H. P. A. H. A. P. J.; Archer R. P. J.; Archer A. P. J.; Archer: Value chain analyses of whole crop harvesting to maximise co-generation. In: *Australian Society of Sugar Cane Technologists Conference*, 2006, S. 37 – 48

[349] In: TIPPKÖTTER, N. : *Grundlagen der biochemischen Umwandlung*. 3. Springer Berlin Heidelberg, 2016, S. 1447–1500

[350] TONG, K. ; GLEESON, M. J. ; RONG, G. ; YOU, F. : Optimal design of advanced drop-in hydrocarbon biofuel supply chain integrating with existing petroleum refineries under uncertainty. In: *Biomass and Bioenergy* 60 (2014), S. 108 – 120

[351] TONG, K. ; GONG, J. ; YUE, D. ; YOU, F. : Stochastic Programming Approach to Optimal Design and Operations of Integrated Hydrocarbon Biofuel and Petroleum Supply Chains. In: *ACS Sustainable Chemistry Engineering* 2 (2014), S. 49 – 61

[352] TONG, K. ; YOU, F. ; RONG, G. : Robust design and operations of hydrocarbon biofuel supply chainintegrating with existing petroleum refineries considering unitcost objective. In: *Computers and Chemical Engineering* 68 (2014), S. 128 – 139

[353] TRAGER, R. ; CHEMISTRY WORLD (Hrsg.): *Bio-based chemicals on the rise in US*. https://www.chemistryworld.com/news/bio-based-chemicals-on-the-rise-in-us/7865.article

[354] TRANSPORTATION STATISTICS, B. of ; TRANSPORTATION, U. D. (Hrsg.): *Railroad Nodes*. `https://www.arcgis.com/home/item.html?id=366792a73ec7451f8a7afa1ec46cc3b3`. Version: 2017

[355] TRINKS, C. : *Auswahl einer robusten Supply Chain-Strategie für Waldhackschnitzel aus dem organisierten Kleinstprivatwald unter Berücksichtigung von Unsicherheiten und eines multikriteriellen Bewertungsproblems*, Diss., 2014

[356] TRIPPE, F. : *Techno-Ã¶konomische Bewertung alternativer Verfahrenskonfigurationen zur Herstellung von Biomass-to-Liquid (BtL) Kraftstoffen und Chemikalien*, Karlsruher Institut fÃ¼r Technologie, Diss., 2013

[357] TRIPPE, F. ; FRÃ¶HLING, M. ; SCHULTMANN, F. ; STAHL, R. ; HENRICH, E. : Techno-economic assessment of gasification as a process step within biomass-to-liquid (BtL) fuel and chemicals production. In: *Fuel Processing Technology* 92 (2011), Nr. 11, 2169 - 2184. `http://dx.doi.org/http://dx.doi.org/10.1016/j.fuproc.2011.06.026`. – DOI http://dx.doi.org/10.1016/j.fuproc.2011.06.026. – ISSN 0378–3820

[358] TRIPPE, F. ; FROEHLING, M. ; SCHULTMANN, F. ; STAHL, R. ; HENRICH, E. : Techno-Economic Analysis of Fast Pyrolysis as a Process Step Within Biomass-to-Liquid Fuel Production. In: *Waste and Biomass Valorization* 1 (2010), Dec, Nr. 4, 415–430. `http://dx.doi.org/10.1007/s12649-010-9039-1`. – DOI 10.1007/s12649-010-9039-1. – ISSN 1877–265X

[359] TRIPPE, F. ; FROEHLING, M. ; SCHULTMANN, F. ; STAHL, R. ; HENRICH, E. ; DALAI, A. : Comprehensive techno-economic assessment of dimethyl ether (DME) synthesis and Fischer-Tropsch synthesis as alternative process steps

within biomass-to-liquid production. In: *Fuel Processing Technology* 106 (2013), 577 - 586. http://dx.doi.org/http://dx.doi.org/10.1016/j.fuproc.2012.09.029. – DOI http://dx.doi.org/10.1016/j.fuproc.2012.09.029. – ISSN 0378–3820

[360] TURHOLLOW, A. F. ; WEBB, E. G. ; DOWNING, M. : Review of sorghum production practices: Applications for bioenergy. In: *Oak Ridge National Laboratory, Oak Ridge, Tennessee* (2010), S. 37831–6283

[361] TYE, Y. Y. ; LEE, K. T. ; ABDULLAH, W. N. W. ; LEH, C. P.: The world availability of non-wood lignocellulosic biomass for the production of cellulosic ethanol and potential pretreatments for the enhancement of enzymatic saccharification. In: *Renewable and Sustainable Energy Reviews* 60 (2016), 155 - 172. http://dx.doi.org/https://doi.org/10.1016/j.rser.2016.01.072. – DOI https://doi.org/10.1016/j.rser.2016.01.072. – ISSN 1364–0321

[362] UNIT, E. R. ; AGRICULTURE, U. D. (Hrsg.): *Sugarcane for sugar : price per ton, by state*. https://www.ers.usda.gov/data-products/sugar-and-sweeteners-yearbook-tables.aspx. Version: 2017

[363] URYASEV, S. : Conditional value-at-risk: Optimization algorithms and applications. In: *Computational Intelligence for Financial Engineering, 2000.(CIFEr) Proceedings of the IEEE/IAFE/INFORMS 2000 Conference on* IEEE, 2000, S. 49–57

[364] U.S. ARMY CORPS OF ENGINEERS ; U.S. DEPARTMENT OF TRANSPORTATION (Hrsg.): *Demands on the Transportation System*. https://ops.fhwa.dot.gov/freight/freight_analysis/freight_story/demands.htm. Version: 2017

[365] U.S. Army Corps of Engineers ; Rock Island District (Hrsg.): *Navigational Charts*. http://www.mvp.usace.army.mil/Missions/Navigation/Locks-Dams/. Version: 2017

[366] US Department of Agriculture: *US Biobased Products Market Potential and Projections Through 2025*. 2008

[367] US Government Printing Office: *Energy Policy Act of 2005 Public Law 109 - 58*. August 2005

[368] USDA: *Table 12–Corn: Cash prices at principal markets*. http://www.ers.usda.gov/data-products/feed-grains-database/feed-grains-yearbook-tables.aspx#26954

[369] Uslu, A. ; Faaij, A. P. ; Bergman, P. : Pre-treatment technologies, and their effect on international bioenergy supply chain logistics. Techno-economic evaluation of torrefaction, fast pyrolysis and pelletisation. In: *Energy* 33 (2008), Nr. 8, 1206 - 1223. http://dx.doi.org/https://doi.org/10.1016/j.energy.2008.03.007. – DOI https://doi.org/10.1016/j.energy.2008.03.007. – ISSN 0360–5442

[370] Vadas, P. A. ; Digman, M. F.: Production costs of potential corn stover harvest and storage systems. In: *biomass and bioenergy* 54 (2013), S. 133–139

[371] Vahidov, R. ; Kersten, G. E.: Decision station: situating decision support systems. In: *Decision Support Systems* 38 (2004), Nr. 2, S. 283–303

[372] Vaswani, S. : Bio-based Succinic Acid / SRI Consulting. – Forschungsbericht

[373] Vauck, W. R. A. ; MÃ¼ller, H. A.: *Grundoperationen chemischer Verfahrenstechnik*. 2000

[374] VESELY, W. E. ; GOLDBERG, F. F. ; ROBERTS, N. H. ; HAASL, D. F.: *Fault Tree Handbook.* 1981

[375] In: VOGEL, F. : *Hydrothermale Verfahren.* 3. Springer Berlin Heidelberg, 2016, S. 1267–1337

[376] WALDHEIM, J. ; NEWS, I. (Hrsg.): *US July ethylene contracts settle down 1.25 cents/lb, not market-wide.* https://www.icis.com/resources/news/2017/08/03/10062158/us-july-ethylene-contracts-settle-down-1-25-cents-lb-not-market-wide/

[377] WALL, J. S. ; ROSS, W. M. u. a.: *Sorghum production and utilization.* Westport, Connecticut: AVI Publishing Company, Inc., 1970

[378] WÄRMEATLAS, V. : *11. Auflage.* 2013

[379] WATERNEWS ; BLUE circle o. (Hrsg.): *Price of Water 2015: Up 6 Percent in 30 Major U.S. Cities; 41 Percent Rise Since 2010.* http://www.circleofblue.org/2015/world/price-of-water-2015-up-6-percent-in-30-major-u-s-cities-41-percent-rise-since-2010/. Version: 2015

[380] WATERS, D. : *Supply chain risk management: vulnerability and resilience in logistics.* Kogan Page Publishers, 2011

[381] In: WATSON, S. A.: *Wet-Milling Process and Products.* 1970

[382] WEINTRAUB, A. ; ROMERO, C. : Operations research models and the management of agricultural and forestry resources: a review and comparison. In: *Interfaces* 36 (2006), Nr. 5, S. 446–457

[383] WERPY, T. ; PETERSEN, G. ; (PNNL), P. N. N. L. (Hrsg.) ; (NREL), N. R. E. L. (Hrsg.): *Top Value Added Chemicals from Biomass: Volume I - Results of Screening for Potential Candidates from Sugars and Synthesis Gas.* U.S. Department of Energy Energy Efficiency and

Renewable Energy. http://dx.doi.org/10.2172/15008859. http://dx.doi.org/10.2172/15008859

[384] WEST, C. T. ; LENZE, D. G.: Modeling the regional impact of natural disaster and recovery: A general framework and an application to Hurricane Andrew. In: *International regional science review* 17 (1994), Nr. 2, S. 121–150

[385] WHYTE, A. V. ; BURTON, I. : Environmental Risk Assessment / Scientific Commitee on Problems of the Environment (SCOPE) of the International Council of Scientific Unions (ICSU). Version: 1980. https://dge.carnegiescience.edu/SCOPE/SCOPE_15/SCOPE_15.html. John Wiley and Sons. – Forschungsbericht

[386] WOOLCOCK, P. J. ; BROWN, R. C.: A review of cleaning technologies for biomass-derived syngas. In: *Biomass and Bioenergy* 52 (2013), 54 - 84. http://dx.doi.org/https://doi.org/10.1016/j.biombioe.2013.02.036. – DOI https://doi.org/10.1016/j.biombioe.2013.02.036. – ISSN 0961–9534

[387] WORTMANN, C. ; KLEIN, R. N. ; SHAPIRO, C. A.: NebGuide: Harvesting Crops Residues / University of Nebraska. 2012. – Forschungsbericht

[388] WRIGHT, M. M. ; DAUGAARD, D. E. ; SATRIO, J. A. ; BROWN, R. C.: Techno-economic analysis of biomass fast pyrolysis to transportation fuels. In: *Fuel* 89 (2010), S2 - S10. http://dx.doi.org/http://dx.doi.org/10.1016/j.fuel.2010.07.029. – DOI http://dx.doi.org/10.1016/j.fuel.2010.07.029. – ISSN 0016–2361. – Techno-economic Comparison of Biomass-to-Biofuels Pathways

[389] WRIGHT, M. ; LIMA, I. ; BIGNER, R. : Stability and Use of Sweet Sorghum Bagasse. In: *Sugar Tech* 19 (2017), Nr. 5, S. 451–457

[390] WU, C. ; HUANG, G. ; LI, W. ; XIE, Y. ; XU, Y. : Multistage stochastic inexact chance-constraint programming for an integrated biomass-municipal solid waste power supply management under uncertainty. In: *Renewable and Sustainable Energy Reviews* 41 (2015), S. 1244–1254

[391] WU, X. ; ZHAO, R. ; BEAN, S. ; SEIB, P. ; MCLAREN, J. ; MADL, R. ; TUINISTRA, M. ; LENZ, M. ; WANG, D. : Factors Impacting Ethanol Production from Grain Sorghum in the Dry-Grind Process. In: *Cereal Chemistry* 84(2) (2007), 130 - 136. `http://dx.doi.org/10.1094/CCHEM-84.2-0130`. – DOI 10.1094/CCHEM–84.2–0130

[392] XIE, F. ; HUANG, Y. ; EKSIOGLU, S. : Integrating multimodal transport into cellulosic biofuel supply chain design under feedstock seasonality with a case study based on California. In: *Bioresource Technology* 152 (2014), S. 15 – 23

[393] YEH, K. ; WHITTAKER, C. ; REALFF, M. J. ; LEE, J. H.: Two stage stochastic bilevel programming model of a pre-established timberlands supply chain with biorefinery investment interests. In: *Computers & Chemical Engineering* 73 (2015), S. 141–153

[394] YOU, F. ; WANG, B. : Optimal design and operations of cellulosic biofuel supply chains under uncertainty. – cited By 0

[395] YOU, F. : Design of biofuel supply chains under uncertainty with multiobjective stochastic programming models and decomposition algorithm. In: *Computer Aided Chemical Engineering* Bd. 32. Elsevier, 2013, S. 493–498

[396] YUE, D. ; YOU, F. : Modelling of multi-scale uncertainties in biofuel supply chain optimization. In: *Chemical Engineering Transactions* 52 (2016), 205-210. `http://dx.doi.org/10.3303/CET1652035`. – DOI 10.3303/CET1652035. – cited By 0

[397] Zamar, D. S. ; Gopaluni, B. ; Sokhansanj, S. ; Newlands, N. K.: Robust optimization of competing biomass supply chains under feedstock uncertainty. In: *IFAC-PapersOnLine* 48 (2015), Nr. 8, S. 1222–1227

[398] Zamar, D. ; Gopaluni, B. ; Sokhansanj, S. b. ; Newlands, N. : A quantile-based scenario analysis approach to biomass supply chain optimization under uncertainty. In: *Computers and Chemical Engineering* 97 (2017), 114-123. http://dx.doi.org/10.1016/j.compchemeng.2016.11.015. – DOI 10.1016/j.compchemeng.2016.11.015. – ISSN 00981354

[399] Zhang, B.-Z. ; Zhang, S.-P. ; Zhao, S.-T. ; Xu, Q.-L. ; Yan, Y.-J. : Pretreatment of Sweet Sorghum Stalk Using Dilute Acid. In: *Energy Storage* 36 (2014), Nr. 16, S. 1835 – 1842. http://dx.doi.org/10.1080/15567036.2011.59689. – DOI 10.1080/15567036.2011.59689

[400] Zhang, B.-Z. ; Zhang, S.-P. ; Zhao, S.-T. ; Xu, Q.-L. ; Yan, Y.-J. : Conversion of Sweet Sorghum Bagasse Residue to Glucose by Dilute Acid Hydrolysis. In: *Energy Sources* 37 (2015), Nr. 15, S. 1688 – 1696

[401] Zheng, P. ; Dong, J.-J. ; Sun, Z.-H. ; Ni, Y. ; Fang, L. : Fermentative production of succinic acid from straw hydrolysate by Actinobacillus succinogenes. In: *Bioresource Technology* 100 (2009), Nr. 8, 2425 - 2429. http://dx.doi.org/http://dx.doi.org/10.1016/j.biortech.2008.11.043. – DOI http://dx.doi.org/10.1016/j.biortech.2008.11.043. – ISSN 0960–8524

[402] Ziegenbein, A. ; Schönsleben, P. D. P. (Hrsg.): *Supply Chain Risiken - Identifikation, Bewertung und Steuerung*. vdf Hochschulverlag AG an der ETH Zürich, 2007

[403] ZIMMER, K. : *Entscheidungsunterstützung zur Auswahl und Steuerung von Lieferanten und Lieferketten unter Berücksichtigung von Nachhaltigkeitsaspekten*, Diss., 2016

[404] ZIMMER, T. ; RUDI, A. ; MÜLLER, A.-K. ; FRÖHLING, M. ; SCHULTMANN, F. : Modeling the impact of competing utilization paths on biomass-to-liquid (BtL) supply chains. In: *Applied Energy* 208 (2017), S. 954–971

PRODUKTION UND ENERGIE

Karlsruher Institut für Technologie (KIT)
Institut für Industriebetriebslehre und Industrielle Produktion
Deutsch-Französisches Institut für Umweltforschung

ISSN 2194-2404

Band 1 **National Integrated Assessment Modelling zur Bewertung umweltpolitischer Instrumente.**
Entwicklung des otello-Modellsystems und dessen Anwendung auf die Bundesrepublik Deutschland. 2012
ISBN 978-3-86644-853-7

Band 2 **Erhöhung der Energie- und Ressourceneffizienz und Reduzierung der Treibhausgasemissionen in der Eisen-, Stahl- und Zinkindustrie (ERESTRE).** 2013
ISBN 978-3-86644-857-5

Band 3 Frederik Trippe
Techno-ökonomische Bewertung alternativer Verfahrenskonfigurationen zur Herstellung von Biomass-to-Liquid (BtL) Kraftstoffen und Chemikalien. 2013
ISBN 978-3-7315-0031-5

Band 4 Dogan Keles
Uncertainties in energy markets and their consideration in energy storage evaluation. 2013
ISBN 978-3-7315-0046-9

Band 5 Heidi Ursula Heinrichs
Analyse der langfristigen Auswirkungen von Elektromobilität auf das deutsche Energiesystem im europäisschen Energieverbund. 2013
ISBN 978-3-7315-0131-2

Die Bände sind unter www.ksp.kit.edu als PDF frei verfügbar oder als Druckausgabe zu bestellen.

Band 6 Julian Stengel
Akteursbasierte Simulation der energetischen Modernisierung des Wohngebäudebestands in Deutschland. 2014
ISBN 978-3-7315-0236-4

Band 7 Sonja Babrowski
Bedarf und Verteilung elektrischer Tagesspeicher im zukünftigen deutschen Energiesystem. 2015
ISBN 978-3-7315-0306-4

Band 8 Marius Wunder
Integration neuer Technologien der Bitumenkalthandhabung in die Versorgungskette. 2015
ISBN 978-3-7315-0319-4

Band 9 Felix Teufel
Speicherbedarf und dessen Auswirkungen auf die Energiewirtschaft bei Umsetzung der politischen Ziele zur Energiewende. 2015
ISBN 978-3-7315-0341-5

Band 10 D. Keles, L. Renz, A. Bublitz, F. Zimmermann, M. Genoese, W. Fichtner, H. Höfling, F. Sensfuß, J. Winkler
Zukunftsfähige Designoptionen für den deutschen Strommarkt: Ein Vergleich des Energy-only-Marktes mit Kapazitätsmärkten. 2016
ISBN 978-3-7315-0453-5

Band 11 Patrick Breun
Ein Ansatz zur Bewertung klimapolitischer Instrumente am Beispiel der Metallerzeugung und -verarbeitung. 2016
ISBN 978-3-7315-0494-8

Band 12 P. Ringler, H. Schermeyer, M. Ruppert, M. Hayn, V. Bertsch, D. Keles, W. Fichtner
Decentralized Energy Systems, Market Integration, Optimization. 2016
ISBN 978-3-7315-0505-1

Band 13 Marian Hayn
Modellgestützte Analyse neuer Stromtarife für Haushalte unter Berücksichtigung bedarfsorientierter Versorgungssicherheitsniveaus. 2016
ISBN 978-3-7315-0499-3

Band 14 Frank Schätter
Decision support system for a reactive management of disaster-caused supply chain disturbances. 2016
ISBN 978-3-7315-0530-3

Band 15 Robert Kunze
Techno-ökonomische Planung energetischer Wohngebäudemodernisierungen: Ein gemischt-ganzzahliges lineares Optimierungsmodell auf Basis einer vollständigen Finanzplanung. 2016
ISBN 978-3-7315-0531-0

Band 16 A. Kühlen, J. Stengel, R. Volk, F. Schultmann, M. Reinhardt, H. Schlick, S. Haghsheno, A. Mettke, S. Asmus, S. Schmidt, J. Harzheim
ISA: Immissionsschutz beim Abbruch - Minimierung von Umweltbelastungen (Lärm, Staub, Erschütterungen) beim Abbruch von Hoch-/Tiefbauten und Schaffung hochwertiger Recyclingmöglichkeiten für Materialien aus Gebäudeabbruch. 2018
ISBN 978-3-7315-0534-1

Band 17 Konrad Zimmer
Entscheidungsunterstützung zur Auswahl und Steuerung von Lieferanten und Lieferketten unter Berücksichtigung von Nachhaltigkeitsaspekten. 2016
ISBN 978-3-7315-0537-2

Band 18 Kira Schumacher, Wolf Fichtner and Frank Schultmann (Eds.)
Innovations for sustainable biomass utilisation in the Upper Rhine Region. 2017
ISBN 978-3-7315-0423-8

Band 19 Sophia Radloff
Modellgestützte Bewertung der Nutzung von Biokohle als Bodenzusatz in der Landwirtschaft. 2017
ISBN 978-3-7315-0559-4

Band 20 Rebekka Volk
Proactive-reactive, robust scheduling and capacity planning of deconstruction projects under uncertainty. 2017
ISBN 978-3-7315-0592-1

Band 21 Erik Merkel
Analyse und Bewertung des Elektrizitätssystems und des Wärmesystems der Wohngebäude in Deutschland. 2017
ISBN 978-3-7315-0636-2

Band 22 Rebekka Volk (Hrsg.)
Entwicklung eines mobilen Systems zur Erfassung und Erschließung von Ressourceneffizienzpotenzialen beim Rückbau von Infrastruktur und Produkten („ResourceApp"): Schlussbericht des Forschungsvorhabens. 2017
ISBN 978-3-7315-0653-9

Band 23 Thomas Kaschub
Batteriespeicher in Haushalten unter Berücksichtigung von Photovoltaik, Elektrofahrzeugen und Nachfrage-steuerung. 2017
ISBN 978-3-7315-0688-1

Band 24 Felix Hübner, Rebekka Volk, Oktay Secer, Daniel Kühn, Peter Sahre, Reinhard Knappik, Frank Schultmann, Sascha Gentes, Petra von Both
Modellentwicklung eines ganzheitlichen Projektmanagementsystems für kerntechnische Rückbauprojekte (MogaMaR): Schlussbericht des Forschungsvorhabens. 2018
ISBN 978-3-7315-0762-8

Band 25 Karoline Fath
Technical and economic potential for photovoltaic systems on buildings. 2018
ISBN 978-3-7315-0787-1

Band 26 Ann-Kathrin Müller
Decision Support for Biomass Value Chains for the Production of Biochemicals Considering Uncertainties. 2018
ISBN 978-3-7315-0820-5